SKILLS, TIPS, AND GEAR FOR ...

THRIVE

LONG-TERM WILDERNESS
– SURVIVAL GUIDE –

JUAN PABLO QUIÑONEZ

BOREAL CREEK PRESS

ISBN: 978-1-7772838-0-3

Illustrated by Juan Pablo Quiñonez
Copy edited by Lianne Fontaine
Proofread by Nicole Boyse
Cover design by WildEagles'99

This book is available at quantity discounts for bulk purchases. For information, please email sales@borealcreek.press.

WARNING:

This book has been written and published strictly for informational purposes. It is not intended to serve as a manual and in no way should be used as a substitute for actual instruction with qualified professionals. **The author and publisher assume no liability for personal injury, property damage, consequential damage, or loss, however caused, from using the information in this book.**

All survival scenarios by nature are life-threatening, and many activities related to wilderness survival are dangerous. The survival techniques described in this book are for use in dire circumstances only, when the survival of individuals depends upon them. **Many techniques described herein are illegal outside true survival situations.** Some of the information presented in this book, if misused, could help kill you.

The author and publisher urge all readers to be aware of their own outdoor experience and health status, to consult all laws relating to the protection of land, property, plants, and animals, and to consult health care and outdoor professionals before engaging in any potentially hazardous activity.

PREFACE

I've studied hundreds of books related to wilderness survival to prepare for my 180 days in the wild and 100 days in the boreal forest during winter. Unfortunately, none of these books tackle the subject from a modern, long-term perspective; therefore, I decided to write this book.

Here, you'll find advice on developing a strategy and preparing for a wilderness survival situation lasting up to one year. While writing this book, I've asked myself: if I could carry only one book on survival, what information and advice would it contain?

I spent a lot of time gathering and cross-referencing the information and concepts in this book; although they may have appeared in other publications, they have been modified or recreated to best illustrate the points I want to make.

This is the book I wish I had read before embarking on my survival adventures. I wrote it because I felt a personal need for it and to organize the lessons I've learned through experience and research. I hope it becomes a stepping-stone for survival enthusiasts.

Here, you won't find comprehensive information on some topics, such as identifying wild edibles or performing basic wilderness first aid. However, you'll find an attempt to tackle the vast subject of long-term survival from a broad perspective, with an emphasis on a survival mindset.

This book doesn't include a lot of beginner information on survival skills. I do go over various foundational skills, but it is assumed that you have a separate field guide for wilderness first aid and perhaps wild edibles, and that you already own a book or two on wilderness survival.

The next decades will certainly bring numerous challenges caused by climate change and disruptions to ecology and energy sources. Being more connected to our land, water, food, and power will make us more resilient to these challenges. Living in the wild is not the answer to our converging predicaments, but it sure helps to develop resilience and a perspective that will be increasingly useful in the future.

I have a desire to share what I've learned. The result is this book, *Thrive,* which is what it is: a bunch of drawings and notes on long-term wilderness survival.

Juan Pablo Quiñonez

To my parents,
Juan Pablo Quiñonez and Claudia Saldaña,
and my partner,
Jennifer Ford,
for their love and support.

ACKNOWLEDGMENTS

Thrive would never have been written without the support of my partner, Jennifer Ford, and my family. I'd like to acknowledge that this book was written on Indigenous hunting and gathering grounds. I'm grateful for living next to the boreal forest, not too far away from the truly remote wilderness, and having had the privilege to pursue the adventures that form the basis of this book. The outdoors has given me direction and encouraged me to be grounded. It has allowed me to experience the freedom that few people will ever experience. Without nature, there is nothing.

Thanks so much to all my alpha readers for taking the time and making the effort to not just read my drafts, but to send me detailed comments and feedback. This book is far better thanks to you. Special thanks to Adam Riley, Benji Hill (benjihill.com), Bruce Zawalsky (boreal.net), Dave Holder (mahikan.ca), D.J. Tudino (bearessentialsoutdoors.ca), Jessie Krebs (owlsskills.com), Karie Lee (karieleeknoke.com), Nathan Martinez, Robert Weir (panaceax.com), Dr. Teimojin Tan (survivaldoctors.com), Terry Burns, Torjus Gaaren, Trevor Page, and Woniya Thibeault (buckskinrevolution.com).

I'd like to thank my copy editor Lianne Fontaine for all her hard work and attention to detail. You made this book readable. I would also like to thank Nicole Boyse for her diligent proofreading of this book.

I'm grateful to all those who passed down their knowledge in print—people such as Cody Lundin, Laurence Gonzales, Les Stroud, Paul Auerbach, Ray Mears, Mike Pewtherer, Mors Kochanski, Mykel Hawke, and many others. I would also like to acknowledge all the bushcraft and survival bloggers and YouTubers for sharing their knowledge and ideas.

It would be impossible to identify and credit all the sources I relied on for this book. Many of the facts came from various sources, including books, peer-reviewed articles, and websites. You will find a list of selected references at the end of this book.

CONTENTS

INTRODUCTION

This book is not the usual wilderness survival guide, and it's not for beginners. There is a vast difference between a short-term survival situation (typically lasting 72 hours) and a long-term situation (lasting more than 30 days). Most books on wilderness survival focus on primitive skills and bushcraft or on staying alive in the short-term while a search and rescue team finds you. *Thrive* is different. Its guiding idea is: if one had to live in the wild for up to one year with only a single book, what would it contain?

Thrive provides strategies, tips, and techniques that could be used if you need to survive in the wild for an extended period. This book is for survivalists, bushcrafters, back-to-the-landers, and anyone interested in knowing what it takes to live in the wilderness for an extended period of time, including obtaining a significant portion of food through hunting, foraging, trapping, and fishing.

I don't want to discourage the survival- and preparedness-minded readers from putting this book in their bug-out bag, but I want them to know that bugging out during an extended emergency to "live off the land" is not wise. You are better off sheltering in a small community that can withstand natural disasters by feeding itself, protecting itself, and providing its own energy—localization is the main idea. Nevertheless, many of the techniques and information here are helpful in a wide range of situations, including sheltering in place.

This guide is meant to be used for both preparation and reference in the field. It is organized using a pattern common in many survival books, but that shouldn't trick you into thinking its contents are the same. Although I will barely scratch the surface of some topics, others will be covered in depth.

Thrive covers all seasons, particularly winter, and emphasizes survival in the boreal forest. This guide focuses on remote wilderness locations, and is more appropriate for northern areas, such as Alaska, the Northern United States, Canada, Scandinavia, and Russia. Nevertheless, people in more temperate climates will still find information relevant to their local regions.

My partner and I spent six months living in the wilderness in 2016, complementing our rations with food that we harvested from the boreal forest. In 2019, I spent a hundred days solo in the boreal forest during the winter months, foraging to complement my small rations. Most recently, I was a participant on Season 9 of The History Channel's survival series *Alone*.

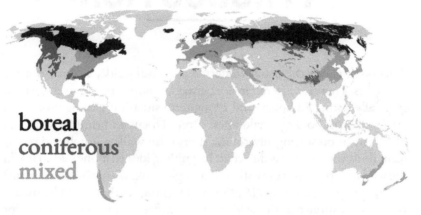

boreal
coniferous
mixed

PREPARATION

"What kept the Baileys, the Robertsons, and Poon Lim alive?
Experience, preparation, equipment, and luck."
— Steven Callahan, *Adrift*

Proper planning prevents piss-poor performance, or at least it aims to. Long-term wilderness survival is tough—you must have every edge to your advantage. That's why a very well-thought-out approach and not falling in love with the original plan is critical. Making a plan will help you spot any holes in your strategy, determine what gear you need to change or acquire, and figure out which skills you need to improve. The bottom line is to always have a plan but never expect it to work out without improvisation.

Having written this, I believe the transformation from knowledge into instinct-like responses through extensive experience is also as important—or even more so—as having a plan.

SURVIVAL PRINCIPLES

Before starting preparations, it's good to consider what I call *survival principles*. The following ideas help guide every aspect of a plan, from gear selection to foraging strategies:

KNOW THYSELF

Be aware of your and your group's strengths and weaknesses. Be mindful of your actual skill level, and take on challenges gradually, according to your experience. Don't start a challenge for the wrong reasons or without being sufficiently prepared.

MURPHY'S LAW

Anything that can go wrong will go wrong. Murphy's Law is not about being pessimistic. It's about proper risk management.

When you are in a situation in which a minor incident can escalate, you must be aware of any potential failures (in your gear, strategy, health, and so on). And you should make plans to deal with those failures. Be ready for unexpected adversity, and be flexible. You can't truly design a resilient strategy with backup plans if you believe it will be all rainbows and sunshine.

Err on the side of caution: if things going south have dangerous consequences, then it's best to be proactive and prevent an incident from happening in the first place.

KEEP IT SIMPLE

This principle goes along with Murphy's Law. If your plans, gear, and techniques have multiple moving parts, they will have numerous points of failure. By simplifying things, you can rely on them more, and your backups will also be more straightforward. Simplicity is better than complexity in rapidly changing situations.

REDUNDANCY

Two is one, and one is none. Redundancy is a buffer that allows you to function if there is a failure. In mountaineering, redundancy is a principle to live by; ignoring this principle means risking death. In wilderness survival, redundancy can be just as vital. It doesn't mean that you must have backups for your backups for everything—you must prioritize. If a component of your plan or equipment is critical, you should have a backup or two.

For gear, it's better to have alternative means of achieving something instead of just having duplicate equipment. The idea is to decrease weight and bulk and have versatile gear.

For instance, you could have an axe and a saw instead of having two axes. If you lose one of them, you can still cut firewood with the other. The combination is much more versatile than having two axes or two saws. Also, having alternative means of accomplishing a task results in less likelihood of experiencing the same failure twice. Diversity is resilience.

TEN ESSENTIALS

Hiking organizations recommend carrying these 10 essentials when traveling in the backcountry: navigation, headlamp, sun protection, first aid, knife, fire starter, shelter, extra food, extra water, and extra clothing. It is a basic list, but it's a helpful reminder when preparing a gear list. As people become more experienced in backcountry travel, they may need less stuff and only pack exactly what they need for regular outings. The problem is that long-term survival is not a typical outing. To compensate for the tendency of only bringing what you need, consider the 10 essentials and add extra gear in each category. It's simple and it works.

RISK VERSUS REWARD

Never seek a reward that is not worth the risk. For example, eating a questionable plant or mushroom that is not found in great abundance. Why risk getting severely sick—or worse—for a meager amount of calories? If your actions carry more risk, it must be because that added risk makes an essential difference in your results. If that's not the case, perform your tasks more safely. For example, cut kindling with a knife and a baton instead of holding the kindling with one hand and using a hatchet.

ENERGY RETURN ON INVESTMENT

Energy is everything. In survival, you'll recognize it as heat in firewood or calories in food. Everything you do in long-term survival should first go through a quick mental calculation: will it give you more energy than you will spend? To increase the energy you are acquiring, you should be efficient with your work and always try to conserve energy. Aim to achieve maximum return for the minimum effort.

Work smart. Avoid working above 60%–70% of your maximum heart rate, for it is less energy efficient. Slow down or take a break if you're short of breath or your heart is pounding. In addition, your body needs fewer calories when asleep, so sleep more. Work with nature, not against it: use natural cycles and animal habits to your advantage. If you don't have to stand, then sit; if you don't have to sit, then lie down. Rest often. Plan things in your mind, and try to find the most efficient way before starting a project. Thinking before acting could save you a lot of energy. In short, if you plan to live off the land, be sure you gain more energy from eating a fish than the energy you used to catch it, prepare it, and cook it.

Something else to keep in mind is the 80/20 principle: roughly 80% of the effects come from 20% of the sources. In business, it is often expressed as: 80% of sales come from 20% of clients. This principle also works in reverse: 80% of your sources will only provide you with 20% of your return. Use the 80/20 principle as a rule of thumb to focus efforts on what will give you the most return. Minimize the energy and effort spent on the 80% of sources that provide you with only 20% of return.

EVERYTHING TAKES MORE EFFORT

Sometimes our minds view things from an armchair perspective and believe that building a shelter or doing a project will be relatively quick or easy. That is far from the truth. You can blame that delusion on being relatively well-fed, living in a modern home, and having many modern comforts. In a long-term survival situation, you should expect to be extremely tired, have limited energy and equipment, and suffer unexpected setbacks. You'll quickly realize you can only work on the most critical things from the list of projects you had initially planned.

YOU NEED EVERY ADVANTAGE

This is one of the most important principles. Don't bring a knife to a gunfight. Set yourself up for success by rigging the game in your favor. Choose the most effective and dependable tactics. Prepare thoroughly and figure things out well in advance. Think fishing nets instead of rods, and steel traps instead of primitive traps.

The fact is, living off the wild is extremely hard. Hunter-gatherers have had to deal with feast and famine, and particularly in the North, they often starved. Those who died were people that had lived their entire lives as hunter-gatherers; they knew the land well and had access to healthy ecosystems. There aren't any emergency handouts in the wild. If the year's harvest is scarce, you may starve. That is the sacred and natural balance.

I roll my eyes whenever I hear or read that if only people had enough knowledge of wild edible plants, they would never starve. Or that some individuals could go naked into the wild equipped with only a knife and survive indefinitely. Ishi, the last surviving member of the Yahi people, might have managed something similar for three years in California in the 1900s (after he was forced to). However, he probably had to steal food from settlers to survive throughout that time. In the end, he could not endure it any longer. He managed to temporarily live alone in the wild only because he had a lifetime of intimate knowledge of his area and total mastery of local hunter-gatherer skills.

NATURE IS NEUTRAL

The bush is neither for nor against you. It is not there to help or harm you. But it sure loves to be unpredictable. Nature is mighty powerful, and you need to adapt to it. It can be quite ruthless or incredibly helpful, but really, it just is. If you have a mindset of man vs. wild, expect to fail. You can't fight nature and expect to win—you can't defeat the infinite. It's best to start from a humble perspective and learn from other earthlings. Nature is the ultimate teacher.

I'm not saying you shouldn't pray to nature for abundance, just that nature helps those who help themselves.

ADAPT

As best you can, adapt your expectations to your circumstances. It often helps to have low expectations. Embrace the suck, and behave like the natives (human and animal). Try to improve your situation continually, unless you are already in a reasonably good position.

BREAK THE RULES

There are no rules in survival, only guiding principles. Many principles are well-founded and time-tested, but don't let them impose limits on what you could be capable of if your life were on the line.

SURVIVAL HABITS

Practice the following habits. They will help you act safer, achieve more, increase your awareness, and improve your mindset.

ALWAYS GIVE 100% EFFORT THE FIRST TIME

Do not rush things when you lack resources and energy. Do a task properly from the start to avoid spending time and effort later redoing the task. Avoid cutting corners unless you absolutely have to.

I've struggled to start a fire in the rain or with a bow drill because I'm taking shortcuts, not fully prepared, or just rushing things. I end up spending more time and energy doing tasks more than once. The irony is that instead of taking shortcuts in difficult circumstances, one should be adequately prepared and give a total effort from the start.

SAFETY FIRST

The more hazards you have around you, the more you need to manage risk. It's not the time to take unnecessary risks, but the time to be extra cautious. It can be challenging, but you must be disciplined and use safe techniques and protective equipment.

Wearing safety glasses when bushwhacking or leather gloves when using a saw might seem overly cautious to some people. It may seem excessive when surrounded by others, with hospitals just a couple of minutes away. But suppose I'm in a remote area relying on just myself or a small group. In that case, I can't afford to have an eye injury or to rip my fingers apart—and neither can my group. I err on the side of caution and wear safety gear and use safe techniques, especially when I'm tired or my mind is not at its 100%.

Having the discipline and humility to take fewer risks allows you to navigate circumstances that others deem too dangerous.

NEVER PASS UP AN OPPORTUNITY

Use different routes when walking to increase the chances of finding something useful. Explore your surrounding area thoroughly: there may be important resources you missed.

Nature works in cycles of feast and famine, so if you catch plenty of food, don't stop—preserve your bounty and keep foraging. And never come back to camp empty-handed: bring back something useful, like firewood or kindling.

FINDING INSTEAD OF MAKING

It is generally easier to find stuff than to make it yourself. Take the time to find the ideal materials, such as a particular tree branch for a bushcraft project.

DON'T LOSE GEAR

Losing gear sucks, but losing something critical like a knife or a fire starter could be devastating (been there, done that). If it happens, don't dwell on it; accept it and party on.

To avoid losing gear in the first place, you can do a few things: paint it with bright colors, attach colored lanyards, and avoid having small items in earth tones. Thoroughly test your tool sheaths and holsters to see if they could fail, always close them properly, and even modify them to hold your tools more securely.

One of the most common times in which a survivalist loses or destroys a fire starter or knife is while lighting a fire.

Always sweep your resting spots, lunch spots, campsites, or anywhere you sit down. To do an area sweep, slowly walk over all the places where you could have left or dropped something; look at the ground and around any tree branches. Finally, when traveling, make sure any item that could fall out of your pockets or off the sides of your pack, sled, canoe, and so on is tied down. Ensure your gear will stay attached even if it hits a branch. When paddling, always tie down your gear to the boat or to something else.

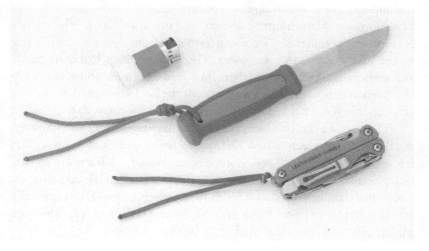

GRATITUDE

When your basic needs are not fully met, it is vital to acknowledge what you have. This will help you stay calm and more satisfied. Read true survival stories. It helps to put things in perspective and think about stories of people who went through much more demanding circumstances. Take the time to enjoy little things like a nice sunset or a drink of water. These moments of gratitude will recharge you.

BE HERE, NOW

Being present is the most important habit for survival and life in general. It is helpful in two ways: as a healthy mental habit and for adaptation. There is no fear or worry in the present. Focus on the present if you want to have a grounded mind during a survival situation. Suppose you're constantly thinking about the future or the past. In that case, the present will pass you by, and it will be harder for you to seize opportunities to be grateful. As a result, your resilience will decrease.

In addition to the benefits of being mindful, being present-minded will increase your awareness of the changing surroundings and environment, and awareness is the foundation of adaptation.

SURVIVAL WISDOM

INDIGENOUS APPROACH AND PRIMITIVE TECH

It is important to analyze Indigenous peoples' approaches for survival in your local bioregion. Many hunter-gatherers lived sustainably in their bioregions for centuries or millennia. We all can learn a lot from their approaches, but we can't survive the same way today. Their regions likely had more plants and animals, and the habitats where they lived were more abundant. They also lived in tribes and their knowledge of the land was passed down over generations. What worked for them won't work for you today.

The use of primitive technology has advantages and disadvantages, much like modern technology. The main benefits of primitive tech are that it is sustainable (it doesn't need nonrenewable resources); it is relatively easy to repair, maintain, and create; and it is mainly made from local materials. Some disadvantages are that it tends to deteriorate sooner, it is generally less effective, it requires more knowledge and skill, and it needs more maintenance and care than modern technology requires.

As you get more experienced and skilled, you might use primitive technology more. Still, for long-term survival, it is best to have it as a complement or backup to modern technologies. You might not get the importance of this point initially, particularly if you like primitive technology, but nature will emphasize this point pretty quickly.

REVISE YOUR PLANS CONSTANTLY

I've learned the hard way that you must revise your entire approach on an ongoing basis. For example, if your plan gets delayed and your time frame changes, you need to adjust the whole plan, not just a few things. You may need gear for a different season, more rations, warmer clothes, warmer shelter, or even an entirely different approach. For example, you may have to pull a sled instead of paddling a canoe or use an alternative route.

You must also revise specific plans, like building a shelter. Maybe there aren't as many materials out there, or the project requires more effort than previously thought. Maybe there's too much or not enough snow.

Sometimes nature will give you strong hints for you to do a task now or later depending on various conditions.

ROMANCE VERSUS REALITY

Reality can be harsh. It's easy to read a book or watch a show and fantasize about living off the wild—being "one with the forest," asking for and receiving bounties from Mother Nature, or living off a few deer and rabbits. Things don't work that way: you starve, you get cold, and you get chronically tired.

Don't get me wrong, it can be a unique, life-changing experience, but the romance will quickly vanish. Doing some trial runs helps get rid of this delusion.

LOCATION

Location, location, location. I can't stress this enough. Location is paramount; that's why many hunter-gatherer societies were nomadic and moved from area to area in search of abundance and seasonal resources.

At the risk of oversimplifying, the ideal place for a hunter-gatherer camp is near the junction of a big river and the ocean. It provides access to a large territory: the sea, the land, the water upstream, and opportunities for foraging, fishing, hunting, and trapping.

Inland, the next best thing is a very large lake with a big inlet stream and with a major outlet stream leading to the sea. Another alternative is a large river that leads to the sea. Water is a theme here, and so is change or transition. Other locations won't be as good, but they could still sustain you.

Life is more abundant in transition zones: where the land meets the air, a lake meets a river, a forest meets a prairie, the mountains meet the plains, the coast meets the ocean, and so on. For instance, a relatively recent wildfire provides berries in the summer and creates transition zones along a forest.

However, coastal areas or rivers often entail close contact with civilization. So being in a more remote and less desirable place—at least to civilization—as well as in a warmer climate (less need for calories and work) with greater plant and animal diversity makes sense for a modern hunter-gatherer.

WATER AND FOOD

Choose a location that has clean water and abundant fish and mammals. A lake with many inlets and outlets has more fish, and the bigger the lake or river, the more fish it will have. Find out how the local Indigenous peoples in your area fed themselves 500 years ago. Did they hunt bison? Did they grow maize, beans, and squash? What were their main staples? These questions can give you hints about which areas are best. The major staples in my neck of the woods were wild rice, moose, caribou, and fish. So an ideal location in my area has habitats for those.

Transition zones have more food, so naturally, an ideal place has numerous types of terrain with diverse and healthy populations of plants and animals. Look at maps or statistics of ungulate or predator populations to give you a better idea of the viability of an area.

VEGETATION

A place with varied terrain offers different vegetation and provides more food. A site with various species of coniferous and deciduous trees will provide better shelter materials and resources than a place with just one or two species of trees.

ACCESS

The location should be relatively accessible (in and out) but still remote enough. Ideally, there should be snowmobile routes or paddling routes nearby. The more remote an area, the less likely you are of encountering others, but the harder it will be to get rescued or walk out. In an emergency, poor access and continually changing conditions could be a deadly combination.

CLIMATE

Gather information on the local climate, including temperatures, precipitation, wind, freeze-up and breakup seasons, water levels, and snow cover. Your notes will help you visualize the challenges you might face and allow you to plan accordingly.

TEMPERATURES

Look at graphs of both monthly mean temperatures and extreme monthly temperatures of the nearest weather stations or towns. Those should give you a good indication of what kind of weather you should prepare to deal with during different seasons.

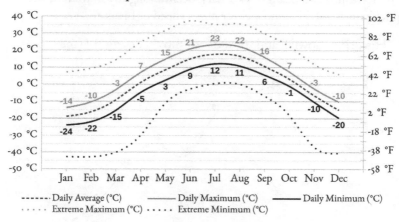

Historical Temperatures 52.36° N 97.02° W (1981-2010)

Data: Environment Canada

To find a diagram of your local weather station, check out **meteoblue.com** or **weatherspark.com** and search for its historical temperatures.

RAIN

In places with plenty of rain, you should find out how many days it rains each month and how much rain you should expect. Look for monthly rainfall averages and average precipitation days. Rain can be a big factor—particularly when coupled with cold. It really intensifies the challenges of staying warm, drying gear, and finding firewood.

WATER LEVELS

Suppose water is your method of transport in and out of the wild. In that case, traveling when the water is high might be better, depending on the existence of rapids on your route and how water levels affect their difficulty. Be aware of dropping water levels throughout the year because some fishing and trapping methods will have to be adjusted as the levels change. Of course, you'll be wise to have a tide table on the coast (or a watch with a tide table feature).

SNOW

Find out the historical snow depth profiles, as they will let you visualize how deep the snow is at different times of the year. The profiles could help with timing trapping, hunting, and travel activities. In the boreal forest, snow starts to accumulate in October, around the same time as freeze-up. The accumulation peaks in February, declines slightly in March, and falls quickly in April. The snow cover melts ahead of breakup.

Historical snowfall and snow depth 51.07° N 93.79° W (1981-2010)

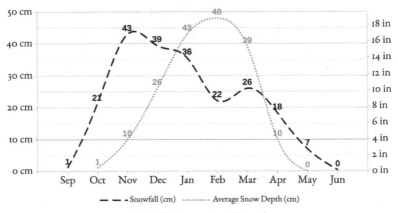

Data: Environment Canada

FREEZE-UP AND BREAKUP

In northern places with lots of lakes and rivers, one of the most important stages of the year is the freeze-thaw cycle. It can be unsafe and almost impossible to travel during these times of the year, and it can disrupt foraging activities—like fishing. Both animals and humans are greatly affected.

I didn't leave early enough before the freeze-up in my winter expedition. I paddled, and after rounding one of the first curves in the river, I had to turn back. Ice had accumulated at the river bend and the river was frozen over. Leave at least 10 to 15 days as a buffer of time when planning something around freeze-up or breakup.

Air temperature is a huge factor in the freeze-up and breakup dates. The time between the first ice and total freeze-over averages 19 days on rivers and 13 days on lakes, but this changes from location to location and year to year. Generally, rivers freeze later and clear up earlier than nearby lakes due to their currents. Often, before lakes freeze over, a full or partial ice cover will form and then melt.

Medium-sized lakes require two to three weeks to freeze over after the mean daily temperature drops below freezing. Breakups generally begin with the ice softening before the final thaw. Most lakes thaw completely two to six weeks after the mean daily air temperature rises above 32°F (0°C).

After the mean daily air temperature drops below freezing, it takes rivers four to five weeks to freeze over, and some small rivers only take two weeks. Breakup on rivers usually occurs three to four weeks after the mean daily air temperature has risen above 32°F (0°C). You can check weekly satellite imagery from multiple satellite constellations at the Sentinel Playground (bit.ly/sentinel-hub) to better understand freeze-up and breakup times for a specific region. Check this map (bit.ly/freez-up) if you live above the 49th parallel.

WIND

Knowing your local prevailing winds is helpful for keeping your camp sheltered and for minimizing campfire smoke. Awareness of the different prevailing winds throughout the seasons can help you make better decisions. Both weatherspark.com and windhistory.com provide historical wind directions and speeds for specific months and seasons.

SUNLIGHT

Another variable to be aware of is daylight hours. You can find charts for your area by searching for a sun graph or daylight hours graph on timeanddate.com.

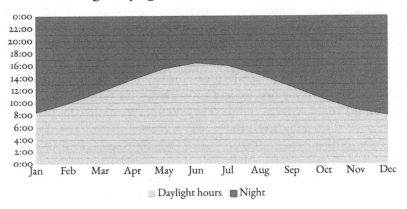

Average daylight hours for 51.0° N -95.7° W

BUGS

It is quite helpful to know when the season is for mosquitoes, ticks, sandflies, and horseflies in your area. If mosquitoes are a major nuisance, check out the Google search interest of your region (bit.ly/mosq-to) to know when to expect the worst periods.

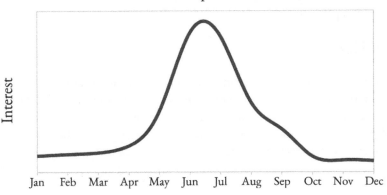

Search interest in mosquitoes, Minnesota

TRIP INTEL

MAPS

Waterproof topographic maps are more expensive, but they are worth it because they withstand folding, dirt, water, and other field abuse. You can search online and buy a ready-made map, but a custom map is the best option. The benefit of a custom map is that you can customize the scale and the area it covers so that the map aligns better with your purpose.

The scale I recommend for a custom map is 1:25,000 to 1:50,000 for navigation. 1:25,000 is more detailed but doesn't cover as much of the area. For a general overview of the area, I recommend a scale of 1:100,000 to 1:250,000. You could use the former scale for navigation in a pinch, but the latter would be difficult to use.

Either way, you should still mark areas of interest and routes. Here are some useful things to mark in your map that may or may not be already included:

- primary and alternative routes to and from camp
- evacuation routes
- location of water sources (ponds, streams, springs)
- food source locations (fruit trees, fishing spots, animal trails)
- roads, fire roads, snowmobile trails, and winter roads
- location of airstrips and railroad lines
- mines, quarries, and dumps
- electricity lines and antennas
- rapids, portages, and paddling routes
- wilderness lodges and their contact phone numbers or emails
- cabins and boat caches
- hunting and foraging sites and traplines

Locals might be aware of many of the areas of interest above. A few online tools are available to find those points of interest. **Caltopo.com** is great for exploring an area while using different layers simultaneously, such as Global Imagery, USGS Topo, and various topo map layers. If you want a different option than Global Imagery, you can use the Aerial View option in Bing Maps (**bit.ly/2a3rial**) to see an area taken from a different time and with different satellites. The website **strava.com/heatmap** can be used to find trails and routes, but it primarily only covers places near civilization.

When using CalTopo, try out the topographic layers and the MapBuilder overlay. To find hard-to-spot human-made structures and paths, explore the False Color IR base layer.

If you want to dive into a rabbit hole, check out government management plans for the area, as they often include valuable maps and information.

You can also explore Sentinel Hub (bit.ly/sentinel-hub) to see satellite imagery during a specific week and year and see an area change throughout the seasons.

Sometimes I want detailed topo maps of a route, but that requires too many maps if the trip is long. So what I do instead is print a set of maps on regular printer paper. CalTopo is a good tool for this, although it has limitations in the free version.

You can print maps on weather-resistant paper, but I usually use regular paper and a waterproof map case with a rolling closure, as other types of closures leak.

Another option for printing free US topo maps is NatGeo maps (bit. ly/nat7geo).

Finally, if you want full-size custom maps in waterproof plastic or fabric, check out kartamaps.com or mytopo.com.

CANADIAN MAPS

Gissurfer.com is an alternative to CalTopo. Although it's not as good, it has Canadian topo map layers and a third source for satellite images: ESRI.

In CalTopo, you can add a custom source for Canadian topographic maps: select the "WMS" type, and the "URL template" is the URL address that appears after you visit this link (bit.ly/topo2-ca). Additionally, I highly recommend looking at backroadmapbooks.com. Their topo maps sometimes include information like paddling routes, portages, and snowmobile trails.

OTHER INTEL

In addition to maps, print or write down the following information in a waterproof notepad:

Cache reports: Where is the cache located? Write clear instructions on how to locate it. Include a list of the contents, their expiration dates, and other relevant information.

Communications plan: How often will you communicate, and what will each party do if communication suddenly fails? Is there an alternative method of communication? When does it make sense to start a rescue? What phone numbers should be called if there is an emergency?

Radio communication: frequencies, call signs, compass bearings, and contact times. Local NOAA Weather Radio or Weatheradio Canada frequencies for weather forecasts and a list of AM and FM stations in the general area. A tall, improvised antenna made of thin wire can receive AM and FM signals from stations outside the typical range.

GROUP

According to some anthropologists, the ideal number of a hunter-gatherer group is around 25 people, including children and elders. The number of active foragers is about 7–8 people. Based on those numbers and the size of working groups in various settings, a group of 10–12 would be ideal. With modern technology, you could reduce the group size to 5–8 people. Avoid having fewer than that because almost all wild foods are seasonal— you must gather and process them in a relatively short time frame. With many helping hands, you can process more food and preserve it before it spoils. The group can split up in pairs (for safety and support) and work on different places and resources. Small groups have difficulty focusing on different types of foods simultaneously. They may have to prioritize and skip some sources. On the other hand, the larger the group, the larger the need for resources and the more potential for interpersonal conflicts.

Wilderness areas can't sustain big groups like agriculture can. That's why our hunter-gatherer ancestors lived in smaller groups.

Ideally, the group members should have had past bonding experiences and performed under challenging conditions before embarking on a survival situation.

GROUP CONFLICT AND ISOLATION

Conflict will happen when you live in close quarters with a group of people 24–7 and don't have much contact with people outside your group. In a wilderness situation, there will be added challenges. The people in the group will be highly irritable because they will be outside their comfort zones and underfed. This can lead to frustrations and misunderstandings.

Strategies to prevent or address conflict in these circumstances include having a private journal, using satellite communications to contact people outside your group, having solo projects, or having some alone time every day.

Other strategies that may help are playing games, meditating, doing breathing exercises, having hobbies, retreating to a quiet place, and even having a time out. To improve the group's dynamics, it helps to have clear communication and better listening skills. Group conflict is challenging and can make an already difficult situation much worse.

TRAINING

"The more you sweat in peace, the less you bleed in war."
— Norman Schwarzkopf

You should train and practice five major tenets for long-term survival: wilderness first aid, friction fire, navigation, hunting-gathering techniques, and wilderness trips.

WILDERNESS FIRST AID

Wilderness first aid (WFA) courses are nothing like regular first aid courses. In regular first aid, the standard procedure is to call 911. WFA courses teach you to deal with emergencies yourself because you are at least an hour away from help. In reality, even a helicopter could be more than 12 hours away. Stay away from WFA courses provided by standard first aid course providers like the Red Cross; instead, look for courses from organizations that specifically teach WFA. The courses last 16, 40, and 80 hours. If you have the money and time, take the 80-hour course. It's expensive but worth it. Otherwise, take the 40-hour course. Volunteer as a first aid attendant at outdoor events or work as an outdoors guide to practice your WFA skills.

FRICTION FIRE

In an actual long-term survival situation, it's not likely that you'll ever need to start a fire with a bow drill. Yet, it's still worthwhile to be proficient with this skill for two reasons. First, the journey to successfully carving a bow drill kit in the field and starting a fire will ensure you dominate the fundamentals of fire, even under challenging conditions. Second, it will give you the confidence to keep going in the unlikely event you lose all your fire starters.

It's easier to learn how to carve a bow drill kit in the field and start a fire with it from a mentor. Another way that takes more practice is watching videos online and learning through experience. I recommend the video **bit.ly/bow-DR** by Cédrik Grenier as a start.

NAVIGATION

I don't go over the basics of navigation because I'm assuming they're already familiar to you. If they're not, or if you don't feel very confident with your navigation skills, I suggest you take a course on land navigation with map and compass. You should also be familiar with survival methods of navigation without map and compass. In addition, practicing awareness and observational skills complements your map and compass skills.

I suggest you read *Be Expert with Map and Compass* by Björn Kjellström if you want to learn more about land navigation.

HUNTING AND GATHERING

Unfortunately, sometimes it's not easy to practice all the hunting and gathering skills we would like, and often it's almost impossible because of local laws. Still, I think it is wise to practice as many techniques as possible.

WILDERNESS TRIPS

Doing long and remote wilderness trips is an excellent way to get experience and be more comfortable being entirely on your own. It also allows you to practice being resourceful and to develop resilience by being outside of your comfort zone and experiencing challenging situations.

Being familiar with the challenges that could arise makes it easier for the brain to act. If you are way out of your comfort zone and are not familiar with the steps that need to be taken, you could panic or freeze. But if it's not your first rodeo, you can better focus on the whole picture and stay aware of your mindset. A person with less training and experience would be more stressed out and overwhelmed than one who has practiced survival skills to the point where they are almost second nature.

MENTAL PREPARATION

Training your mind is even more important than practicing wilderness skills. In the next chapter, I'll dive fully into the survival mindset. In the meantime, see below for activities you can do to train your mental toughness and resilience.

When you have a good idea of what to expect in a difficult challenge, you're less likely to find the reality overwhelming, so research as much as possible, and read survival stories.

Create a list of your victories and achievements and read it every now and then. Doing this can boost your confidence and rekindle your motivation.

Visualize what your routine is going to look like. Complete your journey mentally: be specific and use your five senses.

Practice discipline and exercise your willpower. Forcing yourself to do something unpleasant, like cold showers every day, will test your determination—especially on the days when you least want to.

PHYSICAL PREPARATION

MEDICAL CHECKUP

Ideally, get blood tests done. The complete blood count and metabolic panel could uncover anemia and other deficiencies in your glucose, calcium, electrolyte, and vitamin levels. Also, get a dental checkup.

NUTRITION

To prevent mineral and vitamin deficiencies, take a multivitamin daily for six months prior to your wilderness adventure. That should help load your body with essential nutrients that you may be lacking later.

Maximize your intake of protein and fat during the months prior to your adventure to train your body to process higher quantities of protein and fat in a short time. Food in the wild appears in cycles of feast and famine, so your digestive system needs to absorb as much nutrition as it can when food is available (mainly in the form of fat and protein).

Experiment with interval fasting to train your body to work efficiently even if you haven't eaten in a while, but don't let this reduce your fat reserves.

BODYWEIGHT

Consider gaining substantial weight. Being fit and active helps you stay strong and be less prone to injury, but being reasonably overweight is an advantage in a long-term survival situation. That's precisely why the human body has that tendency to put on weight. One pound (0.45 kg) of body fat has roughly 3,500 calories. That translates into the energy required to sustain an average person for one to one and a half days.

On the other hand, being more muscular than needed is a disadvantage because the body needs more energy to maintain muscle than to retain fat.

If you want to put on weight fast, one of the most effective ways is to drink a gallon of milk a day and drink shots of olive oil (and eat a bit less than normal).

If you want to simulate what would happen to your body with different amounts of calorie intakes per day, check out bit.ly/A-bwp. In a long-term survival situation, expect to lose about a pound of fat per day (or slightly more) during the first several weeks.

EXERCISE

There are a few functional exercises that help you prepare your body. Cutting firewood with an axe and saw exercises the same muscles and allows you to practice the movements you'll use. It also allows you to improve your technique and safety.

Forget hiking; go bushwhacking instead. Bushwhacking will help you negotiate obstacles and become less likely to fall and injure yourself. Backpacking is a good way to train your body to carry heavy gear over rugged terrain. Nevertheless, it's best to avoid backpacking in a long-term situation; it's very inefficient and restricts the amount of gear you can carry. Paddling through water and traveling on snow are more suitable for unaided travel.

Also, weighted carries of stones, logs, or water is an excellent way to strengthen your grip, trunk, core, and back. Those exercises can also help you prevent injuries and develop better form when doing many everyday tasks of backcountry living.

COLD

There are a few ways to prepare for a cold environment, but the main one is to expose yourself to the cold. Regular cold exposure forces your body to adapt. It trains your blood vessels to contract and dilate more effectively, improving your cold tolerance in your hands and feet. Using less insulation on your feet and hands is a good way to encourage this process.

Another significant way the body adapts to cold is by increasing your metabolism—using energy to keep warm. This shifting of gears is not ideal if you're lacking in energy. That's why, if you're not eating enough, you must do everything you can to keep yourself warm with clothing, sleeping bag, shelter, and fire.

Another way to improve your cold tolerance is by having a diet higher in fat. However, this is not easy in the wild.

GEAR

Before diving into gear later in the book, I'd like to briefly explain the main things you need to look for in equipment.

It should be durable: most outdoor gear is designed to be used only occasionally. Be careful that the equipment you choose will at least last an entire season of hard use. Paying attention to the materials, design, and construction can tell you if a product will last. Still, the best way to know is really through trial by fire. Field testing can show you where potential points of failure are so that you can reinforce them.

Durability often comes with the drawbacks of added bulk and weight. You can't have it all. Unfortunately, lightweight gear compromises affordability or durability. Think carefully about those compromises and decide what's best for you.

Multipurpose items enable you to cope with a broader set of circumstances, but there's a balance to it. If your piece of equipment aims to do too many things, it won't be good at any of them.

RISK MANAGEMENT

"No plan survives first contact with the enemy."
— Helmuth von Moltke

CONTINGENCY PLANNING

Always plan for the unusual and unexpected. It helps to:
1. regularly pay attention to weather conditions;

2. strategize worst-case scenarios;
3. always carry a survival kit (or at the very least, a fire starter); and
4. avoid traveling solo.

Send a detailed copy of your planned route and location with potential evacuation routes and expected return time to *two* emergency contacts. If you want to go a step further, include a GPS waypoint file of your route and the general direction you would take in an emergency if all goes to hell. Establish a date and time with your two contacts to call SAR/911 if you are not back by that time, but leave a generous buffer.

Carry a rechargeable NOAA Weather Radio to receive weather forecasts (this may not work in remote areas). Or keep it simple and observe the wind and sky conditions once in a while. Be vigilant of developing events, such as tornadoes and wildfires. Have a plan.

Avoid traveling solo. Being solo in the wild is not a death sentence, but make sure your skill level is appropriate. And make sure you do everything you can to manage the risks, such as carrying a survival kit on your person if you're solo in a remote wilderness area. The bare minimum you should have is a signaling mirror, a fire starter, and a personal locator beacon.

Scenario planning will allow you to prioritize and execute tasks during an emergency much more efficiently. It pays to stay ahead of potential problems. You should visualize the failure of every critical stage of your plan and piece of equipment, then figure out what you would do in response. Maybe you'll come up with a better approach or add alternative means for certain tasks.

As part of your scenario planning, you must designate self-evacuation routes along your area. You, or your rescuers, might need to use them, so leave a copy with your emergency contacts.

RISK MANAGEMENT

It pays off to do a serious risk analysis for something as challenging as long-term survival:
*   Identify possible threats.
*   Assess your plan's vulnerability to those threats.
*   Determine the likelihood and consequences of specific failures.
*   Identify ways to reduce, avoid, share, or accept those risks.

Potential risks in a long-term survival scenario include injury, starvation, fires, poisoning, harmful wildlife encounters, drowning, cold weather issues, infections, and death.

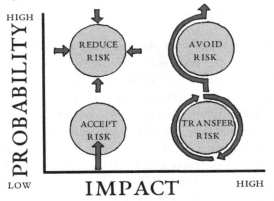

PERSONAL SURVIVAL KIT

A good kit needs to be portable because if you don't have it with you, what's the point? When building your kit, think about the possible scenarios you could use it for. How is it going to play a role? There are seven primary needs that a basic 72-hour survival kit should cover: first aid, navigation, fire, signaling, knife, water, and shelter.

Below are some ideas for building a kit. Adjust the list to your specific needs.

	Quantity	
First Aid	1	Bandage
	1	Duct tape (8 ft / 2.5 m)
Navigation	1	Compass (Ranger SL Silva fits inside bottle)
	1	Headlamp (Fenix HM23 or Petzl e+LITE)
Fire	2	BIC lighters (in a ziplock bag, preferably piezoelectric)
	25	Waterproof storm matches with strikers
	6	Tinder petroleum jelly cotton balls (in a ziplock bag)
Signaling	1	Signaling mirror
	1	Waterproof whistle
	1	PLB (for remote areas, won't fit in bottle)
	1	Orange contractor bag (rain poncho, shelter, signal)
	20 ft	Wire (repairs, snares, smoke generator)
Knife	1	Knife (Mora Eldris fits inside bottle)
Water	20	Water treatment tablets (Aquatabs)
	1	Stainless steel bottle or empty food can
Shelter	15 ft	Paracord (MIL-SPEC)

PERSONAL LOCATOR BEACON

If you want your kit to be as effective as possible, you can't go wrong with a Personal Locator Beacon (PLB). These devices are meant only to be used if your life or limb is in danger. There is no subscription, and you can rest assured it will have a battery. The only catch with a PLB is that you shouldn't get complacent; it could take hours or days to get rescued, just like with any other satellite emergency device. See the chapter on electronics for further information.

EXTRAS

Trying to cover the need for a shelter and keep the kit very compact is not easy. I recommend a sil-nylon poncho tarp (Rab or Sea to Summit).

Unfortunately, space blankets and other disposable shelters can't be relied upon. In buggy areas, head nets are life-changing. I recommend having them. In winter, an excellent addition to a kit is a pot, bottle, or can for melting snow and boiling water (an empty can may be used if the inside lining is burned first). Another item to consider adding is a pocket chainsaw.

THE BARE MINIMUM

When I spent 100 days solo in the boreal forest during winter, I carried a small kit that consisted of a lighter (in a plastic bag), a Personal Locator Beacon, and a signal mirror. That's usually the same kit I carry in my Personal Flotation Device (PFD) when wilderness canoe tripping. The idea behind this minimal kit is that if I'm separated from my gear and my life or limb is in danger, I can fire up my PLB and spend a few nights with just those items waiting to be rescued.

CACHING

Caching gear and food is a time-tested technique used for long expeditions. Cached rations and equipment (woodstoves, steel traps, fishing nets, etc.) are a tremendous asset in a long-term situation. In remote areas where there are no paddling routes and everything has to be carried on foot, caching food and gear makes a lot of sense.

Once you have determined what you'll cache, you can look for a potential site. Topographic maps and satellite imagery can help you pick an area, but you must visit the site to see if it is viable. When visiting potential locations, have a map, compass, tape measure, GPS, notepad, and a small shovel to test the ease of digging if you are burying your cache.

If it will be a long time before you retrieve your cache, place it in a location that is relatively easy to find with instructions. There should be specific landmarks that can be used to take compass bearings and locate the site. Consider the changing seasons and weather conditions with regards to site location. Will changes in the seasons leave the cache site exposed or make it impossible to retrieve? Is the cache difficult for wildlife to access?

Once you have found a suitable location for your cache, prepare straightforward instructions for locating the site. Don't rely solely on your memory. The instructions should be clear enough so that someone who has never been in the area could use them to recover the cache.

The two most practical ways of making a wilderness cache are burial or concealment. Burial is an easy method for a small cache as long as it is packaged in a waterproof container, but a big cache might need to be concealed instead.

Concealment uses natural features to hide the cache, and it requires less effort and equipment than burial. For example, a concealment cache may be hidden beneath a natural deadfall. The primary disadvantage to concealment is the possibility of accidental discovery. Therefore, concealment is best used in remote areas or when rapid access is needed.

There are two main threats to your cache: people and wildlife. It is easier to guard against discovery by concealing the site thoroughly. But animals are harder to protect against, particularly bears. The best prevention is having gear with minimal or no attractive odors. An airtight food cache with flour, grains, sugar, salt, and other powdered foods that don't emit odors should work.

If the main concern is bears, then try one of the following:
- Store your cache on an island or peninsula.
- Have a hanging or raised cache.
- Bury your cache and cover it with big rocks as a deterrent.

A determined bear is a formidable adversary, so it's better to make your cache unattractive in the first place by ensuring there are no alluring odors.

Surplus ammo boxes, buckets with lids (with functioning O-rings), and large diameter pipes are potential cache containers. One of the most practical containers is the five-gallon bucket. Although carrying a bucket is a bit awkward, it holds a lot of stuff, and it's cheap and waterproof. If you use a smaller container, like an ammo box, check that the gasket is in good condition. And check that it is watertight by filling it with water and turning it upside down. Even if you believe your cache is waterproof, you should still place the contents in waterproof bags. For food caches, Mylar bags are a good option. If moisture could be an issue, place silica gel packets inside.

MISCELLANEOUS TIPS

- Keep your gear well organized. Always have a designated place for each item. Never leave equipment down on the snow or ground. Place it in a pack, a pocket, or hang it in a visible spot.
- Prioritize knots that can be easily undone, such as the bowline, friction hitch, or clove hitch; this is particularly helpful in cold weather. Don't cut cordage unless you truly need to.

- Don't discard scraps of plastic, cloth, cordage, or metal. They may be useful later on.
- When scouting an area, instead of covering the area by foot, use a monocular (or binoculars) to save energy.
- To better observe a faraway object with plain sight, form a small hole with your closed fist and look through it.
- To better listen and pinpoint a faint sound, cup your ears with your hands and slowly rotate your head side to side.
- It takes your eyes about 20 minutes in the dark to get dark-adapted. You can't see colors in full dark-adapted mode because you only use *rods* (see below). If you want to preserve your night vision, only use the faintest light possible. In very low light, you can see best by not looking directly at an object but slightly off to the side. If the light is brighter and you start to see some colors, you're beginning to use your *cones*, and your night vision will decrease. It's more important to keep your light source extremely dim than to use specific colors (green is best anyway). If you require color vision—for instance, when reading a map—then use dim light and close one eye to keep it fully dark-adapted.

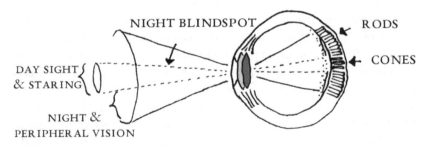

NIGHT BLINDSPOT   RODS

CONES

DAY SIGHT & STARING

NIGHT & PERIPHERAL VISION

MINDSET

THE WILL TO SURVIVE

Survival is 90% mental. Gear and training are useless if you're an emotional wreck. The *will to survive* is the most vital survival aid. It is the fusion of various key mental factors. Some of those factors are purpose, attachment, character, humor, training, and preparation.

This chapter will describe the components of a survival mindset and recommend techniques for strengthening your mental toughness and resilience. In the long run, your mindset is everything.

WHAT IS RESILIENCE?

Resilience is the choice to move through difficulties, find strength in your weaknesses, and serve a purpose bigger than yourself.

It starts by taking responsibility for how you respond to what happens to you. Instead of taking the path of excuses, find the strength and purpose to face the path of pain and hardship, of fear and suffering.

Intelligence, creativity, and motivation allow a resilient person to find ways of coping. To apply those traits confidently and persistently, optimism is needed. Optimism requires finding a sense of control within the chaos. Optimism, intelligence, creativity, and motivation lead to genuine hope, confidence, and resilience.

RESILIENT PEOPLE

Resilient people are exceptionally determined and persistent and will keep going when the only choice is to continue or die. In dangerous, unpredictable circumstances, they can stay focused to attain their goals. After a significant threat passes, their stress response goes back to normal.

They tend to be honest and possess a robust set of values that they strive to follow. Altruism, helpfulness, empathy, and compassion are some of their traits. They turn tragedy into action by helping others. Resilient people often have a good sense of humor. They understand that change is normal and can see it as an opportunity for growth.

People who plan for the future tend to be more resilient. They know life will be hard at times, so they prepare for hardships. They are determined and persistent in pursuing their goals while maintaining a relatively balanced life.

FOUNDATION

IDENTITY

Your identity provides guidance during difficult times. By distinguishing who you are, who you are not, and who you want to be, you can further integrate strengths found in others.

Have role models, and do as they do. Identity is powerful: it guides our actions, and our actions shape our feelings.

PURPOSE

"Those who have a why to live can bear almost any how."
— Friedrich Nietzsche

Why are you in this world? Why is that reason so important that you are willing to go through blood, sweat, and tears for it? What really drives you? Be prepared to have those answers at your fingertips when you hit the walls of hardship and doubt.

Without purpose, we can survive, but we cannot thrive. Your beliefs, assumptions, and expectations about the world and yourself shape your personal meaning. The sense that your life has meaning will enable you to withstand greater adversity. History has proven that having a purpose is an excellent aid to survival.

You must create your own purpose. Finding meaning through tending to others' needs is a good starting point. Often, it boils down to serving something greater than yourself.

Finally, in survival, having a purpose is not enough. It must also be broken down into simple tasks so that you can handle tough times one step at a time.

RESPONSIBILITY

"God grant me the serenity to accept the things I cannot change, the courage to change the things I can, and the wisdom to know the difference." — Reinhold Niebuhr

Taking responsibility for your life is the most important habit to build. The more ownership you take for your actions, life, and happiness, the more resilient you are likely to be.

You are responsible for your reactions, your intentions, and your attitude. We have limited control over the world, yet we are responsible for our happiness. No one else is. The only choice entirely in our power is to accept or reject whatever we cannot control. Focus your power on what you can control.

Even if events are outside their control, resilient people find something to be responsible for. The less power we have over external events, the more crucial it is to practice agency in yourself.

"Everything can be taken from a man but one thing: the last of the human freedoms—to choose one's attitude in any given set of circumstances, to choose one's own way." — Viktor Frankl

CONFIDENCE

Having a realistic belief in your ability to manage challenges is key to a resilient mindset. This belief is forged through training and similar experiences. Resilient people show self-reliance by meeting their needs or solving their problems by themselves, and not depending solely on others. Assessing your strengths—such as the personal, social, and material resources at your disposal—will reduce the stress from your challenges.

Having an inventory of the obstacles you have overcome and remembering what it was like to overcome them will give you a confidence boost.

On the other hand, over-positivity can be toxic and disastrous. There is incomprehensible wisdom in our intuition, so it's extremely important to listen to it.

WORLDVIEW

Survival worldviews are very personal. What works for one person may have the opposite effect on another. Ultimately, you must develop your own worldviews from within.

PRAYER

When things get very tough, people pray. Praying is so common among survivors that its importance can't be ignored. It aids a person's survival by reducing anxiety and keeping hope alive. Prayer unites many tools of resilience: gratitude, perspective, humility, and purpose. Announcing your needs, desires, worries, and goals in a focused attitude can help you become aware of the actions you may need to take.

> "Prayer cannot bring water to parched fields, or mend a broken bridge, or rebuild a ruined city; but prayer can water an arid soul, mend a broken heart, and rebuild a weakened will."
> — Abraham Joshua Heschel

SPIRITUALITY

To endure, you must draw on a belief or emotion for strength—it may be faith in a higher power or a relationship with a significant person in your life. Some draw strength from belief in themselves and their abilities.

When some people get thrown into a new, harsh environment, they become uprooted and disoriented. Their world is gone, and they cannot adapt. On the other hand, people with a solid personal ideal will carry that ideal wherever they go. They are rooted in their ideal. It doesn't have to be religious or intellectual. As long as this belief cannot be shattered, it will be a source of strength.

Spirituality and religion may give meaning to one's suffering, making it easier to adapt to challenges and even see them as opportunities for spiritual growth.

Be open to greater-than-normal assistance. Many survivors report being given a sudden calm, guidance, or presence that helped them deal with a crisis.

STOICISM

"Do not try to make things happen the way you want, but want what happens to happen the way it happens, and you will be happy." — Epictetus, Stoic philosopher

Stoicism is a practical philosophy that aligns well with resilience. One lesson from the Stoics is to focus our attention and efforts where we have the most power and to let the universe run as it will. Distinguishing between what is under our control and what is not will save us lots of energy and worry.

If we have adequate mental health, our behaviors and choices are under our control. Although we may be able to influence it, everything else is outside our control. Our concern should lie with what is under our control, and everything else should just be handled with calmness and self-control.

Another lesson is to constantly examine our impressions and our initial reactions to events, people, and things. Pause and take a deep breath. Realize that if something irritates you, your mind is complicit in the annoyance. Then ask whether what provoked the impression is under your control. If that's the case, you should act on it. If it isn't, you should regard it as not of your concern.

Stoics also reminded themselves of the impermanence of things: whatever benefits us or sets us back will eventually pass. The only constant is change.

Another good habit is to ask ourselves how to match our resources to cope with each challenge—such as facing pain with endurance and problems with patience. Stoics strive to use every occasion to exercise their virtues and become better human beings.

After James Stockdale's plane was shot down in the Vietnam war in 1965, he had a few seconds to say goodbye to his freedom before landing on enemy territory. He whispered to himself, "Five years down there at the least. I'm leaving the world of technology and entering the world of Epictetus." James is the source of the Stockdale Paradox explained later in this chapter.

"If there's a remedy when trouble strikes, what reason is there for dejection? And if there is no help for it, what use is there in being glum?" — Shantideva, Buddhist philosopher

ATTACHMENT TO OTHERS

The strong bonds you have with loved ones and the powerful thoughts about them can be a powerful motivation and a sustaining force for survival. At the same time, thinking about your loved ones can also be quite debilitating when you are isolated (see Extreme Isolation later in this chapter).

TRAINING

TRAINING TO BECOME RESILIENT

Resilience can only be built through practice because it is actions that change who we are. Practice and repetition are necessary to integrate something new into our character.

People who are trained and know what to expect in a survival situation will be more competent should such a situation arise. Training removes the fear of the unknown, and repeated drills enable you to function at an automatic level. It is at this automatic level that most people function during stressful situations.

STRESS INOCULATION TRAINING

Stress inoculation training is based on the idea that you can train your brain to better cope with stressful situations. It is divided into three phases: (1) conceptualization, (2) skills acquisition and rehearsal, and (3) application and follow-through. The details of the three phases are as follows:

1. In the conceptualization phase, the aim is to form a reliable mental picture and fully understand the situation you are preparing for. You can study accounts of others' experiences or expose yourself to realistic yet manageable conditions that give you an accurate idea of what challenges to expect. In this stage, you learn what helps you deal with those challenges and what doesn't.
2. In the skills acquisition and rehearsal phase, you practice problem-solving and develop coping skills while participating in realistic training scenarios. There is an emphasis on emotion-focused

coping—i.e., to relieve the effects rather than the causes of the problems. The purpose of this phase is to acquire and master a set of coping strategies by engaging in gradual exposures.

3. In the application and follow-through phase, you are exposed to more stressful situations where you apply your coping skills. Through gradual exposure, you reach a confidence level that allows you to cope in realistic settings.

This training regimen is how individuals prepare for demanding, stressful situations.

Conceptualization	Form reliable mental picture
	Understand the conditions
	Expose yourself gradually
	Assess upcoming stressors
Skills acquisition and rehearsal	Work on problem-focused solutions
	Practice problem-solving activities
	Work on emotion-focused coping skills
	Develop a set of coping responses
	Engage in gradual exposures
Application and follow-through	Expose yourself to the most realistic experience
	Reinforce appropriate coping behaviors

NEGATIVE VISUALIZATION

Negative visualization consists of intentionally thinking about potential, undesirable scenarios while reminding yourself that they are not as bad as they seem because you have the inner resources to deal with them.

This could be disastrous in challenging moments and should only be done before finding yourself in a threatening scenario, such as a dangerous animal encounter.

Visualize the worst that can happen, and mentally rehearse what you'll do. Instead of worrying aimlessly, use that energy to prepare mentally. Envision yourself overcoming the adversity. This technique may decrease your fear of those scenarios and prepare your mind to deal with them if they happen, and it can also remind you to feel grateful for the good times. For positive visualization, see the Tactics section.

MEDITATION

Meditation is recommended again and again as an aid to resilience. There are countless benefits, but ultimately, regular meditation teaches you that your thoughts are not your mind. Meditation helps you truly integrate that idea and not just understand it at an intellectual level. That is such a simple but powerful lesson. Once you incorporate this understanding, it becomes easier to practice mindfulness (observing thoughts without judging or being caught up by them). This separation from your thoughts allows you to be more effective at staying calm, practicing self-control, and dealing with challenges.

SIMPLE CONCENTRATION PRACTICE

The following is a simple meditation practice that calms and focuses the mind. Find a quiet, comfortable place to sit or lie down. Don't try this if you are tired and will fall asleep. Find a time of day that works. If time is in short supply, set an alarm for 10 or 20 minutes. A simple technique for tracking time is to use meditation beads (a similar idea to pace count beads).

If your mind is agitated, try 10 minutes of square breathing right before meditation (see the next page).

Focus your awareness on the sensations of breathing. Try to focus on your inhalations and exhalations throughout the entire practice. If it helps, count each full breath up to four or ten, then repeat. If you lose track, start over at one. You can also use words such as *in/out*, *inhale/exhale*, or *rising/falling* instead of counting. If you notice your mind wandering, gently return your attention to your breath.

Relax as you breathe. Let thoughts, sounds, and feelings come and go. Don't try to silence your mind. Instead, disengage from your thoughts; neither resist nor pursue them. Simply try to be in the present. Let go of the past, and don't plan for the future. You are setting this time exclusively for meditation. There is nothing to solve and no other place to go. Without effort, see if you can feel a sense of peace and contentment.

With regular practice, you might find that you have fewer distracting thoughts and start to feel separated from them. This sense of separation will allow you to detect when negative thoughts arise and as a result, gently redirect your mind into a positive place. Another significant benefit of meditation is the tranquility gained from being present in the now.

With concentration practice, the aim is not to calm your mind, but this might happen indirectly. You should never try to forcefully quiet your mind because that's like shaking a snow globe to stop the snow from falling. If you want to still your mind, you can focus slightly on your breath and let your "snow globe" calm itself with the help of time and meditation.

DEEP BREATHING

Deep breathing is a ridiculously simple but powerful technique. Breathe in fully and exhale fully. Take a short pause and start again. Doing a series of 10 or 20 deep breaths is an effective way to calm your body and mind. Use it whenever you feel anxiety or stress creeping in.

Breath control is an essential practice for developing mental toughness. You can almost always control your breath, and controlling your breath will help shape your feelings, thoughts, and actions. Slow, deep breaths help calm your body; your mind will soon follow.

Breath control can promote healing, build energy, balance your emotions, and help you perform under stress. Concentrating on a single thing helps calm yourself down and increase your sense of control. It becomes easier to choose what to pay attention to, and to leave worries, stressors, fears, and distractions outside of your focus. In short, breath control helps dial down your body's stress response.

SQUARE BREATHING

Square breathing is a simple yet very effective technique for focusing and calming your mind. This technique is named after its equal intervals of inhalation, retention, exhalation, and suspension.

Square breathing requires more concentration than just taking deep breaths. It is easier to practice in distracting or challenging conditions because it requires more attention. It helps to do a few breathing cycles before

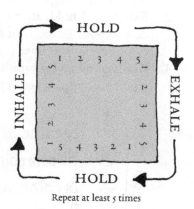

Repeat at least 5 times

doing something way outside your comfort zone or if you need to calm yourself down.

Start by exhaling all the air from your lungs. Inhale through your nose for a count of five, and hold your breath for a count of five. Exhale slowly through your nose for a count of five, and hold the exhaled breath for a count of five. Repeating a powerful mantra on each hold may increase the benefits. Practice square breathing at least once a day for five to ten minutes. This skill is very useful because it can be applied during highly stressful conditions.

POWER BREATHING

This breathing technique developed by Wim Hof uses a combination of controlled hyperventilation and breath-holding to induce a short stress response from your body—the opposite aim of square breathing. This brief stress trains your body to tolerate stress and become more mentally and physically resilient.

It is recommended to practice this right after waking up or on an empty stomach.

This exercise involves hyperventilating, so don't do it in environments where fainting is dangerous, such as around water. Sit or lie down. Follow these steps:

1. **Hyperventilate:** close your eyes and focus on your breath. Breathe in deeply through the nose or mouth, and breathe out unforced through the mouth. Breathe through the belly, then chest, and let go. Repeat 30 to 40 times at a fast pace. It is normal to feel light-headed and a tingling sensation.
2. **Exhale and hold:** after the last exhalation, take a final breath as deep as possible and let it out completely. Hold the exhalation for as long as possible until you can't resist the urge to breathe again.
3. **Recover:** take a big breath in. Hold it for 15 to 20 seconds and let it go; this completes one cycle.

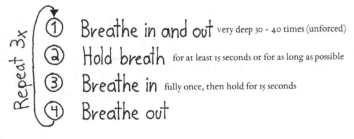

Repeat 3x

① Breathe in and out very deep 30 - 40 times (unforced)
② Hold breath for at least 15 seconds or for as long as possible
③ Breathe in fully once, then hold for 15 seconds
④ Breathe out

Do three to four cycles without pause. Then contemplate your mental state. You may also take advantage of this calm mindset and meditate afterward. The benefits of this breathing exercise come from the induced stress response, including releasing adrenaline, boosting the immune system, and reducing inflammation. Intense exercise provides similar benefits, but it's not appropriate for long-term survival.

When working hard, focus on exhaling fully, and use belly breathing to increase the level of oxygen in your blood. This oxygenates your muscles better and increases your endurance and strength.

SURVIVAL STRESSORS

Strenuous events are not stress; stress is what you may feel as a response. Stressors often stack up and may cause your body to "fight, flight, or freeze." Knowing what stressors to expect and developing strategies to cope with them are essential. Below are some stressors you may experience.

Injury and illness: an ounce of prevention is worth a pound of cure:
- Manage risk, use safer techniques, and wear protective equipment.
- Treat water and cook meat thoroughly.
- Have a comprehensive wilderness first aid kit.
- Avoid being alone.

Uncertainty and lack of control: having a routine and practicing acceptance helps you manage uncertainty and change.

Environment: the weather, terrain, insects, and animals may create a hostile environment; have a plan. Adequate clothing and shelter, and bear spray, are a good start.

Hunger and thirst: dehydration must be dealt with quickly or your body and mind will deteriorate quickly. Starvation will make you weaker and much more irritable.

Fatigue: conserve your mental health and physical strength by any means. Use the most efficient methods, and maximize your downtime.

Isolation: communicate with others, and have an emergency contact. Listen to the radio if possible.

REACTIONS TO STRESSORS

Below are some of the reactions to stressors you might experience in a survival situation. Try to practice your own strategies to address each response.

Fear: is our emotional response to what we believe is dangerous and reminds us to be cautious. You can address fear with knowledge, protective equipment, breath control, and gradual exposure.

Anxiety: is an uneasy feeling we get in hostile situations. Staying busy, being present, and deep breathing may reduce anxiety. In addition, your body could also be telling you that something is wrong and that you need to avoid the situation or do something about it.

Anger, frustration, and depression: frustration may happen after a few failures and may lead to anger. Getting lost, damaging or losing equipment, brutal weather, and challenging terrain are some sources of frustration and anger. Chronic frustration and anger wear down the mind and body and may cause stupid choices and a state of helplessness. So, tackle anger and frustration early on. Breath control, breathing exercises (e.g., deep breathing and power breathing), humor, and a *party on* attitude will help.

Loneliness and boredom: we are social creatures. When faced with multiple stressors, even people who enjoy solitude will find it challenging to cope with loneliness. Keep busy and focus on the present.

HOW STRESS AFFECTS US

When the brain perceives a threat to survival, the nervous system releases adrenaline into the circulatory system. That happens automatically and is the basis for the fight, flight, or freeze response. One of its consequences is an increased heart rate. It is believed that an elevated heart rate impairs first the fine motor skills—such as lighting a match—and then the complex motor skills —such as shooting a bow. On the other hand, gross motor skills—such as running—are barely affected.

In a survival situation, it's essential to stay calm to perceive the situation clearly. Panic impairs your judgment. You need to be able to observe, plan, and act. Here is where square breathing and a powerful mantra help.

"Relax. Look around. Make a call."
— Jocko Willink, former Navy SEAL

Most people under stress can only perform the most basic tasks because stress affects our memory and alters our perception. You make mistakes, see less, hear less, and miss more signs. Some people freeze in place, act irrationally, and are incapable of thinking clearly.

Under extreme stress, your vision and attention narrows, and you may not notice important things. People may imagine they will rise to the occasion, but in reality, they fall to the level of their training.

DEALING WITH FEAR

"Perhaps the greatest survival skill of all is the ability to maintain harmony in the face of seeming chaos."
— Cody Lundin

Keep fear in check by focusing your attention, thoughts, and feelings, and choosing how you speak and act. Being prepared, trained, and aware of your fears will go a long way.
- Stay busy.
- Keep your imagination in check: stick to the facts.
- Control your breath.
- Be present, for there is no fear in the *now*.
- Ask for help. Pray.
- Use humor and party on!

EXTREME ISOLATION

Being isolated is not necessarily negative, but prolonged solitude may turn into loneliness. Many people have been isolated for long bouts of time: polar station residents, submarine crews, prisoners of war, and prisoners in solitary confinement. Reading about their experiences may help you understand what to expect. Research suggests that manual hobbies, music, sports, exercise, communication, entertainment, knowledge of the ordeal's duration, and family photos help.

The ideal team members to have with you during an experience of extreme isolation would be emotionally stable, have strong motivations and abilities, and possess a good sense of humor. They would be kind, share their emotions, help each other, and be sensible toward others.

Both being completely alone and being isolated with a group can be highly challenging. These activities are very helpful when dealing with isolation: communicating with the outside world; listening to shortwave and AM/FM radio; reading; working on a project; embarking on a demanding hunt; journaling; playing games; and listening to music, podcasts, and audiobooks.

Exhaustion can also help you sleep at night rather than dwell on feelings and thoughts.

On the other hand, knowing some of the benefits of solitude can help you see the bright side. It can be an opportunity for freedom, connecting with yourself and nature, reflection, creativity, and feeling more alive.

Avoid thinking about loved ones too much if you're in for the long haul because it will cause debilitating emotional effects. If you can't avoid these thoughts, try restricting them to a specific time and duration.

If you have any emotional loose ends or past trauma, there is a big chance that they will reveal themselves during periods of extreme isolation or stress. So be prepared to confront them.

Your past may cause you to feel lonely, but there's usually something in the present that sets off those thoughts to begin with. Identify those triggers, and have a go-to activity for when you feel loneliness creeping up on you.

OBSERVING

SITUATIONAL AWARENESS

Awareness is crucial because you must know what is happening before acting appropriately. To gain situational awareness, ask yourself: Why am I here? What's going on around me? What am I going to do about it?

Having humility allows your mind to be more open and, as a result, more aware of things you might miss with a know-it-all mindset. Keep all your senses alert. Don't miss an opportunity or a threat.

To have a clearer perspective, avoid self-deception or denial, and avoid being too pessimistic or optimistic. Strive to see the world as it is.

Perform tasks consciously to minimize the time spent on autopilot. There is nothing wrong with being on autopilot during certain situations—especially stressful ones—as training develops muscle memory that helps you act effectively and instinctively when your conscious mind is just not up for the task. But strive to maintain a healthy fluctuation between acting consciously and on autopilot according to the context.

> "Perceive, believe, then act."
> — Laurence Gonzales, *Deep Survival*

S = Stop T : Think O = Observe P = Plan A = Act

THE STOCKDALE PARADOX AND ACTIVE HOPE

> "You must never confuse faith that you will prevail in the end—which you can never afford to lose—with the discipline to confront the most brutal facts of your current reality, whatever they might be." — James Stockdale

You must maintain clarity about your reality, no matter how harsh. But at the same time, you must find a way to retain hope. That's the paradox. Without hope, there's no survival. Yet, hope, an optimistic mindset expecting positive outcomes, is not enough in the face of overwhelming odds. Instead, practice active hope: perceive reality, have a goal, and work towards it. Hope should feed the struggle.

Hardships will eventually end, one way or another. Remind yourself during your most painful moments that things will change.

ATTENTION

> "The best survivors spend almost no time . . . getting upset about what has been lost, or feeling distressed about things going badly."
> — Laurence Gonzales, *Deep Survival*

Recognizing the signs of danger and learning from mistakes is crucial, but dwelling on the negative is counterproductive. If you are not improving your situation, you're wasting your time. And the clock is ticking. Take the time to feel your emotions, then move on.

We command our lives by directing our attention, thoughts, and feelings. Whatever we focus on, *there we are*. We shape our world by focusing our attention and changing what we think, feel, say, and do. Our attitude filters our reality, for good or ill. Everyone sees life through their own uniquely tinted lenses. So, if you find yourself immersed in negativity, gently but firmly turn your attention toward the positive.

Being aware of your mental self-talk and steering it takes effort. Meditation is a significant aid because it helps you witness your thoughts.

Starve the *fear wolf* and feed the *courage wolf* inside your mind by interrupting negative thoughts with a power statement, such as "I've got this." Create a power statement that resonates with you, and use it until it becomes second nature. After your power statement, think of something positive that aligns with your immediate goal. Infuse the thought with imagery and feelings. Then follow through with a mantra.

THINKING

ACCEPTANCE AND MINDFULNESS

Mindfulness is an attention on the present, where thoughts and feelings are observed without judgement. It's an emphasis on the present rather than the future, and on acceptance rather than control. In uncontrollable circumstances, accepting the situation "as is" is a highly effective emotional response. Taking things as they are, including yourself, will help you deal with challenges with less resistance and stress.

In the words of Epictetus: "It is not things which trouble us, but the judgments we bring to bear upon things." The meaning, or interpretation we give to events, is what disturbs us.

"Resignation without giving up. It is survival by surrender."
— John Leach, *Survival Psychology*

BE HERE, NOW

Living in the moment—as it comes and without expectations—is one of the most crucial survival skills. Being present increases your awareness and helps you make the best out of your situation. It keeps you in a better mindset than dwelling on the past and worrying about the future.

It is also a great way of tackling challenges, step by step, which is the best way of accomplishing insurmountable feats. The psychologist Rick Hanson (author of *Resilient*) puts it nicely:

"What's the most important minute in life? I think it's the next one. There is nothing we can do about the past, and we have limited influence over the hours and days to come. But the next minute—minute after minute after minute—is always full of possibility."

Don't take life or its moments for granted. Every day, experience a lifetime.

Being present has been incredibly hard during my adventures, but again and again, it has proven to be essential. The importance of being present can't be emphasized enough.

"If you take care of the minutes, the years will take care of themselves." — Tibetan proverb

LET BE, LET GO, LET IN

Hanson's phrase sums up these powerful lessons on mental resilience: let be, let go, let in. Be with your feelings and experiences, both painful and pleasant. Let go of the negative: prevent, reduce, and stop what's painful or harmful. And let in more of the positive. Create, kindle, and preserve what is enjoyable and beneficial.

FAILURE, ANGER, AND FRUSTRATION

You may likely fail to achieve some short-term goals due to forces beyond your control. But don't let those failures crush your entire endeavor. Breathe deeply, using the abdomen, and repeat your mantra or power statement. Let be, let go, let in. Remember these lessons:
- Be okay with failure, as long as you did everything to succeed.
- Even if you think you'll fail, fail giving total effort.
- Never quit in darkness: don't give up during your lowest point.

"The basic difference between an ordinary person and a warrior is that a warrior takes everything as a challenge, while an ordinary person takes everything as a blessing or a curse."
— Carlos Castañeda

SELF-CARE

MIND-BODY

It's important to understand that our minds do not exist in a vacuum. There is no separation between mind and body—they are wholly interdependent and non-dualistic. Starvation, thirst, drugs, and sleep deprivation make it clear that the mind is hugely affected by the body. And the mind also affects the body. Yet, mind over matter is not always the case. You can't just stop breathing for an hour or stop drinking water for a week. We live in a material world and have few, but very real, material needs. If you treat your mind and body as a whole, you'll be able to make decisions with a more accurate understanding of yourself.

Take care of your body to take care of your mind. That's the first strategy for having a good mindset. Unfortunately, in a survival situation, this isn't always possible. Nevertheless, focus on your most immediate needs, like hydration and warmth. Take action before you find yourself on a slippery slope: dehydration and hypothermia can quickly mess up your mind.

ENJOY THE LITTLE THINGS

Experiencing and absorbing positive emotions becomes more important when life gets tough. Keeping a pleasure diary on paper or in your mind is a simple way to practice this. These experiences give you a psychological time out that restores your mental resources and sustains your efforts.

Deliberately enjoy the little things throughout your day. Highlight them in your awareness. Don't just step over them. Stay with them fully and for longer. These small, ordinary events are not trivial. They are real, authentic experiences that nourish your mind.

Also, recognize your progress towards your goals, especially the small steps. Notice your victories, big and small. Take a few minutes before sleep to remember some of those pleasures and experiences.

SELF-COMPASSION

Treat yourself with the kindness that you would show a friend. Compassion is an inner strength that cares for the pain in ourselves and others. Hanson describes compassion as a warmhearted concern for suffering and the desire to relieve it. This self-care makes you more resilient and capable. Below is a practice from Hanson's *Resilient*:

Remember when you have felt cared for, appreciated, liked, or loved. Relive those feelings and amplify them. Let them sink in.

Think about someone you have compassion for. Get a feel for their struggles. Feel sympathy and concern. Then, have compassionate thoughts, such as, "May your pain ease . . . may you find peace."

Knowing what compassion feels like, apply it to yourself. Sense your burdens, worries, and suffering. Then feel self-compassion. Think: "may I _____."

TAKING REFUGE

Choose something that could be a refuge for you, like the memory of a loved one or an experience in which you felt cherished and loved. Try to experience the emotions and sensations of that refuge. Stay in the experience. Recalling your refuge repeatedly will, with time, make it easier to relive.

HUMOR, LAUGHTER, AND PLAY

"Survivors laugh and play, especially in the harshest situations. Play puts you in touch with the environment and laughter eases frustration and anxiety." — Laurence Gonzales, *Deep Survival*

Humor is seeing the funny side of our predicament and misery. It is vital for long-term survivors. Humor brings relief from the seriousness of a situation and helps distance yourself from a hostile environment. Viktor Frankl summed it up: "Humor is a weapon of the mind in the struggle for its preservation."

TIME OFF

In long-term survival there is always so much to do, so many tasks that seem to take priority. That's why it is important to schedule time off every day or at least every few days. Use this time for low-priority stuff that is fun, rewarding, or satisfying, such as building a chair, crafting a game, or simply allowing yourself to sleep without feeling guilty. Taking time off is an integral part of active-passiveness, covered in the Tactics section later on.

GRATITUDE

Being thankful generates positive feelings and happiness, and it also helps you balance your perspective. Gratitude is about appreciating what we have. There are good things in our lives that we would otherwise overlook, forget, or take for granted if we didn't make an effort to feel thankful. Gratitude also reminds us that we are not alone. Try to practice it once a day. A powerful technique is writing down or reflecting on three blessings before falling asleep.

Reading about the horrific ordeals that some survivors have successfully gone through will help you put your endeavor in perspective and find gratitude.

SMALL ACTS OF KINDNESS

Altruism distracts you from your problems and helps you feel better. Acts of kindness can be performed at any time for people, plants, and animals. It is a straightforward and effective technique that is indirectly related to your self-care. Just don't let your altruism impede your survival.

FINDING BENEFIT

Resilient people avoid seeing things as absolutely negative: they tend to see the positives in negative experiences. How an event is interpreted plays a role in how stressful it feels. Seeing its silver lining and comparing it to worse alternatives will help you adjust to a situation that feels outside your control.

I'm not advocating toxic positivity. Negative thoughts and emotions have their place, but avoid being at either extreme.

COPING

MATCHING STRENGTHS TO CHALLENGES

In *Resilient*, Hanson writes that challenges are best met with multiple inner strengths, but it helps to match a specific strength to a particular need:
- The need for safety may be met with possessing resolve and a sense of agency, feeling protected, being aware of threats, feeling okay in the now, and being calm and relaxed.
- The need for satisfaction may be met with gratitude, pleasure, achievement, goal setting, passion, and contentment.

- The need for connection may be met with compassion for others and oneself, empathy, kindness, and self-esteem.

To help identify the heart of a tough challenge, ask yourself: Deep down, what experience do I still long for? Hanson also suggests trying love as a universal strength.

TACTICS

MANTRA

Survivors make mantras. Powerful and inspiring mantras are a source of strength.

Create your own short but personal mantra. It should make you feel strong and empowered. A mantra can be used to psych yourself up while facing a fear or challenge. Positive affirmations and *I am* statements form great mantras: "I've got this," "Just keep moving," "I am a force of nature," "I am strong," "I can and I will," or "This too shall pass." You might find a mantra to be more effective if it is connected to imagery or your personal experience.

I'm a fan of Cody Lundin's *Party on!* mantra. The power of this statement lies in the fact that you might be forced to become a rational *beast* during survival. You might have to accomplish the insane and smash all your self-limits. But you'll have to do this while being analytical and somewhat detached. *Party on!* embodies this rational insanity. Use this mantra to gear up your mind and body to perform the insane in a calm and calculated manner.

ACTIVE-PASSIVENESS

Successful long-term survivors possess the ability to accept their situation without giving in to it. Active-passiveness is the ability to be active or passive, and knowing when to be so. John Leach (author of *Survival Psychology*) explains that if only one side dominates, the survivor will have a hard time. Not accepting one's situation leads to anger and frustration, and complete passiveness leads to surrender, despair, and apathy.

The key is knowing when to be active or passive and realizing that being passive is also a form of being active. Nature's cycles and your experience may give you guidance. Sleeping also comes with the additional benefit of reducing the length of a difficult experience.

SEGMENTING

"A journey of a thousand miles begins with a single step."
— Lao Tzu

Segmenting is a simple, powerful technique. It consists of breaking down a complex problem into small steps. A seemingly impossible task may be broken down until the smaller steps become doable. Take it step-by-step, day-by-day.

Having small objectives allows your mind to experience small victories. You can focus on the immediate task rather than feel overwhelmed by a bigger, more challenging goal. Once you achieve the small goal, you can focus on the next one.

SMART GOALS

Setting SMART (which stands for *specific, measurable, attainable, relevant,* and *time-bound*) goals is a great aid for resilience. Having a clear vision of what you need to do will make things more achievable. Daily goals also exercise your self-control, and experiencing small victories will give you confidence.

STAY BUSY

Set yourself some goals related to your immediate survival, and put your plan into action. These tasks are necessary, but they also channel your thoughts in a positive direction. Too much idle time may allow your mind to drift to a dark place.

Having an ongoing side project, like writing a book, learning a skill, or making a tool, will help you pass the time. My partner and I spent countless hours brainstorming recipes and baking all kinds of baked goods (with our meager rations) during the six months we were in the wild. We got lots of joy from it, and it helped us pass the time.

VISUALIZATION

Visualization is an effective aid to practice before facing a challenge. Athletes use it regularly while training and before competing. Mental projection is imagining a future personal state, and mental rehearsal is practicing a skill or preparing for a challenge.

Visualizations work best when they are *specific* and your *five senses are engaged*. Visualizations form mental pathways that strengthen your efforts toward a goal, like muscle memory. Practicing visualization also improves concentration because it takes a lot of effort to construct and maintain visual imagery.

Mental projection is painting an image of what success feels like to you. It's visualizing overcoming your challenge and experiencing a victory; this gives you energy and motivation. Mental projection also helps you calm down and relax before a challenge.

Mental rehearsal is about performing a skill or negotiating an obstacle in your mind. Visualizing challenges and deciding how to respond to them helps you be more prepared. It is a powerful way to prepare for pain, fear, and adversity. Your body treats your mental training as real to a certain extent. Mental rehearsal gives you confidence in your abilities and allows you to complement your regular practice.

40% RULE

"Sadly, most of us give up when we've only given around 40 percent of our maximum effort. Even when we feel like we've reached our absolute limit, we still have 60 percent more to give!" — David Goggins, endurance athlete

When your mind tells you "you're done," you are only *partly* done. The percentage in the rule's name is not accurate, but the idea behind it is solid. Your mind will, more often than not, tell you that you're done way before you really are done.

Hitting the wall should be treated as a sign that you're close to half a tank but still have plenty of energy and strength left. It's easier said than done: your body and mind will do everything to convince you otherwise. The body always likes to have a backup reserve of strength and energy, so it will tell you stubbornly to stop. And your mind will rationalize anything to make you stop. Keep in mind that this idea doesn't apply to severe starvation!

ROUTINE

Long-term survival involves monotonous and demanding routines. Routines help establish a sense of control and predictability. Having daily, nightly, and weekly routines, such as gathering water, repairing your shelter, collecting firewood, and checking your traps, will make you feel more at ease. Having routines is crucial, but I don't expand too much in this section because you'll naturally develop your own routines. Just make sure they are helpful.

The most sustainable approach is to structure your days in a rhythmic and punctuated way. For instance, if an activity is very demanding, only do it every other day. That allows you to rest and breaks up the monotony.

KEYSTONE HABITS

In *The Power of Habit*, Charles Duhigg highlights keystone habits. Keystone habits are habits that spill over into other aspects of your life. It's easy to see how a habit like getting drunk every night can create a domino effect in your life. The same is true for a keystone habit like waking up early or meditating.

WILLPOWER AND SELF-DISCIPLINE

"No man is free who cannot command himself."
— Pythagoras

Some research suggests that willpower works like a muscle. Just as muscles get stronger with training, willpower gets stronger when exercised. Nevertheless, the mind will eventually get tired from exerting too much self-control. If you use lots of willpower all at once, your brain will try to ration it, and you will have less self-control available; this is known as ego depletion.

Exercising your self-control regularly is helpful, but also try to conserve it for essential tasks. Exposing yourself to fewer temptations and making fewer decisions helps conserve it. Try to achieve your more demanding objectives early on, while the survival stressors haven't worn you down yet.

Some ways of practicing and strengthening your willpower include performing tasks with your nondominant hand, dieting, taking cold showers, exercising, and doing other activities that require discipline. Challenging yourself to "get out there" when you don't feel like it, when you're tired, or when the weather is not ideal will strengthen your discipline. Willpower could be the only thing standing between improving your situation and becoming a hopeless victim.

MENTAL FLEXIBILITY

Flexibility or adaptability is crucial in survival because you'll be forced to do more with less. Your lifestyle will change, and you'll have to embrace that change. Flexibility is doing whatever your situation demands. Discard your expectations and do as the locals do (human or animal). You might have to abandon notions rooted in self-domestication or civilization. It's okay to be an animal.

SURVIVOR MINDSET

"Gratitude, humility, wonder, imagination, and cold, logical determination: those are the survivor's tools of mind."
— Laurence Gonzales, *Deep Survival*

MENTAL TOUGHNESS

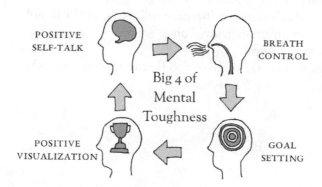

The following skills help increase your mental toughness:

Breath control: use square breathing to focus your mind and calm your body's response. Being calm helps you get stuff done when under high stress.

Positive self-talk: learn to steer your mind and keep your mental self-dialogue positive. Events themselves don't influence your emotions; your thoughts and judgments do.

Visualization: use mental imagery to build confidence, practice skills, and develop a strategy.

Goal setting: learn to set SMART goals and break them into smaller goals if progress is hard. Set *process goals* focused on training and *outcome goals* focused on progress and milestones.

WILL TO SURVIVE

Generally, this is what long-term survivors do:
- Train and prepare.
- Perceive and believe (avoid denial, be highly aware).
- Stay calm (breath control).
- Think, plan, and act (get organized, set up attainable tasks and goals).
- Lead (themselves and others).
- Practice active-passiveness (be bold yet cautious, conserve energy).
- Be grateful for being alive (celebrate victories).
- Laugh (also play and sing).
- Forge a purpose (a mission).
- See the beauty (appreciate the journey).
- Practice active optimism (believe in success, but put in the work).
- Take roots in core beliefs (spirituality, faith, values).
- Pray (religion or not).
- Surrender (acceptance without giving up).
- Do what's necessary (have the will, skills, and be flexible).
- Find motivation in loved ones.
- Never give up.
- When these factors work together and become second nature, they become *the will to survive*.

CLOTHING

Clothing is your first line of defense against weather and bugs, so it is vital. Your clothing should be durable, compact, lightweight, and versatile. Keep in mind that clothing should:

- still fit you as you lose weight;
- be suitable for historical temperature extremes, not just typical highs and lows;
- strike a compromise between being durable and lightweight (unfortunately, lightweight clothing is not very durable, and durable clothing is bulky and heavy); and
- protect you from mosquitoes and other bugs.

Your metabolism slows down when you don't eat as much, drastically lowering your body heat. Bring extra articles of clothing and clothes that are warmer than what you normally need when you're well-fed.

CLOTHING MATERIALS

Clothing materials are grouped into five categories: cotton, wool, synthetics, down, and flame-resistant.

- Cotton has minimal use in the backcountry. It's somewhat useful as an outer layer when around fires because it burns less easily than synthetics. However, this is limited to dry, cold weather only or when there is no risk of getting wet. Another potential use is briefs. Cotton has almost no place in temperate and colder regions because it holds moisture and is hard to dry. As the saying goes, cotton kills.

- Wool absorbs a lot of water but keeps it at the center of its fibers, making it warmer than cotton when wet. That's why wool works great for outdoor socks. It is also slightly more fire-resistant than synthetics. On the other hand, it may shrink if you don't wash it properly.
- Synthetic clothing is divided into two categories: insulated and non-insulated. Insulated synthetic clothing is lightweight like Polartec Power Grid, fleece, and PrimaLoft. Synthetics are slightly more flame-resistant, insulate better when wet, and dry much better than down. However, they are bulkier and heavier.
- Non-insulated synthetic clothing dries very fast, and it's light and compact. For things like shirts and pants, I prefer nylon over polyester, for nylon washes better and is more durable. A drawback of synthetic clothes is that they burn easily.
- Down is exceptionally light and very warm. Nevertheless, it's almost useless when wet. Down clothing also burns extremely easily, and once there's a hole, the down will escape.
- Nomex's and Polartec's fire-resistant clothing is very valuable for survival. Flame resistance is an excellent quality in jackets, gloves, and winter mukluks. Some newer army surplus and military clothes are sometimes flame-resistant (look for "FR" added to the item's name).

Color makes a real difference under the sun in both heat and cold. Wear light earth tones (such as khaki) in hot conditions, as lighter tones reflect more sunlight. Wear darker tones in the cold, for they are warmer and dry faster under the sun.

Color patterns can also make your outline a bit less evident to wildlife. Camouflage and plaid patterns are nice but not entirely necessary.

The common layering system of base layer, insulation, and waterproof shell is not perfect. Gear manufacturers like to think that their products are magical, but they are not—they are full of compromises.

The best approach is to have a versatile system that effectively manages moisture from the body and the environment and still provides a reasonable amount of insulation if wet. A survival clothing system should consist of moisture-wicking, insulating, windproof, and waterproof layers. The emphasis is on synthetic and wool clothing that breathes well and dries fast.

The use of waterproof hard shells is minimized because they don't deal well with sweat and are not as resilient. The clothing system should be able to provide some degree of rain and snow protection without the need for waterproof shells. Clothes with compromises, like down and GORE-TEX, are still used, but strategically. That way they are reserved for when they are truly needed.

THREE-SEASON CLOTHES

SUN HATS

Hats protect your head from the sun, shelter your face from rain, and keep bug nets off your face. Running caps and brimmed sun hats are good options (Outdoor Research makes great sun hats). For rainy environments, wear a GORE-TEX hat.

TUBULAR HEADWEAR

Pack two BUFF tubular styles: a polar model and a regular model. BUFF pieces are very versatile, lightweight, and durable. I sometimes use them as neck warmers, face covers, or beanies in colder weather. On cool nights, these are great for covering your face while sleeping, which warms the air you breathe and keeps your nose warm.

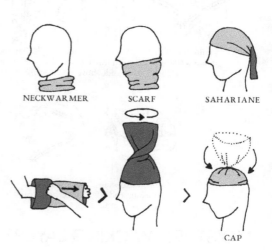

NECKWARMER   SCARF   SAHARIANE

CAP

BEANIE HATS

A two-layered fleece beanie makes a great warm hat without much bulk. In winter, you might have to wear one while sleeping. A beanie may also be used under a fur hat for added warmth in extreme cold. Avoid asymmetrical styles—for instance, with ear flaps—because, if you wear multiple jackets and turn your head, the hat will get disarranged.

SUNGLASSES AND SAFETY GLASSES

Sunglasses protect your eyes from snow blindness during winter. Use a strap to avoid losing them.

In the wilderness, safety glasses help prevent significant injuries. Use them when chopping wood or bushwhacking.

SHEMAGHS

Shemaghs are not ideal headwear for frigid climates. They are, however, versatile and could be used as a last resort for improvised clothes and repairs. Shemaghs are not ideal in moist, cold weather because they are typically made of cotton and take longer to dry. They are also bulky and don't excel at any particular use (except in arid regions for protection from the sun and sand).

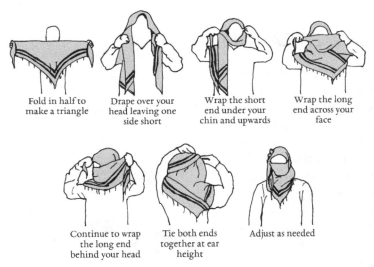

Fold in half to make a triangle

Drape over your head leaving one side short

Wrap the short end under your chin and upwards

Wrap the long end across your face

Continue to wrap the long end behind your head

Tie both ends together at ear height

Adjust as needed

MOISTURE-WICKING LAYERS

The purpose of base layers is to wick moisture away from your skin. Top and bottom base layers are not needed until the weather dips below freezing. Base layers made with Power Grid fabric—such as the ECWCS level 2—are warmer, lighter, and more compact than equivalent synthetic base layers. Merino wool base layers have antimicrobial properties and won't melt to your skin if burnt, but they don't have as good of a warmth-to-weight ratio as Power Grid base layers do.

SHIRTS

Long-sleeved synthetic shirts are the best all-around option for an outdoor shirt. The long sleeves protect you from the sun but can also be rolled up. Choose lighter colors and unbutton the shirt for added ventilation in warm weather. Loose-fitting shirts make it harder for bugs to bite.

PANTS

Synthetic, lightweight, quick-dry pants are preferred. Nylon pants are more durable, and you can sew on reinforcement patches over the knees and the rear. An ideal feature is side zippers for ventilation in warm weather (in environments where you need pants for bug protection). If you are around water a lot, consider convertible pants. If your area gets very cold, you'll need a wider size to accommodate one or two layers underneath your pants.

INSULATED JACKETS

Use fleece, PrimaLoft, and down jackets for cold weather. Each material has its strengths and weaknesses, so having one of each is a versatile strategy.

Fleece (100–200 gsm weight) dries fast and transfers moisture well, so it should be your go-to jacket. PrimaLoft and synthetic down materials don't transfer moisture as well, but they pack very small and are wind-resistant. Down jackets are light and very warm, but they get holes easily and are useless when wet.

WINDPROOF JACKETS

Softshell jackets are wind-resistant and somewhat water-resistant. These layers have a tight weave that traps warm air and prevents it from being carried away by the wind.

INSULATED PANTS

Wear fleece pants (200–300 weight) or synthetic-fill pants over your bottom base layer in cold weather.

RAIN JACKETS

High-quality rain gear makes a difference, but it's costly. Three-layered GORE-TEX and equivalent fabrics are effective and durable. Two-layered

GORE-TEX won't last as long. The issue with cheaper materials is that they compromise waterproofness, breathability, or both. GORE-TEX is not magic—it still traps lots of moisture. Using armpit zippers and opening your main zipper is an effective way to manage moisture. Get a larger size with wide sleeves for wearing layers underneath if you anticipate using the jacket in moist, cold conditions.

Only a quality rain jacket and a poncho will give you complete, sustained rain protection in rain forests. Sil-nylon ponchos are an excellent lightweight option.

RAIN PANTS

With rain pants, breathability is not a big issue as long as there are side zippers; you could make do with cheaper, less breathable fabrics that are not three-layered GORE-TEX. Watch out for fabric durability and waterproofness. You'll likely use these pants in the winter, so they should be able to stretch and fit over insulated pants.

EARPLUGS

Earplugs help you sleep during intense storms when the wind and weather would otherwise prevent you from resting. In addition, it is tough to improvise earplugs in the field (lightly moistened toilet paper works so-so).

WORK GLOVES

Work gloves protect your hands for the long haul. It is easy to injure your hands, so using protective equipment is an excellent way of minimizing injuries. Use work gloves with good dexterity, fit, and breathability.

WATERPROOF GLOVES

Wear waterproof gloves when processing meat to reduce the risk of catching diseases. In addition, waterproof gloves keep your hands warm when working in rain and cold, wet environments.

Use a glove that stays flexible in the cold and has an extended cuff with a drawcord, such as the TEMRES 282-02 (they run small!). The cuff and drawcord are crucial to protect the inside of the glove from rain and wet snow.

WINTER CLOTHES

Always pack additional warm clothing. When figuring out your clothing choices, make sure the layers allow free range of movement and do not restrict your blood flow. Pay special attention to making sure your pants and inner bottom layers don't restrict blood flow to your feet when wearing winter boots and socks. Winter clothing should be clean, loose-fitting, layered, and dry.

INSULATED JACKETS

Have a couple of jackets of different materials that can be layered together. Blanket-weight wool clothing and 200- or 300-weight fleece clothing are good options but are often bulky. Down jackets and synthetic-fill clothing are very light and warm.

You must be able to wear all your cold-weather clothing simultaneously and still stay warm, even if your metabolism is producing much less heat than usual. Choose oversized jackets that can accommodate layering.

Consider that you may, during freezing nights, be forced to sleep with your jackets on inside your sleeping bag. Wool and fleece aren't compressed as easily as down jackets and synthetic fill clothing when you are sleeping in them.

NECK WARMERS

A quality, double-layer, fleece neck warmer is essential for chronic cold weather. The neck warmer can also protect your face from cold wind and pre-warm the air while you sleep. Most neck warmers are too short to use for covering your nose and will let air through the bottom, so I sew a short fleece extension to the bottom to avoid this.

Neck warmers are superior to balaclavas when used with a beanie because, while both will eventually get moist, only the neck warmer can be rotated to keep the fabric next to your face dry.

FUR HATS

For extreme cold, genuine fur hats are best. For maximum warmth, make sure you can wear them over a beanie if needed.

INSULATED VESTS

Vests are an excellent way of keeping your core warm without restricting blood flow to your hands and arms. When your sleeves don't allow you to put on another jacket, you can still wear a vest underneath or overtop your last layer. Vests don't restrict your arms as much as a jacket, as they don't restrict blood flow, and they allow more freedom of movement (for instance, when using an axe). A down or synthetic-fill vest is ideal for this reason.

INSULATED BIB OVERALLS

For frigid weather, bib overalls are a must-have. The main reason is that they provide additional insulation around your core and prevent cold air from getting in where your pants and tops meet.

Army surplus fleece overalls are a cheap option. They can also be layered inside blanket-weight wool, synthetic-fill, or down bibs for extreme cold.

When using tall winter boots, choose a shorter length of bib to prevent restricting blood flow to your feet.

MITTS

Gloves don't perform well in extreme cold, but mitts do. Mitts keep your fingers together, allowing you to rewarm your fingers much better. All your mitts should have removable liners for drying; this also allows you to switch liners among your mitts or use them without them. There are three types of mitts you might want to pack: extreme cold mitts, work mitts, and waterproof mitts. You could get by with just the extreme cold mitts, but they might have to be reinforced and continuously repaired. It helps to have different mitts because the wear and tear is spread out between them.

For extreme cold, I recommend the Canadian military-issue arctic mitts made by Raber.

For work mitts, I recommend an outer mitt made of leather, with gauntlet cuffs and drawstring closures to keep snow out. Sewing full-grain leather mitts to a pair of cheap gauntlet mitts is an affordable option. The liner of the work mitts should be a knitted wool mitt that is easy to take on and off. Wool mitts work great as liners because they insulate even when wet and won't compress as fleece does. You must be able to put on and take off your mitts easily. Sewing on Velcro to keep the liners attached to the mitts helps.

Waterproof mitts are optional. Nevertheless, suppose you expect to handle under-ice nets and fish in extremely cold conditions. In that case, pack waterproof mitts. JokaSafe makes great waterproof mitts, but their removable liners get wear out quickly.

Full-grain leather mitts and gloves can be treated with waterproofing wax to make them water-resistant but not waterproof.

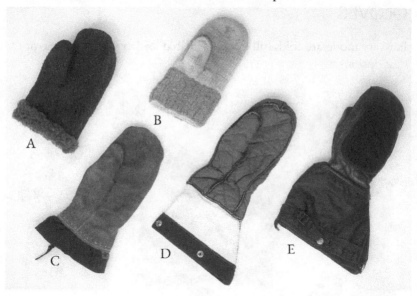

A. JokaSafe waterproof mitts; B. Wool mitts; C. Leather mitts w/ drawstring cuff; D&E. Canadian military-issue arctic liner and mitts

LINER GLOVES

Repeatedly touching metal in the extreme cold will hurt your bare skin. Sometimes you need good dexterity for long periods, and that's why liner gloves are important.

In extremely cold conditions, people often wear liner gloves under their mitts. But I avoid doing this if I can help it because fingers stay warmer and rewarm faster when they touch each other. Moreover, in order to layer liner gloves inside, mitts need to be bigger to accommodate the added bulk—this reduces their versatility and dexterity.

What works for me is to wear arctic mitts without glove liners. I work with bare hands as fast as possible when I need more agility, and if they get cold, I put my mitts back on to warm up my fingers. This technique will also force your hands to acclimatize better. But touching metal is still a problem. One solution is to keep liner gloves in an easily accessible pocket to keep them warm. If you must touch metal, you can put the pre-warmed liner gloves on, get things done, place the liner gloves back in your pocket, and put your mitts back on. Thin, polyester-Lycra (running) gloves work well with this strategy because they are easier to put on and take off.

GLOVES

For very moderate cold, full-grain, insulated leather gloves are one of the best options.

Left to right: Black Diamond Guide Gloves, thin work gloves, TEMRES 282-02, liner gloves

THREE-SEASON FOOTWEAR

It is hard to recommend specific outdoor footwear because everyone has their personal preferences, and the conditions in which footwear is used vary greatly. There are alternatives to explore, but every bioregion and person will have different needs and constraints. I'm not suggesting that having several pairs of outdoor shoes is necessary. I'm just enumerating options. In my area, temperatures mostly swing from 90°F to -20°F (30°C to -30°C) throughout the year, so it's more convenient to have more types of footwear. But someone in an area with less variability will manage with fewer shoes.

There are a few principles to touch on:

- Among backpackers, a well-known rule of thumb is that one pound on your feet equals five pounds on your back. Weight is a significant factor.
- In warm weather, quick-dry shoes are better than GORE-TEX shoes. The reason for this is that waterproof shoes will eventually become moist from your sweat or wet from being submerged, and they won't dry quickly enough.
- You probably can't pack all the recommended shoes, so you'll have some tough choices.

If I could only choose three shoes for a year-round endeavor in the boreal forest, I would pick amphibious trail runners for the summer, Tingley overshoes for early spring and early fall, and waterproof winter boots for late fall and winter.

SUMMER FOOTWEAR

Breathable shoes are preferable in summer, and durable hiking shoes are great options. Contrary to popular belief, boots are overrated for outdoor use in the summer unless you want maximum durability or you need protection against snakes. The advantage of hiking shoes and trail runners is that they are light and dry fast. The main issue is durability, but a sturdy pair of trail runners will last around 600 miles (~1,000 km). They could probably last much longer with repairs. If you want maximum durability, you'll want leather footwear that can be resoled.

For paddling and other water-based activities, choose water shoes or hiking sandals made by Keen, Merrel, Teva, or Chaco. One issue with water shoes and sandals is that they do not protect from bugs.

SPRING AND FALL FOOTWEAR

Depending on how much snow falls during your area's spring and fall seasons, you may want medium-height, lightweight GORE-TEX boots. These boots are waterproof but not very breathable. Paired with gaiters, they handle snow very well. Make sure they can accommodate thick, warm wool socks.

For paddling and other water-based activities in cold weather, the following options are recommended: waterproof hunting boots; Tingley rubber overshoes worn with socks, boot liners, or over shoes; or Xtratuf rubber boots.

THREE-SEASON SOCKS

Wool and wool-blend socks are ideal for outdoor use. Make sure the thickest three-season socks you might wear fit comfortably inside all your shoes. Keep in mind that black socks dry faster in the sun. If you are looking for long-lasting socks, try the T4033 socks by Darn Tough.

WINTER FOOTWEAR

Left to right: Neos Adventurer overshoes, Canadian-issue surplus mukluk, Tingley rubber overshoe

One of the primary considerations when looking at winter boots for survival is how long it will take to dry them. In multi-day endeavors, the ability to quickly dry your shoes is paramount because, in the long run, they will get moist, either from your sweat or from nature. That's why having removable shoe liners is a must.

Your boots must also work well with your snowshoe harness if you use snowshoes. Finally, while warming up by the fire, it is easy to catch a spark on your boots in the winter, so having a fire-resistant or leather boot is a good idea.

WATERPROOF WINTER BOOTS

You need waterproof boots for temperatures above 15°F (-10°C), freeze-up and thaw periods, and the transitions around fall and spring. As the environment approaches above-freezing temperatures, the snow will melt as it touches your boots, and you will likely encounter wet snow and slush.

I've experimented with Tingley natural rubber overshoes, and they are a good option as portable waterproof winter boots. The mid-calf style is the most useful. One of the reasons I like them is because they are rubber, and thus I can stand in water or slush without worrying about moisture seeping through. They are lightweight, can be rolled up, and can dry immediately. Synthetic rubber Tingley overshoes may develop tiny holes after continuous use in severe cold, so make sure you have the natural rubber ones.

A drawback of Tingleys is that they don't have enough space for wool felt insoles when worn with double-layer wool liners. If Tingley overshoes are used in moderate cold, this is irrelevant. If you decide to buy them, bring the wool felt insoles, double-layer wool liners, and socks to the store to get the proper size.

In very frigid temperatures and extreme contexts in which one might be static for long periods, it's best to wear two pairs of double-layer wool liners nested one inside the other. Unfortunately, Tingley overshoes don't have enough space to accommodate this (but NEOS and Army mukluks can).

Another option is NEOS overshoes. These are very light and compact. Instead of being rubber, they have an upper made of tough synthetic fabric lined with a waterproof coating from the inside. Unfortunately, in my experience, the coating eventually comes off. But in the short run, they are an excellent choice.

One footwear option I'm looking forward to is the modern, waterproof military mukluk (AirBoss ECWM), but unfortunately, civilians can't buy them yet.

BREATHABLE WINTER BOOTS

In temperatures well below freezing (under 15°F or -10°C), where the winter is dry and there is not much unfrozen water, breathable winter boots are ideal. Feet produce lots of moisture even in the cold, and breathable boots let that moisture escape. Nevertheless, most of the moisture in both waterproof and breathable boots escapes from the top because of the pumping effect of our feet. The topic of breathable versus waterproof boots is controversial among mukluk fans, but the Canadian military has moved away from breathable to waterproof boots for cold weather, and I agree with the move.

One big drawback of mukluks is that they tend not to be very durable, particularly with harsh use. Some good options for breathable mukluks are Steger mukluks (Arctic) and surplus Canadian military mukluks. The old Canadian Army mukluks are hard to find (search for Chimo shoes by Acton as an alternative). The Steger mukluks are not as breathable as the Army mukluks because they are made with leather. And the military mukluks do have a more rugged sole than the Steger mukluks.

Mukluks tend to have flexible soles. This flexibility allows the toes and feet muscles to move more, thus generating more heat and allowing more blood to flow. That makes them the warmest type of boot and the clear choice for severely cold weather.

In situations where you spend most of the time static in a freezing environment, use an Arctic boot two sizes larger than what you normally wear and insert double boot liners.

The surplus Canadian military mukluks are close to being the ideal shoe for survival in severe, dry cold. However, I wish they were more durable and had Nomex uppers.

DOWN BOOTIES

Down booties are incredibly light and compact. They keep your feet warm at camp and can also be worn inside your sleeping bag. They are not needed, but they are nice to have. The ones with extension cuffs also keep snow out, and booties with synthetic insulation don't lose their insulation as quickly as down when holes are present.

WINTER SOCKS

In severe cold, having high-quality wool socks is crucial. I recommend the Canadian military winter socks and Thermohair socks. I avoid the popular brands of wool socks because they aren't designed for severe cold and tend to constrict blood flow to the feet. One alternative is to buy thick wool socks for diabetics (they are non-constricting).

Under harsh conditions and for sustained use, you need more than three pairs of socks. In those conditions, socks quickly lose their insulation because they aren't as clean and fluffy as if they were regularly machine-washed and dried. So pack as many socks as you can, and ration them.

Some people recommend wearing two pairs of socks, but I think it's best to wear a single pair and have double boot liners instead.

INSOLES AND LINERS

You absolutely need boots with removable boot liners for multi-day use in cold weather; this is even more important if there is a possibility of getting the inside of your shoes wet. Wool boot liners and insoles are essential in their ability to absorb moisture from your feet while keeping your feet dry and warm. You could have a spare set of boot liners for multi-day use to replace moist ones; this is convenient but not entirely necessary, for your liners will rarely get soaking wet.

One of the best mukluk liners for severe cold is the "duffel sock" made by Raber. The wool liner has two layers—one inside the other—that can be spread out for faster drying. You can also wear two nested boot liners for extra insulation in extreme conditions (size up the larger pair two sizes). One disadvantage of these liners is that they quickly get moldy if stored with moisture.

In addition to wool liners, you'll need thick felt insoles. Also, having a mesh insole underneath the felt helps.

GAITERS

Gaiters keep snow out of your boots and are a good option during spring and fall if there is lots of snow. But they are unnecessary when wearing tall winter boots.

WASHING AND DRYING CLOTHES

One way to wash your clothes in the wilderness is to soak your clothes for a day before washing. Then, immerse them in clean water and bring to a boil—add spruce needles or Labrador tea to the water to give your clothes a nicer smell. In order to form a weak lye, boil the water with hardwood ashes. This concoction will act a bit like soap. Young leaves from birch trees can also be added to the water to release a soap-like substance. As soon as the water boils, reduce the heat and soak the clothes in it for a few minutes. Finally, the clothes can be handwashed in clean, warm water and rinsed.

An alternative to washing clothes is to air them out in the sun for a minimum of two hours. Ensure all sides are exposed to the sun: front, back, inside, and outside.

There are a few techniques for drying wet clothes under challenging conditions. One of them is to wring them and wear them until they are dry. The wind is another option: it is very effective at drying clothes, even with no sun. Another alternative is to dry clothes by the fire, but make sure that they are at a distance in which you are comfortable keeping the back of your hand for eight seconds. Place your clothes where there is less of a chance of an ember landing on them, and keep a close watch on them.

DRYING IN COLD WEATHER

It isn't easy to dry clothes in the winter, but there are options. The best option is to dry clothes near a stove, and another option is to place slightly moist—but not wet—clothes in a synthetic sleeping bag while you are sleeping in it. Your body radiates heat, which may dry your clothes, but one drawback is that your sleeping bag may absorb that moisture. Slightly moist clothing may also be dried by placing it between layers of clothes that you are wearing while being active.

Another option (that might not be intuitive) is to sun-dry clothing even in subfreezing conditions. Moisture jumps from a solid to a gas through sublimation. In the freezing cold, you can also let clothes freeze and then beat them with a smooth stick to get rid of the ice.

TRAVEL

Your decision on how and when to travel will impact everything else. It's best to time your travel when the conditions are optimal for moving efficiently and carrying lots of supplies—work with nature, not against it. For long-term survival, waterways provide the best way to travel.

Prepare special meals that are easy to cook and provide lots of calories to fuel you while accessing or exiting your main location.

TRAVEL ON FOOT

Traveling on foot to your main camp is the worst possible strategy, as you can't carry much weight when walking.

Off-road hiking trailers with a single wheel can carry huge loads, but that's nothing compared to a canoe or a sled. Custom expedition trailers, like those used for desert crossings, can transport a lot of gear, but they are not suitable for narrow trails, uneven terrain, or bushwhacking. Walking severely restricts the amount you can carry, and relying on a trailer is precarious. Unless you distribute gear among a large group of people, transporting an appropriate amount of equipment and supplies for long-term survival on your back is naive. On the other hand, if you have placed caches of gear and supplies, travel on foot should work.

Walking is even more unsuitable in places where the cold is severe because the climate requires more clothing and a bulkier sleeping bag. However, pulling a sled in the winter is a great way to travel.

If you choose to travel to your basecamp on foot, you won't be able to carry a significant quantity of food rations. That puts you at a great disadvantage for months-long endeavors.

BACKPACKS

Carrying lots of gear in a backpack sucks, no matter what. Look for a backpack made with fabric of at least 500 denier so that it lasts.

A cheap backpack won't last long carrying lots of weight. Army surplus packs may be a good option. Their volume should be between 80 and 130 liters. The latter size is massive, but the harsher the winter is in your area, the larger your pack should be.

TIPS

If you are carrying lots of weight on your back, use hiking poles or a walking stick. Having a walking stick is also the best way to provide stability and avoid falling, twisting an ankle, or worse.

TRAIL BLAZES

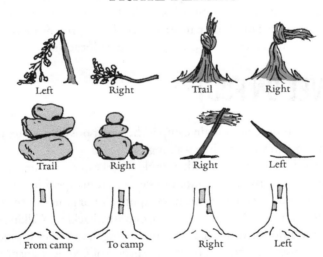

BUSHWHACKING

If you are going to bushwhack in thick forests, wear safety glasses to protect your eyes from branches. Bushwhacking is extremely demanding and exhausting where there is thick vegetation and lots of fallen trees; in waterlogged terrain, wet feet can be a big problem. Try to follow animal trails so long as they take you roughly toward your destination (animals are drawn to water). Traveling along ridgelines and higher ground may be the most efficient way. Having satellite imagery saved on your phone for offline viewing will help immensely. Another option is to plot a set of waypoints based on satellite imagery and topographic maps before heading out and follow the way points with a GPS or a map and a compass—but you won't have as much room for improvisation.

WATER TRAVEL

Water travel is the most efficient way to carry a lot of supplies in the wilderness—that's why it is the best travel method.

CANOEING

A thorough section on canoeing is beyond the scope of this book; nevertheless, I will make some brief comments on canoe tripping.

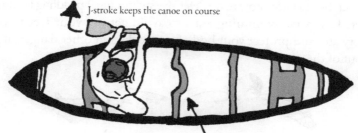

J-stroke keeps the canoe on course

Notice the position of the yoke, bow, and stern for paddling solo

The wind is a major consideration when canoeing because strong winds make travel very slow or impractical. When planning a trip, allow for an extra day every three to five days if you get windbound. Wind can be a considerable aid, particularly in large lakes. A neat trick is to rig a tarp as a sail using extra paddles or sticks. When large lakes get very windy, big waves form, and those waves can swamp your canoe if you lack the skill to negotiate them or if you make a mistake.

Paddlers should learn two essential skills: self-rescue and doing a "T" rescue after a canoe upset.

The most resilient canoes out there are made of T-Formex or Royalex (discontinued). Unfortunately, they are relatively heavy.

Pack paddling gear, such as a repair kit, personal flotation devices (PFDs) with survival kits, a bailer, and a floating rope.

SWIFTWATER

Wilderness paddling may involve rapids. The most appropriate thing in a survival situation is to portage most rapids. Nevertheless, there are a few occasions where that is not an option. That's why it's important to have white water canoe skills. After paddling a few rivers with rapids, take a white water course, and learn from instructors or experienced paddlers. White water paddling can be very dangerous. Some risks include getting trapped underwater by a big wave (hole) or trees (sweepers and strainers).

Consider packing white water helmets (optional), a throw bag, lining rope, and an extra paddle.

A helpful portaging technique, or rather a technique for avoiding a portage, is to "line" the canoe downstream using floating ropes attached to the ends of the bow, stern, or both. Lining is tricky and works best with short "pool drop" rapids. Both paddlers walk on the shore and guide the canoe with the help of ropes. One paddler lets the canoe float downstream with all the gear attached. Another paddler grabs the rope attached to the upstream end of the canoe and accompanies the canoe as it rapidly floats downstream. Having firm footing and a long rope helps.

You should know how to do defensive swimming if paddling in moving water. Defensive swimming aims to avoid getting your feet trapped underwater and protect your body from rocks and other dangers if you fall out of the canoe.

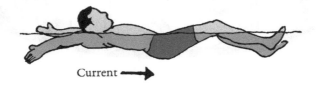

Current ➡

PORTAGING

To portage is to travel overland between lakes or rivers. Portages in remote areas can be pretty challenging, especially if you carry a lot of gear. Resting frequently during long portages helps a lot.

Consider using a tumpline when carrying very heavy loads. A tumpline is a broad strap that rests on the forehead and transfers the load to the spine rather than the shoulders or hips, and they can be rigged to canoes and packs.

A useful technique to use during long portages is to "leapfrog." This technique breaks up a portage into shorter stages, adding rest breaks between carries. One person portages the canoe in one go. The second person brings gear to the midpoint, then returns to the start of the portage for more. The first person collects gear from the midpoint, and the second person finishes the portage.

Five-gallon buckets are cheap containers that easily become waterproof with a watertight lid. A good way to carry a bucket on a portage is to grab its handle and swing the bucket over your head (place it behind your neck, over your shoulders). Having a PFD or backpack on helps keep the bucket stable.

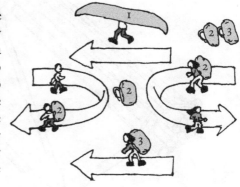

PACKRAFT

Packrafts are a versatile option for water travel. They are available as single or tandem rafts, and they are so lightweight and compact that they can be carried in a backpack. The bag used for inflation is also small and compact. Adventure racers have used packrafts for decades. Some of the best packrafts are found at **bit.ly/pack-raft**, but they are pretty expensive. Stay away from DIY and low-quality packrafts because their construction is not sturdy enough (the type of welding is not as strong). The main problem with packrafts is that they are just not as durable or efficient to paddle as a canoe or kayak.

IMPROVISED CANOE AND RAFT

A last resort for water travel is to improvise a canoe or a raft. But these options are not ideal because they are inefficient, hard to portage with, and take time and resources to build. A raft should be built using standing dead softwood; it's best to choose wide logs.

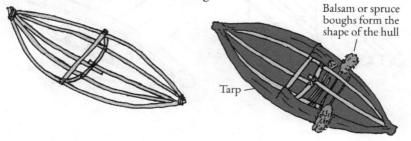

Balsam or spruce boughs form the shape of the hull

Tarp

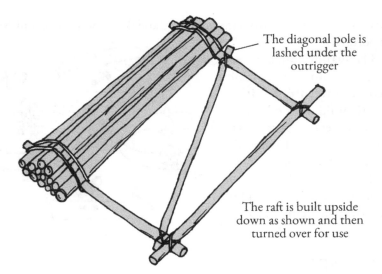

The diagonal pole is lashed under the outrigger

The raft is built upside down as shown and then turned over for use

André-François Bourbeau raft-a-maran

Rugged log raft

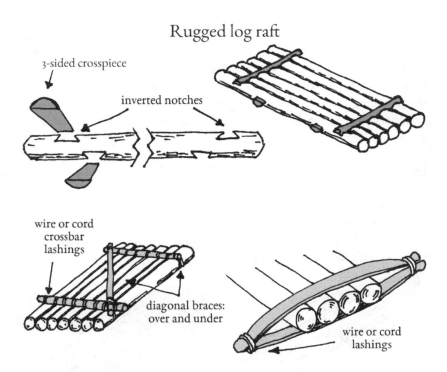

3-sided crosspiece

inverted notches

wire or cord crossbar lashings

diagonal braces: over and under

wire or cord lashings

EMERGENCY WATER CROSSING

An emergency technique is the poncho float. A poncho float is a flotation aid made with a tarp or waterproof material.

Fold in the corners of the tarp to make a watertight bundle.

Tuck in the corners neatly, and wrap a second tarp if available.

Tie the bundle tightly with cordage, to make it waterproof.

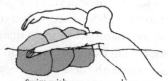

Swim with one arm, and use the float for buoyancy.

WINTER TRAVEL

The snow and ice that form during winter make a wilderness route much more accessible. Winter travel is the next best way to access the wilderness because you can carry much more gear in a sled than in a pack, although it will be much less than what you can bring by canoe.

Aim to travel during the early winter once the ice is safe, or during the early spring when most of the snow is melted but the ice is still firm. These two options are particularly good opportunities for covering long distances over water routes.

In the early spring, when temperatures fluctuate greatly, it is more efficient to travel at night when the snow is hard and crusty. But avoid ice travel at night.

SNOWSHOES

Snowshoes are a must-have for off-trail winter travel over deep snow. Three main styles are practical for winter survival: Huron, bearpaw, and mountain. Choose a snowshoe that matches your weight, local terrain, and snow conditions.

My region is flat, gets lots of snow, and has many rivers and lakes viable for ice travel, so the Huron style is more appropriate. Military magnesium snowshoes are this traditional style, with lighter and more rugged materials.

If you expect to break trail in deep snow, Huron is a good style. Keep in mind that wide snowshoes leave a wide track, allowing for less snow resistance for pulling sleds.

The bearpaw style is a bit in between Huron and mountain snowshoes. It is a style better suited to very wooded areas, as it is more maneuverable and compact.

Finally, modern mountain snowshoes are a good option for uneven terrain and wooded areas with shallow snow. They are quite compact, but they don't have as much flotation and are not suitable for deep snow. MSR Evo and Revo snowshoes are two good options. The Evo is more suited to flatter terrain with less hardpacked snow, whereas the Revo provides better traction over hardpacked snow thanks to its external steel traction. There are optional tail extensions for both models to increase their flotation. A possible issue with these snowshoes is that their bindings may be a weak spot in extreme cold, and they could be difficult to repair.

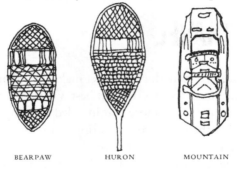

BEARPAW   HURON   MOUNTAIN

SKIS

Skis are often the most efficient way to travel in mountainous regions and where the snow is windpacked. On hilly terrain, use a ski-snowshoe hybrid, such as the Altai Skis, and on flat or off-trail terrain, waxless cross-country skis are best.

In very deep snow, a ski-snowshoe hybrid in the style of Tom Roycraft (long Alaska snowshoe) will provide more snow flotation than Huron-style snowshoes, but ski-snowshoe hybrids are hard to maneuver in treed areas.

SLEDS

One of the most versatile types of sleds is a plastic pulk. These are lightweight, maneuverable, reliable, and cheap. For hilly regions, it's easy to add poles and a harness so the sled won't strike you when going downhill.

Consider the width of the sled: a narrow sled that fits inside the tracks of your snowshoes is easier to drag than one wider than your tracks.

I recommend the Paris sled (60" Expedition Pro) because of its simple design, reasonable cost, and versatility. It is rugged and reliable, and you can easily chain two together if you need a longer sled. If you are dragging your sled over packed snow, tying a Krazy Karpet or snow carpet to the bottom of the sled will help it slide better.

A compact and versatile harness can easily be made with a D ring and strong webbing, or a deer drag (**bit.ly/d-drag**). After you have a harness, be sure to experiment with different lengths of rope because a short one might make it harder to drag the sled.

ICE CRAMPONS

Ice crampons are only needed on icy mountains and glaciers, or if you are traveling on ice shortly after freeze-up or before breakup. During those transition periods, there might not be much snow cover; the ice will be slippery, and pulling a sled or even walking can be a slog.

I recommend carrying 10–18 sheet metal hex-head screws (3/8" or 9 mm in length) per shoe if you anticipate these conditions. If you need traction aids, you can insert the screws around the edges, toes, and heels of the soles of your shoes. This method is cheaper and lighter than ice traction devices. Check **bit.ly/scr-ew** for more information.

I also recommend the IceTrekkers because they last longer than other types of ice cleats and aren't pointed like crampons.

TRAVEL ON ICE

In winter, frozen streams and lakes become the highways of the north, and they provide the most efficient method of travel. However, traveling over ice is dangerous, so you must be extremely careful and observant of any warning signs. You must systematically test the ice thickness if you're traveling over it, especially shortly after freeze-up and before breakup.

TYPES OF ICE

Generally, 3" (7.6 cm) of blue or clear ice will support a person, but 4" (10 cm) leaves a safer margin of error for changing conditions. Blue or clear ice is clear and is void of bubbles, and it is the densest and safest to travel on. Snow ice is half as strong as blue or clear ice. Snow ice is formed by wet snow freezing on the surface; it appears white and is weaker due to its air pockets.

Gray ice is typically refrozen slush and indicates water. It takes six to eight inches of gray ice to support what one inch of blue ice can support.

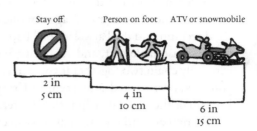

Stay off   Person on foot   ATV or snowmobile

2 in
5 cm

4 in
10 cm

6 in
15 cm

*clear blue lake ice (river ice is 15% weaker)

ICE FACTORS

Ice rarely freezes uniformly: it may be a foot thick at one point and only an inch or two several steps away. Be wary of warm air temperatures. When temperatures vary widely—causing the ice to thaw during the day and refreeze at night—the result is weaker ice.

When the water level of a river lowers, ice may stay suspended in the air. Without the support of water underneath, the ice gets very weak. Keep in mind that ice is generally thinner around logs, rocks, and structures that absorb heat from the sun.

Become familiar with various forms of ice and the factors that affect its integrity—experiment where the water is shallow and you won't get completely wet if the ice breaks.

If you have doubts about the thickness of the ice, carry a long pole and strike the ice hard ahead of your steps. With experience, the vibrations that you feel after hitting the ice may give you a clue about the ice's thickness, structure, and strength. Also, carry a hatchet or an ice chisel and periodically check the ice thickness. Always check treacherous ice before walking on it. The key is to gain experience, be observant, and not make assumptions.

Snowshoes help distribute your weight. If you are in a group, spread out, and don't concentrate your weight in one spot. If the ice is truly unstable and starts to crack, lie down on your belly, stay low, and crawl away.

When in doubt for any reason, don't cross; your intuition might be trying to tell you something.

ICE HAZARDS

There are ice hazards in both lakes and rivers, but rivers are more dangerous. The different water depths and temperatures in streams can result in highly variable ice thicknesses. There is also the risk of falling through the ice and being swept away by fast currents.

In rivers, there are various spots where the ice is weak, so you need to be on the lookout for ice hazards:

- Stay away from rocks and other obstacles, for they create eddies that weaken the ice.
- Travel on the inside bends of rivers, for water flows faster on the outside curves and erodes the ice.
- Avoid rapids.
- There is turbulence when a stream, even a small one, meets another stream or exits from a lake. This turbulence weakens the ice, so walk on opposite sides or the shore. Check a topo map and keep an eye out for any marked streams.
- Deep snow insulates the ice and keeps it warmer, thus making it weaker and thinner—particularly if a river is eroding the ice. Deep snow is also heavy and reduces the weight that ice can support.
- Dark or slushy snow may be a sign of water, and sunken snow may indicate soft ice. Stay away.
- Overflow happens when water seeps up through openings in the ice. Snowfall often hides overflow. Tapping ahead with a pole may help you discover it. Overflow will soak your footwear, and your feet will cool rapidly if your boots aren't waterproof.
- Animals generally go around thin ice, but not always. If they deliberately avoid a spot, you should too.
- Use a 10- or 12-foot-long (3–3.5 m) sturdy pole to strike the ice as you walk and to span a break if you fall in.

River

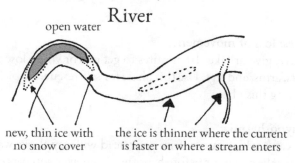

open water

new, thin ice with no snow cover

the ice is thinner where the current is faster or where a stream enters

LAKE

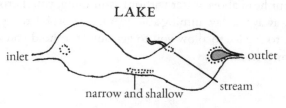

inlet

outlet

narrow and shallow

stream

When venturing on the ice:

- Always carry a waterproof fire-starting kit that won't get lost and is always accessible.
- Carry ice safety picks for self-rescue.
- Be prepared to unbuckle your pack or shed your sled harness quickly should you fall in.
- When with a group, avoid crossing ice in single file or standing together in one spot. Spread out.
- If the ice conditions are unfamiliar, wear a PFD. If you fall in, it will keep your head above water and provide some insulation.
- Carry a personal locator beacon for emergencies.

SELF-RESCUE

If you fall through ice, keep in mind the 1-10-1 guideline by Dr. Gordon Giesbrecht (author of *Hypothermia, Frostbite, and Other Cold Injuries*), which is a way to remember the first three phases of cold water immersion and their approximate lengths of time.

1 Minute: cold shock

Avoid swallowing water: fight the desire to gasp and hyperventilate. Focus mainly on calming down and gaining control of your breathing. The main danger now is drowning, so wearing a PFD is very helpful during this phase.

10 Minutes: loss of movement

You have, give or take, 10 minutes to get out or you'll lose the use of your fingers, arms, and legs. Use this phase for self-rescue. Ice picks are very helpful during this phase.

1 Hour: hypothermia

If you can't self-rescue, ensure your head will stay above water if you faint. It may take one hour before hypothermia makes you pass out. If you can't keep your head above water without swimming, you'll drown once the cold takes away your swimming ability. A last resort is letting your wet sleeves freeze to the ice to allow you to get out or to hold you up until, hopefully, someone arrives.

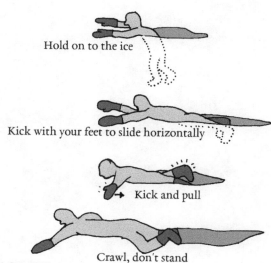

Hold on to the ice

Kick with your feet to slide horizontally

Kick and pull

Crawl, don't stand

AVALANCHES

In mountainous terrain, avalanches are a serious hazard. Most avalanches release on slopes of 30 to 45 degrees, so judging slope angles is an important skill. Some compasses have inclinometers for measuring slope angles.

A good strategy for traveling in avalanche country is to use routes that avoid avalanche zones, but this is difficult and not always feasible. Travel above or below and far away from avalanches.

There are various snow stability tests that may be used to analyze the snow layers and conditions. Avalanche skills are beyond the scope of this book, and reading is no substitution for hands-on avalanche safety training. If you frequent avalanche terrain, I highly recommend taking professional avalanche skills training. You can start by checking out the free online course at **avalanche.ca/tutorial**.

WATER

TO TREAT OR NOT TO TREAT

Assessing the risk versus reward of certain choices is vital in wilderness survival. Treating water found close to civilization is a no-brainer. It is likely polluted with agricultural runoff, industrial waste, and waterborne pathogens.

Suppose you are in a remote place in the wilderness next to a big, clean lake or river. In that case, you may decide that the energy and effort saved from not treating water outweighs the risks in the long run. One of the strongest arguments for drinking untreated water is that it's easier to stay well hydrated, as you don't need to be constantly making a fire or treating water. This is way more relevant the longer you stay out in the wilderness.

It's like choosing to eat questionable street food, but the difference is that if you get sick, you are on your own. And gastrointestinal issues are incredibly tough to diagnose in the field.

I've drank untreated water regularly, including on a 99-day Pacific Crest Trail thru-hike, on innumerable canoe trips, during 180 days in the wild, and on a 100-day winter trip; I've never had anything more serious than diarrhea. Still, I've worked for years on building resistance to questionable water by drinking untreated water whenever I'm on a hike or overnight trip. I also grew up in a country where my immune system had more opportunities to build up resistance. Nevertheless, the risk of getting seriously sick is always there, so this approach is not for most people.

Drinking untreated water can also help you develop resistance against *some* pathogens that are hard to avoid in the wild.

In short: water that is close to civilization should be treated. Treat your water unless you know what you are doing and are comfortable taking risks.

PUREST WATER SOURCES

If you decide to drink water as is, try to get it from deep, big lakes. Lakes are usually better than streams because of a settling effect in which pathogens sink to the bottom.

Water taken directly from springs and seeps is usually fine because it's been filtered by sediments—as long as it is actually groundwater and not surface water channeled underground.

Look for clarity (dilution). Cloudy water is more likely to be contaminated. In rainy seasons and winter, the natural factors that help purify water are less active.

The primary consideration is to ensure that the water source is not directly or indirectly downstream from human or animal activities.

WATER TREATMENT

There are two viable options for treating water for long-term survival: filtering and boiling. Other treatments are not as appropriate for the long-term because they are single-use: chemical treatments, tablets, and drops. UV lights are an alternative that works year-round, although not a very reliable one (due to the need for recharging).

FILTERING

The best filters for long-term use are squeeze filters and gravity filters. These filters are convenient, don't require much effort to use, and can filter a lot of water. Pump filters are not practical because they are slow, have many points of failure, and require much more effort to use. A disadvantage of filters is that they don't remove viruses (but purifiers with 0.02 micron filters do), and they need to be maintained regularly to clear clogs.

I recommend the Sawyer Squeeze (rated to 1 million gallons) paired with the Cleaning Coupling adapter. The adapter allows you to backwash the filter in the field with any standard plastic bottle instead of using a flimsy syringe. And it also makes it easier to use as a gravity filter (pack extra hydration bags because they may burst after heavy use).

The gravity filter I would recommend is the Platypus Gravityworks (rated to 1.5 thousand liters). This filter is convenient for groups, but it's expensive and heavier. A downside of this filter is that it has many different parts that could get punctured.

The Sawyer has a 0.1 micron filter, and the Platypus has a 0.2 micron filter; both remove 99.99% of protozoa and bacteria. Both filters are pretty light, but the Sawyer filter is more versatile, compact, and long-lasting. I would go with the Sawyer Squeeze for a one to two person group and the Platypus for a larger group.

In subfreezing temperatures, filters are out of the question because they eventually freeze or develop cracks. If the filters freeze, they can rupture and allow pathogens to pass through. Using a faulty filter under the assumption it's working is a bigger risk than not having a filter and selecting water sources more carefully. I consider filters useless in the winter due to the impracticality of keeping them unfrozen at all times. Besides, in those temperatures, snow and ice might be the main water sources; thus, boiling makes sense.

BOILING

Contrary to popular belief and outdated guidelines, bringing water to a *rolling* boil at any elevation will kill all intestinal pathogens. You don't need to boil it for a full minute. In the wilderness, the time required to heat water from 131°F or 55°C to boiling point works toward disinfection. Leaving boiled water covered until it cools down enough to drink adds another level of safety. Unfortunately, boiling or filtering water won't remove chemicals (activated-charcoal filters remove some substances). Boiling is also the most popular option in subfreezing temperatures. The disadvantage of boiling is that it requires considerable time and energy.

WATERBORNE DISEASES

The following table is a non-exhaustive list of common waterborne pathogens likely to be encountered in backcountry areas of North America. Those areas near populated places will likely contain a much wider variety of pathogens.

Type	Pathogen	Symptoms	Details
Protozoa	**Cryptosporidium**	Loss of appetite, nausea, and abdominal cramps, usually followed by watery diarrhea, vomiting, and weight loss. See the "Health" chapter.	Extremely common: symptoms usually last about 2 weeks, but some infections in immunocompromised people can be fatal.
	Giardia	Loss of appetite, lethargy, fever, vomiting, diarrhea, blood in urine, and abdominal cramps. See the "Health" chapter.	Extremely common: symptoms generally begin 1 to 3 weeks after exposure and last about 2 to 6 weeks.
Virus	**Norovirus**	Nausea, vomiting, diarrhea, abdominal cramps, headache, fever/chills, and muscle aches.	Symptoms usually last 1 or 2 days. However, people can feel very ill and vomit.
	Rotavirus	Vomiting, watery diarrhea, fever, and abdominal pain.	Symptoms usually last 3 to 8 days.
Bacteria	**Shigella**	Diarrhea, fever, abdominal pain, muscle cramps, vomiting; and blood, pus, and mucus in stools.	Symptoms usually begin 1 to 3 days after exposure, and it usually resolves in 4 to 7 days.
	Campylobacter	Diarrhea, abdominal pain, malaise, fever, nausea, and vomiting.	Symptoms usually occur 2 to 5 days after exposure, and typically last 1 week.
	E. coli	Diarrhea, vomiting, severe stomach cramps, and fever. See the "Health" chapter.	Most varieties of *E. coli* are harmless or cause relatively brief diarrhea, but a few strains can cause severe symptoms.
	Salmonella	Diarrhea, nausea, headaches, stomach cramps, fever, possible blood in the stools, and vomiting.	Symptoms generally occur 6 to 72 hours after ingesting contaminated food or water and last 4 to 7 days.

In addition to the pathogens previously mentioned, water may also contain blue-green algae (cyanobacteria). Some cyanobacteria produce toxins that contaminate water. Drinking high concentrations of the toxins or bacteria can cause gastroenteritis, vomiting, diarrhea, and liver or kidney damage. The algae generally bloom in stagnant or slow-moving warm water rich in nutrients (e.g., agricultural runoff). Neither boiling nor filtration will remove the toxins. Filters with activated charcoal can remove most of the cyanotoxins (but the effectiveness may only last six months from first use).

WATER CONTAINERS

Hydration packs don't work well in subfreezing temperatures and are awkward to refill. Hard plastic water bottles break with hard use and may crack if they freeze. Therefore, only metal and semirigid plastic water bottles (UVPE type) are suitable for long-term wilderness use. Metal bottles are the best type overall because they are tough and can be used for boiling and cooking. Semirigid bottles are the next best type: they can be used as hot water bottles and are very durable. Wide-mouth bottles can be washed thoroughly, and they allow you to use your bottle as a container for things other than water.

Nalgene makes the best wide-mouth stainless steel bottle. The lid is strapped to the bottle with a strong cord, which is convenient for strapping it to a pack with a carabiner, and it can also be quickly removed for boiling water.

A good option for a semirigid plastic bottle is the Ultralite Nalgene bottle made from HDPE/UVPE. This bottle is lighter and cheaper than the stainless steel one, and it won't crack in winter like hard plastic Nalgene bottles.

BOTTLE MODIFICATIONS

The stainless steel Nalgene needs two modifications to become the perfect survival water bottle: an extra metal lid for campfire use (easily improvised from the burned-off metallic lid of a glass jar) and two small holes drilled near the top for use with a free-standing bail handle (made from stiff wire). An alternative for the holes is to mount a ring of wire with two "eyes" for the bail handle. I also substitute the lid's cord with orange MIL-SPEC paracord.

FIRE

FIRE STARTING BASICS

Fire is one of the foundations of wilderness survival. Fire is crucial because fulfilling your basic needs would be very difficult without it. It is a universal aid—from melting snow and boiling water, to washing and drying your clothes, and everything in between. Fire is the reaction that happens when there is a sufficient ratio of heat to oxygen to fuel. When these elements are unbalanced, the fire gives hints; for example, it will smolder. The most reliable way to start a fire is to gather lots of good, dry tinder, enough dry kindling, and some firewood.

Combustible materials are divided into tinder, kindling, and fuel. Nowadays, tinder describes a material that can ignite with a spark from a ferrocerium rod. Tinder is usually very fine—like grass. Kindling is used to sustain and grow a small flame. Kindling's thickness is usually between a pencil lead and a finger. Firewood is generally wider than a wrist, and it sustains a fire.

When you start a fire, the heat source is a tiny flame, so you must feed it with really thin kindling, like red pine needles. Once the burning kindling produces more and more heat, the fire can handle fuel. Gradually feeding the fire with larger fuel—as the fire grows bigger and more capable to consume it—is a reliable strategy. If the fire smokes a lot, blowing on its base will help, as will reducing the size of the fuel.

FIRE SAFETY

Always choose a proper place for a fire. Sometimes roots and organic soil (peat moss) can ignite underneath a campfire and remain smoldering underground for weeks until they find enough oxygen to light up in flames. So make sure you minimize this possibility by insulating the ground below the fire with ashes, sand, or rocks.

Always take the time to fully extinguish a fire. Carefully remove and scatter the remaining wood; ensure it won't start a fire somewhere else. Then, stir up the remaining ashes and embers, and pour water over them until there is no smoke coming up from the ground.

Never use rocks that could contain lots of moisture for a fire ring, such as those near the water line. The fire's intense heat can cause a pressure buildup inside and make them burst violently.

FIRESTARTERS FOR LONG-TERM SURVIVAL

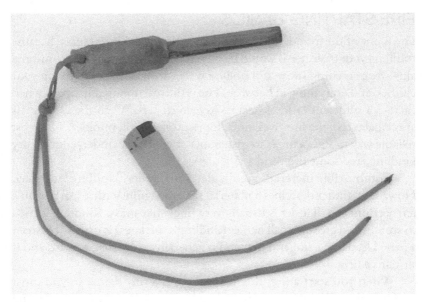

1 – Lighter
Longevity 3 / 5   Durability 4 / 5 Practicality 5 / 5

BIC lighters are extremely easy to use and work very well. Piezoelectric lighters are more reliable than regular lighters because they light up faster after getting wet and are less likely to leak because the button is harder to press. A full-sized lighter can light up to 3,000 fires, and a mini lighter can light up half of that (in practice, the actual number is a fraction of that estimate).

Regular (non-piezoelectric) lighters do need to be fully dry to work. Sometimes you can strike the flint of a moist lighter a couple of times to dry it (or just wait a few minutes).

Lighters stop working in very frigid temperatures, but you can prevent this by keeping one in a warm pocket next to your body. Always remove the child safety of your outdoor lighters for ease of use in challenging conditions.

2 – Ferrocerium rod
Longevity 4 / 5 Durability 5 / 5 Practicality 3 / 5

In theory, a 1/2″ ferro rod can start up to 10,000 fires, and the Swedish FireSteel can start around 3,000. In practice, however, they last closer to only one-quarter of that. One of the main advantages of ferro rods is that they can be wiped dry and used right after getting wet. However, they do require practice and fully dry tinder. Ferro rods are a must-have firestarter because they are so reliable and straightforward.

To avoid losing your ferro rod, I recommend spraying it with high-visibility paint, adding a bright handle (hot glue mixed with paint), and attaching a lanyard.

3 – Magnifying lens
Longevity 5 / 5 Durability 3 / 5 Practicality 1 / 5

You could light unlimited fires with a magnifying glass, but you have to rely on the sun. Card-sized Fresnel lenses work great, and they are incredibly lightweight, simple, and compact, so having them is a no-brainer. Although, they scratch easily—so carry a few.

I don't mention flint and steel or fire pistons because ferro rods have made them obsolete: ferro rods weigh the same or less, are easier to use, and are more practical.

A Swedish FireSteel (or 3/8″ ferro rod), three piezoelectric BIC lighters, and a few card-sized Fresnel lenses make a reliable and compact kit.

FIRE SKILLS

SINGLE-MATCH FIRE

One of the first fire skills to practice is the single-match fire. The challenge is to light a fire using only natural materials, one match, and a match striker. Practicing this helps you push your skill level further and gives you more confidence in challenging conditions. Any remote wilderness traveler should fully dominate the single-match fire in any weather condition.

There are three key points to focus on when starting a fire with only one match:

- Have lots of dry tinder and kindling.
- Choose a location sheltered from wind, rain, and snow (or set a tarp).
- Slowly light the match underneath the tinder bundle.

Preparation is key to starting a single-match fire. If the ground is moist, lay a platform of wood. If everything is wet and you can't find dry tinder under trees or fallen logs, you can carve shavings out of dry wood. The cores of wood will almost always remain dry.

It's best to combine tinder and fine kindling in a bundle. Otherwise, it can light up too quickly without triggering a chain reaction; this often happens with inferior tinder.

Try to strike the match underneath and very close to your tinder bundle. Or build a platform for that purpose. When striking your match, grab it close to the head so it won't break. Once it catches on fire, turn its head downwards to light the match and tinder fully. Avoid making sudden movements.

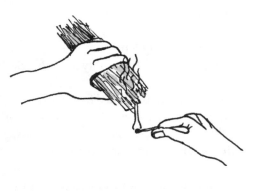

While most people focus on building a tipi, a more reliable strategy is to have lots of tinder, kindling, and fuel at hand, ready to be gradually placed over the fire.

SPLITTING MATCHES

Matches don't cut it for long-term survival. But if you happen to have them, you can split them as a way to ration them. One match can be easily split into two; during WWII, prisoners of war split matches up to six times!

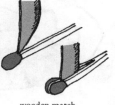

wooden match   paper match

Hold the point of a sharp knife or pin just below the head of a wooden match and press down sharply. The wood will split or run out, but you should have two heads and enough "stalk."

For a paper match, start splitting it at the end opposite to the head with your knife or fingernails. You may have to move your fingers along the stalk and support the head as you split it.

When striking a split match, hold the stalk between the thumb and middle finger, with the tip of the index pressing lightly on the head of the match. Draw the match flat along the striker and take off your index once it lights.

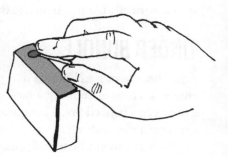

BANKING THE FIRE

Banking a fire is a helpful strategy for conserving your fire starters. It also makes a fire easier to restart.

To bank a fire, you first have to get a good bed of hardwood coals (softwoods make inferior coals). Then, cover those coals with hardwood and add a thick layer of ash, almost to suffocate the fire. If the coals don't get a bit of oxygen, the fire will die out. Either hardwood or greenwood may be placed on top to feed the coals, but greenwood may last longer. The ashes insulate and slow down the burn rate by reducing the amount of oxygen reaching the coals. Circling the fire with rocks or making the fire in a hole may help concentrate the coals and keep the wood and ash over them.

You can bank a fire to keep it burning overnight or if you need to go away for a while. Another way of prolonging a fire if you need to be away is to place punkwood or rotten wood over the fire.

Once you want to restart your banked fire, you just have to find some burning embers among the ashes and, if there is enough heat, place some fine tinder over them. Then you can just let time do its thing or blow steadily toward the embers until the tinder catches fire. If the embers are tiny and there is not much heat, you can place the embers on a tinder bundle and use the technique described in the next section.

One drawback of banking the fire is that you use more wood than you would normally use if you just let the fire die out.

TINDER BUNDLE

A few fire-starting techniques may require you to start a fire from a small ember, such as when using a bow drill, a magnifying glass, or restarting a fire from a banked fire. Therefore, it's essential to know how to make a fire from a tiny ember.

To make an excellent tinder bundle, use two layers of tinder and one of fine kindling. If there aren't many options for materials, you can build it using only two layers, but it might not be as reliable.

OUTER LAYER

The outer layer of the bundle gives it its structure and cradles the inner two layers. This outer layer of fine kindling ensures you can sustain and build a fire once your tinder bundle bursts into flames. Additionally, the outer layer keeps your tinder off the snow or away from the moisture from the ground, and allows you to hold the bundle in your hands without burning them.

Red pine needles work well as an outer layer. But you can use strips of birch bark, dry inner bark, or dry twigs. The point is to wrap the tinder bundle with materials that will catch a flame easily and burn longer.

MIDDLE LAYER

The middle layer should be made of fine tinder that ignites very easily. Dry grass is one of the most abundant tinders for this purpose, but you can also use dry, shredded inner bark or a bird's nest. The point of this layer is to catch on fire when exposed to an ember, so it must be fine and dry.

INNER LAYER

This layer does the job of a coal extender. If you're working with a tiny ember, this layer is critical. Punkwood is the most widespread natural material for this layer. It may be used without much preparation as long as it is dry.

Adequate punkwood is usually found inside rotten tree stumps and dead standing trees. You're set if you find soft and dry punkwood that can be rubbed down into a fluffy powder. Compress the powder tightly and place it in the center of the tinder bundle.

To start a fire from an ember:

1. Place the ember on top of your inner layer.
2. Carefully wrap the tinder bundle around the ember and hold it loosely.
3. Gradually blow into the tinder bundle, or if the wind is strong, allow it to blow through it. The nest should start smoking soon.

Once the smoke is dense, blow onto the ember consistently until it catches on fire. When you need to take a breath, swing the bundle in the air to keep the ember supplied with a steady source of oxygen.

If the tinder bundle is dry and properly made, it should catch on fire as the smoldering tinder grows hotter. Once you see a flame, place the nest on the ground and cover it with thin kindling. Continue adding kindling of bigger diameters, and eventually, fuel wood.

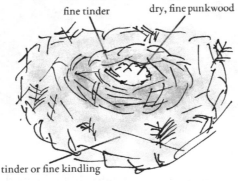

fine tinder   dry, fine punkwood

tinder or fine kindling

MAGNIFYING LENS FIRE

The main reason for using a magnifying lens to start fires is to conserve your fire starter. In addition, starting fires with a magnifying lens is an excellent way of learning how to blow a small ember into a flame.

With patience and ideal conditions, you can improvise many ways of concentrating sunlight , such as using a water bottle or a clear plastic bag. However, I recommend using a magnifying glass of at least 2″ (5 cm) or a card-sized Fresnel lens.

Make a tinder bundle using the instructions from the previous section. Ensure the inner coal-extender layer is thoroughly dried and fluffy. Compress the punkwood fluff to form a small ball and place it inside the tinder bundle. Adding a tiny bit of ash to the coal extender may make it catch on fire faster.

The sun needs to be unobstructed so that its rays hit the tinder with full power. Hold the lens close to the tinder and slowly move it farther until the sun's rays are focused on a small point. It takes seconds to minutes of focusing your magnifying lens on the punkwood ball before it turns black and starts smoking.

Then, focus the beam on the outer edge of the black spot to enlarge it and keep it smoking. Remove the lens once the smoldering black spot is as big as a penny. The punkwood should remain smoking by itself for a few minutes; otherwise, it is not dry enough, or it needs more time under the lens. While being careful not to disrupt the smoldering ember, wrap the tinder bundle around it. Use the same technique described in the previous section to start a fire from the coal.

AUXILIARY FIRE SKILLS

You should always be prepared enough to avoid having to use last-resort fire skills. Nevertheless, stuff happens, and the skills in this section could prove useful.

SPENT LIGHTER FIRE

You can still light a fire with an empty lighter. Hold the lighter sideways over a piece of bark inside the tinder bundle and slowly roll the striker wheel without creating a spark. This grinds the flint into a powder that ignites easily, but don't let it spark, or you'll have to start again. After you have lots of powder, place it in the inner layer of a tinder bundle. Then, use your lighter to throw sparks onto the flint powder; this works only a few times before the flint in the striker runs out.

BOW DRILL FIRE

One of the easier methods of lighting a fire by friction is with a bow drill. It isn't a method to rely on unless you've made dozens of bow drill sets in unfamiliar areas, with materials collected that day and during different seasons and weather conditions.

    Making a fire with a bow drill is not too complicated once you have the right materials and learn the right technique. However, that is precisely what's difficult when starting out: recognizing suitable materials, and learning how to troubleshoot your technique and adjust your bow drill set. Only with the right materials and right technique will you get a fire.

You'll need a strong cord for the bow. The cord should be one and a half to twice the length between your fingers and armpit. Paracord is best because it withstands more abuse than other cord types, but different types also work.

RIGHT MATERIALS

Below is a list of woods recommended for making a bow drill base (board) and spindle (drill), but don't get too fixated on the tree species.

Experiment with dry softwoods in your area. I've often collected spindles or boards from a recommended wood, yet the wood hasn't been dry or soft enough. It really depends on each particular stick. But knowing the suitable types of wood can help you narrow down where to look for your board and drill. Some recommended woods are cedar, willow, poplar, balsam fir, aspen, yucca, sotol, basswood, lodgepole pine, jack pine, and white pine.

DRY WOOD

You'll need to find soft, dry wood for the spindle and board. Your best bet is to find a standing tree that has been long dead and is fully dry. I tend to use a section of wood from the main trunk rather than the branches; the further away the wood is from the ground, the better. The board should be at least two fingers wide or twice as wide as the spindle's diameter. Look for wood without bark, for bark traps moisture. Sun-exposed areas are good places for finding dry wood.

SOFT WOOD

Once you've found a potential piece of dry wood, you must check if it's soft. Different woods are softer than others, but the type of wood does not guarantee that it is a suitable material. It needs to be in a state of decomposition that is

soft enough to produce a fuzzy powder when drilling it, yet hard enough not to crumble.

The thumbnail test allows you to check how soft the wood is. Carve away a small section with your knife and press your thumbnail against the exposed wood. If it barely leaves a mark or is tough to leave a mark, the wood is likely too hard. During my early attempts, I often used wood that was too hard, which only led to disappointments. The best wood is relatively easy to mark but not too easy.

Once you've found soft and dry wood, you must cut the pieces for your board and drill—it's a good idea to use the same section of wood for both. Another option is to look for a piece of wood from the same species that is just as soft.

BOARD

The wood for the base should be two fingers wide by at least a foot long. I like to use a heavy knife or a hatchet to flatten the base quickly. You don't have to flatten the entire top of the board; just flatten the top part where you'll be drilling. I do flatten most of the bottom of the board for stability. At the most, the board should be as thick as your spindle, around half an inch (12 mm) thick.

SPINDLE

The diameter of the drill should be as wide as your finger. Try to find the straightest piece possible for your drill. I cut the spindle as long as my foot. A shorter spindle may be more stable, but it won't last as long.

Having a longer spindle allows you to have a more comfortable position, making the spindle easier to control, press down, and hold in place. Carve the softest end of the spindle to give it a roughly round shape, then carve the other end to a point to reduce the friction on that end. Keep your board and spindle off any moist ground.

If necessary, you can increase the purchase of your cord by carving the spindle slightly squared. But this stresses the cord and spindle, so I rarely do it.

HANDHOLD

Most people recommend using rocks, bones, or hardwood as the handhold for the spindle. Green hardwood also works, and that's what I use because I can always find it nearby. Use the hardest wood you can find.

A large, heavy handhold helps keep pressure on the spindle and use your body weight, and it is more stable. Drill a small hole in the handhold for the top end of the spindle. You may use moss or leaves to lubricate the handhold hole, but the effect wears off almost immediately.

BOW

The bow is the most straightforward piece of wood to find. It should be as long as the distance between your armpit and fingertips and at least as thick as your thumb. If it is too heavy, it can drain your energy while you drill. Look for sticks with a slight curve to keep the bow out of the way when drilling. The stick should be solid and sturdy.

Score one of the ends of the bow, and tie a running bowline knot to secure that end of the cord. The other end is tied like shown in the picture below. You'll often need to adjust how tight the cord is, and being able to change the tension easily is quite helpful.

As a general rule, the cord should be straight but not very tight when first securing it to the bow. If your cord slips when drilling with pressure, it needs to be tighter.

BOW DRILL TECHNIQUE

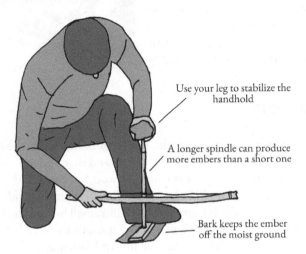

Use your leg to stabilize the handhold

A longer spindle can produce more embers than a short one

Bark keeps the ember off the moist ground

To drill, kneel with your right knee under your center of gravity and step on the board with your left foot.

Holding the wide end of the spindle away from you, wrap the cord around it. If the cord is very tight, try rotating the spindle while wrapping it. Once the cord is wrapped around the spindle, the end of the bow toward you should be higher than the other end.

The spindle should be outside the bow rather than on the inside.

When using the bow drill, you should keep a barrier between the board and the ground; this is where the coal will stay once you finish drilling. You can use bark, a flat stick, or a big leaf; the more moisture there is in the ground, the thicker the barrier should be.

The first step is to predrill the board to help the drill stay in place once the V notch is carved. Predrill until the hole is the same diameter as the spindle. Keep in mind that you don't want your spindle to go toward the board's edge. Don't waste your energy here; do it slowly.

The next step is to carve a V notch, where the ember will form. Try to cut it at a 45-degree angle. Stay a millimeter or two away from the center; otherwise, the spindle will tend to pop out. Cut the notch evenly all the way.

START A FIRE WITH A BOW DRILL

Before beginning to drill, make sure your tinder bundle is nearby. Use your knife to make the pointed end of the spindle a little thinner.

Drill slowly to build up some powder inside the notch and dry out any remaining moisture in the base. Try to use the entire length of the bow, and do full swings. Once the notch is almost full with powder and the base and spindle are smoking, you should gradually increase the pressure and speed.

I usually keep drilling until I can't continue or if I notice that a smoldering ember has detached from the notch.

Once you have an ember still smoking after having stopped drilling, take a well-deserved rest. Take your time to gather your tinder bundle; the coal will stay smoking for a few minutes.

Using your knife, carefully place the coal over the punkwood in your tinder bundle. Without disrupting the coal, wrap the fine tinder over it and start blowing gradually and steadily. I like to move the tinder bundle in the air between breaths. The coal and tinder should begin to glow; just keep blowing steadily until the tinder catches fire.

TROUBLESHOOTING YOUR BOW DRILL SET

If the drill makes a whistling sound or gets polished, there are three things you can do:
- Keep drilling with more pressure.
- Drop a few grains of sand in the hole of the base.
- Use your knife to remove the layer of polished wood.

Check the powder: if the powder is very black but has formed rolls, it's no good. Increasing the pressure might help get a fuzzy consistency instead. If you can't get the suitable powder, try finding softer and dryer wood. The perfect powder is black and sticks together.

If the powder is light brown, you need to increase the speed. If it is brown and dusty, you should increase the speed and pressure.

If you are drilling fast, with pressure, and can't get an ember, try checking your set:
- Is the wood soft enough? Do a thumbnail test.
- Is the cord slipping? Tighten it.
- Is the spindle popping out of the notch? Make a new hole and notch. Try making the notch smaller this time, and keep the base stable and horizontal.
- Is the handhold smoking? Lubricate the handhold or decrease the diameter of the top of the spindle, or do both. Consider getting green hardwood for the handhold.
- Is there not enough speed and pressure? Try a thinner spindle or carve the bottom part of the current spindle thinner.

I continually adjust my set when I'm not getting an ember. But if after all these adjustments you are still struggling, make a new set. The most important lesson for the bow drill is that you'll only get a fire with the right materials and technique. If you are struggling to get an ember, there is something wrong. Don't keep doing the same thing: change your technique, adjust your set, or find better wood. Keep practicing with different sets, and you'll learn the right materials and techniques.

FLINT TINDER

The last emergency fire skill is turning a tiny spark into an ember. This skill could be helpful if you have a source of sparks, like a flint and steel, or if you want to make a ferro rod last longer.

FIELD CHARCLOTH

Charcloth is the tinder of choice for catching sparks from flint and steel because it is easy to make. Field charcloth is made by charring plant fibers, such as cattail fluff, punkwood, inner pith from plant stalks, and tinder fungus, instead of cotton cloth. It's best to place the materials in a metal container with a small hole and place the container in the fire. But burying the fibers and making a fire on top also works. The process is finalized once no smoke comes out from the metal container.

Another faster method that may work with some fibers is to burn them, and then as the flame dies down and the fibers start to glow, place them in an airtight container, or bury them.

CHAGA

Chaga (*Inonotus obliquus*) is the true tinder fungus. It looks like burnt charcoal and lives on birch trees. The inner light brown part of the fungus makes one of the best tinders when it is dried. It can also be used as a coal extender or a board for a friction fire, and it can hold an ember for a very long time.

AMADOU

Amadou is made from the felt-like part of the false tinder fungus (*Fomes fomentarius*). False tinder fungus is commonly found on dead birch and sometimes on aspen, and it is also known as hoof fungus because it looks like a horse's hoof. It's best to collect it when it is young and the crust can still be easily depressed. Many similar fungi can be prepared in the same way. The fungus can also be used as a bow drill base when fully dried.

The cotton-like part of the fungus used for amadou is the tramal layer. First, separate the outer crust and tubes from the trama with a sharp knife. Then, cut the trama into multiple thin slices. Boil it in a slurry of fine hardwood ash, and then pound and stretch the trama to break up its fibers. After it has fully dried, the amadou can be scraped and fluffed up to catch a spark.

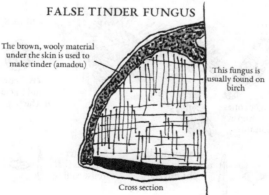

FALSE TINDER FUNGUS

The brown, wooly material under the skin is used to make tinder (amadou)

This fungus is usually found on birch

Cross section

FIREWOOD

BIRCH

Birch is often recognized for its smooth, white, paper-like bark. It is often the only dense and heavy hardwood available in the boreal forest.

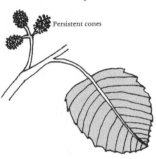

ALDER

Alders may seem like young birches, but they can be easily recognized by the groups of tiny cones that remain after the nutlets have dropped.

SPRUCE

To identify white spruce, look for the following features:
- The twig tips are hairless between the needles.
- The needles roll easily between tightly pressed fingers.
- The cones are relatively long.

To identify black spruce, look for the following features:
- The twig tips between the needles are covered with "hairs."
- The needles resist rolling between tightly pressed fingers.
- The cones are relatively small and spherical.

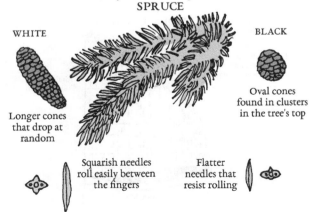

SPRUCE

WHITE

Longer cones that drop at random

Squarish needles roll easily between the fingers

BLACK

Oval cones found in clusters in the tree's top

Flatter needles that resist rolling

TAMARACK OR LARCH

Tamarack is a conifer found in the boreal forest with the unique trait of dropping its needles in the fall. It is often found in wet habitats, but it can also grow in dry places. Tamarack wood is very durable, as it resists contact with the ground and immersion in the water much better than other woods.

TAMARACK & LARCH

Soft needles in tufts of ten or more

LODGEPOLE PINE AND JACK PINE

Lodgepole pines and jack pines are similar and both have moderately soft wood. Lodgepole pines have prickly cones, whereas jack pines have smooth cones.

Jack pine   Lodgepole pine

Smooth cones that point to the branch tip

Prickly cones that tend to point back towards the trunk

BALSAM FIR

The flat and soft needles of balsam firs make this fir easy to identify. Their boughs make the best material for beds, and their soft wood works well for bow drill fires.

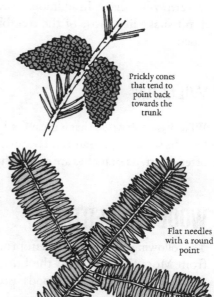

Flat needles with a round point

TREMBLING ASPEN

Trembling aspen (white poplar) is the most widely distributed tree in North America. Its leaf stems are so flexible that the slightest breeze will make its leaves shake.

The leaf trembles with the slightest breeze

In boreal forests, trembling aspen is a popular firewood choice for open fires because it burns well, and the smoke is not unpleasant. In a pinch, trembling aspen may be split and burned green if the fire is hot enough.

BALSAM POPLAR

Balsam poplar tends to be less abundant than trembling aspen. Balsam poplar's bark and trunk are similar to the trembling aspen's, but the leaves have a more pointed and arrow-like shape. In addition, its leaves don't shake like those of the trembling aspen.

WILLOW

Willow is a softwood that is great for open fires. Its smoke is pleasant, and because it's often short, its branches are easy to cut.

WOOD PROPERTIES

The following table is modified from notes from Mors Kochanski on the burning properties of boreal forest woods used in open fires. The most valuable woods for campfires are at the top.

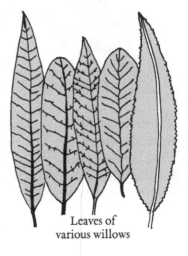

Leaves of various willows

Tree	Advantage	Disadvantage	Smoke	Kindling	Other
Willow (Salix)	The nicest fuel: pleasant smoke, bright flame, good heat and embers, easily gathered without tools.	Found in thin pieces that burn quickly.	Pleasant.	Good.	Great for friction fire.
Trembling aspen (Populus tremuloides)	Available in large, long-burning logs, and it can be burned green.	It can be hard to cut.	Slightly irritating for the eyes.	Dry wood makes good feather sticks.	
Tamarack or larch (Larix)	Burns very hot.	Only available in winter due to wet ground.	Moderate.		Roots smolder and can be a fire hazard.
Alder (Alnus)	Easily gathered and broken without tools.	Burns up the fastest.	Very little.		Green alder is good for smoking meat.
White spruce (Picea glauca)	Large logs make the longest-lasting and strongest heat.	It can be hard to cut.	Bad.	Resin and twigs are good for fire lighting.	
Jack pine and lodgepole pine	Strong heat and fast burning.	Strongly irritating smoke.	Very smoky and irritating.	Red needles are good, water-resistant tinder.	
Driftwoods	Very hot, burning even if wet.	Coastal driftwood (salt) releases toxins when burnt.	Moderate.		
Birch (Betula)	The hottest, nicest-smelling firewood. Burns when green.	Found mostly rotten or green.	Pleasant smoke.	Its bark makes excellent tinder, burns even when wet.	Host of false tinder fungus and chaga.

Tree	Advantages	Disadvantages	Smoke	Kindling	Other
Balsam poplar (Populus balsamifera)	Green wood is the most fire-resistant. Bark makes good coals.	Poor heat.	Moderate. The punky wood is irritating.	Inner bark makes good tinder for embers.	Forms good punkwood.
Balsam fir (Abies balsamea)	The conifer with the least resin.	Poor heat.	Moderate.		Good for friction fire.
Black spruce (Picea mariana)	Adequately hot.	The worst smoke, throws the most sparks.	Worst, irritating smoke.	Resin and twigs are good for fire lighting.	Green wood is good for banking a fire.

EDGED TOOLS AND CUTTING WOOD

SAFETY

Safety is paramount in survival because even a minor injury could snowball into a major issue. It requires discipline to wear work gloves and safety glasses, and to use safer techniques, but being complacent is not an option. If you use cutting tools without protective equipment in a long-term situation, you're just asking for trouble.

CUTTING WITHOUT TOOLS

Cutting without tools allows you to reduce the wear on your metal tools and preserve their sharp edges—plus, sometimes, it is faster and more efficient.

BURNING WOOD

Wood can be burned without cutting it into small pieces, and it can also be cut using fire; this saves you calories. The fire layouts to the right allow you to burn thick, long, uncut firewood.

REMOVING BRANCHES

One of the first steps for cutting firewood is to cut branches off; this is a necessary precaution, as the branches could wound you. Use a green stick—about the length of your forearm—to quickly strike and break off thin branches.

BREAKING FIREWOOD

Thin firewood can be broken by striking with it a rock or a dead tree, and larger firewood can be broken by throwing a rock on top of it. Be careful with both techniques: expect flying sticks and bouncing rocks.

BREAKING WOOD USING LEVERAGE

When two trees are close together, they can act as a fulcrum and allow you to use leverage to snap a thin log. Remember to remove any dangerous branches.

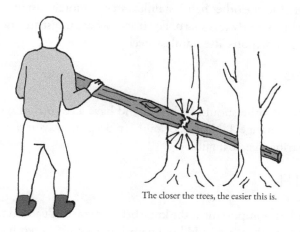

The closer the trees, the easier this is.

KNIVES

A survival knife has to have a fixed blade because folding knives are not sturdy enough. A full-profile tang is preferred because it makes the knife stronger—in smaller knives, a three-quarter tang is enough. Another important feature is a blade with a spine ground 90 degrees sharp for use with a ferro rod and as a thumb rest for pressure and control while carving. Avoid serrated edges because they are harder to sharpen with minimal tools.

I divide survival knives into two categories: big and small. Big knives measure around 9–11" (23–28 cm) point to butt, and small ones measure around 8–10" (20–25 cm). The most relevant difference is weight and shape: big knives are considerably heavier and sturdier.

For long-term survival, small knives are often better. Big knives or *Rambo*-style survival knives are jacks-of-all-trades but masters of none. They are great if you only have that *one* knife as your only tool. Suppose you also have a saw, an axe, and a multi-tool. In that case, you are better off carrying a comfortable and compact knife instead. Small knives work much better at the everyday tasks of wilderness living. Unfortunately, there is no perfect survival knife; there are only compromises.

STEEL

In simple terms, knife blades are made of two main steel types: carbon steel and stainless steel. Carbon steel might cut better, but it needs more maintenance than stainless steel. It's a matter of personal preference. Carbon steel is a harder steel that retains a sharper edge better and is easier to sharpen. On the other hand, stainless steel is more resistant to rust and chipping but slightly less sharp. For places where moisture and water are constant companions, use stainless steel.

COLOR

Your survival knife should be bright and have a color that stands out if lost, such as orange, UN blue, or pink. In deep snow, you should also tie a bright string in case it falls.

SHEATH

The sheath is as important as the knife because you can't afford to lose your knife, and the sheath should hold your knife securely even if you turn it upside down and shake it. The sheath of the popular Mora Companion knives is not secure, but you can add a piece of bicycle tube at the top to secure the knife.

SURVIVAL KNIFE

The Morakniv Kansbol in stainless steel makes a great, affordable survival knife. Another option is the Condor Terrasaur in carbon steel.

FILLETING

If catching fish is part of your survival strategy, pack a filleting knife to speed up the filleting process.

KNIFE SAFETY

It is crucial to have a healthy respect for knives. Prevent accidents by using proper techniques and the blade will miss your body even if there is an unexpected follow-through. Ask yourself, "What if the knife slips?" and handle your knife defensively. Also, it's safer to keep your knife sharp for the reasons explained in the axe section.

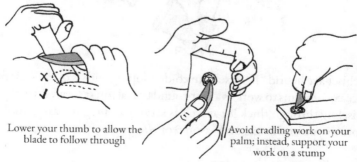

Lower your thumb to allow the blade to follow through

Avoid cradling work on your palm; instead, support your work on a stump

AXE VERSUS SAW

Axes and saws complement each other very well. The axe is simpler and more rugged than a saw, so it takes precedence, but a good kit should include both.

Saws are lighter than axes and are more efficient for cutting wide logs, while axes are more versatile and easier to sharpen. It is easier to learn how to use a saw than an axe, and saws are safer. Suppose your basecamp has a woodstove or a small indoor fireplace. In that case, a saw is a must-have because cutting logs is more efficient with a saw and the saw wastes less wood when cutting.

AXES

A survival axe should be light enough for one-handed work and long enough for two-handed work. It should weigh roughly 2–3 lb. (1–1.5 kg) and measure 18–24″ (45–60 cm). You might opt for a lighter, more compact axe if you have a good saw. I prefer a 16″ (40 cm) axe that weighs about 2 lb. (1 kg) because I can use it more precisely, and it's more portable; the Scaxe2l by Schrade has served me well, but the blade nicks easily.

If you use your axe in winter, consider how easy it is to use with mitts; a heavier axe is harder to grip.

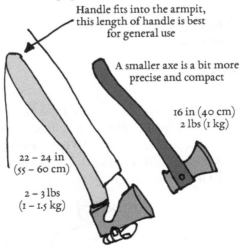

Handle fits into the armpit, this length of handle is best for general use

A smaller axe is a bit more precise and compact

16 in (40 cm)
2 lbs (1 kg)

22 – 24 in (55 – 60 cm)

2 – 3 lbs (1 – 1.5 kg)

The chisel-axe hybrid "JP Paxe" I'm co-developing with Robert Weir from panaceax.com aims to work as a year-round boreal forest survival axe capable of chiseling through thick ice as well as serving as a regular axe. I took the first prototype of this axe on Season 9 of *Alone*.

There are three key innovations we are incorporating into this axe: a drop-leg holster, ice chisel capabilities, and an axe head that can be used without a handle and makes the handle replacement process take less than a minute. The latter innovation also allows you to pack the axe head with no handle into a survival kit; the handle can be readily improvised and mounted in the field.

Boreal forest year-round survival axe and ice chisel hybrid (first prototype).

AXE TECHNIQUES

Axes deserve a lot of respect. It is extremely easy to hurt yourself with an axe, and it is also easy to break their handles or nick their blades. Even experienced users are at risk when they are tired.

Your axe should always be in its sheath when it's not being used. Before using it, always check that the head is not loose, and keep the edge sharp. A dull axe can be dangerous because it can glance off instead of bite into the wood, and you'll have to use more force with a dull axe, thus sacrificing control. Also, check the handle for cracks: a split handle can be quite dangerous. Always carry the axe with the edge away from your body in case you fall.

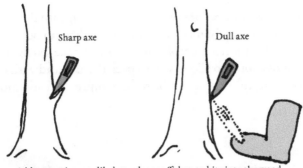

A blunt axe is more likely to glance off than to bite into the wood

AXE STORAGE

PRECISE AXE WORK

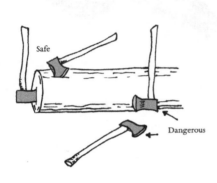

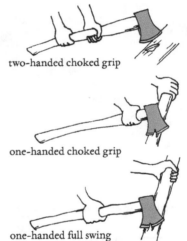

two-handed choked grip

one-handed choked grip

one-handed full swing

CUTTING A LOG

The proper technique for chopping a log that is too big to be rolled is to stand on it with legs far apart and cut between your feet.

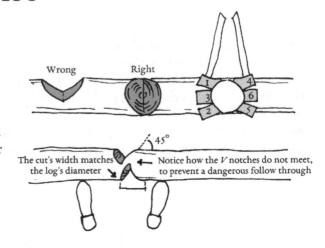

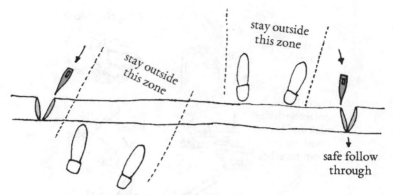

stay outside this zone

stay outside this zone

safe follow through

When cutting small logs either stance works

LIMBING

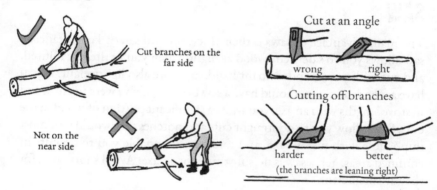

Cut branches on the far side

Not on the near side

Cut at an angle

wrong   right

Cutting off branches

harder   better
(the branches are leaning right)

SPLITTING WOOD WITH AN AXE

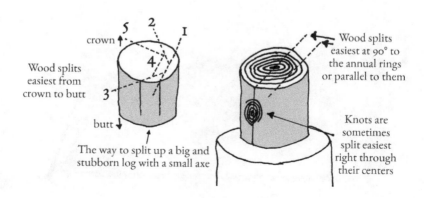

crown

butt

Wood splits easiest from crown to butt

The way to split up a big and stubborn log with a small axe

Wood splits easiest at 90° to the annual rings or parallel to them

Knots are sometimes split easiest right through their centers

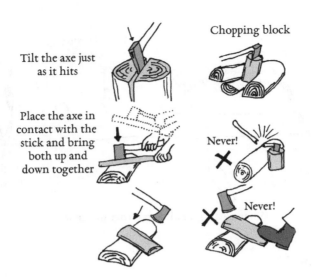

Tilt the axe just as it hits

Chopping block

Place the axe in contact with the stick and bring both up and down together

Never!

Never!

SAW

The main advantage of saws is their efficiency and safety. For instance, a saw allows you to safely cut wood at night, when you're tired or injured, and cut with your nondominant hand. Saws are also lightweight. If you have a woodstove, you should have a saw because, if you were to cut wood in stove lengths with an axe, you waste a significant portion of wood in the cuts. Saws allow you to do straight cuts and notches that would be almost impossible with just an axe, and folding saws enable you to do cuts in confined areas. Yet, a saw is no substitute for an axe. Avoid short saws, for they are inefficient.

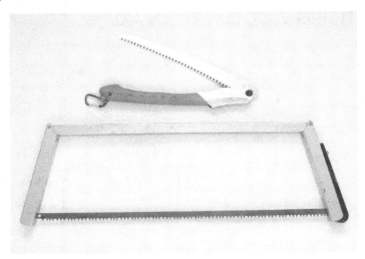

For a portable saw, I recommend the 30″ Tuff Camp Saw by Spring Creek or the 24″ Agawa Canyon saw for camp. If you have to feed a woodstove for the winter, these are the saws to have (with extra blades). These bow saws are light, efficient, and accept standard saw blades. The Agawa is more ergonomic and faster to deploy than the Tuff Camp. And both saws are easy to carry around and ready-to-go.

Suppose you are more interested in versatility and portability and don't expect to cut firewood daily. In that case, I recommend the Silky BigBoy for use outside your basecamp. The BigBoy folding saw is heavier and less efficient than the Tuff Camp and Agawa, but it doesn't need to be set up.

The Original Bucksaw from **bearessentialsoutdoors.ca** is a notable mention in the 21″ bow saw category.

Some people recommend the Silky Katanaboy 650. It is way less portable but much more efficient, with a blade 80% longer than the BigBoy's blade. The problem is that it is designed more for trail maintenance than for cutting firewood—for instance, it is awkward to use with a sawhorse—and it is also expensive.

Finally, another option is to carry a saw blade with two heavy-duty keyrings or bolts attached at the ends to improvise a bow saw in the field. But if you expect to use your saw daily, it's better to pack a good saw—which will be more efficient and practical than an improvised saw.

The previous recommendations are only for portable saws. If you don't need your saw to be portable at all, then the best saw to have would be an old-school crosscut saw or a 36″ bow saw.

SAW SAFETY

Start sawing this way to prevent the saw from jumping and cutting the back of your hand.

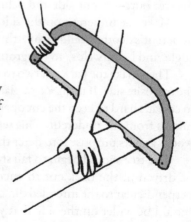

SAWHORSE

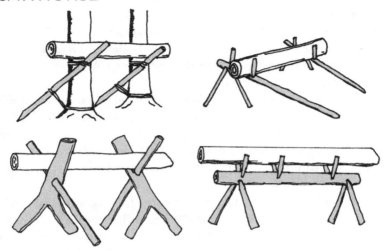

FELLING A TREE

The first step to felling a tree is to determine the direction of its lean or weight. Hopefully, it leans in the same direction you want it to fall. Otherwise, a wedge can be driven in the back cut at the right moment and place to adjust its lean—as long as the lean isn't too strong in the other direction. But if it leans strongly in a particular direction, it's wise to fell it in that direction.

The next step is to clear out an "escape" trail to a safe place away from the tree butt—to one side and behind the direction of the fall.

Make the undercut on the side where you expect the tree to fall: the undercut's depth should be one-third of the tree's diameter, at a 45-degree angle, and be very close to the ground.

Then make the back cut two to three fingers above the undercut and at the opposite side. If using a saw, place a wedge in the cut as soon as possible, in case it's hard to keep the cut open. The back cut should stop about two fingers from the undercut. This separation is the hinge wood or holding wood, and its purpose is to deter the tree from kicking back as it falls.

The tree should begin to fall shortly; otherwise, a wedge (or two) can be driven in the back cut to encourage the tree. If its natural lean is perpendicular to the intended direction of the fall, then the holding wood should be wider on the side that you want to encourage the tree to fall towards. This wider side of the holding wood gives a bit more direction to the fall.

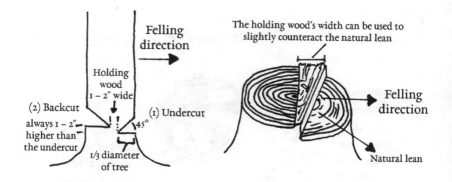

Felling direction

Holding wood 1 – 2" wide

(2) Backcut always 1 – 2" higher than the undercut

(1) Undercut

45°

1/3 diameter of tree

The holding wood's width can be used to slightly counteract the natural lean

Felling direction

Natural lean

Once the tree begins to fall, don't waste time and back away using your escape route. Be careful of swinging branches and trees (widow-makers) that may be launched toward you. Try to anticipate any possible dangers.

Don't stand behind!

MAUL OR MALLET

A maul can be easily carved from a green hardwood branch or tree. Mauls are useful for splitting wood and for safely splitting kindling. A maul can transform your axe into a chisel or a wedge and give you much more control than if you were to swing your axe.

WEDGE

Wedges are used for splitting wood. Make them from green hardwood or the strongest wood available.

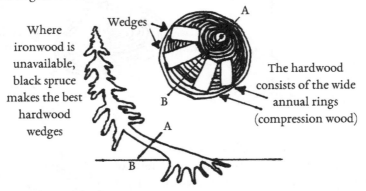

Where ironwood is unavailable, black spruce makes the best hardwood wedges

Wedges

A

B

A

B

The hardwood consists of the wide annual rings (compression wood)

SPLITTING WOOD WITH A WEDGE

SHARPENING

IMPROVISED SHARPENING

A knife's edge can be maintained with sand and smooth stones. Experiment with different stones to determine what works during the coarse grinding stages, and coat a flat piece of wood with wet sand for the finishing phases. The sand may need to be crushed for the last stages of sharpening.

TOOLS

For a minimal sharpening kit, I recommend the double-sided (fine and coarse) Diafold Sharpener by DMT and a Lansky The Puck Dual-Grit

Sharpener for axes. Compact, double-sided sharpening stones are also a good choice. Another option is the Corona Sharpening Tool: a compact and quick sharpener that works well but is quite aggressive.

SHARPENING AN AXE

Axes can be sharpened with an axe stone or similar to a knife.

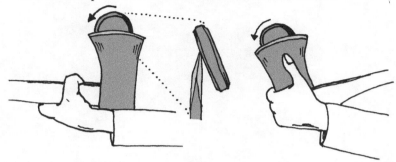

SHARPENING A KNIFE

For wood carving, your knife should be pretty sharp, and for cutting meat and skinning, your knife should be able to shave wet hair from your forearm with one stroke.

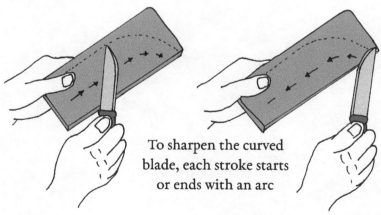

To sharpen the curved blade, each stroke starts or ends with an arc

SHELTER

SLEEPING GEAR

SLEEPING BAGS

A high-quality sleeping bag is one of the essential items to have in a long-term survival scenario. Sleeping bags are a game-changer.

MATERIALS

Down is the number one choice for backpackers because it's highly compressible and has the best warmth-to-weight ratio.

Yet, down is not perfect. A sleeping bag should be moisture-resistant and easy to dry in the field, even in winter. The problem with down is that moisture will accumulate over time in rainy or subfreezing conditions, both from your body and from condensation outside the bag.

Synthetics are a good option for a long-term survival bag, but they are not outstanding. Synthetics retain some insulation when wet or moist, while down is worthless when wet. In addition, it is next to impossible to dry a wet down sleeping bag in the field, while a synthetic bag will dry relatively well.

Although modern synthetic bags are not as bulky as they used to be, they are still pretty bulky and heavy compared to down sleeping bags. That is not as important if you carry your bag on a sled or canoe, but it is likely a deal-breaker for backpacking.

Ultimately, the best all-around approach is a hybrid: a high-quality down sleeping bag tucked inside a synthetic sleeping bag (attached together with Velcro or bra hooks). This approach works over a wide range of temperatures, saves weight and bulk, and retains moisture resistance.

I've had a custom expedition sleeping bag made that is basically a down sleeping bag nested into an integrated synthetic sleeping bag, and I am pretty impressed with its ability to dry off any moisture or condensation.

SHAPE

Stay away from rectangular bags, for those are bulkier, heavier, and colder than mummy bags. Sure, mummy bags are not as comfortable, but they are warmer.

MOISTURE

The problem in freezing conditions is that your body continually produces water vapor. When moisture travels from your body toward the outer layers of your sleeping bag, it reaches the outer fabric—which is way colder than the inside of the sleeping bag—therefore, condensation occurs. Condensation is not an issue if you use the bag for a few days or even a week or two, but it will impact its insulating effect if you go past that.

TEMPERATURE RATINGS

Once you know the lowest temperature you expect to encounter, including historical extremes, you can begin to search for an appropriate set of sleeping bags.

In long-term survival, your metabolism slows down a lot. A lack of a full belly, exhaustion, and many other factors make it much harder for you to stay warm. That's a challenge because sleeping bags work by using the heat your body produces, and if you're not producing much heat at all, the sleeping bag may not keep you warm.

You can check the loft of a sleeping bag by laying it on the ground and then placing a very light stick on top of the middle of the sleeping bag. If you measure the distance from the stick to the ground, you'll have the loft.

I created this chart as a rough guide for choosing a sleeping bag or combination of sleeping bags based on their average loft. This rough guideline is not for regular camping but for situations where your body may be running on fumes.

The chart below is my suggestion for the insulation loft required according to different temperatures in a survival setting.

Sleeping bag loft for long-term survival

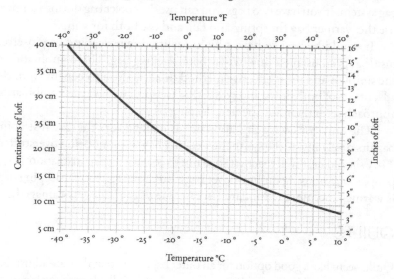

ISO AND EN RATINGS

EN 13537 was a European standard for measuring temperature ratings on European sleeping bags; recently, it has been replaced by an international standard (ISO 23537-1). The tests used are so similar that they are virtually the same for practical purposes. These standards are far from perfect, but they are the best available. They have three main ratings: comfort, lower limit, and extreme.

For long-term survival, the only relevant rating is *comfort*. The comfort rating is the temperature at which an average woman can expect to sleep comfortably in a relaxed position. But beware: many stores will use phrasing such as *comfort limit* and list the EN rating for *lower limit* instead of *comfort*. Many manufacturers won't advertise their EN ratings, but if they sell those sleeping bags in Europe, they must test them. You can usually ask the manufacturer for the EN/ISO ratings or check a European store online. Unfortunately, the EN/ISO standards are not meant for extreme temperatures. Generally, you won't find sleeping bags tested to a comfort rating past -4°F (-20°C).

You should still leave a buffer to account for a slower metabolism in long-term contexts. Don't *just* follow the EN/ISO comfort ratings.

LAYERING BAGS

I highly recommend layering two bags to assemble a four-season sleeping bag system. If you have two bags, you can use the cooler bag during summer, use the warmer bag for spring and fall, and use both for winter.

It would be best to have a high-quality down sleeping bag inserted inside a spacious, high-quality synthetic sleeping bag. This combination is the simplest and most effective method. It allows you to benefit from the advantages of both down and synthetics. Helsport follows this combination approach with their Spitsbergen sleeping bag.

The only trick with this approach is making sure the down sleeping bag fits nicely inside the synthetic sleeping bag without being overstuffed. They should nest well together so as not to compress their insulation. Some people suggest using quilts or over bags, but layering regular sleeping bags is warmer and more redundant (in case one of the bags gets damaged).

QUILTS

Quilts seem like a good option for an outer bag, given that they are adjustable, lightweight, and compact. But a sleeping bag is still a better option as an outer bag because it provides redundancy and full insulation.

The main advantage of using a quilt as an outer bag is that it maximizes the insulation on top and forgoes insulation on the bottom. Thus, a quilt is less bulky and heavy, so it might be a good compromise if you're weight- or space-constrained.

Also, consider the movement of both bags. Most quilt-type over bags utilize various straps to keep both sleeping bags aligned with each other and with the sleeping pad.

TIPS

A practical way of boosting the warmth of your sleeping bag during the coldest nights is to wear warm clothes to bed. Just pay attention not to introduce too much moisture and dirt into the sleeping bag because they will lower its insulation powers. Avoid overheating. Wearing down booties inside the bag is also an excellent way to have warmer feet.

When using a sleeping bag in extreme cold, wear a neck warmer and a beanie. Pull the neck warmer up over your mouth and pull the beanie down over the tip of your nose. Then close the sleeping bag's hood snugly around your face. You might take some time getting used to this, but an added benefit is that the air you breathe will be pre-warmed by the neck warmer.

Down sleeping bags need to have their down regularly worked to redistribute it evenly throughout the sleeping bag and reduce clumping.

Dark colors are preferred for the outside and inside fabrics of sleeping bags because these fabrics dry faster than lighter tones under sunlight; this is even more important in winter.

If you have to sleep near an open fire, use a barrier for sparks. A sleeping bag liner, contractor bag, or a bivvy bag might work as a protective shield.

For remote expeditions in severe cold, your bag should have double zippers for redundancy if the zipper fails (Feathered Friends makes good expedition-grade sleeping bags).

BIVVY BAGS

A bivvy bag is a good complement for your sleeping bag. It prevents your sleeping bag from touching the walls of a snow shelter, and when sleeping under a tarp, it protects the sleeping bag from rain. Even GORE-TEX bivvy bags trap some moisture inside, especially in winter, so that is something to watch for.

I recommend a compact and minimalist bivvy bag like the Special Forces Bivvi by Snugpak or the Co-op Shell Bivy by REI. They make great emergency shelters when coupled with a sleeping bag. Bivvy bags are useful, but they are not needed if you have a fully rainproof shelter.

SLEEPING PADS

Sleeping pads are pretty handy when traveling and when you don't want to spend time collecting materials for a bed. In addition, they can have a significant impact on your comfort level and ability to sleep well.

These are some recommendations for sleeping pads:

- Place clothes between your sleeping bag and pad to reduce condensation in your bag.
- Use a closed-cell foam pad for three-season use because they are quite resilient to sparks and punctures. They are virtually indestructible, but their thickness wears off, and they aren't very warm or comfortable.

- Use a closed-cell foam pad in conjunction with an inflatable sleeping pad for year-round use. This combination is suitable for sleeping in subfreezing temperatures, even over snow.
- Use seam sealant and patches to repair inflatable pads. You can also use hot glue sticks and a lighter to melt the glue over a puncture.
- Keep in mind that ISO and EN temperature ratings are tested with a sleeping pad R-value of around 5. The R-value is a rating that compares the insulation value between sleeping pads: the higher the value, the more insulated it is.

SLEEPING PAD RECOMMENDATIONS

I recommend pairing a Z Lite closed-cell foam pad (R-value 2.6) with a NeoAir XTherm inflatable pad (R-value 5.7). Both sleeping pads weigh around 15 oz. (0.4 kg) each. The NeoAir XTherm is expensive, but it's very compact and light.

CAMP LOCATION

Location is one of the most crucial aspects of a long-term shelter. Below, I'll explain some factors to consider when choosing a basecamp, including the five W's: water, wind, wigglies, wood, and widow-makers.

WATER

Your camp should have easy access to water. Ideally, it should be less than 200 yd. (180 m) from a water source. You will make the trip, at the very least, once a day, so it shouldn't be too long. Ensure you're at an appropriate distance from the water in places that could flood rapidly, such as canyons or tidal zones.

WIND

It helps to know the prevailing winds in your area. Do they come mainly from the west? From the north? How do they change with the seasons?

In addition to checking historical data, observe trees for hints of the prevailing winds (e.g., the side trees lean toward, or if most branches are on one side). Also, consider the breeze created by mountains, valleys, big lakes, and the sea. It's important to be aware of the prevailing winds because they will blow snow, rain, and smoke into or away from your shelter. In addition, the winds will also steal your shelter's warmth, so plan accordingly. Lastly, your shelter should not be too exposed to the wind in case of a strong storm.

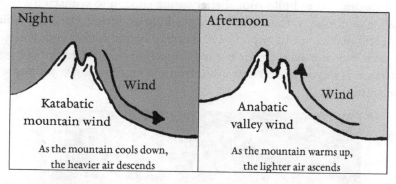

WIGGLIES

If mosquitoes and flies are abundant in your area, carefully choose your location. Don't settle near stagnant water—choose a breezy spot instead. The wind is a significant help for blowing away bugs, but this is counterproductive during winter. Plan for that and make a compromise. Maybe have a day area for cooking and daily activities in an exposed spot, and position your all-season shelter in a protected place. Bugs tend not to like being in exposed areas.

If the bugs are too much to handle and you have no mosquito net, consider setting up an overnight camp on a small island on a lake. Some Indigenous peoples built platforms in the middle of lakes to sleep on during the peak mosquito season. They didn't have the luxury of mosquito netting.

WOOD

There should be enough firewood around to last for the time you'll be there. Estimate how much wood you'll need, then triple that amount; that is a good rule of thumb for how much available wood should be near your camp.

Try some of the following strategies to reduce your firewood use: have a small, well-insulated shelter that requires less firewood to heat; use efficient cooking methods, such as making a wood cookstove from sand and mud or clay and rocks; or use an efficient fire for cooking. In the winter, use a metal woodstove. Finally, if you have a boat, stay close to a waterway to gather firewood from nearby areas.

WIDOW-MAKERS

Some hazards to watch for are falling trees and branches, also known as widow-makers. One preventive measure is to cut down any dead trees and limbs that might fall your way. An alternative—if other options are impractical—is to build your shelter strong enough to withstand a tree falling on top of it. Even if you have a temporary shelter like a tent, you can still make a strong tripod or A-frame to better protect your shelter from a widow-maker. Utilize natural protections to your advantage; for instance, place your shelter near strong trees and big rocks to give you partial protection.

BUILDING MATERIALS

Will you use pine boughs, poles, clay, moss, and so on? There should be abundant materials to make your bed, roof, walls, and other projects—you don't want to haul those materials from a place far away.

SUNLIGHT

The sun provides light, heat, vitamin D, and a necessary morale boost, so make sure your site gets sunlight by paying attention to the cardinal directions and the sun's path. Ensure your shelter will shade you from the sun when it is at its peak during the summer months, when the sun is south and at a high angle. Consider having your shelter facing southeast so that it receives sunlight during the first half of the day during the winter months.

In winter, the sun will rise at a lower angle, so make sure the trees or terrain around your site won't block the morning sun.

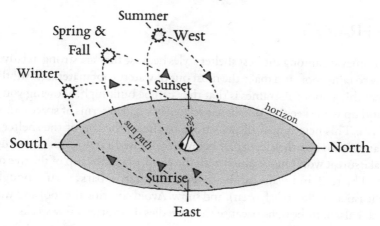

HAZARDS

Your camp must not be in the path of natural hazards, like floods, avalanches, and mudslides. And it should be situated far enough from water so that changing water levels or tides don't flood it. Lightning strikes should be considered as well.

MOBILITY

Your camp should be relatively accessible either by trails or water. Being in an exceedingly secluded spot is not ideal because it may be too hard to do an emergency evacuation or resupply. Also, you will probably have to travel around your area to forage, so make sure it won't be too tough to get in and out.

TRAPPING AND FISHING

Fish will likely be one of your main staples, so pick a camp location near a good fishing spot. A place near some rapids or waterfalls would be great. Set your fishing lines, traps, or nets in a circuit to minimize travel time.

The same guidelines apply for a trapline; ideally, it should be a loop that is relatively close to your camp.

SHELTER CONCEPTS

A-FRAMES

A-frames are among the best shelter styles because they are strong, relatively easy to rainproof, and make the most out of waterproof materials. Another great thing about A-frames is that they can be built high, allowing you to stand up while keeping the shelter relatively small in terms of space to keep warm. This height also allows smoke to rise to the top of the shelter so that you can breathe cleaner air below. If you used a tree for the structure, make sure it won't move much with the wind, or cut the top of the tree off.

The roof and walls can be covered with tarps, bark, spruce boughs, split aspen (split while frozen), and snow. Avoid covering the roof and walls with balsam fir boughs because their needles drop after a few weeks.

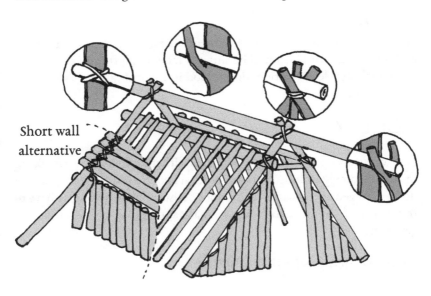

Short wall alternative

When using a tarp as a covering, shave any sharp points smooth on the wooden framework, and think about dealing with condensation. In places with big daily swings in temperature, condensation will form around any thick green poles, so avoid placing your bed underneath those. Keep the roof steep and use vertical sticks to keep the tarp supported so that condensation falls along the tarp unobstructed.

LEAN-TO SHELTERS

Lean-to shelters are well-known because they are simple and effective, but they are not recommended for use for more than 72 hours.

They make great day shelters for cooking under the sun and rain, but they leave you exposed to the elements and offer not much more insulation and wind protection than a tarp. In winter conditions, lean-to shelters require long, large fires, and most of that warmth is wasted due to their open concept.

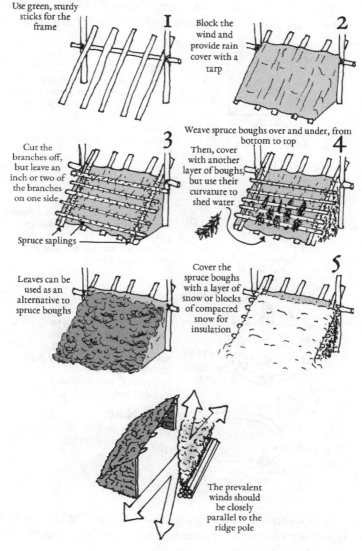

Use green, sturdy sticks for the frame

I

Block the wind and provide rain cover with a tarp

2

Cut the branches off, but leave an inch or two of the branches on one side

3

Spruce saplings

Weave spruce boughs over and under, from bottom to top

Then, cover with another layer of boughs, but use their curvature to shed water

4

Leaves can be used as an alternative to spruce boughs

Cover the spruce boughs with a layer of snow or blocks of compacted snow for insulation

5

The prevalent winds should be closely parallel to the ridge pole

QUINZEES

Quinzees are one of the most practical 72-hour shelters for areas with abundant snow. They can be made with various types of snow, but coarse, grain-like snow doesn't work well.

Quinzees offer excellent insulation and protection from the wind, but they are not warm enough by themselves: if you don't have a sleeping bag or warm clothes, you will still be cold—the inside temperature is usually around 21°F (-6°C) regardless of how cold the outside is. Snow shelters tend to work better when the temperature is below 5°F (-15°C), as clothing won't get too wet during construction and water won't drip down from the roof.

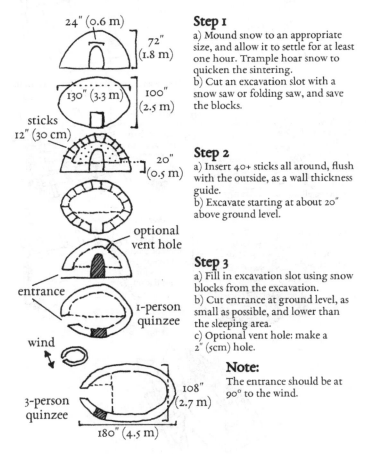

Step 1

a) Mound snow to an appropriate size, and allow it to settle for at least one hour. Trample hoar snow to quicken the sintering.
b) Cut an excavation slot with a snow saw or folding saw, and save the blocks.

Step 2

a) Insert 40+ sticks all around, flush with the outside, as a wall thickness guide.
b) Excavate starting at about 20″ above ground level.

Step 3

a) Fill in excavation slot using snow blocks from the excavation.
b) Cut entrance at ground level, as small as possible, and lower than the sleeping area.
c) Optional vent hole: make a 2″ (5cm) hole.

Note:

The entrance should be at 90° to the wind.

One of the best aids when making a quinzee is a tarp. The tarp can be used to move lots of snow from one place to another and be placed on the floor of the quinzee while it's being built to remove the snow more easily (the snow won't stick to the tarp).

To make a quinzee, shovel a bunch of sticky snow into a large, tall, dome-like pile. Then let the snow stand for a few minutes or hours to sinter (fuse) into a more cohesive pile.

The fastest way of hollowing out a quinzee is to make a large opening and then close that opening with blocks of snow from the interior.

Many survival instructors insist on making a vent at the top; they likely believe there is not enough breathable air without a vent. But this precaution significantly reduces the warmth inside. In practice, there will be enough air available *as long as the inside doesn't ice over*—preventing air from permeating through the snow. Always watch out for ice forming on the walls—scrape it off to make the snow porous again. Or make a vent if ice is a recurring problem. Ensure you don't heat up the inside, for the roof will start to drip. It's crucial not to use a stove or gas lamp inside, for these combustion sources could lead to the risk of carbon monoxide poisoning—this goes for quinzees with or without vents.

I don't recommend using a candle inside the shelter because, with time, the heat it generates may make a hole in the roof.

The downsides of quinzees are:
- They require lots of snow and effort.
- They sag after a couple of days.
- They are not compatible with fires inside the structure.

Those factors make quinzees not worth the effort for long-term use in wooded regions. But they are excellent emergency shelters, and the principle of insulating with snow is extremely important.

Suppose you are strongly considering using a quinzee for long-term survival. In that case, think instead about building a dome-like shelter or A-frame (with poles, boughs, and a tarp) that can bear the weight of snow and use it for insulation. Another option is to make artificial snow blocks and build an igloo.

Artificial snow blocks

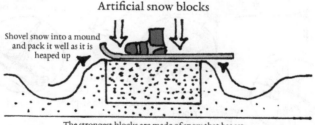

Shovel snow into a mound and pack it well as it is heaped up

The strongest blocks are made of snow that has set overnight, but they may be cut within an hour or two

PIT HOUSE

Pit houses are one of the best types of shelters for cold weather because, since they are partially underground, they provide protection from the wind and take advantage of the ground's thermal mass and relatively warmer temperature. But a lot of time and effort is required to build them. In many areas of the boreal forest, this type of shelter is not viable because of the Canadian Shield rock.

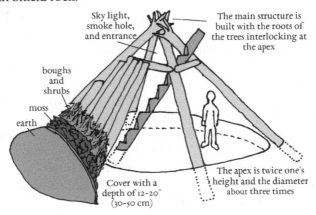

Sky light, smoke hole, and entrance

The main structure is built with the roots of the trees interlocking at the apex

boughs and shrubs

moss

earth

Cover with a depth of 12-20" (30-50 cm)

The apex is twice one's height and the diameter about three times

SHELTER TECHNIQUES

TARP TECHNIQUES

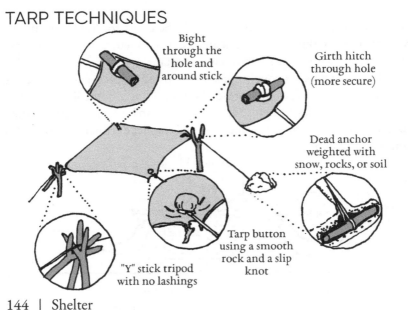

Bight through the hole and around stick

Girth hitch through hole (more secure)

Dead anchor weighted with snow, rocks, or soil

Tarp button using a smooth rock and a slip knot

"Y" stick tripod with no lashings

WALLS

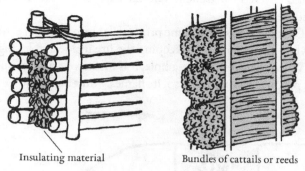

Insulating material

Bundles of cattails or reeds

ROOF

If you plan to build a tarp-based shelter, consider sewing and seam sealing marine-grade clear vinyl for windows. And consider sewing fireproof material for a stovepipe or chimney.

If tarps are not available, a waterproof roof can be improvised with layers of birchbark or other tree bark. The pieces of bark can then be used as roof tiles, held in place with heavy sticks. See the "Bushcraft" chapter for info on removing bark.

INSULATION

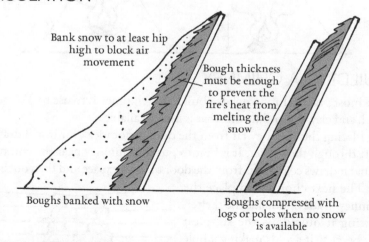

Bank snow to at least hip high to block air movement

Bough thickness must be enough to prevent the fire's heat from melting the snow

Boughs banked with snow

Boughs compressed with logs or poles when no snow is available

OPEN FIRES AND SMOKE

A significant drawback of open fires inside a shelter is smoke. For this reason, the Sami sometimes built air intakes that brought air from the outside of their shelters straight to their fire pits; they dug a trench in the ground and covered the trench. The extra oxygen made their fires burn hotter and cleaner.

The Dakota Fire uses the same principle of bringing more oxygen into the fire while at the same time keeping the fire inside a hole dug into the ground. When the fire is inside a hole, it is insulated and can burn hotter and thus produce less smoke; also, its flames won't be visible to others.

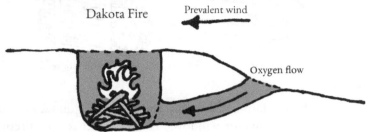

Dakota Fire   Prevalent wind

Oxygen flow

Another technique for reducing smoke in a shelter is elevating the fire to raise the smoke ceiling.

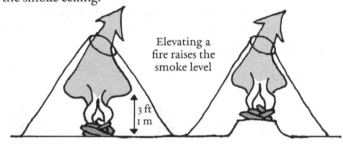

Elevating a fire raises the smoke level

3 ft
1 m

BUILDING A CHIMNEY

The most practical approach for building a chimney is to use rocks, mud, sand, and clay, depending on what is most available.

Placing the chimney far from the door is not ideal, for it will draw a draft through the shelter. It is best to put the chimney near the entrance so that it draws cold drafts from the door to the fireplace and then outside.

The next choice is to place the chimney inside or outside the shelter. Putting it outside is the simplest way because it avoids making a hole through the roof, but it decreases the amount of heat radiated inside. Another option is to place the chimney in the inside corner of the shelter.

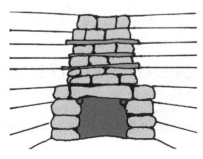

To build a chimney out of rocks and mortar, use rocks featuring a smooth side and place the rocks with their smooth side facing inside the chimney. That method will decrease the soot and creosote buildup and reduce the danger of a chimney fire. Another alternative for using less-than-ideal stones is to build the chimney and line it with a smooth layer of clay.

You can use clay mixed with ash, mud, or sand for mortar. When building rock walls, the rocks should break joints (like brick walls) so that the joints do not line up to prevent vertical cracks from spreading (see the next section).

First, build the fireplace base with stones to keep the chimney off the moist ground. The fireplace should be shaped like a *U* with the opening facing into the shelter. Plaster the mud or clay over the fireplace to form the chimney. You can use bark or wood to temporarily support the mud over the fireplace opening until it dries. If the weather is too humid, you can start a small fire to help speed up the drying process. As the height of the chimney increases, the opening should decrease in size and end at about one-quarter of the size of the fireplace opening.

The mud should be mixed with materials like clay, ash, sand, and fibers so that it won't crack too much as it dries. If clay is the primary material, it may shrink and crack, so temper it with lots of fiber, soil, sand, and ash.

The top of the chimney can be covered with flat stones. A hole can be made on the side while the chimney is still drying to let the smoke escape, or place a few small rocks under the flat stones to create vents. The top of the chimney could extend above the roof to increase the draft and reduce the danger of fires, but this is not necessary.

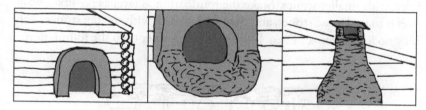

A chimney could also be constructed using greenwood laid cabin-style and lined with tempered clay to seal any air gaps and prevent it from burning down. But this type of chimney must be continually inspected to avoid a chimney fire due to creosote buildup or an inadequate clay liner.

A mud or clay stove can also be improvised by building it over a frame of metal cans, wires, sticks, or a punky log. But the quality of the mud and clay construction must be excellent to withstand the intense heat and avoid cracking.

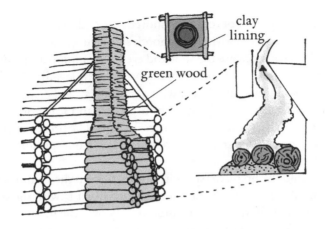

clay lining

green wood

With enough metal cans and materials, it's possible to improvise a full stove and stovepipe without clay or mud.

BUILDING WITH STONES

Stone and mud walls are fairly rain-resistant as long as the top and bottom outer edges are kept dry. The wall's foundation must be made only with stones—without mud mortar—and the roof should have a long overhang to protect the top of the wall from rain. Choose the flattest rocks you can find for the foundation. They should be laid firmly on the ground and have no movement. Smaller stones can be wedged between bigger stones to stabilize them. The space between the foundation's outer and inner rocks can be filled with smaller stones. Make the foundation as level as possible. Walk over it to find loose stones, and then wedge them with smaller stones until they no longer move. Then, build the wall thinner than the foundation.

Lay stones horizontally and fill the middle with small stones and mud

Break the joints as with a brick wall

DOOR

A straightforward and practical way to make a door hinge is just to loosely tie the door to the frame with paracord. Below are some other techniques for improvising doors and hinges.

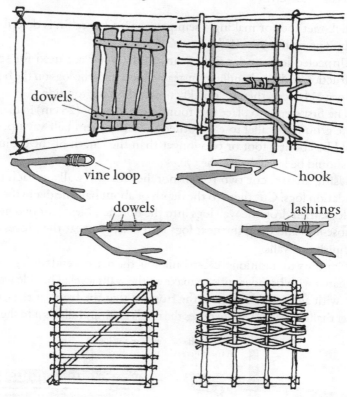

dowels

vine loop

hook

dowels

lashings

HEWING A LOG WITH AN AXE

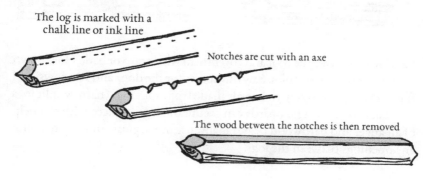

The log is marked with a chalk line or ink line

Notches are cut with an axe

The wood between the notches is then removed

CABINS

QUICK CABIN

A quick method for making a semipermanent log cabin is described in Calvin Rutstrum's *The Wilderness Cabin.*

Unpeeled logs under 6″ (15 cm) in diameter are used for speedy construction and easy handling. Instead of notching the logs on the bottom side to avoid decay, they are quickly notched on the top side.

The first step is to place two foundation logs 10″ (25 cm) in diameter on the ground parallel to each other and bury them halfway up. They should be about a foot or two longer than the length of the cabin, and they should be leveled with the eye.

Using an axe, cut two rough notches for the walls in each of the foundation logs. Cut them to the depth of about half the diameter of the wall logs, then drop the wall logs into the notches. Next, cut two notches in those logs and drop the next logs into place. Repeat the process until you finish the walls.

Contrary to traditional cabin building, the narrow ends of logs are not alternated with broader ends to make all the walls level. The side walls are built with all the wide ends to the front so that the front of the cabin is higher than the back. This increases the roof's pitch and allows it to shed rain.

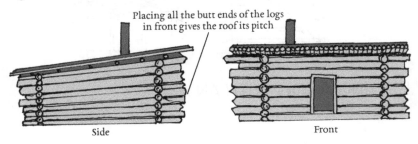

Placing all the butt ends of the logs in front gives the roof its pitch

Side   Front

Lay down poles for the roof and cover them with a tarp or bark. Hold down the tarp or bark with poles. Saw out spaces for the door and windows, and frame those openings with boards made from split logs (narrow split logs are easier to hew). The boards can secure the logs in place with the help of an auger and hardwood pegs. Finally, use moss, grass, and clay to chink any openings between the logs.

No notch cabin

top view

LOG CABIN HAND TOOLS

A log cabin can be built with just an axe, but having a few more tools will help you build your cabin better and faster. Below is a short list of hand tools inspired by Dick Proenneke and *roughly* separated into tiers of importance.

1. First-tier tools include axe, saw, flat chisel, gouge chisel, mallet, and sharpening stones.
2. Second-tier tools include woodworking dividers, drawknife, peeling spud, 1–1.5″ auger, log dogs, adze, files, and small handsaws.
3. Third-tier tools include plumb bob and chalk line, string level, carpenter's square, froe, pencil, ruler, hammer, carpenter's hatchet, spirit level, nails, and tape measure.

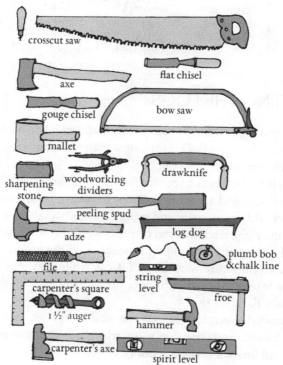

crosscut saw

axe

flat chisel

gouge chisel

bow saw

mallet

sharpening stone

woodworking dividers

drawknife

peeling spud

adze

log dog

file

string level

plumb bob &chalk line

carpenter's square

froe

1 ½″ auger

hammer

carpenter's axe

spirit level

SELECTING WOOD

When building a permanent shelter, it is best to use wood that won't decay quickly. Generally, hardwoods will take longer to decompose than softwoods.

For the pieces of wood that will be in contact with the ground or closest to it, it's best to use wood that resists moisture. Look at which trees remain standing in local marshes and bogs long after they are dead; this will give you clues as to which local species are best. One technique you can use to make wood more resistant to decay is burning the logs' outer layers.

Evergreens like pine, fir, cedar, spruce, and larch make satisfactory cabin logs, but the availability of wide, long, and straight logs will probably be the deciding factor in choosing a type of wood.

Woods very resistant to decay	Woods resistant to decaying	Woods with moderate resistance to decay	Woods that decay quickly	Woods that decay very quickly
Black locust	Butternut	Pitch pine	Ash	Aspen
Cedars	Honey locust	White pine	Beech	Basswood
Cypress	White oak	Yellow pine	Birch	Cottonwood
Walnut	Persimmon	Tamarack	Elm	Balsam fir
	Sycamore	Yellow poplar	Hemlock	Black gum
	Bur oak	Sassafras	Red oak	Jack pine
		Western larch	Lodgepole pine	Poplar
			Norway spruces	Willow

PREPARING THE LOGS

Ideally, all the logs should be straight, undamaged, and about the same diameter. Cut the logs 4 ft. (1.2 m) longer than the cabin so that their ends project at the corners.

Winter is the best time to cut the logs because they have less sap, season faster, weigh less, and are more resistant to decay. Transporting the logs is also easier with snow cover and minimal vegetation. Peeling the logs is easier if done right after cutting, but this won't be any easier in winter. Once the logs are cut, they should be stacked off the ground for three to six months to minimize warpage and decay while they season. The logs will still settle over many months once the cabin is built, so windows and doors should allow for this.

Unseasoned, green logs can also be used right away, but they will be heavier to handle, and the cabin will settle more. That can be accounted for when building windows and doors.

NOTCHING LOGS

The following notches are for building a longer-lasting cabin than the "quick" cabin described earlier. Two notches work well for simple cabins: the saddle notch and the V notch.

The saddle notch can be done with just an axe, but having woodworking dividers, a saw, and a gauge will make the job easier. Only the underside of logs should be saddle notched if you want to prevent water accumulation on the notches.

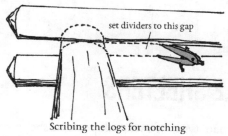

set dividers to this gap

Scribing the logs for notching

The V notch is another alternative that is easier to cut than the saddle notch, but it requires two cuts per log (top and bottom) instead of one. This notch can be cut with an axe by eye, but using a carpenter's square is more accurate.

When cutting the notches and laying the logs, it's best to leave more space between the logs so it's easier to chink them later with wood, clay, and mud.

To compensate for the natural tapering, alternate the butt and top ends. The logs' ends should extend about 1.5 ft. (45 cm) beyond the corners. They can be cut to size later. The door and windows can be cut once the walls are high enough.

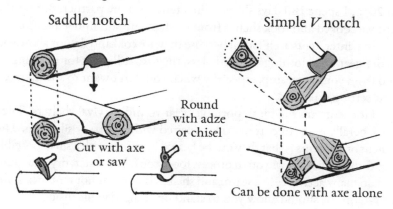

Saddle notch

Simple *V* notch

Round with adze or chisel

Cut with axe or saw

Can be done with axe alone

SHINGLES

Besides using a tarp or bark, another option for roofing is to use wooden shingles. Shingles can be split from sections of logs with a straight grain with a froe or a long knife, and they can be secured to the roof with nails or pegs.

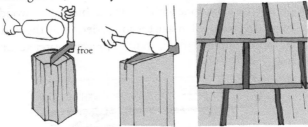
froe

PORTABLE SHELTERS

There are three main types of backpack-portable shelters: tarps, tents, and hot tents.

Tarps are the most portable and compact shelters, but they offer no bug protection unless bug netting is added. It's best to pair small tarps with a bivvy bag to protect your sleeping bag from rain and snow. Due to bugs, a tarp alone is not appropriate for long-term use, but it shines when it becomes the roof of an improvised shelter like an A-frame or a cabin.

Tents are ideal for traveling and three-season use because they are quick to set up and provide complete protection from rain and bugs. The disadvantage is that they are too small for cooking or doing activities inside them, but they are ideal if you want protection from the elements when traveling long distances. Ultralight tents nowadays compete in weight with heavy tarps and heavy bivvy bags (MSR and Big Agnes make good tents). In 2016, I spent 180 days sleeping in a tent with my partner; during the day, we cooked and took shelter from the rain and sun under a lean-to.

In winter, tents aren't ideal because they are cold and do not allow you to dry gear and clothing. Nevertheless, they are still great for traveling to and from your basecamp, especially when you don't want to spend much time setting up camp.

Hot tents are the ideal, portable, year-round survival shelters. They are generally made of cotton canvas (paired with a tarp) or sil-nylon. The benefit of hot tents is that they can be heated in winter with a small portable woodstove. That allows you to process food, cook, boil water, dry your gear, and do many activities in a warm and sheltered space. A hot tent meant for long-term use should allow you to stand up straight while inside.

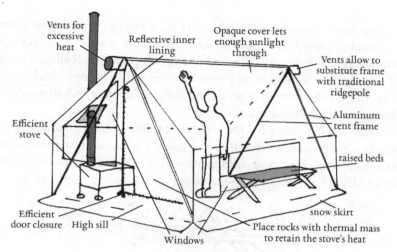

The ideal shelter is difficult to improvise

A cotton canvas tent is too bulky and heavy to be carried solo on a backpack, but a group may be able to do it. Cotton canvas is not waterproof, so it breathes well and thus accumulates less frost in winter. For the rest of the seasons, it can be covered with a tarp to provide rain protection. Canvas tents are the best option for a shelter if you can manage the cost, bulk, and weight. For long-term use for one to two people, I recommend the 10′ × 13′ Outfitter tent by Snowtrekker.

Sil-nylon hot tents are very light and portable, so they make more sense if you are constrained to a backpack. They are fully waterproof, but they accumulate frost and condensation. A lightweight liner can help manage frost, but it will still be a nuisance in long-term winter conditions. The frost and condensation issues with sil-nylon were not intolerable during the 100 winter days I spent on my boreal trip, but it's something to keep in mind. Another advantage of sil-nylon is that it's a cheaper and more available material to source for a DIY tent. Sil-nylon tents come in various styles, like pyramid or tepee, but I prefer a regular wall-tent style because it provides more usable space. If strong winds might be an issue, a tent with a more aerodynamic shape such as a tepee, pyramid, or yurt will hold up better. Seek Outside sells some good options for sil-nylon tents, but a DIY tent is probably best for long-term use.

In the appendix, I provide some plans for making a tent and recommend dimensions and materials.

An addition that I recommend for long-term use is adding a few small windows. The windows should be attached with Velcro to make them removable. In extremely low temperatures, you must carefully warm up the window (with a stove or fire) before it's rolled or unrolled; that's why it should be easily separated from the tent. Marine-grade PVC works well enough as long as it's rated for subfreezing temperatures. Rolling instead of folding the windows helps prevent creases, which become weak spots. The trick is to be extremely gentle and never hit, fold, or unfold windows during very low temperatures.

Windows are essential for avoiding cabin fever, maintaining good morale, and providing natural light. Place the window close to the stove to minimize ice, frost, and condensation. The windows should be placed on a wall that is as vertical as possible to avoid collecting snow and ice.

Banking and winterproofing a tent

PORTABLE WOODSTOVES

Woodstoves are a game-changer for long-term survival, for they allow you to keep your shelter warm during winter. Woodstoves excel over open fires and chimneys because they reduce smoke, produce more warmth, and don't require a big opening. They give you the ability to work and cook in a warm environment and dry your clothes and gear. Although, the hot tent will only stay warm during the day, for as soon as you stop feeding the stove, the tent will cool down (unless there's a fire watch at night). If the woodstove is used in conjunction with an insulated shelter, then the shelter will stay warm for a longer time. The only disadvantage of a woodstove is that you need a good saw and lots of calories to keep the woodstove fed.

When choosing a portable and folding woodstove, look for one that has a flat top for cooking and boiling water. It's essential to have a large woodstove that can accommodate long logs—with a large door that fits wide wood. The longer the woodstove, the less work you'll do with your saw.

The stovepipe should extend about a foot (30 cm) above the top of your shelter. You must clean the stovepipe and spark arrestor once or twice a week to manage the creosote and soot buildup that accumulates when you burn wood that is not thoroughly dried. Check the stovepipe and spark arrestor if you notice the woodstove becoming smoky or hard to keep well-lit. Always have a layer of ashes (or greenwood) at the bottom of the woodstove to protect it from the intense heat of the coals and extend its life.

The ideal woodstove should have a glass window for enjoyment and light; unfortunately, few woodstoves come with windows. An alternative is modifying a regular stove and adding either stove glass or stove mica (a lightweight material used in old stoves) to the door.

Most folding and portable stoves appropriate for backpacking are made of titanium. I recommend the Seek Outside XL stove because of its relatively large size, large door, and flat top. I used this stove for 100 successive days on my winter trip. It performed relatively well with only minor warping.

If bulk and weight are not an issue, I recommend a larger titanium or steel camping stove.

Instead of taking a whole stove, another possibility is just to pack stove jack material (silicone fiberglass), a titanium rollup stove pipe, a spark arrestor, and a stove door. The stove body can be readily improvised in the field with clay.

SHELTER DANGERS

ACCIDENTAL FIRE

Suppose you spend a long time in an improvised shelter with an open fire inside. In that case, soot and creosote will accumulate, and the vegetal and wooden parts of the shelter will also dry out. So a shelter with lots of vegetation will gradually become a tinder bundle ready to ignite once a tiny ember or spark lands on it.

There are various ways to mitigate the danger of fire:
1. Use a woodstove.
2. Avoid leaving the fire unattended.
3. Make the area around the fire as fire-retardant as possible.

Use rocks, green logs, and even a tarp to protect the area around the fire and the roof from sparks and flying embers. Continually inspect the site to keep it safe. Another way to mitigate the danger of fires is to build a cabin-style shelter instead of using boughs and debris.

When using a woodstove inside a tent, secure the stovepipe firmly to the woodstove so it won't get detached if a strong wind moves the top of the tent. Also, secure the top of the stovepipe with wires. Clean the stovepipe regularly.

SHELTER COLLAPSE

Another danger related to shelters is shelter collapse. If necessary, reinforce a shelter to bear the added weight of a big snowfall. It's best to use solid greenwood for the weight-bearing poles.

Another danger to look for is falling branches and trees (widow-makers). Make sure your shelter site is far from weak or dead trees and limbs that could fall during a storm. Keep in mind that a rare storm might knock down a nearby tree, so design and build your shelter to be strong enough to resist it.

CARBON MONOXIDE

Carbon monoxide (CO) is an odorless gas formed by the incomplete combustion of fuels. The inhalation of this gas leads to many deadly poisonings every year. It's important to be aware of the signs of carbon monoxide poisoning because it is a danger whenever there is an open fire inside a shelter—or *anything* powered by combustion.

The early symptoms of CO poisoning include headache, faster-than-normal heart rate (over 100 bpm), and altered mental status. The poisoning is cumulative and may build up over a few days. Some mild effects include fatigue, faintness, and flu-like symptoms. The effects worsen into severe headaches, nausea, and decreased mental abilities.

An excellent way to prevent CO poisoning is to have a well-ventilated shelter with an influx of fresh air. That can be accomplished by having one or more holes 3–4″ (7.5–10 cm) in diameter at the base and top of the shelter. In extreme cold, you wouldn't want to have a very well-ventilated shelter, so a balance must be made.

If you have a woodstove, you can help prevent CO poisoning by keeping the woodstove flaming and drawing well so that the fuel combusts completely (thus forming less CO).

Carbon monoxide poisoning doesn't have to be a mysterious and scary threat. Carbon monoxide has no smell, but the fuels that feed fires usually produce an odor or smoke. It's easier to be aware of the potential for CO to accumulate if you pay attention to the smell in the air. However, smokers and people that spend a lot of time around smoke or combustion engines might not have as much sensitivity. Once you know that the air is not quite fresh, you should pay close attention to your body for any signs of CO poisoning. One of the first symptoms might be a headache. If you feel any symptoms, take action right away: increase the ventilation in your shelter and go outside for a walk. Breathing fresh air for at least four hours will reduce the amount of CO in your system by half.

If you constantly monitor the air and pay close attention to your body, you might be able to make do with a less ventilated shelter—this is not recommended but may be the reality of a survival situation. Awareness and self-monitoring are required. If you are going to sleep, you need to either have adequate ventilation or make sure the fire goes out right away. Never sleep with questionable ventilation because you can't monitor your symptoms or the air.

FOOD AND FORAGING

EDIBILITY

One myth I'd like to dispel is that edible plants are abundant: they are not. At least not in higher latitudes. The majority of plants labeled as *edible* in wild edibles books are highly seasonal, low in energy content, generally only found in insufficient quantities, or hard to digest in high amounts.

TESTING FOR EDIBILITY

The universal edibility test (UET) found in many survival manuals is not practical. That's why it's not included here. It's best to think about the UET as a way to test if you are allergic to an edible plant, but not as a practical way to test if an unknown plant is edible. The UET takes a long time. It requires you to only test one plant at a time and eat exclusively from that plant, so if you happen to have other food around, you can't eat it until the UET is finished.

In response to the UET (and inspired by Graves' and Hawke's tests), I've come up with a common sense edibility test for trying wild plants that seem familiar and are likely to be edible, but aren't entirely identified. The common sense edibility test (CSET) is not for the uninitiated. It must be used with extreme caution and not-so-common common sense. No test will ensure 100% that a questionable plant is edible—and not deadly poisonous.

The first part of the CSET is to see if the plant is abundant. That is the risk versus reward equation. It is not worth the risk to eat a questionable plant that will only give you a tiny amount of nutrition if edible. Even if it is relatively abundant, it should provide you with more than just a couple of meals to be worth the risk. Take into account that even if plentiful, many wild edibles are actually only marginally edible and can only be eaten in small quantities.

The second part is to assess its familiarity. Does it look like something you've eaten before? Or something you know?

The third part is to observe, smell, touch, and taste the "edible" part of the plant, one step at a time. As primates, our bodies have evolved ways to try to detect potential poisons. The first one is sight. If the potential food looks familiar, healthy, and clean, it may be edible. The next safeguard is smell. If it smells okay, you can proceed with the next sense and touch it. Touch your lips to the plant for a minute to feel for a burning or itching sensation. If no sensation occurs, then taste it for a minute without swallowing. If it tastes all right, it is probably edible. If you sense any burning, acrid, milky, rotten, or unpleasant flavors, avoid it. You should eat only a tiny portion and gradually increase the amount over the following days if no adverse effects occur.

When doing the taste stage, be aware of flavors of almond, bitterness, or extreme acidity: these are signs of danger.

Numerous toxins are found in wild plants, but two are particularly relevant. One is hydrogen cyanide (hydrocyanic acid), which tastes like bitter almonds. It is a dangerous poison that dissolves in water. If you find this taste in a plant, question its edibility—unless you are sure what it is and know safe methods for preparing it.

The other poison is calcium oxalate and can be recognized by a sharp stinging, burning, or numbing sensation caused by tiny barbs irritating the tongue, mouth, and lips. For example, this poison is found in relatively small quantities in rhubarb leaves.

Calcium oxalate can cause intense pain and swelling of the tongue, throat, and lips. Poisoning from swallowing oxalate-containing plants is rare because the intense mouth pain prevents people from eating significant quantities.

Other poisons may have no distinctive flavors and may be fatal. The only warning signs they give are severe symptoms after it's already too late. *All plants are edible, some only once.*

The fourth part of the CSET is that an edible plant is one that tastes relatively good and is somewhat pleasant to eat. Marginally edible plants and "emergency" wild edibles are not a good source of sustenance.

This common sense edibility test should only be used on things that are very likely food, such as berries, nuts, and other plants that are not likely poisonous. One should observe, smell, and then taste only a minimal amount without swallowing if the plant seems okay. If one of the warning tastes is present, spit it out.

Generally, the dose makes the poison. But some plants like water hemlock can be lethally poisonous even when minuscule amounts are eaten.

Many edible plants will fail the taste test because they need to be processed or cooked (often by boiling) to make them edible, so you may want to taste test the plant again after boiling.

This common sense edibility test should never be applied to mushrooms and plants closely associated with poisonous species. The onset of symptoms from eating poisonous mushrooms may occur 6 to 24 hours after ingestion (in some species, up to 21 days afterwards), and fatal mushroom poisoning is generally associated with a delayed development of severe symptoms. Kidney or liver failure may be one of the first severe indications of mushroom poisoning. Never eat raw mushrooms regardless of species.

WILD FOOD SEASONALITY

Another myth I'd like to dispel is that a survival expert can just go into the wild and live off mushrooms, berries, lichen, and inner bark. Getting a meal that provides half the calories your body needs for a day is not easy, let alone providing the total amount of calories, day after day, rain or shine, winter or summer.

A handful of insects, mushrooms, and rodents is not a full meal, and it won't even cover one-quarter of the daily calories a person needs. It doesn't matter much in short-term survival if you eat a few calories or not, for the bulk of your energy and nutrients will come from what the body has already stored: fat.

Wild foods are highly seasonal, and more so the farther north you are. Weather and animals ensure that most highly productive wild edibles don't remain available for long. Not only are practically all wild edibles and animals seasonal, but they also have good and bad years. For instance, you are out of luck if you count on snaring hares and you happen to be at the low point in their decade-long cycle.

SURVIVAL FORAGING CALENDAR

The calendar below is intended for the boreal forest. It's best to make your own calendar based on your region; nevertheless, this calendar can be helpful. Find out what is available in your area and note the optimal times for harvesting food (check your local regulations).

SPRING

Collect cattail rhizomes and wapato tubers.
Collect young cattail shoots.
Collect birch or maple water.
Fish for pike, trout, walleye, and catfish (with rods, setlines, trotlines, and nets).
Hunt waterfowl (late spring).
Trap muskrats (late spring).
Hunt and snare snowshoe hares and rabbits (early spring).
Hunt large animals (early spring).
Hunt grouse.

SUMMER

Gather currants, saskatoons, bunchberries, raspberries, and blueberries.
Collect cattail pollen, immature cattail pikes, and cattail laterals.
Collect crayfish.
Fish for pike, walleye, and catfish (with rods, setlines, trotlines, and nets).
Gather hazelnuts (before the squirrels do).
Gather acorns (late summer).
Harvest wild rice (last week of August to the first week of September).
Trap beavers and muskrats.
Hunt waterfowl.
Hunt grouse.

FALL

Process wild rice and acorns.
Collect cattail rhizomes and wapato tubers.
Fish for pike, trout, walleye, whitefish, and catfish (with rods and nets).
Hunt and snare snowshoe hares and rabbits.
Hunt large animals.
Trap small animals.
Hunt waterfowl.
Trap beavers and muskrats.
Hunt grouse.

WINTER

Fish for pike, walleye, and catfish (with nets).
Hunt and snare snowshoe hares and rabbits (early winter).
Trap small animals.
Trap beavers.
Hunt grouse.
Hunt moose (late winter).

FORAGING STRATEGY

When figuring out a foraging strategy, the first step is to determine what foods are available, in what quantities, and how easy or hard it is to gather them.

For instance, fish generally have the largest biomass per area of all animals in the boreal forest. Fish populations are pretty stable throughout the seasons and over the years—that's why they are an excellent food source. Hares can be super plentiful or not at all: their populations fluctuate a lot throughout the year and, more importantly, over several years. Although the population density of moose is low, their large size makes them an excellent source of food.

A vital concept for foraging is to work with the rhythms of nature: gather foods when they are at their peaks and when they are more easily collected.

Another essential concept to consider is optimal foraging theory. Optimal foraging theory states that foragers spend their time and energy searching for and gathering foods with the highest energy payoff and with the least risk. Optimal foraging also means conserving calories whenever possible; therefore, resting is essential.

Although foragers know and utilize hundreds of edible plants and animals, few food sources are plentiful enough and provide enough calories to be considered staples. These staples are the basis of a forager's diet, and foragers focus most of their time and energy on gathering them.

Along the same lines, the strategy for optimally foraging food patches is to leave a patch when the gathering rate drops to the average rate of the habitat. For example, suppose you are working on a patch of berries, and your gathering speed drops to the average in that area. In that case, you should move to a more productive patch.

What are the major sources of food for long-term survival: small or big animals? The consensus for short-term survival is small animals, but for long-term survival, your efforts should focus on medium and big animals. To subsist long-term on small animals, you would have to catch a ridiculous amount, day after day. Small animals tend to be quite low in fat, meaning you may have to deal with protein poisoning if you are eating a ton of them (see "Health" chapter). Hunting large animals is risky, for you might spend a lot of time hunting and return empty-handed. Yet, if you happen to get one, the reward is enormous.

Plot your local animal species by population density and energy content on a graph. You'll get clusters of medium-sized, relatively abundant animals in the middle. You should focus most of your time on trapping these medium-sized animals and fishing.

Big and small animals should be hunted opportunistically. If you happen to see either during your day, seize the opportunity. That is why you should always carry a hunting weapon. Large animals should also be hunted deliberately during their peak seasons.

Another thing to think about is using active versus passive techniques. For instance, fishing with a rod is active, while fishing with a trotline is passive. You shouldn't focus exclusively on one or the other. Instead, you should be opportunistic and switch back and forth depending on which technique has the most potential reward for the time and energy invested in those circumstances.

STAPLE FOODS

An integral part of a foraging strategy is identifying the staple foods in your area. One way to do this is by researching what the staples were for the local Indigenous populations in your area before contact with Europeans; however, this will only give you clues because the availability and quantities of wild foods are different now.

Habitats of staple animals		
Animal	Associated patch or vegetation	Notes
Moose		
Winter	Aspen-birch forest, recent burn, lake margins	Deep snowfall intensifies the winter patch association
Summer	Aquatic vegetation, lake margins	Low water, heat, and insects strengthen the summer patch association
Caribou		
Winter	Closed black spruce forest, pine forest on outcrop, lichen woodland	Deep snowfall intensifies winter patch association, especially for open jack pine forests
Summer	Peat bog	
Beaver	Aquatic vegetation, lake margins	
Muskrat	Aquatic vegetation	
Hare		
Winter	Aspen-birch forest, recent burn	Association with specific patches increases during fall, winter, and spring, and when populations are low
Summer	Various	
Ruffed grouse	Aspen-birch forest, recent burn, lake margins	
Spruce grouse	Closed black spruce forest, spruce-aspen-birch forest	
Fish	Aquatic vegetation, open water	Association with shallow-water habitats is influenced by temperature and increases in spring and fall with spawning

Modified from *Boreal forest adaptations*

In the boreal forest, fish and large animals formed the foundation of survival. In southeastern areas, wild rice was crucial. Bear, beaver, hare, and waterfowl complemented the diet. Wild edibles, such as roots, tubers, nuts, and berries, were also gathered despite their thin distribution and seasonality.

In terms of edible plants, only tubers, roots, fruits, nuts, and seeds contain enough calories to serve as staples.

NUTRITION

The biggest challenge in the wild is obtaining calories. For hunter-gatherers, it is easy to get enough protein from meat and vitamins from raw greens or the stock from boiled meat. But it is hard getting enough calories, and that is why fats, oils, and grease are essential. While starch and protein contain only 4 kcal per gram, fats contain more than double at 9 kcal per gram.

In a survival situation in which you have minimal equipment and you're strained in various ways, I recommend only hunting lean animals opportunistically and focusing exclusively on fishing and on hunting and trapping animals with fat reserves.

CALORIES

Determine how many calories you need to maintain your body weight to help plan rations and check if you are meeting your energy needs.

Start by determining your basal metabolic rate (BMR). This is the body's energy requirement to function at rest, not accounting for physical activity.

This formula can be used to estimate your basal metabolic rate: BMR in kcal/day = $(10 * \text{weight } kg) + (6.25 * \text{height } cm) - (5 * \text{age}) + S$. In this formula, S is $(+ 5)$ for men and $(- 161)$ for women. For reference: 1 lb. = 0.453 kg and $1'' = 2.54$ cm.

Once you know your BMR in kcal/day, you can multiply it by ~1.8 to guesstimate your total energy needs in a wilderness survival context. That is your entire daily energy requirement. Children and the elderly need fewer calories, and large people and fit people need more.

One of the best online calculators for getting these estimates is the *Body Weight Planner* (bit.ly/b-wpl in advanced mode) because it provides long-term weight and body mass index projections.

Something to consider is that, if you lose a lot of body weight, your energy needs will also decrease. Your body will burn 40%–45% of your energy through activity in a wilderness context, and the other 55%–60%

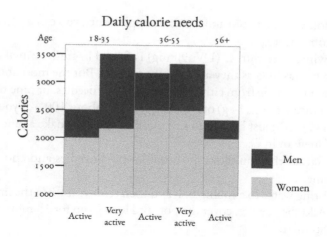

Daily calorie needs

will be spent on just keeping the body functioning, so conserving your energy by resting and sleeping is essential.

For instance, if you target hares for food, keep in mind that energy is everything. Make sure you consume more calories than you spent making, setting, and checking the snares as well as processing and cooking the hare.

VITAMINS AND MINERALS

Taking multivitamins for the months before participating in a long-term survival situation is a good way to ensure your body won't start with a deficit. The average person has about a 28-day supply of vitamins in their body, and vitamin C is one of the first that will need to be replenished.

Women are more likely to suffer a deficit of vitamins and minerals, so carrying a multivitamin is a good idea (it should contain iron, zinc, folate, vitamin B6, and calcium). Multivitamins often contain relatively low amounts of calcium, so women may benefit from an additional calcium supplement for a total of 1,000–1,300 mg per day.

Getting enough micronutrients may be difficult if you are not eating enough food. For this reason, the following supplements on top of a multivitamin may be helpful: potassium, magnesium, and sodium chloride (2.5–5 g of salt per day). The amounts in your supplements should be close to 100% of the daily value (DV) or less. Exceeding that may be counterproductive. Keep in mind that just because you consume a multivitamin it doesn't mean that you are necessarily absorbing all the vitamins in it. Vitamins A, D, E and K can only be digested efficiently when consumed with fat.

If you don't have vitamin and mineral supplements, you can try to obtain them from nature.

In winter, vitamin C (DV: 90 mg) is found in fresh animal organs and fish roe (as long as they are not overcooked). But the most abundant source is a tea made from either rosehips, spruce needles, or pine needles. A half-ounce serving (14 g) of rosehips provides about 100% of your daily vitamin C needs; just be sure to spit out the seeds. To make a pine needle tea rich in vitamin C:

1. Gather the youngest, most tender pine needles and chop them finely.
2. Bring water to a rolling boil and then remove it from the fire.
3. Add the needles, cover the pot, and let it steep for 15 minutes.
4. Strain it.

In summer, vitamin C can be easily obtained from fresh greens and berries.

Vitamin D can be obtained from fish oils, fish roe, and sunlight.

Some sources of potassium (DV: 3,200 mg) include raspberry leaf infusion, wapato tubers, bur oak acorns, nuts, stinging nettles, chickweed, algae, kelp, seaweed, meat, and fish.

Magnesium (DV: 420 mg) can be obtained from raspberry leaf infusion, wild rice, seaweed, chickweed, stinging nettle, dandelion, and seawater.

Sodium can be obtained inland from meat and blood and, on the coast, from seawater and seaweed.

Calcium (DV: 1,000 mg) can be obtained from raspberry leaf infusion, stinging nettle, broadleaf plantain, pigweed, bone marrow, and bone broth.

Iron can be obtained from stinging nettle, meat, and cooking food on cast iron cookware.

There is a chart of the daily recommended intake of vitamins and minerals in the appendix.

RATIONS

Rationing food for an extended time without meeting at least a thousand calories per day is not a good strategy because your body will run at a massive deficit. Such a deficit quickly saps your energy, and your condition will deteriorate. Instead, it's best to eat an amount of calories closer to your basal metabolic rate and at least above a thousand calories. This way, you'll have more energy to gather food.

When the duration of an ordeal is unknown, it's best to set your timelines and ration according to your supplies and the seasons.

If you are preparing rations in advance, one of the first things you'll need to determine is how many calories you must bring. During the 180 days in the wild project, my partner and I brought rations of 1,180 kcal per person (one-third to one-half of our daily needs). We brought olive oil, brown rice, flour, whole milk powder, and honey. For my 100 days solo winter trip, I brought 2,150 kcal per day (around one-half of my winter energy needs), consisting of navy beans and lard. Based on those experiences, I think it's wise to cover about half of your energy needs (at least 1,500 kcal for the summer and 2,000 kcal for the winter)—particularly if you haven't survived in those circumstances for that length of time, or if you are alone.

For rations, the foods I recommend are olive or coconut oil (or butter), lard for winter, brown rice, navy beans, flour, whole milk powder, sugar, half salt (salt and potassium chloride blend), baking powder, yeast, and spices. If stored properly in their original packages, these foods can last at least a year; to make these foods last much longer than that, use Mylar bags and long-term packaging methods. The downside and upside of flour is that you may spend a long time baking all kinds of stuff. Spices don't take much space, but they will significantly enhance the taste of wild foods.

Buckets work well as ration containers, and they can be waterproofed with Gamma seal lids or regular bucket lids with O-rings. Your rations could be cached on a small island, placed under a pile of rocks, buried under an uprooted tree, or stored in a proper bear hang. Most of the foods I recommended above don't give off strong odors, so you may not have to worry too much about large animals, but your mileage may vary. In winter, you can store your dry rations in your shelter because bears won't be active, and they shouldn't be too interested in dry goods anyways.

PREPARING ANIMALS

Avoid touching raw meat directly because it can carry diseases. Wear gloves if you have them; otherwise, wash your hands thoroughly after touching raw meat.

SMALL ANIMALS

The preferred method for skinning a rabbit is called glove skinning, and it is illustrated below. For this method, you can tie, peg, or nail the rabbit's feet to a tree or pass a branch through its foot tendons and hang it.

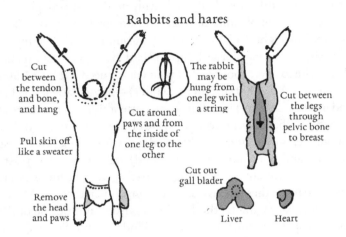

Rabbits and hares

Cut between the tendon and bone, and hang

Pull skin off like a sweater

Cut around paws and from the inside of one leg to the other

The rabbit may be hung from one leg with a string

Cut between the legs through pelvic bone to breast

Remove the head and paws

Cut out gall blader

Liver   Heart

The head of snowshoe hares can be skinned and boiled for its meat and brain, and the long finger bones can be used to make a gorge hook, an awl, or a primitive sewing needle. In addition, their tendons and sinews can be twisted into snare cordage.

If you snared a rabbit or hare in winter and it's frozen solid, you'll have to thaw it before skinning it. Thawing can be done by a fire, but I prefer submerging the frozen rabbit in water. If you have access to a river or lake, place a rock and the rabbit in a bag, tie the bag closed, tie it to the shore, and leave it submerged overnight. If the body of water is frozen, cut a hole in the ice, tie the bag to the long end of a T-shaped stick (to avoid cutting the line during retrieval), and submerge it overnight.

In addition to the method illustrated to the right, squirrels can also be skinned like a rabbit if you plan on using their hides. Some fat might come off with the hide if you are not skinning very carefully.

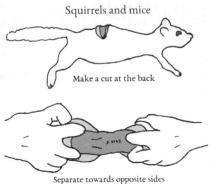

Squirrels and mice

Make a cut at the back

Separate towards opposite sides

If the hide won't be used and you want to eat the skin, an alternative method is to burn the fur off and cook the animal in its skin.

LARGE ANIMALS

To skin and butcher a large animal, hang the animal by its hind legs. If the animal is too big to elevate or you prefer skinning on the ground, skin one side towards the backbone and spread that skin out on the ground to keep the meat clean when you roll the animal over to the other side. A tarp comes in handy for this.

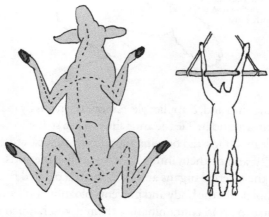

Animals usually bleed out by the wound that kills them; otherwise, it's recommended to cut the jugular vein in their necks (if done early enough). It's worthwhile to collect the blood and cook it later for its sodium and micronutrients. Thorough bleeding will help the meat keep better.

Pull up the paunch and work carefully to avoid cutting the entrails

Insert two fingers between the skin and the membrane enclosing the entrails

Place the blade between the two fingers and extend the cut to the chin

Repeat on the abdominal membrane starting at the sternum, in the opposite direction

Remove the hide, and be careful not to puncture the entrails. Minimize the use of your knife and cut with the edge away from the animal. If you are going to use the hide, be careful not to damage it.

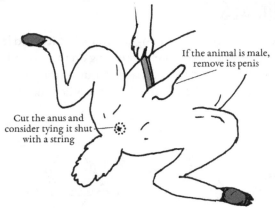

If the animal is male, remove its penis

Cut the anus and consider tying it shut with a string

Cut around the anus and, if applicable, remove the penis by making parallel cuts to the skin around it. Tie the anus shut with a string to keep the meat and organs clean. Or instead of tying the anus shut, separate the intestines from the cavity, and tie them into a knot just above the anus.

Remove the internal organs and keep them separated from the meat. That helps cool down the body and prevents bloating. Pull any organs you plan to eat first to avoid contaminating them if you happen to break the intestines or stomach. The removal of organs from small animals and birds may be done later at camp. Cut large animals into more manageable chunks.

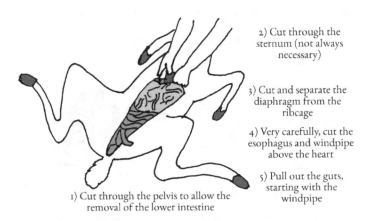

2) Cut through the sternum (not always necessary)

3) Cut and separate the diaphragm from the ribcage

4) Very carefully, cut the esophagus and windpipe above the heart

5) Pull out the guts, starting with the windpipe

1) Cut through the pelvis to allow the removal of the lower intestine

BIRDS

Birds can be skinned or plucked. Plucking preserves the fat-containing skin; nevertheless, in some circumstances, you might opt for skinning instead, which is simpler and faster.

There are two methods for plucking: wet and dry. Dry plucking is likely what you'll do, particularly if you don't have a large container to scald the birds. Additionally, scalding may tighten the feathers of waterfowl and seabirds. It's best to pluck the bird right after you kill it. Some birds have thin skin that tears easily, so be careful. Use your thumb and index finger to grasp a feather or three, and swiftly pull up while holding the skin down with your other hand. It takes patience and time. The remaining small feathers can be singed off by burning them quickly over a fire.

A grouse can be quickly field-dressed or skinned by stepping on its wings and pulling its feet until the lower part of the bird comes off. Then cut the wings off. Separate the legs from the bottom part and deglove them (skin them) while they are warm.

EDIBLE PARTS OF ANIMALS

BLOOD

Blood should be eaten first, as of all the edible parts of an animal, it is the most perishable and hardest to store. Blood is very high in protein, calories, iron, sodium, and potassium. It is easier to eat when mixed with other foods. Blood carries pathogens, so it should be cooked.

If you avoid perforating the stomach and intestines, you'll sometimes find some blood pooled in the chest cavity. Scoop it out. Then, cut the large vessels around the heart and pump them to extract more blood.

Blood clots quickly upon contact with oxygen, making it easier to handle.

The easiest way to preserve blood is to dry it in a container in the sun. Once dry, it will turn into dark, solid chunks.

ORGANS

Organs are some of the most nourishing parts of an animal, and they should be eaten as soon as possible, for they spoil faster than meat. In survival, almost everything in the chest cavity is regarded as an edible organ except for the gallbladder (which is nonexistent in antlered animals). The following organs are edible: heart, liver (except from polar bears and bearded seals), kidneys, lungs, stomach, spleen, thymus gland, pancreas, blood vessels, connective tissue, intestines, mammary glands, eyes, tongue, bladder, testicles, and ovaries. In addition, the stomach content of hooved animals is also edible.

Check the organs—and the liver in particular—to see if they look healthy or not (spotty or old). This may give you clues about the health of the animal. Discard the organs if they look off.

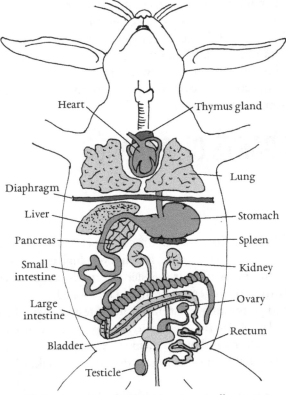

Illustration not to scale nor anatomically correct

If there's a gallbladder, it should be removed. It is a small, thumb-shaped gland attached to the liver that contains bile. To remove it, pinch the duct connecting the gallbladder to the liver and cut the gallbladder off, then pull the duct off. Spilling bile on the surrounding meat could make it unpalatable. Gather any fat surrounding the intestines. To prepare the intestines for consumption, cut them into short lengths, turn them inside out, and scrape off the inner lining.

The intestines can be turned into storage containers for pemmican or fat:

1. Scrape off the slimy inner lining.
2. Tie off one end.
3. Fill up loosely with dry grass.
4. Hang up to dry.

To prepare the stomach, turn it inside out and scrub thoroughly. Simmering it in water may help the taste.

The bladder can be processed like the intestines and stomach.

FAT

Fat should be eaten or processed early on because it's essential and can spoil quickly.

The brain is a significant source of fat; it can be cooked or rendered. The spinal column also contains fat between the vertebrae.

Bone marrow is also high in fat: crack open the long bones and cook or render the fat. Hooves can be boiled to extract some fat as well.

Beware of species that carry prions (e.g., chronic wasting disease), such as antlered animals. Avoid harvesting an animal that appears sick or acts abnormally. There are no known cases of human CWD. However, the general advice is to refrain from handling and eating meat from a CWD-infected animal. The brain, spinal cord, spleen, and lymph nodes may contain prions, and prions can't be neutralized by any cooking method.

BIRDS

In birds, the heart and liver should be eaten if they are in good condition. Discard them if they look old (pale brown), are spotted, or have parasites. Keep the seeds and berries found inside the bird to use as bait.

CARRION EATERS

Carrion eaters, such as vultures, are more likely to transmit pathogens because of their diets. They should be boiled for twenty minutes to ensure thorough heating and a wide margin of error.

FISH

Fish heads can be cooked into a nourishing soup. Many parts of the head are nutritious, such as the tongue, eyes, brain, and cheeks. The heart and liver (found close to the heart) are edible and sometimes have sacks of visceral fat around them. The sperm sacs (milt) and fish eggs (roe) are edible and nutritious. Keep in mind that the eyes, brains, and internal organs usually concentrate accumulated pollutants, particularly in saltwater fish.

FILLETING FISH

You don't necessarily need to remove the skin or scales; fish fillets can be cooked over a fire with their skin on. Just place the fillets meat-side up over the coals. This method is straightforward and delicious, particularly with oily fish. Watch out for dripping oil. Remember these points:
- Fish skin is very nutritious and high in fat.
- Save the head and skeleton for boiling into stock.
- Eat the meat from the cheeks.

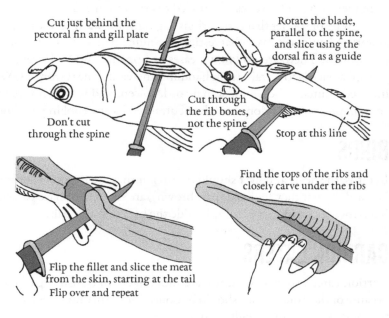

Cut just behind the pectoral fin and gill plate

Rotate the blade, parallel to the spine, and slice using the dorsal fin as a guide

Cut through the rib bones, not the spine

Don't cut through the spine

Stop at this line

Flip the fillet and slice the meat from the skin, starting at the tail
Flip over and repeat

Find the tops of the ribs and closely carve under the ribs

Y-BONES

To fillet pike, trout, and similar fish with Y-bones, process them like any other fish: remove the guts and ribs, leave the skin on, and follow the illustration to the right to remove the Y-bones.

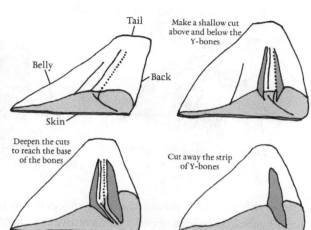

CATFISH

Skinning large catfish is time-consuming; it is easier to fillet them like a regular fish. Catfish often have a good chunk of meat in their cheeks, so scoop it out.

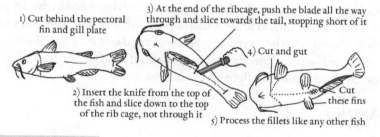

COOKING

COOKING METHODS AND NUTRITION

BOILING

Boiling is the best method of cooking meat for survival. It is the most nutritious and safest method of cooking. Boiling is advantageous because:

- it avoids wasting nutritional drippings, which often happens when roasting or grilling;
- it requires less fuel than other methods; and
- if you drink the broth, you get close to the total nutritional value.

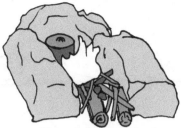

This U-shaped fire setup provides warmth and can burn big logs

The rocks block wind and provide a pot warming shelf

The three stone fire setup can be very efficient when it's tended closely

Although it's not as efficient as a rocket stove, it is up there

Unlike other cooking methods, boiling makes it easy to confirm that the meat has reached a high enough temperature to neutralize pathogens and harmful toxins. To ensure all meat is adequately cooked, keep the chunks equal in size. If you are eating questionable meat or meat from a carnivore or omnivore, cut the chunks into thinner slices to ensure the center of the pieces reaches a high enough temperature.

Braising is another good option for cooking wild meats. It is a combination-cooking method in which the meat is browned in the dry pot first. Then, water is added halfway up the pot and the meat is boiled-steamed with the lid on. This helps tenderize the meat and give it a roast-like flavor.

One of the most efficient cooking methods with a pot is to place it between three stones and light a fire underneath.

BAKING

Baking preserves a lot of nutrition, but it uses more firewood than most methods. Baking every once in a while is an excellent way to introduce some flavor diversity. As with roasting, it is hard to ensure meat reaches a pathogen-killing internal temperature. Ovens can be quickly improvised by making a small cave of plain rocks.

Make a fire inside the stone oven, and after an hour or so, remove everything

Place the food inside the oven and cover the opening with a rock

ROASTING

Roasting is an easy cooking method, and the results are pretty tasty, but it causes some nutritional waste. Unfortunately, roasting may reduce some nutritional value because the nutrients are exposed to direct heat.

After the small animal or fish has been cleaned, spike it on a green stick and place it beside a fire. The fire should produce as little flame and smoke as possible. Turn the meat occasionally to cook all sides evenly.

A big downside of roasting is that a significant portion of the nutritional juices may drip. That can be avoided by:

- placing the meat very close to the fire at first to form a hard crust;
- putting a shallow plate underneath the meat to catch the drippings; and
- placing the meat in an angled pan beside the fire.

BROILING

Broiling is a simple way of cooking fish. To broil, place a layer of small stones over hot coals and lay the fish fillets on the top. It's unnecessary to scale the fish or remove the skin, and tiny fish don't need to be gutted. Fish taste pretty good when cooked this way. Crabs, lobsters, and crayfish may also be broiled.

Another way of broiling is to lay the meat on a flat wood or stone plank and prop it up by the fire. You may need to turn the meat over to cook it thoroughly.

FRYING AND GRILLING

Frying is not generally recommended in most survival manuals because some nutritional value is destroyed. But this is true with *all* cooking methods, and the effects are not as detrimental as commonly thought.

Frying is an acceptable survival cooking method. It helps change the monotony and improve the flavor of your meals every once in a while.

Grilling is frowned upon in survival situations because of the wasted drippings; nevertheless, it can provide some highly valued variation.

BAKING BREAD

Baking bread can be a great pleasure in the wild. It's an excellent way of boosting morale, and the opportunities for creativity are endless. One downside of baking bread is that it may use up a lot of your time, which could be better spent foraging for food.

Below, I illustrate some ways of baking bread over an open fire. A rock oven is another option, but it's less practical. Tin cans, like those of stove fuel, make good, improvised ovens; just place a few glowing coals underneath the oven and some over it. As an alternative, dough can also be fried on an oiled pan.

If you can count to eight, the pan is at a right distance

Place most of the coals at the top and leave only a few at the bottom

COOKWARE

The most important piece of cookware is a pot. Wide pots are much more versatile than tall ones, for they can be used for catching fat drippings, frying, baking, or broiling. Titanium and stainless steel pots are best, but avoid those with a Teflon coating, as Teflon can't withstand the high temperatures of campfires.

I recommend the MSR Alpine StowAway pots. They have long handles that won't melt. In addition, they can be closed tightly for food or water storage.

If you have the space, I would also add a tall pot, which will make it easier to boil water and pour it out. I also recommend packing an 8" (20 cm) frying pan. Another optional item is a grill: campfire toasters from a dollar store make cheap and lightweight grills.

In terms of utensils, use titanium forks and spoons. Stay away from anything plastic, for it breaks easily, and it takes only a few distracted seconds for it to melt. Spatulas can be easily crafted in the field.

If you have rations of beans, it might be good to have a small pressure cooker, but only if you can carry or cache one. A pressure cooker will cook beans much faster and use less fuel than a regular pot, saving energy and time. I recommend the 1.5 L Classic Hawkins with a spare O-ring and safety valve.

You don't need to pack washing implements because you can scrub your dishes using sand, moss, horsetail, and other plants.

FOOD PRESERVATION

Don't preserve food unless you are consistently meeting around two-thirds of the energy you need in your current condition, or you foraged far more than you can eat within a couple of days. Starvation is a slippery slope, and it's best to avoid getting too far down that slope. Don't try to take care of your future self if you can't take care of your present self. Avoid getting sucked into a vicious cycle: the more you starve, the less energy and strength you will have for foraging.

When deciding which preservation method to use, think about how much time and energy you will spend with different techniques. Use the easiest and simplest methods first.

COOLING

An easy way to keep meat short-term is to store it in a rodent-resistant container in a cool place—a hole in a riverbank, lakeshore, or hillside covered with vegetation or sod will work. Another option is inside the hole of an uprooted tree. I've stored fish this way with no problems for up to three to four days.

HANGING

Hanging is a good way to store meat for a few days, depending on the weather. In theory, the wind and sun should dry the outer layer into a hard crust. This crust protects the inner meat. In practice, it's a battle against rain, flies, birds, and mammals. Try to keep the meat as high as possible off the ground to minimize the number of flies landing on it and to keep it away from scavengers.

Placing your meat inside a game bag is an easy way to prevent flies from depositing their eggs on the meat. Otherwise, if you don't have a game bag, you can dry the outer layer by exposing it to the sun or a fire. Sticks and debris may be used to make a barrier for birds, and you can use tarps and plastic to cover the meat when it's raining. But try not to decrease the airflow and do not let moisture stay on the surface of the flesh.

It's best to keep the pieces of meat as large and intact as possible to reduce their surface areas and aid the preservation process. Keep them separated from each other because they may start to mold or rot if they are in contact. In warm weather, hang the meat in the shade. If the weather and circumstances cooperate, you may be able to keep meat this way for a long time. If the outer layer starts to mold or gets maggots, just scrape them off and use the rest.

SUBMERGING

If the weather is above 60°F–65°F (15°C–18°C), consider submerging your meat inside a waterproof dry bag. During the day, place the meat inside a contractor bag (without the game bag), and put the whole thing inside the waterproof dry bag. At night, remove the meat from the bags and hang it to dry. This last resort allows you to store meat for a few days in hot weather, but it's far from ideal.

On a completely different note, our hunter-gatherer ancestors would sometimes submerge meat in peat bogs for preservation. The acidity of the water helped preserve the meat. Archeologists have found mammoths, mummies, and butter kept this way.

WATER COOLER

Foods can be refrigerated with an improvised water cooler: place a waterproof container in a shallow creek and cover it with a wet cloth large enough that its ends are touching the water. The stream will cool down the container through convection and the cloth through evaporation.

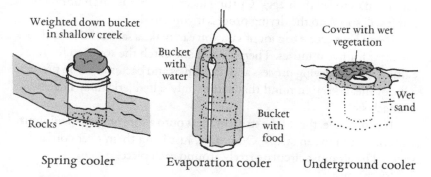

Spring cooler   Evaporation cooler   Underground cooler

DRYING

Drying is one of the simplest and easiest methods of long-term food preservation. Jerky is made by dehydrating meat gradually under the sun or over a slow fire. Keep in mind that this only works with lean meat—fatty meat will go rancid—so cut off all the fat.

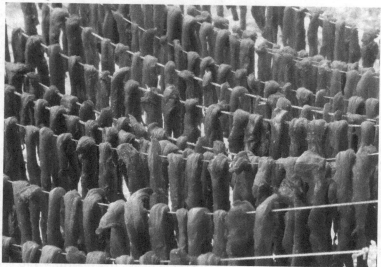

The meat should be fresh. Slice it across the grain into thin strips of around 1/4″–3/8″ (0.5–1 cm) thick. The thinner, the better.

Flies are an issue because they will lay their eggs on the meat, but there are ways to prevent this. Smoke can be used to deter flies at first until the surface of the flesh dries. Once the surface is dry, flies won't lay their eggs on it, so smoking is unnecessary. The other alternative is to cut the slices of meat into extremely thin strips of 1/8″ (3 mm) thick so that the slices are too thin for flies to lay their eggs. Cutting meat this thin is often impractical, but it will speed up the drying process if you can do it.

If you have access to a lot of salt, you can make a salt solution and soak the meat for five minutes. Then drain it and catch the solution for reuse. Salting aids the drying process and deters flies and bacteria. If you preserve a lot of meat, keep in mind that eating only salted jerky may make your stomach sick.

If you're able, thread the strips of meat onto a wire or cord to minimize any contact between strips. Otherwise, just hang them over cordage or sticks. The air must circulate freely around each piece.

To dry the meat:

1. Hang the meat over a slow fire. Make sure it's not too close. Avoid cooking the meat, for that will reduce its shelf life.
2. The surface may take anywhere from an hour to a day to dry. Once it's dry, hang the meat in the sun.
3. If the weather is not cooperating, keep the meat over the fire. It may take anywhere from a day to three days to dry.

Don't add resinous wood to the fire to produce smoke. Use birch, willow, alder, or other woods that won't leave oily residues or soot on your meat. Smoking meat in an enclosed space is an optional process that will coat the meat's surface with flavor and preservatives.

Choose a warm, dry, and sunny day, and start early. Sun-drying may take a day in ideal conditions or a couple of days if the air is humid. Use a tripod or a rack to keep the meat exposed to the wind and sun. Drying must be done as fast as possible while the weather is ideal. Once the meat is brittle and cracks easily, the process is done. If it's rubbery, it needs more time; otherwise, it will mold.

Dried meat is still raw, so it may contain pathogens such as trichinella. Omnivorous and carnivorous animals are more likely to carry pathogens, so avoid making jerky from their meat or take preventive measures, particularly with bear and cougar meat. If the animal is herbivorous and looks healthy, you may choose to take the risk and forgo preventive measures, but keep in mind that even strict herbivorous animals might carry parasites in their meat or eat potentially infected meat once in a while.

Some preventive measures, such as salting and freezing dried meat for 14 days, may neutralize most pathogens, but they won't work for trichinella. To neutralize trichinella, the meat must be heated to 170°F (75°C). You can attempt to reach this temperature by heating the jerky on a frying pan or over hot coals for three minutes, to the point where the jerky is too hot to hold. An optional step before the drying process is to dip the slices of meat one at a time in a boiling pot before they are hung to dry (this also speeds up the drying process). Finally, you can also heat the finished jerky to 170°F (75°C) or boil it briefly before eating it.

To store jerky, you have two general options depending on the weather. If the air is dry, pack it in a breathable, open weave bag. If you pack the jerky in plastic, condensation and mold may form. If the air is humid, pack the thoroughly dried meat in an airtight container to

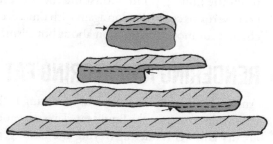

Butterfly cut for making jerky

prevent it from reabsorbing moisture from the air. Properly dried and stored meat will keep for a few years, but expect something closer to six months in the field. The dried meat from fish and other animals can also be ground and stored as a powder.

BURYING

A less conventional but straightforward method of preserving meat is to bury it. Burying was used extensively by hunter-gatherers worldwide, and it can be used to preserve meat for weeks or months. Keep in mind that, if the meat is stored for too long, it will "ferment" and have a very strong taste. Due to the danger of botulism and other pathogens, you must take extra precautions.

To bury meat for storage, make a pit 1.5–2 ft. deep (45–60 cm) in a well-drained spot. Salty or sandy soil works well. Line the pit with a thick layer of sphagnum moss, grass, or leaves. The important thing is to let oxygen circulate. Leaving the skin on the meat helps preserve its juices and keeps it cleaner. Lay the meat on the grass, and cover it with another thick layer of grass; this prevents soil from getting on the meat. Fill the pit with dirt, and cover the spot with rocks or logs to prevent scavengers from digging it up. Typically, you may store meat like this for a month or two.

One of the main risks with this method is botulism. There are ways to minimize the risk, but it will still be there. Never use plastic bags or containers with this method because they increase the potential for botulism. Salt helps inhibit botulinum bacteria, so use it if available. Bury the food when the ground temperature is cold, ideally below 36°F (2°C). Wash your hands and the meat to keep it as clean as possible.

Finally, cooking the meat in water heated to a rolling boil before eating destroys the botulinum *toxin*. The internal temperature of the meat must reach the boiling point. Consume the meat immediately after cooking because toxins could develop again with time. See the section in the "Health" chapter for more information about botulism.

RENDERING AND STORING FAT

Animal fat is stored in cells, and rendering is the process used to rupture those cells to extract the liquid fat. Two relevant methods of processing fat are dry and wet rendering (frying and boiling, respectively).

For the dry method, dice the fat into small chunks—the smaller, the better—and fry over low heat, stirring frequently, until the pieces become crisped and shriveled. Strain them to separate the hot oil from the nourishing cracklings. Avoid overheating: don't let the fat caramelize or the cracklings turn brown because they will not keep as long. Store the fat in a container that vents moisture out, unless the fat will be stored very cold.

For the wet method, just prepare the fat as you would for frying, but place the chunks of fat in a pot and cover them with water. Bring the water to a boil for several minutes, or let simmer for a few hours. Remove from heat. As the mixture cools, the fat should solidify at the top. Skim it off and place it in a pot over low heat to evaporate any residual water (until there is no condensation on the pot's lid). That will help the fat keep longer. This method can also be used to extract fat from greasy bones.

The result should be semi-solid fat or oil, which won't spoil quickly if appropriately stored, unlike raw fat. If the fat is rendered correctly and there is no moisture content, bacteria won't grow. Leaving the fat uncovered allows moisture to evaporate. The other thing to watch for is oxidation, so airtight containers will help in the long run. Store the fat in a cool, dry, dark place to lengthen its shelf life. The more solid the fat is at room temperature, the longer it is likely to last. It should keep at least between two to six months.

PEMMICAN

Pemmican is a trail superfood because it's rich in energy and protein and provides nearly complete nutrition (recipes with berries also provide vitamin C). To make pemmican, you'll need *completely* dried meat and rendered fat. Oil also works, but it's not ideal.

The dried meat must first be pulverized into a cornmeal consistency. This step is easier if the meat is roasted briefly over hot coals—right after it finishes drying—and pulverized immediately afterward. If you use stones for grinding, choose hard, fine-grained ones to avoid creating grit. Then melt the rendered fat and pour it into the pulverized meat. The fat should be warm, but not hot. Mix it in and gradually add more until you can form clumps or balls. Store the pemmican as if it were lard, and keep it protected from insects and rodents.

FREEZING

In an area that stays consistently below freezing, preserving food through the cold months is easy. The challenge is thawing the food and keeping it away from scavengers.

When freezing meat or fish, it's best to separate the meat in meal-sized portions so that everything doesn't freeze into one big clump.

If the weather is well below freezing, and you don't want to freeze your fresh kill immediately, you can bury it in the snow to keep it around the freezing point.

If you have a huge bounty and a few months of subfreezing temperatures, you can slice up the meat and store it securely over the winter to let it freeze-dry. Make sure the meat is lean, for fatty meat will become rancid.

Thawing can be easily accomplished if there are rivers or lakes around. Just submerge the meat overnight in a secure bag.

FRUIT LEATHER

Fruit leather is not only quite tasty, but it is also a simple way of preserving berries. You'll need one or two warm and sunny days to dry the berries thoroughly. To make this vegetarian jerky, mash a bunch of berries into a purée and sun-dry immediately. It's best to start early in the morning. If the fruits have big seeds, pick them out. Pour the purée over a smooth material, like a layer of plastic, a contractor bag, or a clean tarp (avoid smoked tarps). Spread the purée about 1/8"–1/4" (3–6 mm) thick. The thinner it is, the faster it will dry. Spread it as evenly as you can so that it dries uniformly, thus preventing some spots from sticking when you flip the leather over. Depending on the weather and thickness of the purée, it may take five to eight hours to be ready for flipping. Scare away any curious flies and wasps. Flip the fruit when the top is dry and the bottom is still moist. After flipping, dry the other side under the sun for another three to six hours. The leather is done when it is not sticky anymore: it should be supple, not crispy. You can cut a piece to check if the inside is dry. If the fruit leather is not fully dried, it may mold in a few weeks or months, but it may last a year or more if it is properly dried.

This method is an especially good way to use prickly berries (slit the berry and squeeze out the berry goo to make the purée).

FOOD CACHES AND STORAGE

When choosing a food cache, consider which animals pose a threat and what kind of food is stored. Suppose you are caching powdered foods, nuts, grains, legumes, vegetable oil, jerky, or fruit leather. In that case, rodents could be an issue, depending on the container. But you probably don't have to worry about larger animals, for they don't usually recognize most of those items as food. And the ones they might recognize—like nuts and jerky—don't have much odor. On the other hand, if you are storing foods like fresh meat, fish, fat, or other smelly goodies, you might have to deal with birds, bears, and other critters.

Think of your cache not as animal-proof but as a deterrent. And add more barriers according to the threat. For instance, placing your cache on a small island makes it harder for animals to discover it. And if you encounter "problem animals," flip things around and use that problem as a hunting or trapping opportunity.

ROCK CACHE

A rock cache is a long-term cache that works as a deterrent for large animals. The food is stored above ground or is buried. If the weather is warm, you can use soil and moss to cover the containers to keep the food cooler. Then, cover the containers with logs and sticks to protect them from sharp rocks and to distribute the rocks' weight. Choose larger stones if the threat is from larger animals. But remember that it's not the weight of the rocks that slows them down, but how interlocked they are.

In winter, you may decide to reinforce a cache with icecrete. This method makes the cache highly secure, but it won't be easy to retrieve until the spring. Icecrete is made with a mixture of snow, ice chips, soil, gravel, sticks, and wood chips. Water is added so that the mixture freezes solid. Icecrete is stronger than ice, but it will melt faster. Another approach is to shovel some snow over the rocks and pour water on top: the water will freeze and the ice will "glue" the stones together throughout the winter.

BEAR HANG

Bear hangs can be very practical and effective if done properly. In a long-term situation in bear territory, you should have the skill and gear to do a proper bear hang. The neat thing about a bear hang is that once you put in the effort to have a good setup, you can hang and retrieve your food easily, day after day. Also, if you only have to guard against rodents, then a small bear hang is quite convenient and practical.

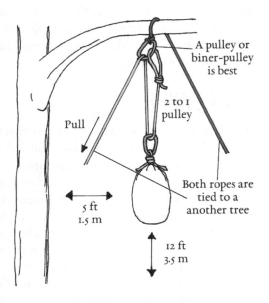

If you are hanging something very heavy, you'll probably need to use carabiners and pulleys to get some leverage. I recommend packing one or two Petzl Rollclip pulley-carabiners (or Petzl Ultralegere pulleys coupled with oval carabiners) and one or two wiregate carabiners for the bear bag. Use paracord for the rope and a solid rainproof bag or container for the food. Test your carabiner, pulley, and cord combination beforehand to ensure it works.

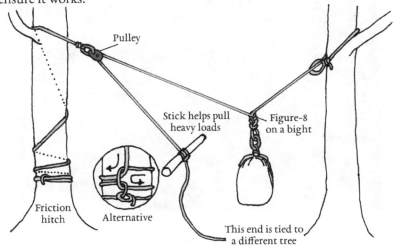

It's often hard to find a tree with a branch that allows you to set up a "textbook" bear hang. Another problem is that bears have learned to defeat most bear hangs in some high-use areas, but that shouldn't be much of a problem in remote areas where bears have had less practice.

A more realistic alternative to the hanging method described above is to use two trees. With the rig in the second illustration, a bear hang can be used by one person to raise two or three fully loaded buckets.

BEAR-RESISTANT CONTAINERS

In addition to a bear hang, there are two popular and effective bear-resistant containers: the Ursack and the BearVault. The Ursack is a bag made of Spectra fabric, and the BearVault is a rigid plastic container. Both are pretty effective against bears, but they are expensive. I recommend the Ursack because it's lighter and more portable. Nevertheless, I think it's more practical to use a bear hang than bear-resistant containers, particularly if you have food inside a bucket or food barrel.

CABIN-STYLE CACHE

This cache design is a small log cabin "cooler" created by Roland Welker. It is meant for protecting food from winter creatures, such as wolverines. This style is not ideal for summer storage unless the walls and top are well chinked against rodents. The walls are built below the ground (to deter critters from digging underneath). In winter, the sides can be chinked and reinforced with icecrete.

This cache style makes sense if you have butchered a large animal and it is too difficult to store the meat with other methods.

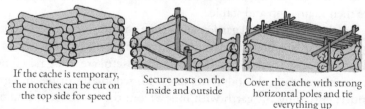

If the cache is temporary, the notches can be cut on the top side for speed

Secure posts on the inside and outside

Cover the cache with strong horizontal poles and tie everything up

RAISED CACHE

A raised cache can be built by cutting the tops off of three to four trees close together so they all measure 12 ft. (3.6 m) high, then constructing a scaffold on top. Ideally, the trees should be strong enough to support substantial weight but small enough in diameter to make it hard for bears to climb. Sawing off the tops of the trees can be very dangerous (keep yourself and the ladder clear of the falling top). Once the treetops have been cut, you can debark a long section of the upper tree and chop off all the lower branches to slightly deter animals from climbing. Then, fell any surrounding trees that could be used to get into the cache. You may want to leave one tree standing a few meters away from the cache so that you can lean a ladder against it to save energy and effort.

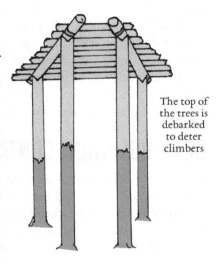

The top of the trees is debarked to deter climbers

The floor can be built using lashings and sawed-off notches. A broad-based ladder can be fashioned from two poles tied at the top. The rungs can be secured with nails, dovetail notches, or notches and lashings to prevent the rungs from moving.

SURVIVAL GARDEN

In multi-year wilderness survival, having a garden may be crucial. This section will briefly scratch the topic of survival gardens in a wilderness environment because it only makes sense for a situation spanning multiple seasons. The Lykov family spent over 40 years isolated in the Russian boreal forest. Their garden was fundamental for their survival because potatoes were their main crop and staple.

Developing a survival garden takes time and effort because forest soil may be inadequate. Nevertheless, soil can be improved by adjusting its pH and fertility. Some techniques that might be useful are using raised beds; using compost to build soil; fertilizing with wood ash, urine, and green manure; enriching the earth with muck from the bottoms of bodies of water; composting fish discards; and planting your garden in Hügelkultur beds (mounds of soil over piles of rotting logs).

Regarding which plants to grow, focus on calories and resilience, not on nutrients, for nutrients are widely available in wild foods while calories are scarce. Plants such as potatoes have the most potential, and your efforts should be focused on them.

EDIBLE PLANTS

Most edible plants are overhyped. A handful of collected greens is not a meal. The truth is that in temperate regions, most wild edibles can only complement staples like meat and fat, and in practice, they won't provide many macronutrients. Only a few dozen species of edibles can serve as a decent and practical source of nutrition, and only a handful of those have the potential of becoming true food staples. Knowing this, you don't have to spend time learning about marginal food plants. Instead, focus on learning which edible plants are the most useful as a food source. Only tubers, roots, fruits, nuts, and seeds contain enough calories to serve as staples.

Even though most greens don't provide many calories, they are still a good source of micronutrients and constipation-preventing fiber.

I include the profiles of some of the most valuable wild edibles found in the boreal forest because there are only a few, and they are truly useful as a source of nutrition in a real-world survival situation.

The edibles relevant to your location will be different from those below. My advice is to research the main staples of the Indigenous hunter-gatherers in your bioregion and focus on those food sources.

There are a few edibles that I don't cover thoroughly because, in most areas, they generally won't be abundant enough to form a substantial part of a survivor's diet. Still, I'd like to highlight them below so that you can learn to recognize them.

Gooseberries and currants can be a bit sour, but they are pretty easy to identify, and they are one of the first berries to ripen. Saskatoons (serviceberries) taste better than blueberries and ripen earlier.

Edible plants | 195

Raspberries need no introduction. A significant drawback of raspberries is that they are very fragile and usually won't stand being stored in a container. Their fresh or dried leaves make a very nutritious tea. Harvest the leaves in spring before flowers emerge and the leaves turn bitter. If you want the full nutritional value of the tea, let the leaves stand in cold water overnight.

In winter, depending on your latitude, you may be limited to stored edibles and what you can harvest year-round. A few vitamin-rich teas that I recommend for their taste or nutrition are:

- Spruce needle tea from young needles
- Wild rosehip tea (high in vitamin C)
- Juniper needle tea
- Labrador tea (found in mid-US to far north)

ACORN

Oak *Quercus* spp.
Range: US and Canada.
Calories: 387 kcal / 3.5 oz. (100 g) raw acorns (shelled).
Harvest: Gather in the fall, when the acorns turn dark brown and fall. This period usually happens from late August to October and may last a couple of weeks.

Abundance: Acorns can be very bountiful, but bountiful trees tend not to be common in the heart of the wilderness.

Identification: Oaks are hardwood trees 65–130 ft. (20–40 m) tall (shorter in the north). Their acorns have a woody, scaly cap. They can be roughly divided into red or black oaks and white oaks. Red and black oaks have leaves with pointed tips and lobes, and their acorns contain high amounts of bitter tannins. On the other hand, white oaks have leaves with rounded tips and lobes, and their acorns contain fewer tannins, and some are considerably less bitter.

Habitat: Oaks are found in open woods, deciduous forests, and dry prairies.

Preparation: Acorns found on the ground with the cap still attached likely have worms. Discard those, as well as those with obvious wormholes. Usually, the first acorns to fall are damaged. You can also drop them in water to separate good and bad acorns. Acorns that have sprouted are okay—as long as the nutmeat hasn't turned green—just break off the sprout.

Drying the acorns by a fire (slow, *low* heat) or under the sun makes the shells easier to crack. Crack the nuts by pressing or whacking with a wooden spoon for containment.

Red, black, and white oak acorns contain bitter tannins that must be leached. But some white oaks may be less bitter and require no leaching (but they will still contain tannins). There are two basic processing methods: repeated boiling or cold water leaching. Keep in mind that having more surface area exposed makes the tannins leach out faster. You'll have to experiment. Use the following methods to process the nutmeats.

Boiling: Boil the whole or *lightly* chopped nutmeats in various changes of water until the water remains clear or lightly colored. Have the changes of water already boiling before adding the acorns or the bitter taste will remain. The acorns should change color from yellowish-white to dark brown and lose all of their bitterness. If the acorns are still bitter, they are not done leaching. This method is not recommended because of the labor involved, and some of the nut oil may be lost.

Cold leaching: Leave the coarsely ground nutmeats in a porous bag or basket in a running stream for several days until the raw acorns are no longer bitter. Or soak them over a couple of days, rinsing the acorns and changing the water at least daily until it no longer darkens and the nutmeat is not bitter.

The "sweet" or leached acorns can be eaten raw, roasted, boiled, or as porridge.

Storage: Acorns store well in their shell. Don't shell the nuts unless you'll process them right away. Once leached, dry or roast the nuts and store them in a cool, dry place.

BLUEBERRY

Blueberry, huckleberry *Vaccinium* spp.
Range: US and Canada.
Calories: 60 kcal / 3.5 oz. (100 g) berries. The average berry weighs 0.3 g.
Harvest: Summer, particularly in July.
Abundance: They can be quite abundant in prime locations. Based on my experience, one person can gather around 5.5 lb. (2.5 kg) of *lowbush* blueberries per day in a moderately good area, which amounts to ~1,500 kcal. Use a very wide container for speed.
Identification: A shrub or bush with small whitish to pink flowers and thin oval leaves 0.4"–1" (1–3 cm) long. The berries are whitish-green before turning blue.
Habitat: Blueberry bushes grow in forest openings and other exposed areas. Look for the best patches on south-facing slopes, sunny and rocky hills, and recently burned areas.
Storage: Store undamaged berries in a bug net or highly breathable container for a few days. Sun-dry into fruit leather for long-term storage.

BUNCHBERRY

Bunchberry, dogwood *Cornus canadensis*
Range: Mid US to the far north.
Calories: 52–76 kcal / 3.5 oz. (100 g) berries.
Harvest: Mid-summer, July.
Abundance: These plants are relatively common. Each produces one to twelve berries in a tight cluster, and they can be easily picked in quantity.
Identification: Bunchberries are a small shrub that grows up to 8″ (20 cm) tall. Early in the season, the plants can be identified by the telltale white flower with four 0.4″–0.7″ (1–2 cm) long petals and the four or six leaves near the top. The leaves are 1.6″–2.8″ (4–7 cm) long. When ripe, the berries are bright red (scarlet) and form one tight cluster where the flower once appeared. Their flavor is neutral, and their seeds are crunchy. Like with other berries, eating many at once may cause diarrhea.
Habitat: Bunchberries grow in moist woods, bogs, woodlands, and mountains, and they are commonly found on the forest floor of spruce and fir forests.
Storage: The berries are pretty sturdy and easy to store; just dry off any leftover moisture.

CATTAIL

Cattail *Typha angustifolia, T. latifolia*

Range: North America.

Calories: 25 kcal / 3.5 oz. (100 g) young shoots (the average shoot weighs 19 g). 266 kcal / 3.5 oz. (100 g) flour. 304 kcal / 3.5 oz. (100 g) pollen.

Harvest: Collect rhizomes in April and October to mid-November; shoots in mid-May to mid-June; immature spikes in mid-June to mid-July; pollen in late June to July; laterals in mid-July to mid-September.

Abundance: Cattails can sometimes be found in huge patches around lakes and rivers, but your bounty may vary greatly.

Identification: Cattails have a very distinctive, fluffy seedhead that persists through the winter. It grows 5–9 ft. (1.5–3 m) tall and is usually found in dense, pure patches near water. Its stalk is straight and round.

Habitat: They live on wet ground, often near water.

Shoot cores: The bottom core of the leaf base can be collected anytime from spring to mid-summer. But it's best to gather them in late spring or early summer when the plant is only 50% to 75% fully grown, and the flower stalks are still not formed. To cut the bottom, grab the cluster of leaves—except for the outer two leaves—and pull firmly. You can also use a knife to cut the bottom. Then separate the outer leaves from the tender, white core. The edible part is usually only the first 4″–10″ (10–25 cm) from the bottom of the stalk. The shoots may be eaten raw, but some find them slightly irritating. It's best to cook them, and their taste has a hint of cucumber.

Spikes: In the early summer, the plants develop a spike enveloped in thin leaves. The bottom part of the spike is what later will turn into a fluffy seedhead. The top half of the immature spikes is good to eat, and its flavor has a hint of corn. Boil it briefly, add it to soups, or eat it raw. The nutritional value of spikes has been said to be questionable.

Pollen: Later in the summer, the top part of the spikes releases pollen. An excellent way to collect this is to cut a small hole in the side of a container and carefully shake the spike into the container. The pollen can be eaten as is or added to flour.

Laterals: The lateral shoots of the rhizomes are white or cream-colored and have a smooth, root-free exterior. The laterals are the new lateral shoots of the cattail before they mature into rhizomes, and they are much easier to prepare than rhizomes. Collect them after the cattail has flowered, but before it dies and turns brown. To collect them, reach into the muck at the base of the cattail, and feel for the rhizomes until you find one heading to an area with no stalks. If it ends in a pointed tip that doesn't turn upwards, it's a lateral. Be careful because they break easily. Feel back toward the cattail and cut the lateral at the point where you feel roots. It's easier to collect laterals at the edges of a cattail patch in soft muck, but they are also found throughout the patch. Eat the laterals raw or boiled.

Rhizomes: The cores of the roots (rhizomes) of the cattail contain starch among their thick fibers. The rhizome is edible, but it's like trying to eat sugarcane without the sugar. The rhizomes are found 2″–6″ (5–15 cm) under the mud, and they connect to multiple cattails. The best time to gather them is from fall to late spring, when the plant has the most starch stored for the winter. It's easier to dig up rhizomes in areas where the cattails are sparse and the mud is soft and near the water's edge. Use a knife to cut the rhizomes from their stalks. Then remove the spongy outer layer from the rhizome cores. Use your thumbnail to push in a scraper-like manner, and once you get a strip started, peel it off. You can chew and suck the starch out of the core's fibers in a pinch, but most people use them to make flour.

Rhizome flour:

1. Cut sections of the cores and twist them vigorously to separate the fibers and loosen the starch.
2. Rub the fibers in your hands to loosen the starch further.
3. Submerge the cores in a bowl of cold water and work the fibers until all the starch has separated.

4. Remove the fibers, and let the starch settle to the bottom of the bowl over several hours.

5. Carefully pour off the top slimy water. You'll be left with a thick white sludge.

You may pour it into a different container and let it settle again to condense it further, or just use it like that. Mix wheat flour into the sludge to make batter or dough. Or use it to thicken a soup. There are other methods for making powdered flour, but cattail flour can't be used like regular flour. It must be mixed with wheat flour to be useful for baking. So if you are baking in the field, the sludge method makes the most sense. Collecting rhizomes and processing them to make flour is very labor-intensive; don't expect this to be a regular activity.

Leaves: The leaves can be used for anything from mats to hats.

Storage: Most edible parts can be stored in a cool place for several days. The rhizomes, pollen, and flour should be dried for long-term storage.

HAZELNUT

Fungus Guy / CC BY-SA 3.0

Beaked and American hazelnut *Corylus cornuta* and *C. americana*
Range: California, eastern US, and from the mid-US to mid-Canada.
Calories: 628 kcal / 3.5 oz. (100 g) nuts (the average nut weighs 0.4 g).

Harvest: July to September. There is a lot of competition for hazelnuts, so they should be gathered early in the first or second week of August, or earlier before squirrels eat them up. The nuts can then be stored to ripen in a safe place.

Abundance: Hazelnuts are often found in dense stands of shrubs. Nevertheless, there aren't many nuts per shrub.

Identification: Hazelnuts grow on shrubs that reach 3–15 ft. (1–5 m) tall. It can be hard to spot the nuts hidden underneath the leaves, but they are pretty distinct. Beaked hazelnuts have prickly, beak-looking, toothed husks that can be two to five times longer than the nut, and American hazelnuts are enclosed in two leafy, toothed husks. The nuts (without the husks) look similar to an acorn, and they are about 0.4″–0.8″ (1–2 cm) in diameter.

Habitat: Hazelnuts grow in dry open woods, forest margins, well-drained streamsides, and areas associated with oak trees. And they are generally found at 300–1,600 ft. (100–500 m) of elevation.

Preparation: If you are dealing with prickly husks, use gloves to peel them. There are other techniques for dealing with the prickly husks:

- Bury the nuts in the damp ground for several days to let the husks decay.
- Place them in a sack and pound them against a rock or with a pole to loosen them up.
- Store them for a long time until they turn brown.

The nuts can then be cracked and eaten raw, but they taste much better roasted. If you find many empty shells, drop the nuts in water to separate the floating (empty) ones, but verify that you are not discarding any good ones.

Storage: The nuts should last a year or more if kept in their shell without husks in a cool place.

WAPATO

Wapato, arrowhead *Sagittaria spp.*
Range: North America from coast to coast.
Calories: 99 kcal / 3.5 oz. (100 g) raw tubers (the average tuber weighs 12–25 g).
Harvest: Fall and spring. Wapato can be harvested starting in late summer, but most tubers won't be fully grown until the plants begin to turn brown and die. Typically, the tubers grow fully from late September to early October. They can also be harvested during winter in places where water doesn't freeze. Spring is another possible time for harvest, but the water is usually deeper and colder than in the fall. The tubers shrink and die around late spring to early summer.
Abundance: Wapato can be found in small patches up to patches of a few acres. Each plant produces two to eight tubers.
Identification: The wapato or arrowhead is an aquatic plant commonly found on wetlands, with arrowhead-shaped leaves. The most widely harvested species is the broad-leaved arrowhead, *S. latifolia*. Its leaves are usually around 10″ (25 cm) long. The *S. cuneata* is another common species—but it is smaller. Its leaves are 4.7″ (12 cm) long, and its tubers are smaller as well. There are plants similar to wapato, but they don't have any part resembling wapato tubers. Tubers range in size, and they are generally about 1″–2″ (2.5–5 cm) long, and their shape is spherical or oval. The

tubers are usually a brilliant purple color, but they can also be dark purple, reddish-brown, or white.

Habitat: Wapato and arrowhead plants grow in ponds, slow streams, and slow or stagnant wetlands. Wapato is often found near cattail and wild rice stands.

Preparation: Harvesting can be hard work. Usually, the plants deposit their tubers at least 6″ (15 cm) deep in the mud, and bigger tubers may be up to 2–3 ft. (60–90 cm) deep. A common way to gather the tubers is to use a rake to break up the deep muck and let the tubers float to the surface. But the most efficient way to collect them is to wade in, and stomp and work the mud with your feet to loosen the tubers. This method may be intense if the water is too cold.

Wapato tubers can be cooked like a potato, and they are pretty tasty fried. Most people peel them to improve their flavor, which also helps spot spoiled ones.

Storage: Undamaged tubers (in perfect condition) keep for several weeks to months. But it's best to cook, slice (or mash), and dry them for storage.

WILD RICE

Wild rice, manoomin *Zizania aquatica, Z. palustris*
Range: Northeastern US and eastern Canada, but the range has been
greatly reduced by human industry and encroachment.
Calories: 357 kcal / 3.5 oz. (100 g) raw wild rice (the average cup of raw
wild rice weighs 160 g).
Harvest: Third or fourth week of August to the first week of September.
River wild rice tends to ripen a few days earlier. Check the maturity of the
rice stand regularly, and harvest the wild rice once it begins to fall when
knocked. Gather every two to five days during the harvest period, which
typically lasts 10 to 14 days.
Abundance: Wild rice can be very abundant and productive in specific
areas. In those limited areas, in a good season, wild rice has the potential
to cover at least half of your energy needs for several months and up to a
year. In a few hours over a single day, my partner and I managed to gather
around 66 lb. (30 kg) of kernels in a good patch during our six-month trip.
Identification: Wild rice is an annual, tall aquatic grass that grows 3–7 ft.
(1–2 m) above the water. The delicate plants float on the surface during
June before they develop enough to stand straight. The rice hulls are often
empty in plants that won't have a crop. In plants with rice, the grains start
green and darken as they ripen.

Habitat: Wild rice can be bountiful at the margins of shallow and clear rivers and lakes (with some water movement but stable water levels). They develop best at a depth of 24″–48″ (60–120 cm) and perform poorly if the water levels are high. But don't get your hopes up if you find extensive stands in streams or lakes where the water level fluctuates significantly. In those places, the harvest will likely be disappointing or nonexistent. It's best to research if an area has a history of successful harvests.

Preparation: Gathering wild rice can be a fantastic experience, particularly if you're hungry. To gather wild rice, you'll need a canoe, a paddle, a helper (preferred), a pair of knocking sticks, a long pole, a few gunnysacks, and a tarp (preferred). The long pole should measure about the same length as the canoe, and it's best to make it with lightweight softwood. It's best to splice or attach a V-fork to the pole's end so it doesn't get stuck as often. The knocking poles should measure about the same distance from your armpit to your fingertips; lightweight wood is best. Past the handle, they should narrow immediately to about 1″ (2.5 cm) thickness and gradually taper to a 3/8″ (1 cm) thick tip. The tarp can be tied to the gunnels or other canoe parts to form a catchment area and keep the kernels clean from sand or grit.

You'll need to push the canoe with your pole to move it through the wild rice stand. But first, reverse the canoe so that the front becomes the back. The *knocker* should sit in the stern, and the *poler* must stand in the bow facing the stern. The poler should stand in a "fighting" stance to stay balanced. The poler must push the pole into the muck to propel the canoe. To prevent getting the pole stuck, do a short and quick jerk back toward the front at the end of each stroke. Keep a constant rhythm to maintain momentum. The rice is ready for harvest once it falls into your canoe just because you're moving through the patch.

To "knock" the rice, use one knocking stick to lean several plants over the canoe. Try not to touch the seedheads to avoid knocking the kernels into the water. Using the other stick, gently tap the stalks to knock the kernels into the canoe, alternating sides as the canoe moves. It's important not to damage the plants so that you can harvest them again in a few days. Ricing solo is not recommended because it's very slow; nevertheless, it's doable. It's best for the knocker to place a tarp on their legs and wear a rain jacket and rain pants, for the rice tends to stick to clothes and scratch the skin.

Gathering wild rice is easy, but finishing rice manually is hard work. Wild rice must be dried, parched, "jigged," and winnowed to make it palatable.

Look for kernels infected with ergot fungus throughout the process and discard them (see the "Health" chapter).

Drying: Unfinished wild rice contains a lot of moisture. To stop mold from growing on the rice and worms eating it, it's best to dry it as soon as possible. Spread the wild rice on a tarp and leave it under the sun for two full days to dry. Stir it throughout both days so it dries evenly. Sample a few kernels to check that they are fully dried. Remove their husks and check if they bend or if they are stiff and brittle (fully dried). Dried rice stores for a very long time.

Parching: Parching is the process of heating the kernels to harden and slightly shrink them and to make their husks more brittle. You can do this by placing a small amount of rice at a time in a tilted metal basin over a small fire. Keep the heat low and steady, and stir with a big wooden spoon to prevent the rice from burning. It may take several minutes. To know if the kernels are ready, sample a few by rubbing them hard between your hands: some kernels should come free of their husks. Over-parching won't make the husks easier to remove, so avoid it. Only parch the quantity of rice you are ready to hull immediately or it will reabsorb moisture and turn brittle.

The traditional method used before metal was to dry the rice over a fire. A long and narrow scaffolding (*abwaajigan*) was built with green sticks, about 3–4 ft. (0.9–1.2 m) high. Cedar slabs, hay, reeds, grass, willow, or horsetail mats were laid on top to prevent the rice from falling. This method combined the drying and parching process into a one- or two-day process. The downside was that the rice had a smoky flavor, so this method was entirely abandoned as soon as metal was available.

Treading or jigging: The rice should be threshed soon after being parched to remove the hulls. Treading is the most labor-intensive part.

To jig the rice:
1. Line a small pit with a strong tarp or skin. You may also place four wide logs to form a square and place the tarp inside to form the "pit."
2. Place some rice in the pit, and "dance" over the rice by stepping and rotating your feet in place.
3. Use the friction of your feet and the ground to dislodge the hulls; the rotating motion is essential.
4. Wear clean shoes with no traces of grit or sand.
5. Experiment with varying amounts of rice to learn what is optimal.

Often two poles were lashed to a nearby tree to give the "jigger" more stability.

Winnowing: On a windy day, the loose hulls can be removed by repeatedly pouring rice from chest height into a container in the ground. Some of the husks and debris (chaff) should blow away each time. Adjust the height and position continuously to avoid losing kernels. You can also use a birch bark tray to swing the wild rice upward in a circular motion while letting some of the chaff fall outside the tray, but this is not easy. Pass the rice through another round of jigging once most of the loose chaff is gone. Continue winnowing, jigging, winnowing, and jigging until the fraction of rice with husks is tolerable.

Cooking: Wild rice should be cooked for about 40 minutes in a 1:3 ratio of rice to water. You may also fry a few kernels to make "popcorn."

Tied rice: If there are relatively few wild rice plants or you foresee a scarce harvest, you could tie the rice stalks into bundles with bark fibers, grass, or roots. This was usually done in the first days of August. It maximizes the amount of rice you can harvest but requires more effort. Binding rice may not be legal in your area.

Storage: The sun-dried rice should be stored in a cool, dry place in gunnysacks. Traditionally, it was kept in birch baskets.

FISHING

Where fish are plentiful, they usually make up a significant portion of the available food. There are a few reasons for this. Fish can reliably be caught year-round. Fish are limited to bodies of water (versus land animals), so they can be "ambushed" in specific spots. And fish usually make up a large percentage of the wild food biomass in a given area.

In places where fish migrate, hunter-gatherers would secure most of their fish during the fall runs. The hunter-gatherers would set weir traps in rapids upstream where fish ascended to spawn. For some species, the heaviest runs occurred at night. By November, almost no fish would be migrating, so some hunter-gatherers would travel to large lakes with ample fish populations to spend the winter.

FISHING LOCATIONS

General rules of thumb regarding fishing locations:
- Ninety percent of the area in a body of water holds no fish.
- Take the time to sit and observe. Notice the subtle clues on land and on the water's surface.
- Fish are often near cover, or *structure*, to live and commute.
- Fish tend to concentrate in areas with good cover.

- Inactive fish are more likely to be in heavy cover or deep waters (try passive fishing techniques there).
- Fish tend to stage in areas where they can spend the least energy while having the highest chance of having food brought to them.
- Be mindful of how you approach any body of water (think of it as hunting).
- Notice the sun direction—avoid casting a shadow on the water.

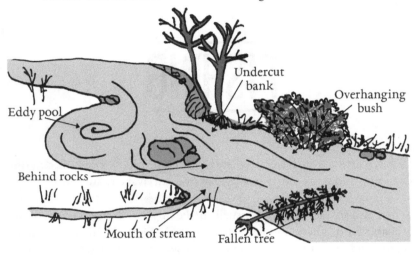

SEASONS

	Spring	**Summer**	**Fall**
Rivers	Walleye, trout	Trout	Trout, salmon, char
Lakes	Shallow water: pike, trout, walleye, bass	Shallow water: pike, bass Deeper water: trout, walleye	Shallow water: trout, pike, bass
Time	Any time of the day (as the water warms it gets better)	Morning and evening fishing is best at higher temperatures	Any time of the day

FISHING STRUCTURES

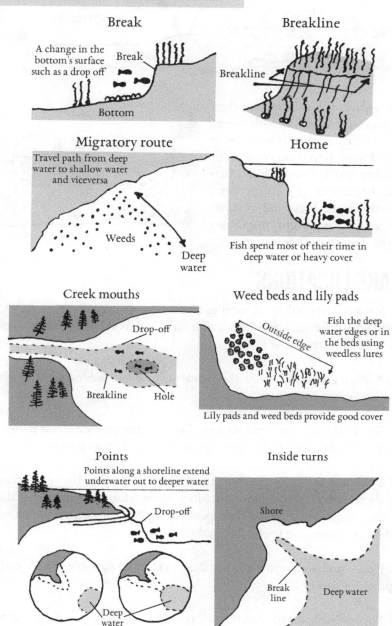

Break

A change in the bottom's surface such as a drop off

Break

Bottom

Breakline

Breakline

Migratory route

Travel path from deep water to shallow water and viceversa

Weeds

Deep water

Home

Fish spend most of their time in deep water or heavy cover

Creek mouths

Drop-off

Breakline

Hole

Weed beds and lily pads

Fish the deep water edges or in the beds using weedless lures

Outside edge

Lily pads and weed beds provide good cover

Points

Points along a shoreline extend underwater out to deeper water

Drop-off

Unproductive

Deep water

Ideal

Inside turns

Shore

Break line

Deep water

Strong winds push cool water and insects to shore, attracting fish to feed.

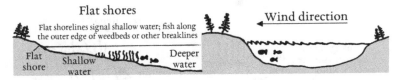

Irregularities on the lake or river bottom provide fish with cover, or structure, throughout their travel from deep waters (home) to shallow waters (work). Fish often use breaklines (e.g., drop-offs, weedbeds, or logs) and channel edges as their commuting routes from deep to shallow waters.

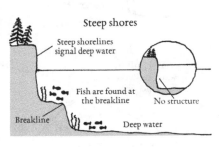

LAKE LOCATIONS

1. Stream inlets: inlets are excellent fishing spots because they bring in food for baitfish and game fish, and usually have good hiding spots, such as weeds, deep holes, or rocks.

2. Rapids: above and below the rapids are excellent fishing spots. Large fish are often near rapids.

3. Points: fish the ends and corners of points that provide access to deep waters. Big fish tend to hang out around the tip of those points.

4. Weedbeds and lily pads: these are excellent areas when they give access to deep waters. Weedbeds produce food (indirectly) for baitfish and also provide cover—fish the shallow edges in spring and fall. Fish use the deeper edges as commuting routes due to their cover.

5. Reeds: reeds that connect to marshes or creeks are excellent spots in early spring for bass or pike.

6. Stream channels: in lakes that are part of a river system, a deeper main river channel may provide a commuting route from deep to shallow waters. The edges of this channel are excellent fishing areas.

7. Submerged rocks: rock piles are excellent fishing spots if they provide cover and access to deep waters. Shallow rocky areas are usually good for fishing as well.

8. Ridges and ledges: the edge and base of a ridge are good fishing areas.

9. Deep holes: most fish will be along the edges of the hole.

10. Submerged or fallen trees: fallen trees, dead brush, and stumps can be excellent fishing spots if they provide shade and access to a breakline or deep waters.

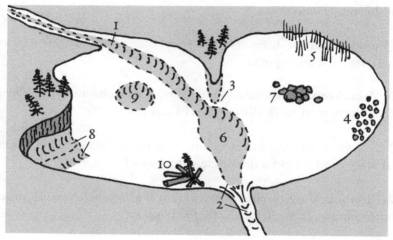

STREAM LOCATIONS

1. Rapids: above and below the rapids are excellent fishing spots. Large fish are often near rapids. Fish the rock-covered areas along the shore and the first eddies immediately above or below the rapids.

2. Eddies: eddies provide food and cover, and they can be fished from a canoe or the shore.

3. Bars: raised bars or humps provide spawning grounds in early spring. Catfish and walleye lurk in humps near rapids.

4. Points: points form eddies downstream, which are good fishing spots.

5. Bays and backwaters: spots with little or no current provide spawning grounds for walleye, bass, and northern pike. Fish them in early spring.

6. Stream inlets: great areas to fish for pike during early spring and throughout the summer.

7. Rocks: the downstream edges of rock piles provide good cover for fish lying in ambush. A good strategy is to fish above the boulders and let bait float downstream. Target also the still water in front of the rocks or other obstructions.

8. Islands: fish the sides of the islands opposite the main channel and along the downstream points.

9. Outside bends: the shores of outside river bends, where the current flows faster, are good fishing areas.

10. Main channel edges: the edges of the main river channel are excellent fishing areas, particularly downstream of rapids.

11. Current seams: the current seams, where faster water meets slower water, are good places for fishing closer to the surface.

12. Riverbeds: there are current breaks near the bottom where fish stage, conserving energy, while waiting for food to come.

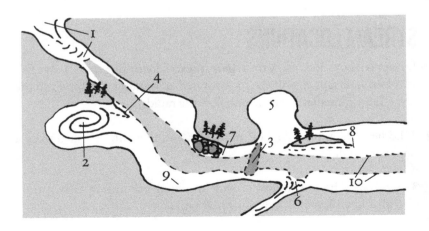

FISH BEHAVIOR

General rules of thumb regarding fish:

- Fish are creatures of habit. Learning their habits is the key to finding them.
- Fish can see, hear, and smell.
- Natural and unnatural colors (e.g., bright or shiny) and movements (e.g., rapid or erratic) attract fish.
- Fish are scared by too much flash, noise, and fast-moving shadows.
- In lakes, fishing is more successful in low water than high water. In streams, medium or slowly rising water is best.
- Fish in rivers always face the current; approach from downstream to avoid being noticed.
- Fish are cold-blooded, so they are more active when the water is warm and less active when the water is freezing cold.
- Fish are susceptible to weather changes, so learn how they react to them.
- Too much wind, mud, or water clarity is counterproductive to fishing.
- Fish don't necessarily bite because they are hungry; figure out why they bite (e.g., aggression or instinct).
- Dawn and dusk are good times for fishing.
- On cloudy days, fish are more likely to be in shallow areas, and on sunny days, they are more likely to be in deep or shaded spots.
- Some fish may bite more frequently when it's raining (light or moderate showers but not pouring).
- The wind can be good for fishing; fish in wind-exposed areas.
- One of the best times to go fishing is right before a storm or cold front hits.
- Capitalize on air pressure changes in which fish may feed more aggressively.

PIKE

Pike are aggressive fish that can reach enormous sizes (up to 40 lb. or 18 kg in Canada). They bite anything that looks like food. Lures such as spoons and spinners work well, and plugs are excellent. Make sure you use metal leaders when you're in pike territory. You'll find pike in shallow bays with plenty of water lilies and weeds. If you can't find weedbeds, look for drop-offs and submerged trees and rocks.

CATFISH

Catfish are bottom-feeders with a strong sense of smell, and they are not picky. They can be caught day and night, but they feed more at night. Place your bait at the bottom or just above it, and leave it there until a catfish bites. For those reasons, trotlines work well for them. Live baits and stink baits are good for catching catfish. A nice thing about catfish is that they are often reasonably large, and some have lots of fat.

ACTIVE FISHING

The main disadvantage of active fishing is that it is dependent on the weather. For example, fish tend to bite only in specific weather conditions, and wind and waves make it hard to fish and be out on the water.

FISHING RODS

Fishing rods are not the most effective fishing method, but they are great for fishing while traveling and when the conditions are ideal. Pack at least one fishing rod per person. A nice thing about fishing rods is that they can help you get the ball rolling. For instance, you can catch a fish with a lure and then use its meat as bait for trotlines, setlines, and land traps.

Something to keep in mind is that catching enough fish with a fishing rod is not as easy in the wilderness as it is at the edge of civilization. You'll be less effective because you won't have access to a motorized boat or store-bought bait, and you will have to be much more careful to avoid losing your tackle.

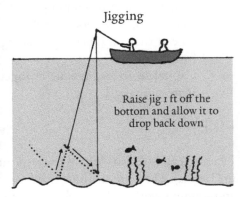

Jigging

Raise jig 1 ft off the bottom and allow it to drop back down

One downside of fishing rods is that if you are not careful, you might lose many hooks and lures to snags, so bring lots. Bobbers might help you minimize this.

I recommend the Emmrod Packer Rod (with six coils) because it's compact and won't break. However, it won't cast as nicely as a full-length rod. Ugly Stik is a good option for a nearly unbreakable full-length fishing rod. Another option is a telescopic rod, but it could break easily. Pack monofilament or braided fishing lines of various weights (e.g., 6 lb., 10 lb., 20 lb., and 50 lb.).

HANDLINE

Handlining is a simple fishing method that uses minimal gear. The basic setup consists of a sinker, a hook, a mono fishing line, and something to wrap the line around.

The sinker is important because it is needed for casting. It is usually rigged at the end of the line, but it can also be tied above the hook. A mono line rated to 35 lb. or more is used because it's easier on the hands and can withstand the stress of handlining. Gloves are sometimes used to protect the hands from cuts when pulling in a fish. Hooks can be easily rigged with a Palomar knot. The classic handline rig uses a glass Coca-Cola bottle, but you can improvise something similar with a wide driftwood stick.

When handlining in the dark, use a light or improvised torch to attract fish.

The *Cuban yo-yo* is a simple plastic tool that makes casting and wrapping the line easy. If you don't have a fishing rod in your kit, I recommend at least having a Cuban yo-yo. In addition, it also works well for setlines.

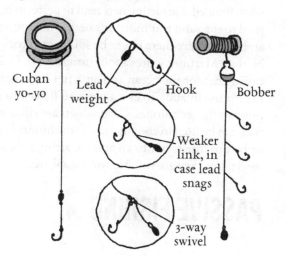

Cuban yo-yo

Lead weight

Hook

Bobber

Weaker link, in case lead snags

3-way swivel

PLANER BOARD

A planer board is a simple device used to position a hook and line farther into a stream. The attachment point of the line needs to be fine-tuned, and the line must be off the water for the planer board to work well.

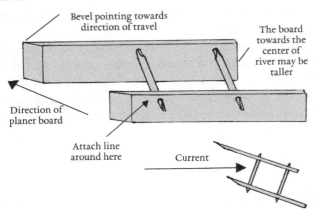

Bevel pointing towards direction of travel

The board towards the center of river may be taller

Direction of planer board

Attach line around here

Current

CASTING NET

The casting net is an efficient tool in places where fish form dense schools. Casting nets are circular nets with dozens of weights embedded around the edge, and have various lines running from the mainline—located at the net's center—to the edge of the net. That allows the net to entrap fish when the mainline is pulled in.

Casting nets are typically made with braided nylon or monofilament lines. Braided line casting nets tend to perform better overall; however, they tend to snag and tear more. It's best to use a mono line casting net in rivers and lakes where there might be submerged rocks and trees. In *Subsistence*, Nathan Martinez writes about using a 14 ft. (4.2 m) diameter braided line casting net for the ocean and an 8 ft. (2.4 m) diameter mono line casting net for use inland. To cast a net, you'll need to take the time to learn and practice the techniques. Casting nets are efficient at catching baitfish, and they can be used in conjunction with chumming (using chopped fish parts or bait to lure fish into an area). Casting nets are not ideal for the boreal forest, but they are suitable for coastal areas.

PASSIVE FISHING

WEIRS

Fishing weirs were one of the primary fishing methods used by hunter-gatherers. Traditionally they were built or activated during the fall spawning migrations and were designed to trap fish as they traveled upstream. Hunter-gatherers would often use spears or nets to catch the fish trapped in the enclosures of the weirs. Weirs were also built with rocks to trap fish in coastal areas as the tide receded. Weirs can also be adapted to trap fish at other times of the year, using the current to funnel fish into a *pool* or a basket trap, which is hard to escape from.

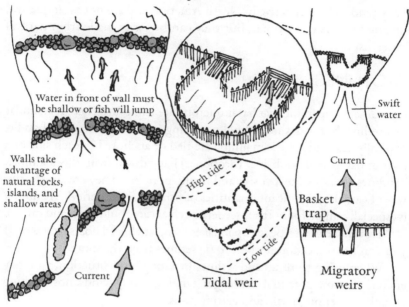

Water in front of wall must be shallow or fish will jump

Walls take advantage of natural rocks, islands, and shallow areas

Current

Tidal weir

High tide

Low tide

Swift water

Current

Basket trap

Migratory weirs

BASKET TRAPS

Basket traps can be improvised with roots and green sticks. The Lykov family used this type of trap during their 40 years in the taiga, for they didn't have nets.

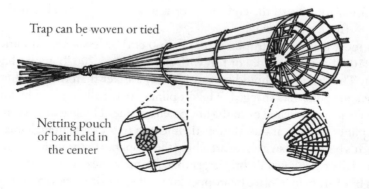

Trap can be woven or tied

Netting pouch of bait held in the center

These traps usually need smelly bait to attract fish. Place chopped bait in a netting pouch or inside a perforated plastic container. The bait should be securely tied in the center of the trap, regardless of the trap's position.

You'll also need rope and a float to set and retrieve the trap. The funnel should be tied in a way that is easy to undo.

These traps work best with currents, natural "bottlenecks," or a weir. They tend to be ineffective in North America, and are not as simple and effective as nets or trotlines, but they can be easily made from natural materials.

TROTLINES

A trotline is a mainline that has numerous hook lines attached. It is similar to a setline, but it has more hooks, making it more awkward to handle. Typically, the ends of the mainline are tied or anchored to each side of a river or bay, baited hook lines (droplines) hang down from this mainline. Trotlines are fairly inexpensive and highly portable. They are an effective way of catching significant quantities of fish in a short period. Trotlining is especially suited for bottom-feeders, such as carp, bullheads, and catfish.

Trotlines can also be set up in lakes using anchored floats or stakes. If you don't have a canoe, it's best to rig setlines from the shore.

When using trotlines and setlines in a long-term situation, you may encounter some potential challenges: tangles, strong winds, not catching or gathering enough bait, and getting hooked.

To make a small 80 ft. (24 m) trotline for small streams and lakes:

1. Use a 100 ft. (30.5 m) long, durable tarred braided nylon line of 200 lb. test (Catahoula #30).
2. From the center, tie 1–1.5 ft. (30–45 cm) long droplines every two to three feet.
3. Work toward the ends, leaving at least 10 feet of the braided line free for anchoring.

For most fish—and droplines of 2 ft. (60 cm) or less—a mono line of 50–100 lb. can be used. For fish with sharp teeth, a 200 lb. mono line is best. The droplines should be considerably weaker than the mainline in case a dropline gets snagged. The droplines are usually secured by knots or plastic stops melted onto the line on either side. The space between the droplines must be at least double their length to prevent entanglements.

It's best to use swivels for attaching the droplines to the mainline. If the swivel diameter is just slightly larger than the mainline diameter, the swivel can be easily held in place by stopper knots. Rig the droplines to allow you to attach and remove them quickly. This can be very helpful for baiting, repairing, and dealing with difficult fish or tangles. It's recommended to use trotline *snaps* for this purpose, but the girth hitch or Prusik knot work in a pinch (although not as well).

The mainline can be improvised from a paracord's outer sheath. The droplines can be made with three-stranded paracord's inner cords or a two-stranded inner cord twisted into two-ply cordage with a rope twister.

When targeting bottom-feeders, let the mainline sink close to the bottom of the lake or stream. If surface feeders are the target, stretch the mainline tight. Floats are often used along the mainline to prevent fish from pulling the line below the feeding area or into underwater obstructions. It's best to use floats every few hooks.

Circle hooks are recommended for trotlines and setlines because they tend to be more effective, don't need "setting," and are safer to handle. They also help remove fish and reset the trotline rapidly (digging out J or treble hooks from a gut-hooked fish takes too long). Circle hooks with an offset often catch more fish, and stainless steel is preferred because it's more durable. Use 5/0 to 8/0 size circle hooks for catfish, or use larger hooks if you're targeting larger catfish. For circle hooks to be effective, the gap must be wide enough for the fish's mouth, and the point must not be blocked by the bait. If you don't have circle hooks, trebles will do.

Bait the trotline with worms, crayfish, minnows, frogs, stink baits, fish parts, or leeches.

Where there are lots of catfish, wooden "buttons" may work as lures. Cut slices from a round stick and drill a hole near the edge. The hole should be just slightly larger than the hook's wire so that the barb can keep it in place. These lures are effective and efficient. Some people also soak or boil their dry wood pieces in fish oil to make them more attractive.

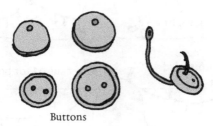
Buttons

If your droplines are easily disconnected, you can store them by hanging them from a line running around the inside of a plastic container or from its rim.

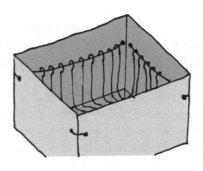 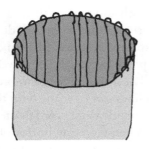

Trotlines can also be stored in a magazine, allowing the lines to be quickly set. The magazine can be built using two parallel rods. The trotline must be stored properly, or you'll make a mess trying to set it. You will also need some sort of boat to set it up. Tie one end of the trotline to a fixed point near the edge of a bank, like a stake, a big rock, or a submerged tree. Stretch the line and tie it to either the opposite shore, a stake, or an anchor. The trotline must be tight but not too tight.

Side view

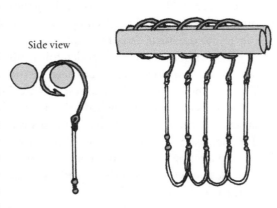

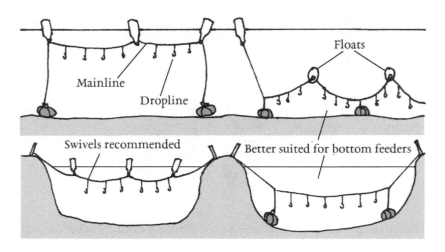

Leave enough slack to keep it at the desired depth. Sinkers can also be used near the ends to weigh down the line. Finally, pull your canoe along the mainline, and attach the baited droplines.

Trotlines can be set at any time, but they are usually set in the evening and checked in the morning. The longer the line is left unattended, the more time fish have to escape. A gaff is handy for checking the mainline. Place a landing net under the fish before bringing them out of the water, or you'll risk losing them.

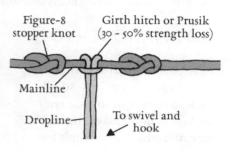

SETLINES

Setlines are a compact and effective way to fish passively, and they can be set from land or a canoe. As with trotlines, these setups are more effective for bottom-feeders attracted to smelly bait. One of the advantages of setlines is that they are easy to deploy and retrieve and can be used while traveling.

Stick to simple designs. For instance, setting up an L-7 trap trigger to hook the fish onto a J hook is likely more trouble than it's worth. In practice, the L-7 will just alert you of a bite rather than hook the fish.

Use hooks that will keep fish hooked overnight: barbed circle hooks are best, but barbed trebles will also work. Typically, setlines are tied to a stake, tree, or branch on one end and an anchor on the other. If you place a setline away from shore in a shallow lake, use a solid stake and heavy anchors to prevent hooked fish from circling the stake and getting unhooked. A netting bag makes a versatile portable anchor when filled with rocks.

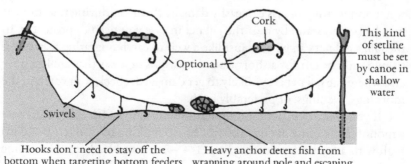

It's important to use swivels on a setline. If you don't have swivels, use a perfection loop or a non-slip loop knot. And keep in mind that you may need a heavy mono line or wire leader if northern pikes are around. You may add improvised floats and sinkers to adjust your setline.

AUTOMATIC YO-YO

The mechanical fisher or automatic yo-yo is a small, durable contraption that reels the line in and "plays" the fish once triggered. Many people use them successfully in setlines and limblines.

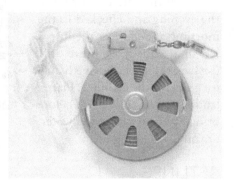

GILL NETS

For long-term survival, gill nets are a must-have. Gill nets are one of the most efficient methods of catching fish. That's why commercial fishermen use gill nets in rivers and lakes, in summer and winter, in freshwater and salt water. Gill nets are so effective that they are outlawed in most places. The "tax stamp" or commercial permit can be pretty expensive. Check your local regulations.

The advantage of a gill net over other techniques is that you don't need bait, and the net will work even if fish are not biting at the time. The disadvantage of gill nets is that they may get tangled or break if you are not careful. Gill nets must be used with respect and without compromising the present and future fish populations.

Gill nets are very effective in rivers during early spring, but the high water and floating debris can easily damage them. So during that time, it may be best to stand by near the gill net in case you need to protect it. In the fall, a gill net can be used just like a weir to catch migrating fish, but it should only be left for a short time. In seasons or areas that are less busy and where the gill net is less likely to get damaged, check your catch in the mornings, evenings, or preferably both.

If you want a gill net for long-term survival, my advice is to purchase a monofilament line net 65–100 ft. (20–30 m) long by 3–6 ft. (1–1.8 m) high with a foam-core floating line (1/4″–3/8″) and lead-core sinker line

(3/16"–1/4" or #20–#30). It won't be very compact, but it will be effective. Or buy a cheap mono line net, and add a float line and a lead-core line.

MONO OR MULTIFILAMENT

Mono nets tend to catch two to four times as many fish as multifilament nets, and that's why mono nets are popular. The main reason for this is that they are less visible, and fish are more likely to get caught by the gills rather than just by entanglement. Usually, mono nets are more durable, easier to use, and tangle less, but they are harder to repair.

A standard thread size for multifilament nets is 210/3, with a breaking strength of 10 lb. Both mono and multifilament nets are tough to weave by hand with the thin lines used by manufacturers. And the knots are also complicated to make right; they will usually slip. So if you are weaving your net, I suggest you use, at the minimum, 0.3 mm multifilament or 0.2 mm mono. Avoid using a braided fishing line because it has a coating that makes knots slip. Test the knots as you go to avoid unpleasant surprises.

MESH SIZE

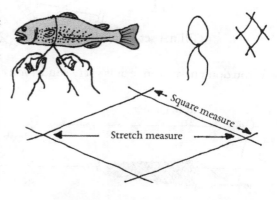

Guesstimate the average size of fish you would like to catch to determine the optimal mesh size. Measure the fish's girth by wrapping a cord around the thickest part of its body—you need a mesh size about one-quarter smaller than the fish's circumference.

Square measure

Stretch measure

The good news is that you may catch bigger fish by entanglement. For survival, it's wise to go with a *slightly* smaller mesh size because a smaller mesh size may catch bigger fish, but bigger mesh sizes won't catch smaller fish.

Mesh size may be confusing because it is expressed as *square* or *stretch* measure. Here I only use the stretch measure, which is the length of the stretched mesh. The square measure is the distance between two neighboring knots of the mesh, and it's half of the stretch measure.

For an area with whitefish, lake trout, catfish, and pike, I suggest a 5"

(12.5 cm) stretch size, or 5.5" (14 cm) if you are targeting bigger fish. For areas with small suckers, lake herring, yellow perch, carp, or bass, a 3" mesh is more appropriate. And for big salmon, steelhead, sturgeon, or carp, a 7" mesh may be ideal.

LOCATION AND SET UP

Place your gill net in a place that takes advantage of natural funnels, migration runs, or currents that encourage fish to swim through the gill net. A simple way to set up a gill net is out from the shore toward the center of a lake.

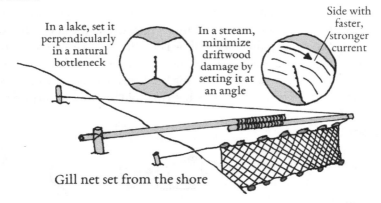

In a lake, set it perpendicularly in a natural bottleneck

In a stream, minimize driftwood damage by setting it at an angle

Side with faster, stronger current

Gill net set from the shore

If you don't have a canoe or it's very windy, you can rig a clothesline system

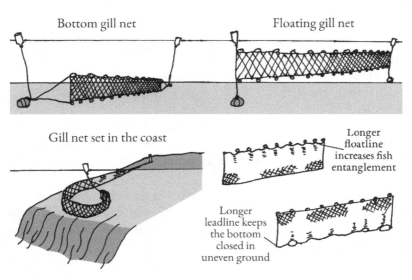

Bottom gill net

Floating gill net

Gill net set in the coast

Longer floatline increases fish entanglement

Longer leadline keeps the bottom closed in uneven ground

for your gill net: find a narrow bay and walk around it while pulling a line over the bay. Another technique for deploying and pulling the gill net in is to sink an anchor attached to a clothesline rig.

When using a canoe, set the gill net downwind. It's best to work in pairs. Tie the top line of the gill net to a tree or stake and gently pull the gill net out. Then pull some slack and tie a buoy and an anchor. Set your gill net loose at the top or bottom of the lake to make fish more likely to get tangled. If you're not catching enough, experiment with different parts of the lake, closer or further from shore. Avoid setting it near vegetation, for you'll spend a long time cleaning it. Use a landing net when retrieving the gill net to avoid losing fish.

To avoid entangling your gill net, it may help to use a Y-shaped stick to coil the float line in one forked end and the bottom line in the other end.

MAKING A NET

I encourage you to pack a well-made custom gill net because it will be more effective and easier to use than one made in the field. Nevertheless, you may be forced to improvise one with found materials.

To make a gill net, you'll need lots of time and cordage. Keep in mind that the gill net's effectiveness is greatly affected by the visibility of the mesh. Cordage may be improvised with paracord inner strands, unwaxed dental floss, or fishing line.

There are two main ways of making a gill net. If you are working with less-than-ideal cordage, the knots will likely slip, so I recommend using the well-known "survival" method when using this kind of cordage.

SURVIVAL METHOD

Most instructions on survival gill net making don't cover the importance of having floats and sinkers. Floats and sinkers help position the gill net so that it is effective. And they also help prevent the net from getting too tangled when a fish is caught.

Traditionally, floats made of wood, cork, or plastic are strung along the top line and lead weights are strung or crimped onto the bottom line. Unfortunately, both floats and sinkers tend to get tangled within the mesh. Nowadays, foam-core float lines and lead-core lines are preferred because these types of floats and sinkers don't get tangled in the gill net. However, gill nets can still get nastily tangled even with float lines and lead lines.

Ideally, for each float on the float line, the corresponding sinker should weigh three to five times more than what the float can lift. Try to have floats and sinkers with consistent flotation or weight, and distribute them evenly so that the gill net is as straight as possible.

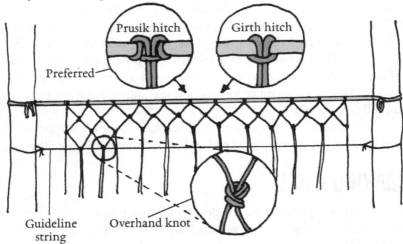

SHUTTLE AND GAGE

You'll need a shuttle and a gage to make a woven gill net. To carve a shuttle, cut a hardwood or birch stick to about the width of your wrist and split it in half. Then, thin down one piece and carve the point of the shuttle. Afterward, mark and carve out two parallel holes on each side. And finally, join the parallel holes toward the tip and carve out a hole at the bottom of the shuttle. You can also carve a shuttle out of plastic.

The gage should be smooth and carved thin or round and measure half of your intended stretch mesh size. It's essential to make it out of hardwood so it doesn't get scored when tying the knots tightly.

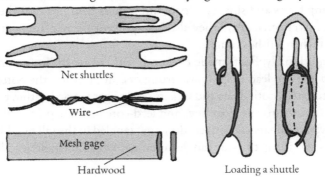

WOVEN METHOD

The woven method is a faster method of making a gill net. Another advantage is that it can be done in a small space, like inside a shelter, as the process is a bit like knitting. The downside of this method is that you must carve a shuttle and have cordage that won't slip, and it requires a bit more practice and experience.

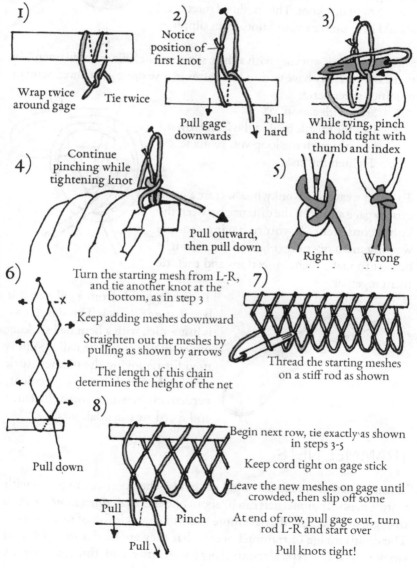

1) Wrap twice around gage   Tie twice

2) Notice position of first knot
Pull gage downwards   Pull hard

3) While tying, pinch and hold tight with thumb and index

4) Continue pinching while tightening knot
Pull outward, then pull down

5) Right   Wrong

6) Turn the starting mesh from L-R, and tie another knot at the bottom, as in step 3
Keep adding meshes downward
Straighten out the meshes by pulling as shown by arrows
The length of this chain determines the height of the net
Pull down

7) Thread the starting meshes on a stiff rod as shown

8) Pull   Pinch   Pull
Begin next row, tie exactly as shown in steps 3-5
Keep cord tight on gage stick
Leave the new meshes on gage until crowded, then slip off some
At end of row, pull gage out, turn rod L-R and start over
Pull knots tight!

With thin, smooth cordage, and when first learning to weave gill nets, it's likely that your sheet bend knots (weaver's knot) will get tied improperly (below the *V*) and slip as a result. One way to prevent this is to do a double knot by passing the cord through the *V* underneath the not-yet-tight first knot. This modified sheet bend should help prevent your knots from slipping.

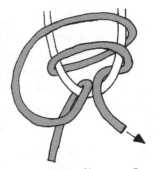

Suppose you are working with a thin, slippery line, like monofilament. In that case, you may have to do a knot after you've done your sheet bend or modified sheet bend:

1. Start with a loop.
2. Pass the shuttle behind the *V* and toward you, through the loop you've made.
3. Tighten the knot.

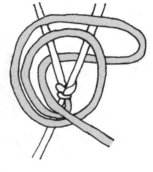

To avoid weaving a wonky mesh, craft a good quality gage and keep the distance between the knots consistent. If you're having trouble weaving mesh openings of equal size, it might be best to make them in sections and then tie them together.

To untangle fish from a gill net, it is best to use a fish pick. This simple tool is just a stick with a bent nail sticking out from one end. The nail's point is used for removing the meshes stuck around the fish. It is very convenient, particularly in winter when efficiency and speed are essential.

TRAMMEL NETS

Trammel nets are practically a gill net sandwiched between two nets with a larger mesh. Trammel nets can be about one and a half times more effective than gill nets because they are more likely to entangle fish of various sizes. The disadvantage of trammel nets is that they are harder to repair and tangle up more. A typical trammel net has an outer mesh three to five times larger than the inner mesh.

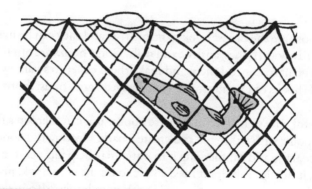

IMPROVISED GEAR

It's best to have ready-made gear, but you'll need to improvise gear using found materials in many circumstances.

LANDING NET AND GAFF

Having a landing net is a must when fishing for subsistence because you can't afford to lose any fish. I recommend packing the net portion of a landing net. The net's frame can be quickly improvised out of a Y-shaped branch, and the fork can be spliced onto the ends with a flexible green stick. It's best to use a fairly symmetrical stick or it will swing to the heavier side. If you don't have a net or want to save cordage, you can weave a "basket" onto the frame with wet spruce roots.

A wooden fishing gaff is a handy tool for checking trotlines and setlines, but it's not great for landing fish.

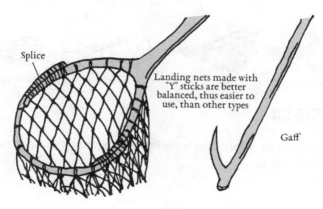

Splice

Landing nets made with "Y" sticks are better balanced, thus easier to use, than other types

Gaff

HOOKS

Gorge hooks are the easiest hook to improvise, and they can be made with carved hardwoods, bones, antlers, and nails. Gorge hooks are often inserted into a soft bait to conceal them and make them easier to swallow.

J-style hooks can be improvised with carved hardwoods, thorns, bones, and wire.

Use stiff wire or nails to make wire hooks. You can sharpen a flattened end to a point with a thin file and create a barb. Heating the hook to red-hot in a coal fire and submerging it in water may help temper it, but it can also turn it brittle. You don't need a hole to tie the wire hook; just flatten the shank. Another alternative style with wire hooks is to make a barb similar to traditional thorn and bone hooks.

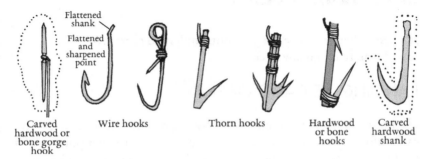

Carved hardwood or bone gorge hook

Wire hooks

Thorn hooks

Hardwood or bone hooks

Carved hardwood shank

LURES

Lures can be improvised with rope fibers, strips of cloth, feathers, plastic strips, thin wire, aluminum, tin cans, spent cartridges, tape, or foil. It's best to smear the lures with mashed liver (or blood) from the first fish caught to make them more enticing. Adding maggots and worms should also help.

Paracord

Feathers

Nylon cord

Plastic or rubber

FISHING LINE

Fishing line can be improvised with inner paracord strands, dental floss, and natural cordage.

FLOATS AND SINKERS

You may improvise floats by using softwood pieces, rolled birch bark, dry birch conks (polypore mushroom), plastic, or corks. Devise sinkers with rocks, bullets, shotgun shells, washers, hex nuts, lead molded in a spoon, or even donuts made of fired clay. Small net bags filled with rocks work great as portable anchors for gill nets, setlines, and trotlines.

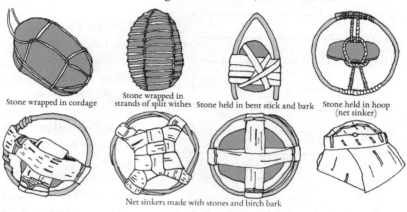

Stone wrapped in cordage   Stone wrapped in strands of split withes   Stone held in bent stick and bark   Stone held in hoop (net sinker)

Net sinkers made with stones and birch bark

HOOKS

The most appropriate hooks for *passive* fishing are circle hooks and trebles, as they keep fish trapped for a long time. For *active* fishing, use J hooks, jigs, and lures.

It's best to have stainless steel hooks, for they will last longer. Colored hooks are preferred because even if you don't have enough bait for all your hooks in the water, the color could attract fish.

In *passive* fishing, circle hooks tend to catch more fish than trebles, likely because they stand out less. In addition, they are also easier to unhook from the fish. Trebles almost guarantee that any fish hooked will stay hooked, and even if one of their points break, there are still two more. Trebles are superior to circle hooks for fast, predatory fish like trout and pike.

It's helpful to think about how many hooks you might be able to bait daily and consistently for passive fishing; this might be 25–50 hooks per one or two people. So, 60–100 hooks should be enough to replace damaged hooks for multiple months.

HOOK SIZES

See below for hook size recommendations based on species of fish:

Hook number	Hook length (inches)
13/0	4
12/0	3 - 3/4
11/0	3 - 1/2
10/0	3 - 1/4
9/0	3
8/0	2 - 3/4
7/0	2 - 1/2
6/0	2 - 1/4
5/0	2
4/0	1 - 7/8
3/0	1 - 3/4
2/0	1 - 5/8
1/0	1 - 1/2
1 - 1/2	1 - 3/8
1	1 - 1/4
2	1 - 1/8
4	15/16
6	13/16
8	11/16
10	9/16
12	7/16
14	11/32
16	9/32
18	7/32
20	5/32

Crappie/White Bass: Sizes #4–2/0 light wire hooks

Walleye/Sauger: Sizes #6–#1 light wire hooks

Yellow Perch: Sizes #8–#4 light wire hooks

Muskellunge/Pike: Sizes 1/0–6/0 forged steel hooks

Stream Trout: Sizes #10–#1 Aberdeen or baitholder hooks

Striped Bass: Sizes 1/0–6/0 forged steel hooks

Catfish: Sizes 1/0–7/0 forged steel hooks; #8–#1 light wire; 5/0–8/0 circle; #6–#2 treble

Note: hook sizes are determined by shank length, excluding the eye.

LURES

There are many types of effective lures. A jig is one of the most versatile and productive lures for fishing with a casting rod. Jigs are worked on the bottom, and they are well-suited for rocky lakes. Jigs can be used as an all-purpose hook for natural bait or rubber worms. There are also weedless jigs that can be used around weedbeds.

Plugs are another excellent type of lure. There are surface, wobbling, and diving plugs. Unfortunately, plugs are expensive and bulky, and they don't work well around weeds. When using wobbling plugs, it's generally better to go with smaller sizes unless you're fishing for large pike. Diving plugs are used in deeper water, and surface plugs work better at night than other lures. Plugs may be used occasionally in setlines if you don't have bait. On bright days, use plugs, spoons, and spinners.

Weedless spoons are the best lure for fishing around weedbeds and lily pads.

Use spoons in muddy water, on both dark and bright days, or when targeting pike. One clear advantage of spoons is that they are easier to cast into the wind than plugs. Spinners are good for use around weedbeds and muddy water.

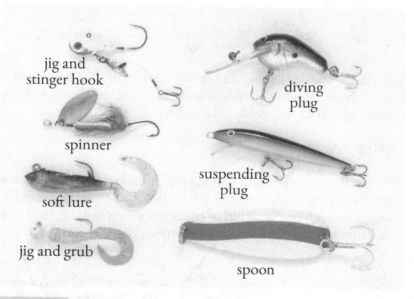

jig and stinger hook

spinner

soft lure

jig and grub

diving plug

suspending plug

spoon

BAIT

When fishing for subsistence, one of the first things you can do is check the stomach contents of the fish you catch. That will give you ideas of which bait is effective and locally available, and you may even be able to reuse some of it.

Below are some drawings and ideas for hooking bait to a casting rod. On setlines, you'll have to adapt those techniques to hold live bait more securely.

FISH PARTS

Fish parts make great bait because they are widely available if you catch fish consistently. The eyes, belly skin, tail fin, tough skin under the tongue, and intestines may be used as bait. You can use any part of the fish that has meat as long as it is tough and leathery enough so that it won't dissolve when submerged for long periods. If used for active fishing, the bait should have tough skin to withstand being casted. Note that using parts of game fish as bait is illegal in many places.

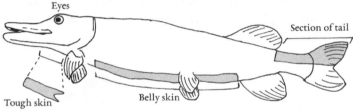

You may also use fine netting as a bag for chopped baits, similar to spawn sacks. Pieces or entrails of oily fish are best: the oil and blood escaping from the bait will attract scent feeders like catfish.

MINNOWS

Minnows can be caught with a casting net, minnow dip net, or minnow trap. To make a minnow trap, punch holes into a plastic bottle and cut it, as shown below. Place small bits of bait and a weight inside it, tie it to a rope for retrieval, and check every 30 minutes.

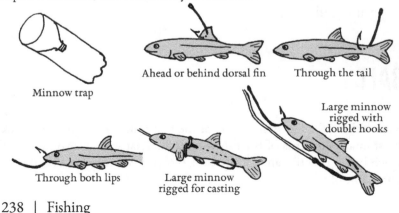

LEECHES

Leeches can be plentiful and easy to trap in some areas. Punch small holes in a metal or plastic container, fill it with fish discards, sink the container overnight, and pull it out the following day. Or just leave a fish carcass in clear, shallow

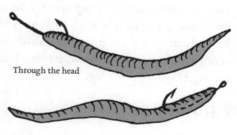

Through the head

water, and check it now and then to trap any leeches feeding on it. Keep leeches in a closed container filled with the water and place the container in the shade to keep them cool, and change their water daily.

OTHER BAITS

Various insects can be found inside rotting logs lying on the ground.

Catch grasshoppers early in the cool of the morning, for they are slower when the temperature is below 60°F (15°C). Sometimes, they climb the stalks of tall plants and spend the night there, and they can be picked in the early morning while they are still dormant.

Crickets are easier to catch than grasshoppers, and they can be found under rocks and logs.

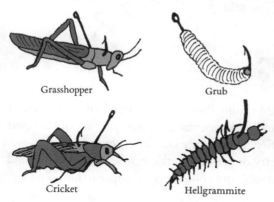

Grasshopper

Grub

Cricket

Hellgrammite

WORMS

Look for worms under logs and rocks in wooded areas, and dig for them in damp humus, especially after rain.

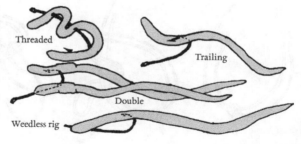

Threaded

Trailing

Double

Weedless rig

FROGS

Frogs are excellent bait. They often come out after rain, and can be caught with a hat or your hand. Keep them for a short time in the shade in a well-ventilated container. To fish with them, hook them through both lips or a leg.

CRAYFISH

Crayfish are more active at night, so that's the best time to catch them. Tie bits of fish organs to a string, and once the crayfish grabs them, quickly pull the crayfish to shore before it releases the bait. Or use a lift net or a minnow dip net to capture the crayfish.

During the day, look for them under rocks, and keep in mind that they move backward rather than headfirst. You may find them burrowed in the mud near shallow waters; watch for the telltale "chimney" breathing hole.

FISHING KNOTS

Monofilament and braided fishing lines require special knots because of their different structures and smooth surfaces. When tying any of the knots below, moisten the lines first, and test the knot after securing it.

Due to their simplicity or versatility, the first knots I recommend learning are the Palomar, double uni knot, dropper loop, and non-slip loop.

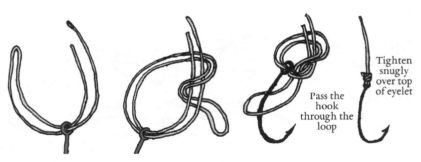

Pass the hook through the loop

Tighten snugly over top of eyelet

PALOMAR KNOT

The Palomar knot is an easy-to-tie and simple knot used for attaching lines to swivels, sinkers, and tackle. It's solid and reliable with both mono and braided lines, and it has a small profile. It has a breaking strength of 90%–95% and can be used with mono lines up to a 20 lb. test.

DOUBLE UNI KNOT

The double uni knot can join lines of similar or different strengths and types (e.g., mono-mono and mono-braid). When joining braided line to mono line, do eight wraps with the braided line and five turns with the mono line. This knot can be tied on a bight to increase its strength.

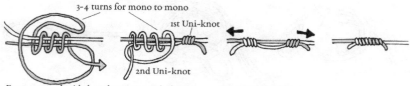

3-4 turns for mono to mono
1st Uni-knot
2nd Uni-knot
For mono to braided, make 5 turns with the mono and 8 with the braid

DROPPER LOOP KNOT

The dropper loop knot can create a loop right in the middle of the line, angling away from it. It is handy when working with multiple hooks. Avoid making the loop too long or it may twist.

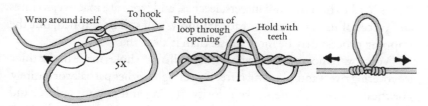

Wrap around itself
To hook
Feed bottom of loop through opening
Hold with teeth
5X

NON-SLIP LOOP KNOT

The non-slip loop knot creates a solid loop at the end of the line. This knot is useful for attaching a lure and allowing it to swim freely. Wrap the line about six times when using a weaker line and four times with a stronger line.

ALBRIGHT KNOT

The Albright knot is used to join lines of different types or diameters, such as when joining mono with braided. It is slimmer and stronger than the double uni knot.

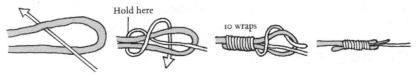

SURGEON'S END LOOP KNOT

The surgeon's end loop knot is a simple loop knot that can be used at the end of the line for interlocking two loops together.

ICE FISHING

In northern latitudes, fishing can be a significant challenge during the winter: fish are less active, and the cold makes fishing difficult and slow. Bait is hard to find because insects, leeches, and frogs are inactive, so lures and pieces of fish are used instead. Minnows can still be trapped, but the trapping process may be more hassle than it's worth.

Very low temperatures may present challenges: holes made in the thick ice covering rivers and lakes will refreeze overnight, either partially or entirely. For these reasons, gill nets take priority. Jigging and rigging setlines and tip-ups are generally reserved for late winter and early fall, when the ice is thinner and the weather warmer.

LOCATIONS AND BEHAVIOR

In winter, fish still need shelter, food, and oxygen, so those needs dictate where they are found. In bright, high-pressure conditions, fish tend to feed less than during overcast, low-pressure conditions.

Depth charts (bathymetric charts), like those found at webapp.navionics.com, help identify areas for fishing, but they are generally not available for remote areas.

Fish reside in deeper waters and move to shallow waters to feed. They use contours and structures such as drop-offs, saddles, and peninsulas as pathways to their feeding and resting locations. Try to locate their commuting route.

At 39°F (4°C), water is at its densest and sinks to the bottom. But in winter, colder water rises to the surface and, as a result, deeper water tends to be more comfortable for resting fish, as long as it is well oxygenated. This also means deeper waters tend to be the most productive for fishing.

The ideal lakes for ice fishing are large and have many distinctive features. Different features, structures, and depths fulfill specific needs for fish throughout the winter. For instance, shallow areas can be pretty active in early winter, and deep areas become more important later in the season. The perfect lake offers a mix of rocks, bars, points, and weeds.

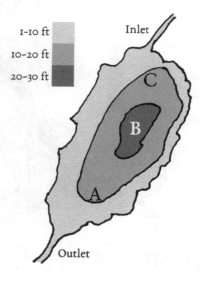

In lakes with a single basin like the example to the right, you can try areas A, B, and C. In this instance, the third area may be slightly better because the inlet brings oxygenated water.

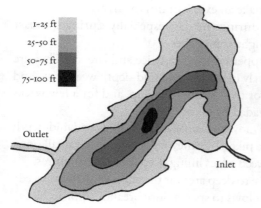

In lakes with a more punctuated basin, the prominent area in the center may be the most productive.

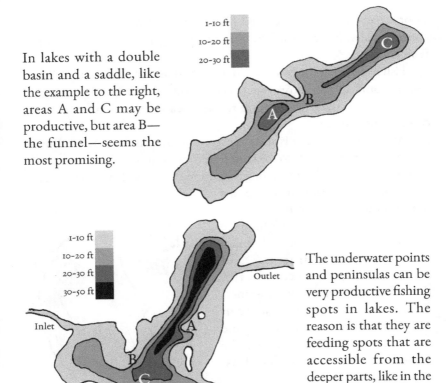

In lakes with a double basin and a saddle, like the example to the right, areas A and C may be productive, but area B—the funnel—seems the most promising.

The underwater points and peninsulas can be very productive fishing spots in lakes. The reason is that they are feeding spots that are accessible from the deeper parts, like in the lake to the left.

NORTHERN PIKE

Pikes are highly active throughout the winter months, and they can be quite large. Naturally, they make an excellent fish to target.

Pikes consistently bite during the day, especially during overcast conditions, and feed less as night approaches.

Most of their activity happens during early ice and late ice. They are often found feeding aggressively in shallow and mid-depth weedy bays and on bars and points. A week or two before freeze-up, and for a few weeks afterward, these areas are invaded by pikes.

During midwinter, pikes move to deeper areas. Shallow and mid-depth weeds may still contain some pikes, but they will primarily be small ones, and large fish will be along weed edges lining deep areas or structures.

In late winter, pikes move to deep areas at the edges of shallow, weedy spots. They go into these shallows to spawn once breakup approaches.

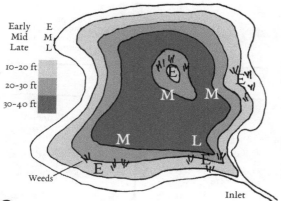

Early   E
Mid   M
Late   L

10-20 ft
20-30 ft
30-40 ft

Weeds

Inlet

JIGGING

In traditional jigging, the fishing line and jig are tied to a short stick, allowed to sink close to the bottom of the lake, lifted 1–1.5 ft. (30–45 cm), and allowed to sink again close to the bottom. After a pause, the motion is repeated. Use a thin jigging spoon, jigging plug, or bait when jigging. When using bait, slow down your movements even more to avoid spooking the fish.

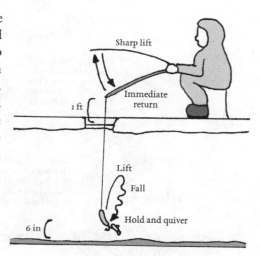

Sharp lift

Immediate return

1 ft

Lift

Fall

Hold and quiver

6 in

SETLINE

You can use J hooks in sizes 9/0–11/0 for large pike and lake trout, but trebles may be better for hooking and holding pike. Use sizes 1/0–3/0 trebles for larger pike and #4–#1 for smaller pike.

Use at least 40 lb. test braided line or heavier braided nylon twine for setlines.

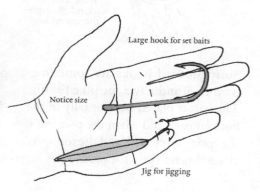

Large hook for set baits

Notice size

Jig for jigging

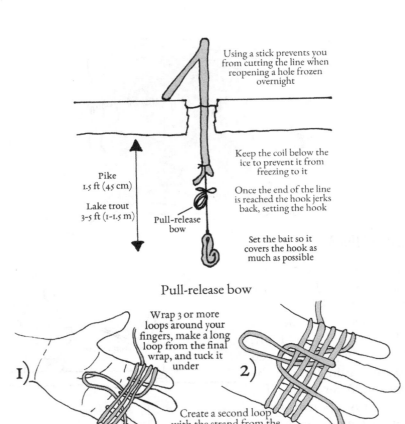

Using a stick prevents you from cutting the line when reopening a hole frozen overnight

Keep the coil below the ice to prevent it from freezing to it

Once the end of the line is reached the hook jerks back, setting the hook

Pike
1.5 ft (45 cm)

Lake trout
3–5 ft (1–1.5 m)

Pull-release bow

Set the bait so it covers the hook as much as possible

Pull-release bow

1) Wrap 3 or more loops around your fingers, make a long loop from the final wrap, and tuck it under

To hook

2) Create a second loop with the strand from the long loop, and pass it over the wraps and around the long loop

3) Pass a third loop, form the same strand, through the second loop

4) Tighten the third loop to create a snug bow

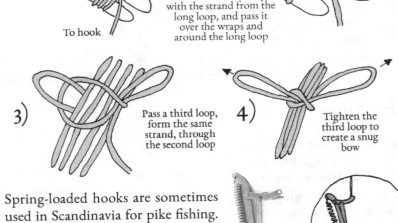

Spring-loaded hooks are sometimes used in Scandinavia for pike fishing. The bait is placed horizontally in the bottom part, and when the pike bites, the spring is released, and the top spike closes down to grip the pike.

Use bigger bait if you want to catch bigger fish; oily and smelly bait is best. Large pikes are usually caught in relatively shallow water, usually 5–10 ft. (1.5–3 m) deep. Use a 40 lb. test braided nylon line and a thin wire or a strong mono leader for your setlines and tip-ups. If there are huge fish around, you may need a stronger line. Make a coil of a few dozen feet (or even a hundred feet) of line and tie a bow; this will release the coil when it's pulled by a fish. Keep the coil below the ice to keep it from freezing.

Place the bait about 1 ft. (30 cm) underneath the ice. In deeper water, you may also place the bait about one foot off the bottom; nevertheless, try at least one set right under the ice.

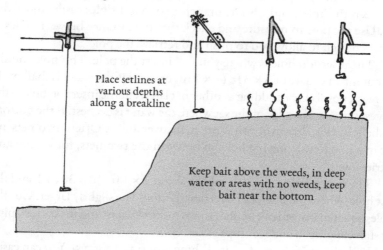

Place setlines at various depths along a breakline

Keep bait above the weeds, in deep water or areas with no weeds, keep bait near the bottom

GILL NETS UNDER ICE

In cold weather, monofilament nets are more challenging to repair and handle, but they are less visible, easier to clean, and more durable.

The traditional way of setting a gill net under the ice is to cut a series of holes in the ice, pass a pole and rope under them, tie the net to the rope, and pull the net below the ice. I'll explain first the method for setting a gill net under a lake and later, under a river. The technique I describe allows a single person to set the net, but I highly recommend having extra helping hands—things will be faster and easier, and you'll be able to skip some steps.

CUTTING HOLES

The first step is to choose a location. Follow the same principles as regular gill nets, but choose wisely because changing spots takes a lot of time and effort. It is also helpful to choose a place that allows you to extend the gill net in the future if you choose to add another one.

Ice chisels are much more portable than ice augers, and they are well-suited for setting a gill net because they can cut through very thick ice and make large holes. A skilled individual with a sharp chisel can make a 1.5 ft. (45 cm) diameter hole in 10 minutes in ice 2–3 ft. (60–90 cm) thick. When you're close to breaking through the ice, always use a wrist strap to avoid losing the chisel. You'll have to cut a series of holes about 10–12 ft. (3–3.5 m) apart.

Find a straight pole about 3 ft. (1 m) longer than the planned distance between the holes, and trim its branches so that it slides easily under the ice. Use the pole to measure and check that the distance between holes is short enough to allow you to push and retrieve the pole.

The insertion hole is where you will insert the pole. This hole should be cut into a square of 3 × 3 ft. (1 × 1 m) or more if the water is shallow. If there is a possibility of adding another net later, cut the insertion hole—the largest one—at the edge of the set where the water is deepest. If the bottom is shallow, this also gives you more maneuverability. Often, two nets are set in a line to use one big hole, in between the two nets, for setting and retrieving.

The intermediary holes should be about 1 × 1 ft (30 × 30 cm), and the last hole, where the line will be retrieved, should be slightly larger. Cut the holes squared instead of circular: this is more efficient and makes scooping or shoveling slush and ice chips easier.

Pack the scoop part of an ice fishing scoop and a screw. You can easily screw the plastic scoop to a stick in the field. In the winter, you'll use the scoop daily for fishing and collecting water.

Another very helpful tool is an aluminum avalanche shovel. You'll use the shovel to clear the snow when cutting holes in the ice and to remove the snow that accumulates with the wind.

If you are alone or you might take longer than one day to cut the connecting holes, cut one hole in the middle and measure the ice thickness. Then cut the rest of the holes 0.5 ft. (20 cm) short of breaking through. This way, you can finish the next day without having to cut through refrozen holes.

SETTING THE LINE

Tie a strong synthetic rope to the front end of the pole. Make sure the knot is secure but easy to untie underwater. If the ice is not too thick, you may be able to undo the knot easily; otherwise, you'll have to cut the ice a bit so that your hand can reach the rope. The rope should be longer than the length of the net, and if you are solo, it will have to be twice as long. Make sure the cord is not badly twisted or it may twist and tangle the net. Tie the rope's end to the net or to something secure to prevent it from falling under the ice.

Tie bright flagging tape near the back end of the pole to signal when the end is close; this helps you avoid pushing the pole too far and starting again from the beginning.

Find a sturdy Y-shaped stick that fits through the intermediate holes. You'll use it to move the pole under the ice. It's best if the forks of the *Y* are close together so that they can grip the pole with more friction. You'll also need a stick shaped like the number *7* that won't fall through when placed inside the intermediate holes.

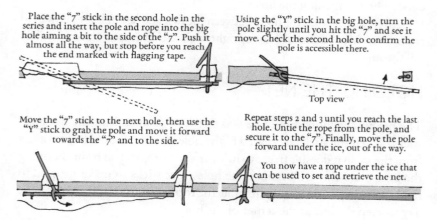

Place the "7" stick in the second hole in the series and insert the pole and rope into the big hole aiming a bit to the side of the "7". Push it almost all the way, but stop before you reach the end marked with flagging tape.

Using the "Y" stick in the big hole, turn the pole slightly until you hit the "7" and see it move. Check the second hole to confirm the pole is accessible there.

Top view

Move the "7" stick to the next hole, then use the "Y" stick to grab the pole and move it forward towards the "7" and to the side.

Repeat steps 2 and 3 until you reach the last hole. Untie the rope from the pole, and secure it to the "7". Finally, move the pole forward under the ice, out of the way.

You now have a rope under the ice that can be used to set and retrieve the net.

SETTING THE NET

It's best to peg a tarp in place at the edge of the insertion hole so that the gill net can be easily dragged in and out of the water and to prevent the gill net from catching the edges of the hole and tearing. The hole's walls should also be chiseled smooth to avoid any tangles.

If the rope under the ice is twisted, place a swivel to prevent it from twisting the gill net. If you are alone, stand near the big hole and pull the long rope from the last hole to pull the net under the ice. Guide the gill net as you pull, positioning the sinkers to one side and the floaters to the other and ensuring the gill net doesn't get caught by the ice—this is easier with two people.

To leave the gill net tied overnight and keep the top away from the ice, you'll need two sticks shaped like the number 7 that are two to three times as long as the ice thickness. Tie the end of the net to one stick before you pull the entire length under the ice so that you don't lose it. Once the net is below the ice, tie both ends to the two sticks and the anchors. Drop the anchors, ensuring that the sticks remain over the ice. The net should be set a bit loose like an entangling net.

An essential function of the lead line and end anchors is to keep the net and floats away from the ice. Keep in mind the ice grows downward throughout the winter, sometimes as many as a few inches overnight if it is extremely cold. Set the net far enough from the ice; otherwise, it could be rendered useless.

Never wrap the rope used to set and retrieve the nets into a coil, for it will twist. It's best to leave it on the snow where it won't be cut by your chisel when reopening the holes.

After the net is set, the holes between the first and last hole are allowed to freeze over. Mark them with an upright stick so that you don't accidentally fall through.

HOLDING THE NET

The net and anchors should be tied to the bottom ends of the 7-shaped sticks. When the sticks are placed in the hole, the line should be well away from the ice so it doesn't freeze to it. That also prevents you from chopping the lines every time you reopen the holes. Use sticks to make a tripod to hold the 7-shaped ones upright while the top layer of the hole freezes over. Try to keep the line at the center of the holes.

Always be careful to secure the rope that is under the ice because, if it goes underwater, you'll have to recut the whole series of holes and do the entire lengthy procedure again.

If the weather is around -5°F (-20°C) or colder, the holes may freeze overnight as thickly as the surrounding ice. You may slow this down by letting a thin top layer of ice develop over the hole and covering it with snow to insulate it from freezing further.

If you have plywood around, use it. Cut the plywood pieces a bit bigger than the holes. Then, cut them in half—so that you can place the two halves around the 7-shaped sticks—and cut a small opening for the sticks. Cover the plywood with a heap of snow to insulate the holes. The plywood also makes it easy to remove the snow when reopening the holes.

You can also use spruce boughs and a layer of snow on top to cover the holes, but keep the branches off the water; otherwise, they will freeze to it and you will dull your chisel trying to cut them out of the ice.

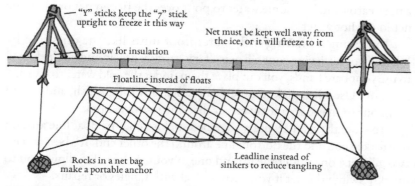

RIVER METHOD

Setting a net is a bit harder with a current under the ice. You'll have to cut the holes closer to each other and much wider. You'll also need a long pole with a hook at the end. Depending on the ice thickness, you can drop a weighted line and retrieve it using the hooked pole, or you can make a loop in the rope and use a long pole to position the looped end closer to the next hole and use the hooked pole to retrieve it.

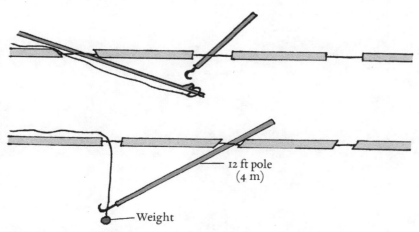

TIPS AND TROUBLESHOOTING

Having a tarp pegged at the edge of the hole makes it easier for you to pull the gill net out of the ice. In freezing weather, spread out the gill net as soon as it is out of the water, or it could freeze into a mess. Once it's extended for a minute or so, the water will freeze, and you'll be able to pull it without having the mesh freeze. If the gill net does freeze in a tangle, put it back underwater for a couple of minutes to thaw it. You can also light a fire nearby and boil some water to pour over the frozen net or place the net in the hot water.

I recommend having truly waterproof mitts like the ones sold by JokaSafe for retrieving your gill nets. If it is extremely cold and you're forced to use your bare hands, you can place them under the cold water to "warm" them up. Use a fish pick to quickly untangle any caught fish, and spread them out to freeze separately rather than into a single brick.

To store the gill net, use a Y-shaped stick to coil the float line around one forked end and the bottom line around the other end. It's best to have two gill nets: one under the ice and one in your shelter; this allows you to quickly switch the net if you need to deal with tangles or repairs.

TRAPPING

Check your local regulations! Many tools and techniques described in this chapter—and book—may be illegal in non-survival circumstances.

Trapping is passive, but there is a lot of work involved. Traps need to be constantly checked and adjusted for the changing weather conditions. A lot of experimentation needs to happen to find what works and what doesn't.

Trapping animals for food is different from trapping animals for fur, particularly if you don't have a motor vehicle. Your trapline will be short, so your catch will be much more limited. As with everything else, always think about calories in versus calories out.

Find natural bottlenecks or funnels along animal corridors, and set up your traps in those "ambush" areas. It may be good to add sticks or logs to reinforce the funnels.

To prevent animals from accessing your bait from behind the traps, incorporate a fence or barrier (backing) around them: use rocks, sticks, logs, debris, trees, or stumps. For clarity, the funnels and backing are not depicted in the relevant trap illustrations.

In survival, almost everyone recommends focusing on small animals. But for long-term survival, that is not the only way to go. Be strategic and target the animals that can give you the most calories for your effort. Those will often be medium and big animals, as well as rabbits and hares if they are in peak years.

There are many different traps shown in this section for thoroughness—but I don't have experience with all of them. I used countless sources to cross-reference and confirm that the information is as accurate as possible.

I included many illustrations of primitive traps and snares, but this isn't an endorsement. It's good to know how to make them as a complement or backup for modern traps. Do you think it's more effective to fish using primitive hooks and lines or modern fishing gear? The same is also valid for trapping and snaring techniques.

PRIMITIVE TRAPS

Primitive traps are not as easy to use or as effective as modern traps. They require time and effort, and they can be complicated and finicky to set up. Rain, wind, and weather often trigger or disrupt the functioning of the trap. And animals that are not your target species—such as rodents—can steal the bait or trigger the traps and leave you empty-handed.

Treat primitive traps as a backup or a last resort, but not as part of your main strategy. Having said that, primitive traps are truly sustainable, and if you stay in one spot for a long time and have the energy and effort, they could be worth the trouble.

For clarity, not all the illustrations of deadfall traps below have a hard bottom (rock or log), but having a solid bottom (anvil) is required to provide a hard surface for the deadfall to lethally "sandwich" the target.

A disadvantage of some of the traps shown below, such as the figure-4 and Paiute, is that stone slabs are not generally easy to find. The traps that work with a log deadfall may be more practical.

SMALL TRAPS

This section introduces various improvised traps for small animals. The Paiute, Arapuca, and hook traps are the most versatile and practical. For medium animals, or when stone slabs are not available, log deadfalls like those shown in the next section are the best option.

FIGURE-4 DEADFALL

The figure-4 deadfall is one of the most well-known traps, but its popularity is not due to its efficiency or ease of use. Paiute traps are usually better because they are faster to make, but they require cordage.

Fence the sides of the figure-4 trap. The upright stick can be driven into the ground for stability, but it must not be below the weight.

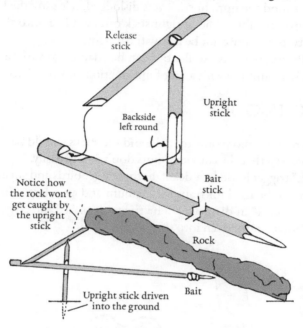

MODIFIED PAIUTE DEADFALL

The modified Paiute deadfall is very quick to make, and it can be set in a way that can be triggered very easily. A disadvantage is that it needs a short

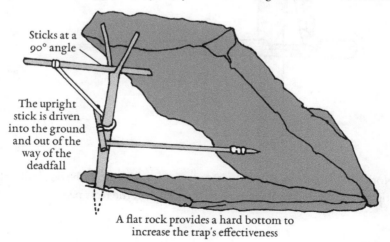

piece of cordage. The bait is placed on the horizontal baited stick, as in the figure-4 trap. Once the horizontal baited stick is disrupted, the tethered stick wrapped around the upright stick gets dislodged, releasing the lever stick that rests over the fork. The upright stick can be driven into the ground for stability, but it must not be below the weight.

The Paiute trigger is excellent; it can be adapted to various traps for small and large animals with a bit of imagination and creativity.

"SLICK" TRIGGER

This trap requires more time to make and the sticks should be carved out of hardwood so that the contact points don't round easily.

The "slick" trigger is used for deadfalls that target birds and small animals, but it can also be used for traps for medium and even large animals (the trigger must be 1″ in diameter). The trigger is placed directly under the deadfall, but it's not driven into the ground.

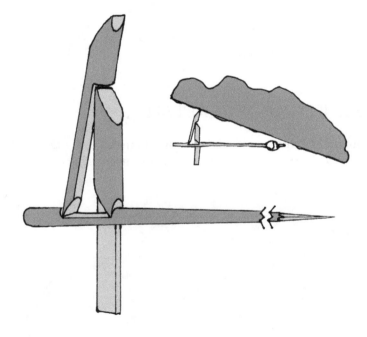

Notice how the animal could escape fast enough to avoid the deadfall if the trigger is activated by its mouth in the setup on the next page.

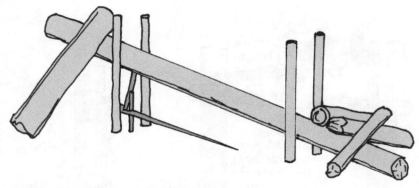

MCPHERSON DEADFALL

This trap (created by John McPherson) uses cordage and a "spring" stick. The trigger is baited at the top. As the animal moves the bait to the sides of the peg, the trigger and upright sticks get released. The main advantage of this trigger is that it can be set before the deadfall is positioned.

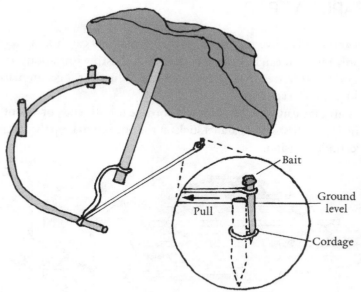

Bait

Ground level

Pull

Cordage

KOOLYOMKA TRAP

The Koolyomka, which originated in Siberia, was shown in the documentary *Happy People*. It is used for trapping martens and sables for fur, and its clever trigger can be adapted for deadfalls. When the bait stick is dislodged, the two upright trigger pieces collapse and get launched out of the way for the weight to fall on the animal.

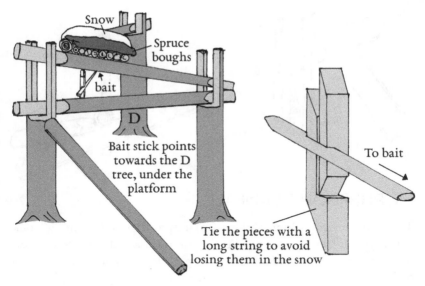

Snow

Spruce boughs

bait

D

Bait stick points towards the D tree, under the platform

To bait

Tie the pieces with a long string to avoid losing them in the snow

ARAPUCA TRAP

The arapuca is a live trap used by the Guaraní to catch small animals (mainly birds). It can be built very quickly and used with various triggers. It's good to tie a weight to the trap when catching stronger animals that could push the cage over.

This cage can be made with less cordage if both ends of a bent stick are tied to the first set of parallel sticks at the bottom to keep the rest of the sticks under tension.

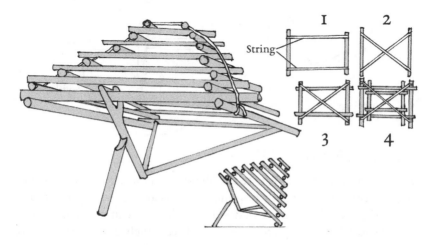

String

1

2

3

4

HOOK TRAPS

Seagulls, ducks, and geese swallow their food quickly; therefore, they can be caught with baited fishing hooks and gorge hooks. Use aquatic plants for bait, and tie the hooks securely to a weight or stake. As shown below, this trap can be easily modified to become a drowning trap. And it may also work with turtles (use hooks sized 4/0 or 3/0 and a wire leader).

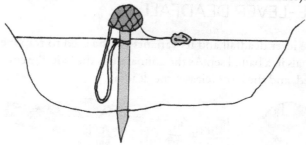

BIG TRAPS

Warning! These traps can be extremely dangerous and could crush your hands or feet—or worse. Be extremely cautious when setting up any primitive trap intended for medium to large animals.

KICKER DEADFALL

The kicker deadfall mechanism can be adapted for medium to large animals.

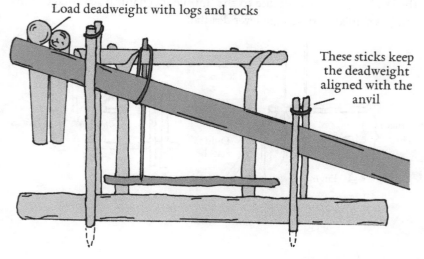

Load deadweight with logs and rocks

These sticks keep the deadweight aligned with the anvil

The tread trigger can be a bar, or a board made from sticks or bark laid over the tread bar. Once the tread bar is pressed down, the vertical stick tied to the deadweight is released. This trap can be built as a blind set on an animal trail or as a baited cubby set with a U-shaped enclosure to force the animal to step on the trigger.

SINGLE-LEVER DEADFALL

The single-lever deadfall and its variants can be used to trap medium to large animals in a baited set. As the animal pulls the bait, the cord and peg are released, and the lever releases the deadfall.

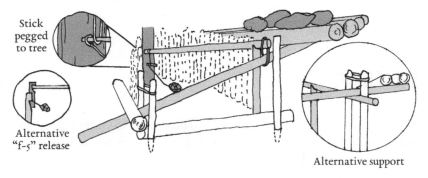

Stick pegged to tree

Alternative "f-5" release

Alternative support

DOUBLE-LEVER BEAR DEADFALL

The double-lever bear deadfall is used for large animals because it reduces the strain on the trigger due to the double mechanical advantage. This setup is similar to the single-lever deadfall.

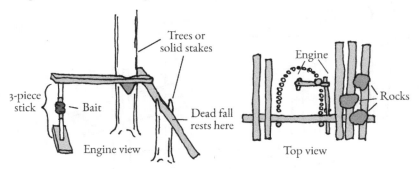

Trees or solid stakes

3-piece stick

Bait

Dead fall rests here

Engine view

Engine

Rocks

Top view

SAMSON POST DEADFALL

The samson post deadfall is used for medium to large animals. This trigger—and its multiple variations—is easy to make. The setup relies on skillfully balancing the support and trigger sticks. There must be a round "anvil" log underneath the trigger for the trap to work. The bait stick may be round or flattened as shown (thinner is better), and the upright stick should be rounded at both ends.

SPLIT-STICK TRIGGER

The split-stick trigger is a simple trigger that can be used for bear traps, path traps, and small deadfalls. Take into account that this trigger is not very sensitive.

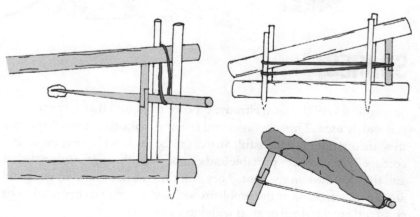

PIT TRAPS

Pit traps have been used worldwide to trap animals such as elk, caribou, bears, and wolves. For instance, the Lykov family used pit traps to trap animals in the taiga. Pit traps are very labor-intensive, and their location is critical for success.

Traditionally, these traps were often used along with fences or human-looking cairns and were set in natural funnels. Hunters would spook or drive animals such as caribou into the traps.

Pit traps are usually camouflaged with thin branches, moss, and debris. When trappers want to target predators, they place bait at the center. Spikes can be added to these traps to make them lethal. The pits are generally lined with logs cabin-style or stones to form an inner wall. In many places of the boreal forest, the ground is inadequate for these traps due to the Canadian Shield rock.

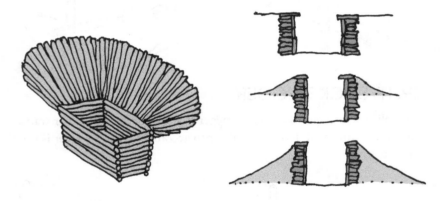

SNARES

Snares are one of the most effective types of traps, and that's why they are still widely used. They are easier and faster to make than most traps, and they are often more successful. Snares can be made with wire, cable, and cordage. They are very portable and can be partially built inside a shelter and then finished on the spot. They don't need bait or lures to work and are easy to set. Some of the problems with snares are that they need to be constantly maintained in areas with lots of snowfall.

Primitive snares made with cordage often lift the animal as a way to prevent it from biting through the snare. These primitive snares need more skill and time to be set properly.

Wire and cable snares are more straightforward to set. Unfortunately, modern snares meant for animals larger than a rabbit can only be used once or a few times (depending on the animal) before the cable gets too mangled for use.

The snares should be placed along animal trails or runs; funnels may be added to encourage the animals to go through the snares.

Snaring is a numbers game. You need lots of snares, and one catch per 10 snares is considered a very good day. Check your snares daily for bigger animals or if there are scavengers around. For small animals, such as hares, you could check the snares every other day, as long as other predators aren't checking them before you. Lifting poles may deter other predators from hunting your trapline.

LOCATION OF SNARES

Some locations generally work better for different animals, so for:
- coyote, fox, and badger, set snares on unused trails, ditches, fence lines, ridgelines, and clearings' edges;
- bobcat and lynx, snares are best set at bases of cliffs, ridges, and passes (set traps near the cover of bushes and trees);
- raccoon, opossum, and skunk, set snares on stream beds and banks, as well as on trails along stream beds, ponds, lakes, and streams;
- beaver and muskrat, set snares around their food caches under the ice; and
- rabbits and hares, set snares along runs and trails in thick willow stands.

Generally, use an enclosure set (cubby) for bobcat, raccoon, marten, fisher, opossum, and skunk, and use a trail set for coyote, fox, mink, and rabbit. This depends on multiple variables and it may be worth it to experiment with an enclosure set instead of a trail set and vice versa. For instance, coyote and fox may be snared with a cubby set.

CORDAGE SNARES FOR SMALL ANIMALS

TIPS FOR PRIMITIVE HARE SNARES

Hares must be lifted off the ground, or they might bite through the snare's cordage. Always attach the noose straight to the lifting line because the trigger stick may break.

Heavy mono and braided fishing lines work well for cordage snares for rabbit-sized animals, and they work better than cordage.

Set traps slightly inside the forest—not on a transition zone to a clearing, but inside, where the animal is less cautious. The best place for snares is in well-used runs where there are natural funnels that can be built up. It's best if the hares are moving fast through the run. If the run contains droppings and not a series of prints, they are not moving fast enough. Place the snares right in the middle of the small prints in the snow, not the big ones. Build double-sided funnels using unattractive branches (e.g., dead spruce twigs) to prevent the hares from slowing down to eat. Try setting the snare in the middle of the spot where they land, not where they jump.

The snare's opening should be about the size of a closed fist and about three to four fingers off the ground. Ensure there is an "ear dropper," or a stick above the snare to prevent the hare from pushing the cord away with its ears. If the snare is too small, the hare will twist free or avoid it entirely. Use sticks split at one end, and grass, pine needles, hair, or tiny twigs to hold the cordage in place.

If there are recent signs of hares, but there aren't any apparent runs, place bait on both sides of the snare. Use two or three of the smallest and most tender shoots of birch or tamarack for bait. Trembling aspen, birch, and balsam poplar buds also work.  Making a fence and leaving a snared opening is also a good strategy. Another option is to build an enclosure set (cubby) and place the bait inside.

Build most of the trap parts inside your shelter where it's more comfortable. Avoid peeling the bark off the trap sticks to make them less visible.

The state of the ground, snow cover, and the availability of saplings will dictate which type of triggers and lifting rigs will work for each circumstance. The Dené toggle, Paiute trigger, and release-knot sets are more practical in deep snow and frozen ground. And the pencil and "L7" will work better in unfrozen areas and deep soil. If you have a small diameter auger, you may be able to craft numerous pipe snares and set them just like a modern snare.

LIFTING POLE SNARES

Lifting pole snares are generally better than spring poles because they won't lose any lifting power if they are set for too long. And they can also be rigged even if there are no suitable saplings around.

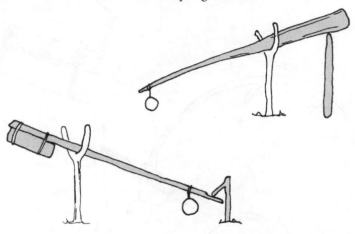

SPRING POLE SNARES

The spring pole snare is similar to a lifting pole snare but uses a bent sapling. Use tall, solid, young trees for spring pole traps; otherwise, the sapling may quickly lose its springiness. Spring poles tend to be less effective in winter when trees become less flexible.

"L7" ROLLING SNARE TRIGGER

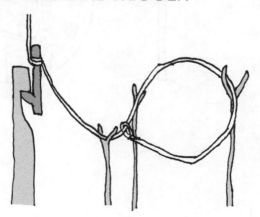

DENÉ TOGGLE SNARES

The Dené toggle snare can be set two different ways: with a horizontal anchor stick or with a vertical anchor. This type of snare works for small animals like hares and marmots.

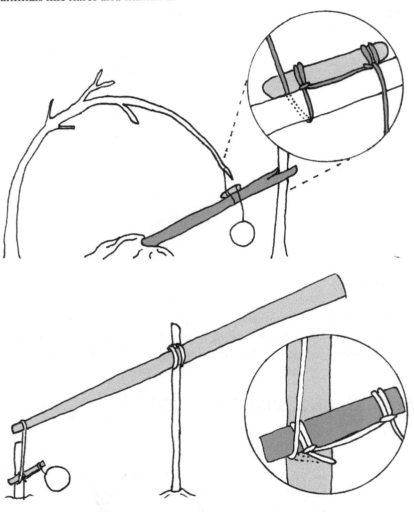

RELEASE-KNOT SNARE

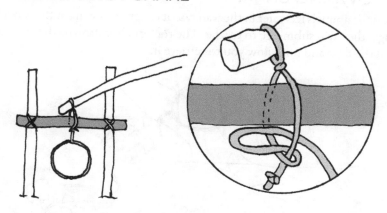

PAIUTE-TRIGGER SNARE

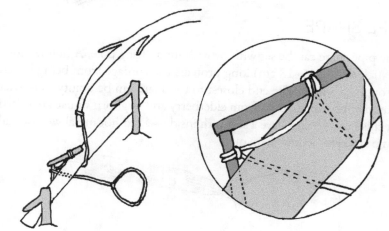

PENCIL SNARE

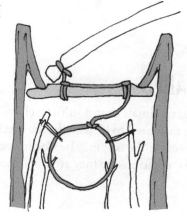

DROWNING SNARE

Aquatic animals feel safer in the water, so if caught in a snare at the water's edge, they will submerge to escape. The rock anchor drowns the animal, and the float and line allow you to retrieve it.

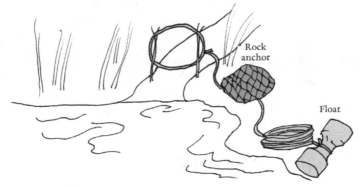

PIPE SNARE

The pipe snare can be set with or without a lifting pole. A hollow bone or stick 6"–7" (15–18 cm) long protects the cordage from being bitten through by a hare. The end closest to the snare can be pointy to restrict movement further. Sticks from elderberry and staghorn sumac are suited for this because they have a soft pith inside—a red-hot metal wire or nail can be used to hollow them out.

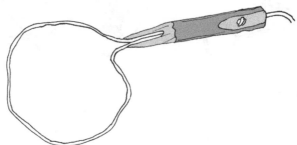

BAITED SNARES

In order to attract animals that don't travel on obvious trails, such as predators, snares may need to be baited. The need for bait requires more effort and time because the bait may be stolen by other animals, so snares must be checked daily to ensure they are still baited.

BAITED TWITCH-UP SNARE

The baited twitch-up snare needs to be fenced and covered (cubby set) so that the animal is forced to get the bait through the snare. There are many variations of this twitch-up. For instance, the Paiute and kicker deadfall triggers can be adapted for this snare.

MODIFIED MOJAVE SCISSOR SNARE

This trap is like a primitive body grip trap for rabbits and other rodents. Often, it has the advantage of killing quickly. If the trigger is not working smoothly, instead of using a single 7-shaped stake, use two 7-shaped stakes with a horizontal stick as in the original Mojave trap.

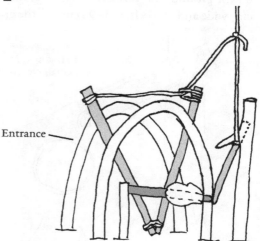

Entrance —

CORDAGE SNARES FOR LARGE ANIMALS

Use a fixed snare or a drag snare for large animals, depending on the likelihood of the snare to strangulate the animal effectively versus catching the animal by the wrong place, such as a limb or antler. Approaching a trapped, large animal that is still alive is extremely dangerous. If you can ensure your target animal won't break the snare or tether, use a fixed snare.

Drag snares are sometimes used because an animal is less likely to fight as hard to get rid of the snare if it perceives that it has a chance to escape. This principle is even more important with large and powerful animals.

This doesn't mean the snare shouldn't aim to stop the supply of oxygen to the animal's brain. It means that in case you fail to lethally snare the animal, it won't destroy the tether and anchor. Set the drag either by lodging it or tying it in a way that it strangulates the animal effectively, but allows the drag to break free with strong enough effort.

A drag snare should make it very difficult for the animal to make any progress—it should tangle up easily and leave behind an obvious trail. The drag pole should be made with solid greenwood of appropriate diameter for the animal. And it should be scored, or the base of the branches should be left on so the rope won't slip out.

ANTLERED ANIMAL DRAG SNARE

Moose snares should be about 3–6 ft. (1–2 m) in diameter and 3 ft. (1 m) off the ground, and for deer or caribou, they should be about 2.5 ft. (70 cm) wide and 1.5–3 ft. (45–90 cm) off the ground.

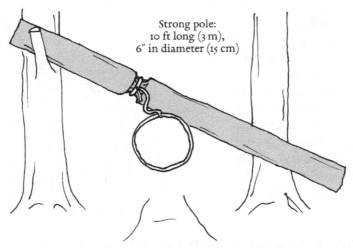

Strong pole:
10 ft long (3 m),
6" in diameter (15 cm)

DRAG AND TETHER SNARES FOR BEARS

An appropriate drag slows down the bear and makes it easier to track and kill. The noose should be about 2 ft. (60 cm) wide and 1.5–3 ft. (45–90 cm) off the ground.

In the illustration on the next page of the snare labeled "C," once the bear pulls hard on the snare, the heavy log is lifted slightly and the pole that supports the log against the tree falls. The bear is then pulled upward by the falling log.

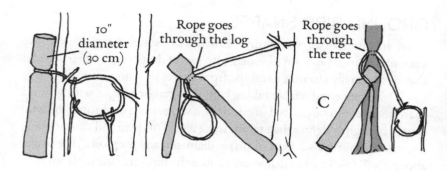

APACHE FOOT DRAG SNARE

Dig a hole 12″ deep and as wide as the animal trail. Place a sheet of thick birch bark with an *X* cut over the hole. Tie the snare to a heavy log and place it over the bark. Then, conceal the trap with leaves and soil. The bark will help keep the snare around the animal's foot as it closes up. As shown below, the birch bark can also be substituted with a "bull's-eye" of green twigs pointing toward the center. Camouflage the snare with loose debris. The animal will tire itself out and leave a trail behind as with other drag snares. This trap is not ideal because it traps the animal by its foot. It's better to use a different type of snare.

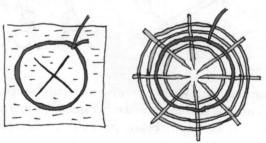

BIRD SNARES

GROUSE NOOSING POLE

Grouse can be snared with a pole when they are on a tree branch. The noose can be made with spruce roots and has to be firmly tied to the end of a long, lightweight stick. Mono line 50–80 lb. test also works. Once the noose is placed around the grouse's neck, the pole is swiftly pulled down to close up the noose, and the flapping grouse can be lowered to the ground. Sometimes this snare works because some grouse feel safer when they are on a tree and won't fly away while you attempt to snare them.

GROUND BIRD SNARES

There are multiple ways of snaring birds; to start, simply hang snares above a popular branch (look for a branch with lots of droppings). Keep in mind that birds usually attempt to escape from snares by flying forward.

If birds are comfortable taking bait, they can be caught with ground snares. Snares can be tied to lashed sticks, a stake, or an enclosure; the wire should be slightly lighter than rabbit snare wire. For quail and similar birds, use snares about 1.5"–2.5" (4–6 cm) in diameter, and for grouse, use snares about 2"–3" (5–8 cm) in diameter. To lure the birds in, bait is placed near the snares as well as in the center of the snared enclosure. Marginally edible berries or sand can be used as bait; check the bird's stomach contents for ideas.

Snares can also be set at the entrance of a pen with young birch twigs as bait. For waterfowl, set them around islands.

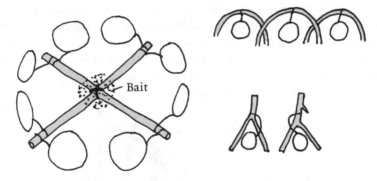

If you are working with weak, primitive materials—such as roots and fibers—when making bird snares and other snares for very small animals, make the noose knot as shown below. Notice that a short strand is added to the main strand for strength.

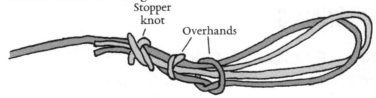

LINE "SNARE"

Thread six or seven berries onto a thin but strong line 5 ft. (1.5 m) in length, and tie it to a stake. The bird cannot escape once it has swallowed most of the bait.

ANISHINAABE BIRD SNARE

A neat thing about the Anishinaabe bird snare is that it can be effective with or without bait because a tall stick is a natural place for birds to land. The landing stick can be baited (as shown) or the bait can be place on the upright stick. It helps to carve a small groove for the cord on the upright stick so that there is more contact and the landing stick stays in place. Use a heavy log or rock as a weight instead of using a spring pole because counterweights don't freeze up or lose their spring over time.

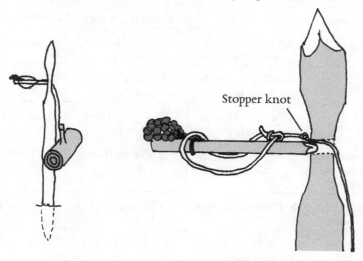

Stopper knot

WIRE AND CABLE SNARES

Always tie the snare to an anchor or heavy drag that can hold the largest animal that could get into it. A lifting pole can help close up the cable snare for large animals such as deer.

For predators and other animals that travel in less predictable ways, use bait and make an enclosure or funnel for the snares.

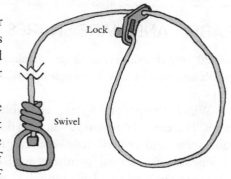

Lock

Swivel

For medium and large animals, cable snares are not ideal in the long term because they will only work a couple of times. If you can, cache a lot of cable snares beforehand, as having a large supply is pretty valuable. In terms of traps in general for large animals, snares are the only portable option.

In a long-term survival context, two good targets for modern cable snares are rabbits and hares because their snares can be reused a couple of times. In addition, rabbit snares are lightweight enough that carrying dozens is not impractical.

SNARE SIZES

Animal	Noose size	Ground clearance	Cable diameter
Squirrel	2.5″–3″ (6–8 cm); four fingers	0.5″–1.5″ (2–4 cm); two fingers	1/32″–1/16″
Rabbit	4″–6″ (10–15 cm); one fist	1.5″–4″ (4–10 cm); four fingers	3/64″–1/16″
Hare	4″–6″ (10–15 cm); one fist	3″–4″ (8–10 cm); one fist	3/64″–1/16″
Groundhog, opossum, skunk	5″–6″ (13–15 cm); eight fingers	2″ (5 cm); three fingers	1/16″
Fox, bobcat, wolverine	8″ (20 cm); two fists	8″ (20 cm); two fists	1/16″–3/32″
Raccoon	6″–8″ (15–20 cm); fist with the thumb up	2″–4″ (5–10 cm); one fist	5/64″–3/32″
Coyote	10″–12″ (25–30 cm)	10″–12″ (25–30 cm)	3/32″
Wild hog, wolf	18″ (45 cm)	10″–12″ (25–30 cm)	3/32″–1/8″
Deer	16″ (40 cm)	15″–20″ (38–50 cm)	3/92″–1/8″

RABBIT AND HARE SNARES

Use 20 gauge (stronger) or 22 gauge stainless-steel snare wire for single-use rabbit and hare snares. Fishing leader wire at 60 lb. test or stronger may also work.

Wire is cheaper and lighter, but cable snares can be reused multiple times. Therefore, I recommend carrying dozens of 3/64″ or 1/16″ diameter cable snares and a roll of snare wire. The 1/16″ snares are generally better because they can be used for other animals and will kink less. Nevertheless, cable snares will only work for a couple of catches of medium-sized animals before the wire becomes too mangled. So, if you want something that will last for years, you'll need commercially made 110 conibear traps (described later).

Don't just set the snare in the first set of tracks you see. Follow the tracks to find where they join a more well-used run. Place the snare right in the middle of a small print in the snow; don't set it between prints or in the large ones.

An effective technique for snaring hares is to cut a 5 ft. (1.5 m) section from the top of a small jack pine or spruce and place it across a runway to quickly make a fence. Cut the branches off from the lower portion of the tree section—the one right over the runway—to create an opening for the snare. Use sticks and branches to improve, reinforce, and shape the fence or funnel. Keep in mind that the hare may come from either side. Put sticks below and around the snare to encourage the hare to lift and pass its head through. Use tiny Y-shaped twigs or sticks with an end split to hold the snare in place. That will also help keep the snare in position despite wind, rain, and snow. When setting a snare, avoid disturbing the hares' runs; otherwise, they may take alternative paths. Use flagging tape to mark your traps.

A practical approach is to attach your snares to strong, green sticks at camp and carry a bundle of them to your trapline. Just place the sticks in a place where they will snag easily. Instead of wire, I use metal cable clamps and wood screws as a lightweight and reusable way of attaching cable snares to the anchors or drag sticks.

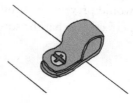

SNOWSHOE HARES

In the boreal forest, hare populations fluctuate in cycles of about 10 years. The peak population estimates are about five hares per acre (1300 hares/km²) and the lowest population estimates are one or two hares per 250 acres (1–2 hares/km²). Hares are much more numerous in the summer and decline by about 70%–90% through the winter.

In abundant years, snares can compete with net fishing and hunting big animals in terms of energy return, but don't plan on relying on hares unless the population is currently high. You may have to set up 100 snares or more to catch a hare a day in lean times. In addition, hares are extremely lean, so protein poisoning is an important consideration (see "Health" chapter).

Hares prefer bushy habitats that include trembling aspens, small conifers, conifer marshes, burned areas, alder marshes, and young jack pine areas. They usually avoid mature forests.

Hares avoid movement when there's rain, wind, or clear nights. Warm, calm, overcast nights are good for snaring. Hares can be trapped year-round, but late spring and late fall (after freeze-up) are the best times, and they are generally hunted in late spring. Hares are abundant and active in the fall, and the shallow snow cover makes it easy to spot their runs. In midwinter, hares become less active and their numbers decrease, so they are harder to snare.

SQUIRREL POLE

One way to trap squirrels is to lean snare poles against the trees where they hang out, but this type of trap won't produce much food unless the squirrels are plentiful. Try using pinecone seeds or spruce twigs for bait if the squirrels aren't approaching the pole.

Use 22 gauge wire made into a 2.5″–3″ (6–7.5 cm) loop—or smaller for small squirrels—and place the loops 0.5″ (1.2 cm) above the pole. Once snared, the squirrel must not touch the ground or it could stay alive and break the snare. If the pole's angle is too steep, they might grab the pole and remain alive. If the pole is too close to the ground, predators may steal the squirrels. Set the loops far enough apart so that they don't tangle, which would prevent the squirrel from dying. And make sure the loops line up perfectly so that the squirrel won't avoid them.

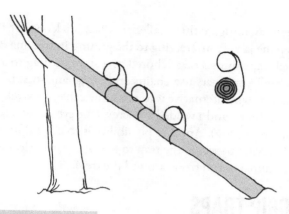

STEEL TRAPS

Steel traps are relatively simple to set, and they can be very effective. Unfortunately, traps for medium-sized animals can be heavy, bulky, or both, so you may need to make tough choices and compromises.

Contrary to popular opinion, avoid steel traps for small animals because trapping small animals for food is a numbers game. It's best to have dozens of cable snares and extra snare wire for hundreds of snares than only a few steel traps.

For long-term survival, the targets of your steel traps should be medium-sized animals. Large traps are not portable, so they are not an option. Medium-sized traps can potentially give you a worthwhile energy return, even if you don't have too many. Overall, they are the best compromise.

If bulk and weight are not an issue, bring a multitude of steel traps and cable snares for small, medium, and large animals. Cable snares may be more effective and practical than steel traps for medium animals, but the problem is they can't be reused repeatedly.

For steel traps, you also need to consider additional items to carry—like stakes, anchors, and cables—to prevent losing the traps, or as part of drowning sets. That is one of the reasons why a body grip trap (conibear) would be a better option for long-term survival. Because body grip traps are very likely to kill medium animals once triggered, they have huge advantages over leg hold traps. For this context, body grip traps are generally better than leghold traps, and they are more respectful and simpler.

One important thing to consider with steel traps is that the triggers may freeze in winter if they are set close to the ground or near the water. Waxing the triggers may mitigate this challenge. Place sticks under the bottom jaws to keep the jaws from freezing to the ground in freezing conditions.

All steel traps should be anchored to a stake or drag to avoid losing them. Generally, trappers use chains and metal anchors, but those are heavy. A lightweight alternative is to use some cable, a swivel, a screw pin shackle or carabiner, and a welded eye screw (the eye screw can be screwed to a tree or a heavy log). Another possibility is to use a doubled piece of strong bailing wire to secure the trap to a drag or a tree (loose enough to allow a live animal to run freely around the tree).

BODY GRIP TRAPS

The body grip trap or conibear is like a giant vertical two-way rat trap. Unfortunately, conibears don't always kill, hence the name *body grip*. It works by having two parallel metal squares close up to trap the animal once the trigger releases the tension springs. Conibears come in various sizes, but the most popular are 110, 220, and 330. The 110 is used for squirrel, rabbit, muskrat, mink, and similar-sized animals. Placing bait in a rag tied to the 110 trigger works well with squirrels. The 220 is used for catching raccoon, goose, skunk, small beaver, badger, muskrat, fisher, marten, nutria, opossum, otter, lynx, and other similar-sized animals. And the 330 is used for beaver and wolverine.

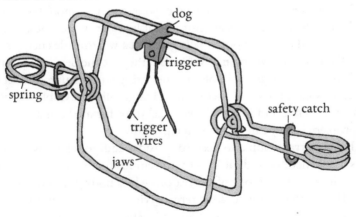

The only body grip traps that are worth carrying or caching for long-term survival are double spring 220s and 280s. But they are big and heavy. Most people consider 110 conibears as the must-have survival trap. But if you're carrying the traps and don't require them to work indefinitely, you're better off pound for pound with 1/16" or 3/64" cable snares instead. The 280 conibear can trap beaver, otter, lynx, bobcat, and raccoon, but it weighs 3.3 lb. (1.5 kg) and needs to be set with a rope to compress the springs. The 220 conibear is lighter, weighing 2.2 lb. (1 kg), and some people can set them without tools.

Popular conibear sizes			
110	120	220	330
Muskrat, weasel, squirrel	Muskrat, mink, marten, skunk	Muskrat, marten, skunk, fisher, raccoon, otter, beaver, lynx	Otter, beaver, lynx, wolverine

Often the wire trigger is placed at the top and set so that the upside-down *Y* will brush against the head or shoulders of the animal. But the trigger wires shouldn't be too far apart, or the trap will close upon the animal's stomach instead.

New conibear traps and cable snares should be treated to prevent rust, deodorize them, and add natural odors.

First, boil the traps and snares in one tablespoon of wood ash per gallon of water for 15 to 30 minutes, and then rinse the traps in plain boiled water to remove their grease and a bit of their odor. For snares, the boiling and dyeing can be accomplished at once.

To dye the traps, boil them with tree bark, moss, spruce needles, and leaves. Dyeing darkens the traps and masks their scent. Commercial dye adds corrosion protection as well. Traps can also be spray painted, but that is not as effective as dyeing.

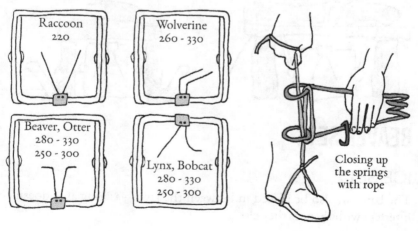

Raccoon 220

Wolverine 260 - 330

Beaver, Otter 280 - 330 250 - 300

Lynx, Bobcat 280 - 330 250 - 300

Closing up the springs with rope

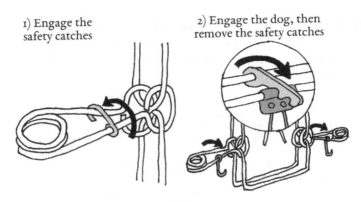

1) Engage the safety catches

2) Engage the dog, then remove the safety catches

GENERAL CONIBEAR SETS

Conibears work well in cubby sets; these sets can be made by piling up rocks, sticks, or brush to form walls and a roof.

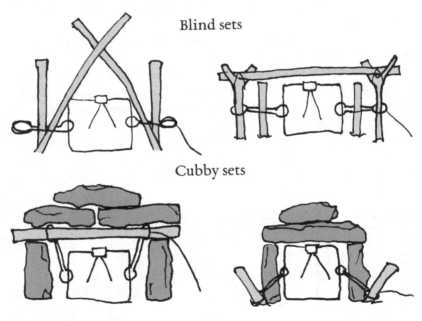

Blind sets

Cubby sets

BEAVER SETS

ICE SET

The bait can also be placed in between the jaws—as long as it doesn't interfere with them as they close.

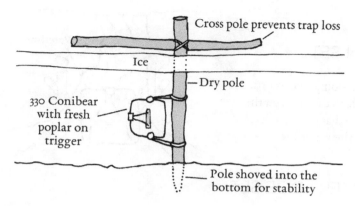

Cross pole prevents trap loss

Ice

— Dry pole

330 Conibear with fresh poplar on trigger

Pole shoved into the bottom for stability

DAM SET

Beavers can be trapped using a dam set. Open a hole in the upper side of the dam about 18"–24" (46–60 cm) wide and 2–3 ft. (60–90 cm) below the water level; this should be done in the morning. If the trap is set right away, the water level may drop too low, rendering it ineffective, or floating debris may trigger it. Wait and set the trap in the evening when the beavers are more active.

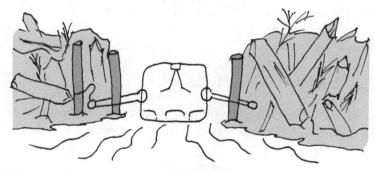

Stake and anchor the conibear 12"–18" (30–45 cm) in front of and on the dam's upstream side. Beavers are very perceptive to the sound of running water, so they will attempt to repair the dam. Make a funnel with debris to channel the beaver toward the trap. Set the trigger in the least sensitive notch to prevent branches from tripping it. Move the trigger a bit to the side for the same reason and to avoid catching smaller animals.

Alternatively, if a beaver path is on top of the dam, the trap can be placed there (camouflaged with grass, sticks, and leaves) instead of breaking the dam.

RUN SET

When doing a beaver run set like to the right, set the trap so that the top is level with the waterline.

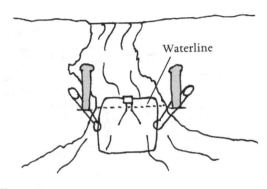

WATER EDGE SET

For a water edge set, submerge the trap not more than halfway. Use grass and twigs to conceal the spring, but leave the jaws clear. Try to place the trap where beavers are coming out instead of into the water—they may be carrying branches that can trigger the trap.

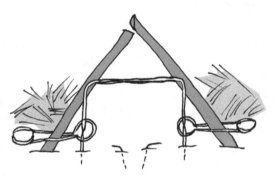

LODGE AND BANK HOLE SET

Look for bank holes, dens, and freshly chewed twigs. Set the trigger at the top if the hole is above the waterline or at the bottom if it is underwater.

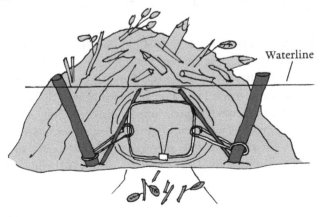

CANAL SET

The canal set is very effective. Improvise or use wire to secure the pole to the anchor stakes in the banks. The stick should touch the water surface so that the beaver dives under it. If the canal is wider than 16″–18″ (40–45 cm), place vertical sticks to funnel in the beaver. Bend the trigger as shown to avoid spooking the beaver: the trigger can be at the top or the bottom.

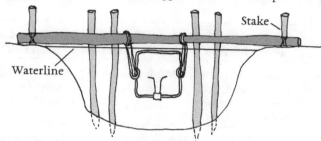

RAT TRAPS

Some survivalists recommend trapping squirrels and mice with rat traps because they are lightweight, effective, and cheap. Generally, mice are not worth trapping unless they are a nuisance inside your shelter. They offer little nutrition and may carry hantavirus in temperate regions. But squirrels might make a good snack if abundant in your area. For this reason, having one or two metal rat traps might be a good idea. Don't get regular wooden rat traps because those don't last under field conditions (they split, and the staples come out). Make sure to secure rat traps to an anchor like any other trap.

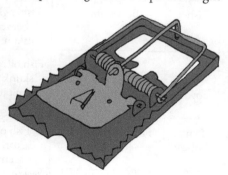

TRAP LURES

With traps that rely on bait and lures, it's essential to keep the prevailing wind direction in mind. Ideally, the wind should carry the scent toward the trap entrance.

Fish oil is a component of many lures used for trapping, and it can also be used alone. Fish oil works well with raccoons, mink, skunks, and foxes.

To make fish oil in the summer, cut a fatty fish into chunks and place them in a glass jar. Then add water to cover the pieces. Leave the lid loose enough so that gases can escape but not so loose that flies get in. Keep the jar in full sun. After several weeks, a layer of oil will rise to the top. Pour the oil into a container, and return the jar where it was to produce more lure. Use about 20 drops of oil per set.

Animal	Bait	Scent	Visual
Beaver	Green aspen, willow, birch	Beaver castor, or beaver oil glands	Partially peeled sticks behind the trap
Muskrat	Cattail or lily pad roots, sweet flag, bulrush, wapato, or other marsh plants	Muskrat musk glands	Floating objects, the sight of bait, light from a hole in the ice
Mink	Fresh fish, fresh muskrat, or beaver flesh	Fish oil, mink gland scent, beaver castor, muskrat musk scent	Hanging wing, dark hole
Otter	Fresh fish	Fish oil, otter gland scent	Whole fish
Marten	Squirrel, rabbit, and beaver flesh	Marten glands, beaver castor	Dark hole
Fisher	Beaver meat	Fisher gland scent, beaver castor, muskrat musk scent	Dark hole
Fox, wolf, coyote	Beaver meat (spoiled or fresh), entrails	Fish oil, gland lures, skunk oil, urine from target animal	Unusual but natural features (e.g., dirt holes, a clump of grass)
Lynx, bobcat	Fish, beaver meat, rabbit	Fish oil, beaver castor, and other scent glands	Wing or feather moving with the wind; dark cubby

Modified from *Saskatchewan Trappers Training Manual*

RABBIT-SKIN BLANKET

This section is mostly based on *desk* research, so you'll have to adapt these rough directions greatly to make them work.

Rabbit and hare skins rip easily, so they are traditionally turned into "rabbit cord" in order to utilize them for insulation. It's a good idea to harvest the rabbits and hares in late fall or winter when their furs are at their prime.

For skinning, it helps to drive two nails into a tree, and then hang the rabbit upside down by poking the nails between the Achilles tendon and the bone of each leg. Use gloves to avoid tularemia. Make a slit from the hind foot down the leg, past the genitals, and up the other leg. And cut around the upper part of each foot. Gently peel the skin toward the head to "unglove" the rabbit. Be careful to keep the pelt intact.

Keep the pelts or strips of fur frozen or in a cool, damp place until 60 to 70 skins are collected.

The rabbit-skin cordage should be made before the skins dry. However, dried skins can also be dampened and then cut into strips.

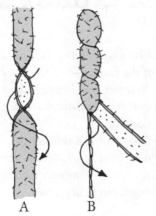

The strips are cut off in a continuous spiral starting at the eyehole if possible

Raw skin cord is traditionally cut starting near an eyehole so that the next skin can be attached with a sheet bend.

A hide can yield 8–12 ft. (2.5–3.5 m) of wide rabbit cord with skillful cutting. To maximize the length, cut the stronger areas of the pelt (i.e., the back and thick parts) a bit narrower at 0.5" (1.5 cm), increasing the width to 1" (2.5 cm) in the belly and thinner portions of the hide.

At warmer latitudes, the skins may be more fragile, and in this case, it is a good idea to coil the skin strips around fiber cordage. Wrap the strips in a spiral so that the end of a piece holds the beginning of the next. The coiled skin is then left to dry in the shade and shrink around the cordage. To join each successive skin, a small three-quarter-inch slit is cut about one inch away from the end of the strip. Then, slip one end of the new strip into the slit or eyehole of

A. Stronger skins can be twisted by hand or with a rope twister.

B. Weaker skins should be twisted around a cord.

A   B

the last strip, and pull the new strip through its own slit. Pull tightly to lock the strips together. A sheet bend can also be tied as an alternative way of joining weaker skins. The joined skins will eventually complete a fur chain.

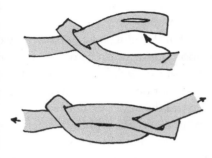

The next stage is to twist the fur chain by tying the chain to a tree and rolling the cord along the thigh or by using a rope twister. With enough twisting and gentle stretching, only the fur side should show; just don't overdo the twist. As an alternative, the skins can also be individually twisted and then chained.

The fur chain can be wrapped around horizontal poles and hung to dry in a place protected from rain. Secure the ends as it dries so the twist won't unwind. And cut off the ears because they harden up.

Once the rope is dried or slightly stiff, the blanket can be weaved. Build a wooden frame of dry, peeled poles.

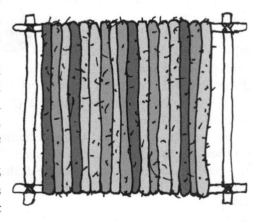

The weave mesh should allow two fingers to be poked through it at the most. A smaller mesh will be warmer, heavier, and require more skins.

A blanket measuring 6 × 5 ft. (1.8 × 1.5 m) requires between 70 and 100 rabbit skins.

Traditionally, the rabbit-skin cordage is the warp element—attached to the top and bottom of the frame—and the fiber cordage is the weft or horizontal component. Warmer and heavier blankets can be made with rabbit-skin cordage as both the horizontal and vertical weave, but twice the amount of pelts are needed.

Cordage must be woven on both sides of the vertical strips of rabbit fur, as shown. This twining is very important because it helps keep the fur in a twisted and uniform way. You may have to tie knots in the cord regularly to stop everything from falling apart.

Finished blankets are about 1″ thick, and they are relatively light and much warmer than wool. Making a sleeping bag out of rabbit-skin blankets is also possible.

Expect the rabbit skins to shed hair continually. To prevent this, you can sew an inner and outer shell of cotton or nylon around the blanket.

HUNTING

When preparing for a hunt, practice as much as possible. Put in the effort to ensure good shot placement and a quick kill. Study shot placement frequently, including different profile angles. Practice shooting in real-world scenarios, including the following: from uncomfortable angles, including uphill and downhill; through trees; near brush; or from a stand or blind. Practicing diligently is a way to pay respect.

HUNTING STRATEGIES

AMBUSH

Ambush or stand hunting consists of waiting in a stand or near a spot where animals are likely to come. Animals are creatures of habit, so their patterns and movements can be predicted. Once a watering hole, feeding area, well-used trail, or funnel has been identified, the hunter positions themself in a spot within a comfortable shooting distance. They must be able to see the animal clearly without being seen, heard, or smelled. An ambush is an effective way to hunt deer, geese, bears, and moose.

In long-term survival, you have to use ambush hunting sparingly, and only when you have the maximum chance of having a successful hunt.

Animals usually spend most of their time resting, feeding, or traveling between resting and feeding spots. It's best to avoid targeting resting or bedding areas because they are usually sheltered among thick vegetation (making shots difficult). Moreover, animals don't tolerate being disturbed there and will leave the site for good if they don't feel safe.

Focus instead on feeding areas; those are easier to identify and predict. They tend to be more open and enable better shot opportunities. When animals are feeding, they move around, thus providing multiple angles and shooting positions.

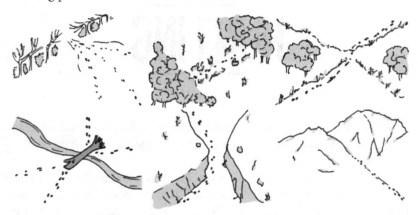

Observe the landscape to predict any natural ambush funnels and choke points.

Take advantage of natural choke points. If pinpointing a feeding spot or watering hole is difficult, concentrate on well-used routes from the resting to feeding grounds or between feeding areas. Another good strategy is to use bait or call the animals in.

Hunters usually wait in a blind or on a stand. Blinds are setups that provide visual concealment. They can be built out of local materials. For example, a dome shelter (wigwam) can be made with a frame of green poles and covered with interwoven pine or spruce limbs. A short cabin-like wall also works. If rain is a possibility, it's best to set a tarp. Some pit blinds take advantage of depressions or are dug in the ground.

Stands are usually elevated, such as a tree stand. Sitting high in a tree is effective because few animals look up. A stand can be improvised by securing horizontal logs to strong branches or weaving a platform with green sticks. It must be comfortable so that you can spend a long time sitting motionless on it.

You don't necessarily need a special setup. You may use a large tree to obscure your outline or lie flat on the ground in tall grass or dense brush, as long as you have a clear view. Below are some useful tips.

Movement: Stay as still as possible when waiting in ambush. It's best to position yourself so that you won't make any movements—or where you can minimize them when taking a shot. If you have to move, wait until the animal is facing away, until its head is behind a tree, or until it's eating. Move slowly and steadily.

Outline: It's also crucial to hide or blend your silhouette. Use terrain or sparse vegetation to cover your front, and use a complex or uneven backdrop to break up your outline. Wearing camouflaged clothing helps.

Sound: Minimizing noise is easy and essential. Do a few jumps with all your gear on to find potential noisemakers and address them. Soundproof your stand by clearing branches that may catch on you and make noise. Practice aiming in various directions to notice any likely noisemakers.

Smell: Use the wind to your advantage. Position yourself downwind from the trails, and have alternative ambush spots if the wind changes direction. Use campfire smoke to mask your odor.

Animals are usually most active right around sunrise and sunset, so get in position an hour earlier. Listen carefully. Noise may alert you in advance of an approaching animal.

Be warm, dry, and comfortable. Have extra ground insulation and clothes to keep you warm and still. If you must take a nap, remain in a slightly uncomfortable sleeping position to wake up easily. Be prepared to stay in ambush from dawn to dusk.

STILL-HUNT

Still-hunting consists of carefully choosing and planning a route and moving through it very slowly and stealthily with the intention to encounter animals. This technique is demanding: the hunter must stay still most of the time, listening and observing. It's like being permanently on the final approach of a stealthy stalk. Naturally, places where it's challenging to walk silently are not conducive to still-hunting.

Your route should take you through prime habitat. In addition, it should allow you to walk quietly while enjoying enough visibility to spot animals ahead of you. Open forests, ridgelines, and edge habitats make great locations for still-hunting. Edge habitats attract animals because they are close to food and shelter. Often, you can travel quietly on ridgelines, and they may allow you to observe both sides from a high elevation. Paths and animal trails that go through feeding and resting locations are also great because you can travel quietly, but sometimes visibility is too short. Always be on the lookout for parts of animals: an eye, the flick of an ear or a tail, a furry back, or antlers. Look for a horizontal line (like a belly or back) in a sea of vertical lines.

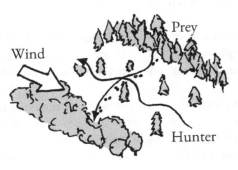

Try to have the sun at your back, where your visibility is best. Binoculars are a great aid because they narrow your focus in addition to zooming in. Below are some tips.

Smell: Managing your human odor is essential when still-hunting. If the wind is not in your favor, wait for it to change, or modify your route. Ideally, the wind should be in your face, but a 90-degree angle from your direction of travel is enough. If the wind is blowing toward your side, focus your attention on the upwind landscape.

Movement: Slow way down. Carefully scan ahead every time you take a step or two. If the bushes are thick, crouching close to the ground may give you a much better view. Move as if you were vulnerable prey in hostile territory. Take a few steps and then pause. Listen and observe for a few seconds, then repeat. To take silent steps, slowly plant your toes first, then gradually lower your heel. Use the soles of your shoes to feel for sticks, rocks, or leaves that could cause noise. Choose your route carefully to maintain a backdrop at all times: use trees, brush, and terrain to minimize your silhouette and avoid being skylined.

Noise: Minimizing noise is vital. Avoid making an unnatural noise at all costs. For instance, stepping on a stick is not that bad, but the sound of metal will make animals wary. Choose routes over bare ground, rock, or soft vegetation to diminish the noise of your footsteps. You might be able to slightly disguise the sound of your steps by imitating the sound of deer: listen to the sound they make when walking and replicate it.

If you make a loud noise, stop. Wait motionless for one to five minutes, then proceed.

Also, consider using soft-soled footwear. Wearing traditional moccasins or going barefoot is an alternative way to slow down your pace and minimize noise (carry lightweight shoes in a pack).

Sometimes, weather conditions like rain, soft snow, or strong winds reduce or mask your noise. In addition, strong winds also make your movements less obvious.

Camouflage clothing is not as crucial as being still and quiet, but using gloves and covering your face with a head net or bandana is important.

During your day-to-day survival activities, learn to recognize when the conditions are right for still-hunting. If you are traveling and realize that the wind, the ground conditions, and other circumstances are in your favor, consider still-hunting. If you are paddling, similar circumstances may arise. For instance, strong winds may prevent moose from hearing and smelling you until you get pretty close.

If you're hoping to still-hunt small animals, you have to spot them before they spot you. To do this, move very slowly and carefully observe any spots where animals could be hiding. Instead of trying to flush small animals out, your aim should be to shoot them before they run. It may take you a couple of hours just to travel a mile in this way. Keep in mind that some small animals, like rabbits hiding in dense cover, may need to be flushed out.

With small animals, you may also try out the opposite strategy. Animals can read your body language and energy exceptionally well. If you are in stalking mode, birds, squirrels, and other animals may notice right away, and they may sound the alarm or just become more attentive. So try projecting a nonchalant vibe instead of a predator vibe; move as if you were out for a stroll. Pause now and then—paying a subtle attention to your surroundings. Pretend to feed, and be in your bubble, minding your own business. Then, once you're within shooting range, swiftly change your mood.

SPOT-AND-STALK

Spot-and-stalk hunting is one of the most demanding hunting strategies. This style is best used in relatively open spaces where you can spot your quarry at a distance and approach the animal within shooting range while staying unnoticed.

Position yourself at a lookout, and use binoculars to observe a large expanse of land. This technique also allows you to assess an animal before committing to pursue it.

If there aren't any elevated lookouts around, you may need to climb a tree, but this is not ideal. It's best to locate a comfortable spot to allow you to stay put for a long time. Sites such as ridgelines connected to other high points are excellent. Choose a location that is accessible enough that you can reach a potential quarry in a reasonable amount of time. Use a topo map to identify possible feeding grounds, travel corridors, and lookouts.

Once you're on a lookout, mentally break up the landscape into manageable chunks. Use your binoculars to scan large open areas first. Start with the easy stuff. Then move to smaller, harder-to-scan areas; you may need to stabilize your binoculars. Thoroughly observe any places where animals could be. Check multiple times and take it slowly. If the terrain is relatively uniform, divide it into a grid, or use a combination of zones and grids.

Emphasize areas that provide shelter, food, and water for your quarry. Food is often found in clearings and sites that provide enough sunlight for grasses, shrubs, or berries. Whenever you see an animal, try to figure out why it is there; learn its patterns.

Many large animals are active primarily during sunrise and sunset, so that's when you should be at your lookout spot.

Break up the landscape while glassing

If you've spotted an animal, the next step is to determine if attempting to stalk it makes sense given its behavior, distance, time of day, route, and wind direction.

During the breeding season, males—who are looking for females or a fight—will stick around longer. A nervous animal or one on the move is not likely to stay in one place for long. The odds are better if it's resting or feeding. If a group of animals is grazing and facing in a particular direction—often toward the wind—it's likely that they will continue to travel that way. In the evening, animals tend to stay in the same place until dark, and in the late morning, they move to their resting areas.

If you've located an animal, but you think it may get spooked as you try to stalk it, you can let it go rest while you set an ambush. Begin the stalk once the animal has stayed put at its resting spot for about half an hour or more. Keep in mind that the animal may be moving around. Remain watchful.

Don't attempt to hunt the animal in its resting grounds. Once you're relatively close, find an area where the animal will likely emerge again, and stage your ambush there.

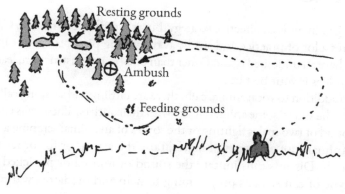

The first step before stalking your quarry should be to either take a mental note of its location, memorize nearby landmarks, take a picture, or mark a GPS waypoint. Then, plan a route that is fast enough and provides sufficient cover.

Animals rely mostly on scent, motion, and sound to detect predators, so if you remain still and your outline is broken up by vegetation or camouflage, you'll probably go unnoticed. Use the terrain and vegetation for concealment. You may have to move on all fours or crawl on your stomach at times. Or you may only be able to move when the animal is busy feeding or facing away. If an animal turns your way and you feel you've been spotted, freeze. Wait until the animal turns away before even considering moving.

Always consider the wind direction, and remember that even a faint wind will carry your odor. Concealing your odor is even more important than avoiding being spotted. Wood smoke may help disguise your scent, but wind direction is your best aid. If the wind is unfavorable, stop and reassess. An animal may question its eyesight, but never its nose.

Stalking with a bow: A hunter must get much closer to the animal when using a bow. If there are loud noises from gusts of wind or other animals, take advantage of those moments to close in on your quarry. Even the slightest noise could spook your quarry, so choose the quietest route. Pay close attention to feet placement: step on soft grass or dirt instead of dry leaves or loose rocks. Move sniper-slow. Once you are within range, use the terrain or vegetation to cover you as you draw your bow, and then move within view to shoot.

CALLING

Calling animals is an effective strategy, but it is difficult to master. Calling requires a lot of practice and study, as the wrong pitch, tone, or cadence could have an undesired effect. Other than one-on-one instruction, learning with videos is your best bet.

In addition to vocal animal calls, there are rattling and scraping calls that imitate the sound some animals make with their antlers. These calls emulate the sound of two males fighting or the sound of an animal scraping a bush.

Animals use calls to find mates, raise the alarm, or for other social purposes. Distress calls imitate the sound of injured or panicked prey; this type of call attracts prey coming to help and predators wanting to take advantage. Social calls attract animals looking for company or food.

Some calls—like those of a moose—can be made without aids. Commercially made calls are easy to learn how to use and are extremely effective.

DRIVING

Driving is the strategy of flushing animals toward an ambush. Driving must be done in teams, usually of four to eight hunters. For this reason, there must be careful and safe coordination.

There are two groups in a drive: the drivers and the standers. The drivers aim to find animals. They use the wind, the terrain, and their knowledge of animal behavior to flush them toward the standers. The standers wait patiently in a concealed place in range of the main escape routes, and they position themselves to have their zone of fire away from the drivers.

Drives work best in places with a block of cover surrounded by open areas because animals will try to stay in the cover until they are driven to the edge. Then, the standers can take a shot. Corridors like streams and canyons also make good places for driving.

By observing the animals during a drive and studying their tracks afterward, you can learn to predict their behavior.

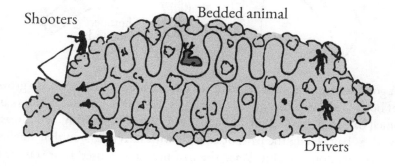

Shooters   Bedded animal

Drivers

BIG ANIMALS

SPECIES

BEAR

The best seasons for hunting black bears are the spring and fall—when they are at their most hungry—either during the first weeks after hibernation or the four to six weeks before. Hunting a bear in the fall is best because the bear is much fatter.

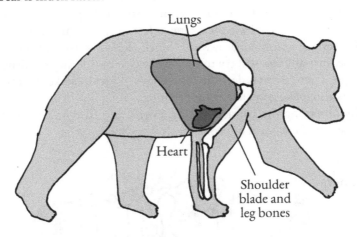

A good strategy is to set a stand near a natural food source, such as a grove of beech, oaks, or a berry patch. Baiting is also quite effective, as bears can smell bait from up to 3 mi. (4.8 km) away. Piles of guts, fish, or a carcass work as bait. Hang the bait, or cover it with heavy logs, so that smaller scavengers don't steal it. Place the bait near a well-used bear trail or a natural food source. The area should have enough cover to make the bear feel secure enough to visit the bait during the day. Bait a site a few times so that bears get familiar with it.

Bears feed the most during cool morning and evening hours, and they avoid being in direct sunlight during hot days due to their dark fur. Bears are not generally very abundant, averaging only one bear for every 2 sq. mi. (5.2 sq km).

Use at least a .30-caliber cartridge and bullets that weigh at least 165 grains (10.7 g) for bear hunting. Set a stand nearby, and always keep the wind direction in mind. Needless to say, bears can be unpredictable and dangerous. If you are using a bow, you may have to get real close for a good shot.

MOOSE

In the boreal forest, moose are one of the most important foods. A large bull can weigh about 1,200 lb. (540 kg), and just one moose quarter can weigh over 220 lb. (100 kg).

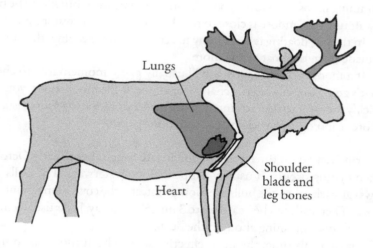

Moose eat a wide variety of vegetation, but willows and trembling aspen are their main staples during the winter months. For this reason, moose stay in shrubby habitats in the winter, and wet bogs and areas with shallow marshy waters in the spring and summer. They are found in aquatic habitats, eating aquatic vegetation and taking shelter from bugs and the heat. In the fall, their diet shifts back to twigs and buds. In winter, their range shrinks considerably, especially if the snow is very deep.

The peak times for moose hunting are during the rut (late September to early October) and late winter (late March to early April). Moose are mostly seen on clear, calm days. Rain, snow, and strong winds keep them bedded down. In the boreal forest, moose are rarely visible or shot from a distance greater than 160 ft. (50 m).

In summer, it's best to wait for conditions that force moose to go near the water, such as a hot, still afternoon. A canoe can be used to scan the shores where moose may be feeding and taking refuge from the heat and bugs. Low water levels are better for summer moose hunting because they force moose to move from swamps and bogs into streams and lakes.

Floating in a canoe can be a very productive way of hunting during the ice-free months, and it provides a very stealthy means of traveling. Start early in the morning and float until dark. Floating is convenient because you can paddle right up to a moose and shoot from the boat, or you can land and proceed with a stalk. Moose don't get spooked as easily by floating objects. And transporting meat over water is infinitely easier than over land.

In the past, Indigenous hunters would sometimes hunt swimming moose from their canoes, but pulling a moose out of the water is difficult. A swimming moose provides a good shooting opportunity, but it may be best to wait until the moose is close to the shore or out of the water for a shot.

In the fall, floating is a great way to access a spot for calling: the call can be made from the boat or the shore.

If a moose gets surprised, it will usually pause momentarily to check what's going on; this offers a chance for a shot. If the moose bolts, you can quickly follow it to take advantage of its tendency to travel a short distance before stopping and assessing the situation again.

The rut is a two- to three-week period in late September to early October when mating occurs. It usually happens along waterways. The bulls and cows call each other: the bulls use a low grunt, and the cows a long trembling moan. Their calls can be heard up to 3 mi. (5 km) away. Bulls usually make a lot of noise thrashing about in the bush.

During this time, the most effective way to hunt moose is to use a megaphone—often made of rolled birch bark—to call bulls by imitating cows or other competing moose. This technique requires much patience and skill. You can make many calls without success, but persevere and have faith. It's a good idea to make calls near your camp for a few days.

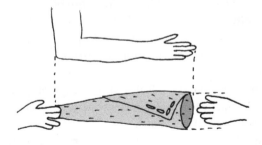

A pin can be used to close the cone.

Often, hunters use a dried moose scapula to emulate the antlers of a bull scraping the brush; a plastic liquor bottle with its bottom cut off works as a substitute. The scapula scraping call works well during the pre-rut season and can be used as a call in itself or to enhance a vocal call; at this time, bulls seek out other bulls to have shoving and pushing matches.

The cow call can be complemented by pouring water from a height to imitate a urinating cow.

Success at calling depends on the population of moose in an area. Moose are less abundant than you may think, with a population of about one animal per 6–11 sq. mi. (10–18 sq km).

For example, a moose call can be started with a cow call (for one hour), then pause for 15 minutes or more, and proceed with a bull call. Break some sticks and imitate the scraping and brush thrashing that a bull would make when demonstrating his dominance when closing in on an area. Pause for a few seconds and then make three to five grunts. These calls aim to motivate a bull to compete with "the other bull" for the female.

Wait patiently for a bull to come; it may take more than half an hour. A bull can be very quiet, so stay put.

In winter, expect to travel over several days and cover up to 30 mi. (50 km) when hunting moose in the traditional intensive style.

To locate a track less than two days old, assess the following signs: the freshness of nearby poop, the moisture and state of the soil in the hoof prints (if possible), and the newness of the ends of eaten twigs. Fresh snow makes it easier to estimate the age of the track and will also muffle the sound of your steps.

Wind

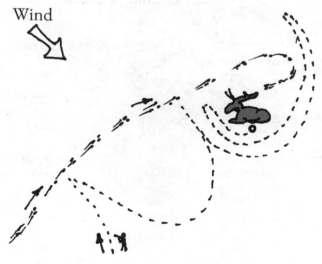

Deep snow facilitates moose hunting because a hunter on snowshoes can move more efficiently than a moose. Crusty spring snow is ideal because it hurts the moose's legs and slows it down.

The wind is the most critical factor in moose hunting because it directs odors and covers sound. If the wind stops, so will the hunt.

Moose take precautions, especially in winter, by circling downwind of their trails or feeding areas. This way, they can smell any predators following them; it's a similar strategy to what soldiers do in dense jungle or snow.

Traditionally, hunters perform a sidetracking stalking technique as a counteraction. The hunter follows the trail in a series of arcs, staying on the downwind side. Once the hunter outpaces the moose (because the moose paused to rest), the hunter backtracks again in progressively smaller, downwind arcs. It may take hours to cover a few hundred yards doing semicircular tracking.

Most hunters use large-caliber rifles and high-velocity ammunition to penetrate the thick skin and heavy bone structure of moose. If you can get a close shot, aim at the base of the ear to drop the moose immediately—this may not be ideal if the moose is on a riverbank.

If you are bowhunting, a draw weight of at least 55–60 lb. is recommended. Shot placement with a bow is paramount, and the ideal shot is through both lungs with a broadhead. Aiming for the heart is too risky because of its proximity to the shoulder.

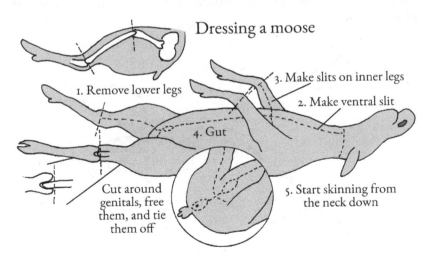

Dressing a moose

1. Remove lower legs

2. Make ventral slit

3. Make slits on inner legs

4. Gut

Cut around genitals, free them, and tie them off

5. Start skinning from the neck down

DEER

White-tailed deer feed mainly on buds and twigs from shrubs and saplings, and they graze on grasses and other plants. Deer usually live at the edges of forests or in open woodlands where sunlight can penetrate and maintain the plants they feed on. They thrive particularly well in forested areas near civilization, where their main foods are plentiful, and the populations of other big animals are reduced or nonexistent.

Deer are more likely to be seen when feeding or moving between resting and feeding areas. They tend to feed more before sunrise and after sunset, and they typically rest during midday. Deer usually move more when it's warm and clear versus when it's cold and cloudy.

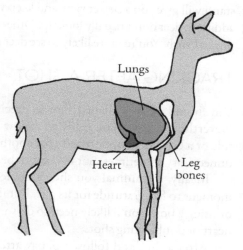

Most white-tailed deer are harvested through still-hunting, ambush hunting, or driving, but antler rattling and stalking are also effective.

Be aware that ungulates keep their rumps into the wind, so they can see what they can't smell and smell what they can't see. Use this knowledge to thwart that.

The wind is not only crucial for diverting your smell, but it can also provide background noise to make your footsteps less noticeable. Light rain also makes background noise and softens the leaves, making travel quieter.

Minimize your scent by using clothes that have been left out in the open or wood-smoked.

White-tailed deer mate between October and January, but their rutting period is shorter in the north: from mid-October to mid-November or December. During the rut, both males and females are less cautious. Here are some tips:

Antler rattling: During the rut, take two antlers and rub, knock, and rattle them together to imitate the sound of fighting bucks. If no buck shows up after 20 to 30 minutes, move stealthily to another place.

Lure: The tarsal glands from a dead buck or doe can also be used as a scent lure during the rut and year-round. These glands are located on the deer's rear legs, at knee-level, beneath a dark patch of hair.

Ambush: Scout the area before setting an ambush to ensure there are recent signs of deer activity. A prime location for a stand is near the intersections of well-used deer trails or in an area with fresh scrapes in the trees. An elevated stand will give you a better view and keep your scent above the ground; in addition, deer don't usually look up. Otherwise, just hide behind a tree or a pile of brush. You're more likely to see deer during the day's final moments.

TRACKING AFTER A SHOT

You should make your first shot as precise and well-placed as possible. Nevertheless, always be ready to follow up with a second shot with a rifle or a bow. If an opportunity for another shot arises, take it. It may be unnecessary sometimes, but it's best to be sure.

Ideally, the animal you shot will die in its tracks; if it does, take a moment to feel gratitude for its gift. But if you're hunting a larger animal or using a bow, you'll likely need to do some tracking, even with a perfect heart or double-lung shot.

After a shot and follow-up, pay attention to the placement of the wounds, the animal's movements as it runs away, the location where it was standing and last seen, and the direction it took. These insights will help you with tracking. Look for a spot of blood on the animal for evidence of shot placement; this will be obvious if an arrow was used. A shot limb would be bad news. If the rear legs or all four legs fold, you probably hit the spine and may need to shoot again at the head, neck, or lungs.

The next step is to wait. If you're confident of your shot placement, you should wait about half an hour before approaching the impact site; if you're not so sure, wait 45 minutes to an hour.

Stay attentive to any noise the animal makes as it flees. Make a blaze to mark the location you took the shot from, and take the time to observe and memorize the features of the spot where the animal was when it was hit.

Waiting is essential because you don't want the animal to stand up and run far away. If the animal feels secure, it will likely just find a spot nearby and lie down to die. If it might rain or snow soon, you'll need to start tracking earlier because precipitation will obscure the signs.

After the waiting period is up, go to the impact site where the animal was shot. Mark the site with a blaze and search for any signs. Look for blood or hair on the ground or vegetation. Assess the clues to determine how much time you should wait before proceeding to track the animal. Even if you don't find signs of a successful hit, show due respect by tracking it down for a while in case you see signs of a wound later on.

Neither the amount of blood nor its absence will provide definitive clues about the shot's lethality or even indicate a miss. It's entirely possible that the bleeding is primarily internal.

Hopefully, you'll find a trail of blood. The color of this blood may give you hints about the wound. Frothy, pinkish blood indicates a lung shot, and rich red blood—but not frothy—suggests bleeding from a major blood vessel. Dark blood mixed with what appears to be stomach or intestinal contents indicates a stomach or gut shot. As a rule of thumb, wait four to five hours before tracking an animal shot in the stomach, and 10 hours if it was shot in the intestines.

Following a blood trail requires patience and discipline.

If the trail seems to have ended, mark the spot with a blaze for reference. Systematically follow different directions for a short distance in search of any signs. Get down on your hands and knees to look, but be careful not to disturb the signs.

If you can't find blood, look for other signs, such as tracks, disturbed ground and vegetation, and overturned leaves. Don't search for blood exclusively on the ground; look for it on foliage, logs, and tree trunks as well. Be open to unconventional signs, and think outside the box.

Wounded animals sometimes head toward water or move erratically. Two people may track faster if one focuses on the blood trail, and the other looks around for signs of a change in direction. If you find your prey still alive, approach it stealthily, and be ready to shoot.

HANDLING MEAT

The internal organs of a large animal should be removed soon after it dies to cool down the meat. This slows down the growth of bacteria and prevents the meat from spoiling quickly. Removing the hide and placing it over the meat also helps it cool down.

If you cannot relocate the meat to a secure spot, or camp at the site of the kill, you'll have to leave some of it unattended overnight. Prioritize packing the fat, organs, and meat with high fat content. Remove the guts and place them in a pile, away from the rest of the meat and prized organs. This gut pile will serve as a decoy. Scavengers often devour the gut pile and ignore the meat. Leave the carcass with the fur still on in a hidden spot, and place a bunch of spruce boughs or leaves over it. If you have a rope, you might be able to hang some of the meat from a tree. You may also try weak deterrents such as peeing on the ground around the meat or improvising a crude scarecrow out of your clothes, trash, or tarp.

When storing meat in camp, keep three concepts in mind: cool, clean, and dry. Ideally, hang and air-dry the meat if the insects are not a huge issue. Air-drying builds up a dry crust that protects the meat; this is better than placing it straight away in a game bag—and in dry, breezy conditions, this dry crust may develop quickly. Otherwise, if the bugs are plentiful, place the pieces of meat immediately into breathable game bags and hang them in a shaded and breezy area. Ensure the meat stays in the shade throughout the day.

Air should be able to flow between the quarters and large pieces of meat. Don't place them close together because there will be moisture trapped between them. If you cannot hang the meat, place it on the ground over a base of rocks or sticks to allow air to circulate underneath. If you are using plastic or a tarp to protect the meat from precipitation, ensure you leave space or a buffer made of brush to keep the material from touching the meat. If you are transporting meat in a non-breathable bag, such as your pack or a dry bag, take the meat out and hang it to dry as soon as possible.

If you have a canoe, you can take advantage of the cooler temperature of the water by placing the meat inside the canoe and over a pile of brushes; this makes sense primarily when traveling.

RIFLES

.22 LONG RIFLE

Many consider the .22 Long Rifle (LR) to be the ultimate survival round. It is inexpensive, versatile, relatively quiet, and accurate at ranges under 50 yd. (45 m). The advantage of the .22 LR is portability: .22 rifles are lighter than center-fire rifles, and a pack of 500 rounds weighs 3.7 lb. (1.7 kg) and takes up the same space as a pack of 150 .223 REM rounds.

During day-to-day activities, you're more likely to encounter small animals (e.g., grouse, squirrels, or rabbits) than large animals. Nevertheless, suppose you spot a large animal. In that case, you could still kill it if you're at close range and exercise proper shot placement. The .22 doesn't have the kinetic power of center-fire rifles, but if necessary, it can kill deer-sized animals at 50–75 yd. (45–70 m) with a well-placed shot.

Many survivalists agree that the capabilities of the .22 are often underestimated. Putting regulations and skill aside, the .22 has been used successfully to hunt every land mammal in North America.

You should always have your rifle handy because you never know when an animal might show up. Therefore, portability and weight are crucial.

If you can only have one survival rifle, you should probably choose a .22—but if there are many abundant large animals around, a center-fire rifle may be best.

Rimfire rifles are often sighted at 50 yd. (45 m) because even high-velocity .22 rounds have a significant drop at longer distances (~2" for 75 yd. and ~6" for 100 yd.).

Trajectory of 22 LR Bullet (rifle zeroed at 50 yds.)

- ∎ 22 LR CCI Mini-mag (SH 0.8") ∎ ∎ 22 LR CCI Mini-mag (SH 1.5")
- ▬ 22 LR CCI Standard (SH 1.5") ▬ 22 LR CCI Standard (SH 0.8")

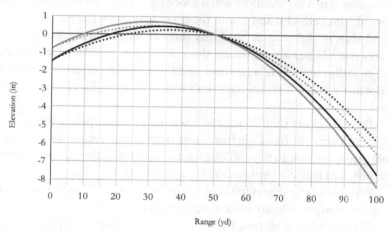

Range (yd)

Because of the parabolic arc of the bullet, at ranges from 20–40 yd. the point of impact of a high-velocity .22 round (Mini-Mag 40 gr.) sighted at 50 yd. on a scope (sight height of 1.5") will be up to 0.25" (6 mm) above the target. On an iron sight (s.h. of 0.8"), at ranges of 15–40 yd., it will be up to 0.5" (1 cm) above the target.

The point of impact of a standard-velocity .22 (CCI std.) sighted at 50 yd. on a scope (s.h. of 1.5"), at ranges from 20–40 yd., will be up to 0.5" (1 cm) above the target. On an iron sight (s.h. of 0.8"), at ranges of 10–40 yd., it will be up to 0.8" (2 cm) above the target.

For distances between 70–100 yd., it's important to adjust for bullet drop by aiming 1.5"–6" above the target with high-velocity rounds or aiming 2"–8" above with standard-velocity rounds. Another option is to learn to adjust your scope for drop or use one with MOA/MIL marks.

The .22 round is such a low-powered round that choosing appropriate ammo and proper shot placement is critical. Stick with high-velocity loads for general purposes, and for medium to large animals, high- and hyper-velocity rounds only.

Avoid using hyper-velocity rounds (>1,400 fps) with small animals because these rounds damage the meat too much, except with headshots. Solid points work best on small animals.

For medium- and large-sized animals, use hollow-point bullets for heart and lung shots, and solid points for headshots. High-velocity loads (e.g., CCI, REM, WIN) work well. Hyper-velocity rounds are louder, but they pack more kinetic power than high-velocity loads.

Never target the shoulder when shooting a .22 round at large animals. Instead, aim behind it and low in the chest, just above the elbow.

A shot to the heart or head may drop an animal immediately, but it is very risky. Never attempt these shots unless you're a skilled marksman, you're really close, there is no wind, and the animal is perfectly still. Never shoot at the back of an animal's skull with a .22 round because that is its thickest spot.

If you're closer than 25 yd. and a headshot is appropriate, then follow these instructions: from the front, aim right at one eye, or imagine lines going from each ear to the opposite eye and aim where they cross; and from the side, aim halfway between the eye and the ear.

A double-lung shot is the least risky target with a .22 rifle: use a high-velocity or hyper-velocity hollow-point bullet.

Having written all this, I want to be clear: using a .22 rifle on large animals is *never* recommended. It is illegal in most jurisdictions, and there is a high risk of severely injuring—but not killing—the animal. Be respectful, and use common sense.

.22 RIFLES

The topic of survival rifles can be a rabbit hole, so I'm just going to scratch the surface. You'll have different opinions and needs. I will discuss .22 rifles specifically, but many of the points below apply to center-fire rifles.

I will consider only those rifles compact enough to be carried inside a pack for our purposes. Takedown rifles aren't the only option for a survival rifle, but in my opinion, their portability makes them the preferred choice. Takedown rifles are easier to transport, don't draw attention, and can fit inside a waterproof pack or barrel. A takedown rifle certainly has more moving parts and, therefore, points of failure, but I feel the benefits outweigh the risks. Generally, in the field, the rifle is assembled and carried on a sling; it's never taken down and held in a pack.

It's best to have a magazine-fed .22 rifle rather than a break action rifle to avoid fumbling with another cartridge in case of a miss—particularly in winter. A bolt-action rifle is fine. I also prefer a magazine-fed .22 rifle because I can carry two magazines with different types of rounds and switch according to the circumstances.

The magnification a scope provides is helpful but not necessary. If the survival rifle is scoped, it should also have backup iron sights. One thing to consider is that the scope may interfere with its portability, as with the AR-7 survival rifle, and that you may need to take extra care when packing a disassembled, scoped rifle. A good takedown rifle (scoped or not) should stay zeroed even after being taken apart, transported, and put back together a couple of times. Consider using quick detach rings in conjunction with a Weaver rail or a Picatinny rail if you want to be able to detach a scope and retain some sort of zero.

Nowadays, there are four takedown .22 rifles for survival:
- The Henry U.S. Survival AR-7
- The Ruger 10/22 Takedown
- The Marlin 70PSS
- The Savage 64 Takedown

I'll just briefly write about the three most popular ones. The AR-7 is incredibly lightweight, and it is super compact because the action and barrel can be stored inside the stock. Those—and the fact that it's pretty inexpensive—are its best attributes. What I don't like about the AR-7 is its toy-like peep sight and its budget-build quality. Current models work best with high- and hyper-velocity rounds and may have problems cycling lower-velocity cartridges. A friend has had three plastic "action spring guides" from his AR-7 consistently fail in temperatures under 15°F (-10°C).

The Marlin 70PSS is in the same category in terms of weight and price as the AR-7 and is a better option for use in cold weather.

The original Ruger 10/22 is considered one of the most reliable .22 semi-automatic rifles. The takedown version is likely less accurate and reliable, but it is very well designed and built. The coupling mechanism is much more tight and secure than that of the AR-7. The difference in quality is noticeable, but that makes sense since the Ruger costs about twice as much. I recommend the Magpul X-22 Backpacker aftermarket stock because it keeps the barrel and the stock secured when disassembled and allows you to store three magazines in the stock. In addition, for scoped use, I recommend installing the MSP See Through Picatinny Mount and quick detach rings.

Top to bottom: Ruger 10/22 takedown, U.S. Henry AR-7

LARGE-CALIBER AMMO AND FIREARMS

The main advantage of a large-caliber rifle is that it can be used to hunt large animals, which is crucial. A center-fire rifle is not suitable for hunting small animals, so it's best thought of solely as a large-animal hunting rifle.

Shotguns are one of the most versatile firearms, but they are not ideal in a long-term context due to the bulk and weight of their shells.

It's best to stick with a widely available cartridge appropriate for the large animals in your region. As a rough, general rule, use a round with a *striking* energy of 900–1,500 foot-pounds (ft. lb.) to kill deer; 1,500–2,500 ft. lb. for elk or bear; and 2,100–3,500 ft. lb. for moose or large bear. The lower figures are the minimum, and the higher figures are the preferred kinetic energy *at the point of impact*. What kills an animal is severe damage to vital organs, not kinetic energy. That's why shot placement, deep penetration, and decent bullet expansion are critical. As another rule of thumb, use anything larger than the .223 caliber, up to the .30-calibers for deer and similar-sized animals. For general purposes, use anything between and including the .270 to .30-calibers.

A .308 WIN rifle is a good option because it's the second most popular center-fire rifle caliber in North America (after the .223 caliber). For comparison: the .308 round packs 2,200 ft. lb. of kinetic energy at 100 yd.; 1,760 ft. lb. at 200 yd.; and 1,400 ft. lb. at 300 yd. Compact rifles such as the Steyr Scout, Sig Cross, and Ruger Scout are good choices for a center-fire survival rifle due to their portability and versatility.

The .223 REM rifle could be another option due to its popularity, but it's not recommended for large animals. Many hunters assert that it doesn't have adequate kinetic power for deer (the .223 round exerts ~900 ft. lb. at 100 yd.). If you're going to carry a center-fire rifle, you might as well have one chambered in a cartridge more powerful than the .223 round.

The 7.62 × 39 round is another possible option with a kinetic energy of ~1,150 ft. lb. at 100 yd. But it's not recommended for anything larger than a deer.

A reasonable compromise for long-term survival in the boreal forest may be having a compact .308 bolt-action rifle for large animals and a .22 semi-automatic pistol for small animals. Finally, I'm not suggesting you pack both a .22 rifle and a center-fire rifle; you may have to make a difficult choice and compromise.

FIREARM CONSIDERATIONS

Firearms have various advantages over bows: more kinetic energy, extended range, and greater accuracy. It's more comfortable and practical to daily carry a slung rifle than a survival bow and arrows. Nevertheless, the rifle's weight and the need for ammunition can be significant disadvantages.

In the wilderness, it's impossible to store a rifle in a fully dry, temperature-controlled environment. The temperature will swing from low to high, and if the air is humid, the firearm will begin to rust. To minimize condensation and rust, store it in the driest spot available and wrap it in a breathable gun sock or a breathable and moisture-wicking fabric, such as wool. In addition, regularly take apart, dry, and clean your gun.

Pack some gun oil and cleaning tools: a green scrub, cotton swabs, and a bore snake or other barrel cleaning tools. As a lightweight tool, I use a strong cord and pull a small patch of fabric through the bore. Here are some tips:
- Use tape or water balloons as "muzzle condoms" to stop snow, rain, and dirt from getting inside the barrel.

- Carry two accessories with you: a dependable scope and a good sling.
- Avoid bringing your rifle inside a warm place in cold weather or condensation will form. Remove any oil from your firearm and substitute it for graphite powder.

ARCHERY

Bows are the other main option for a hunting weapon. Their main advantages are that arrows can be reused and that they are silent. Some of their disadvantages are their shorter range and that shooting accurately requires more skill and practice.

Compared with a .22 firearm, the advantage of reusing arrows is not as crucial because packing 500–1,000 rounds is not hard. The fact that bows are pretty quiet is generally not that important, but it's a nice feature when there's a group of small animals.

I'm not considering crossbows or compound bows for these purposes because they are not as compact or lightweight, and their designs are not as resilient and straightforward as a traditional bow.

Takedown recurve bows work well for survival. The takedown feature is not crucial, but it does make it easier to transport.

Recurve bows are shorter and more compact. But recurve limbs are less resilient and may break when twisted or if the bow is strung without a stringer tool.

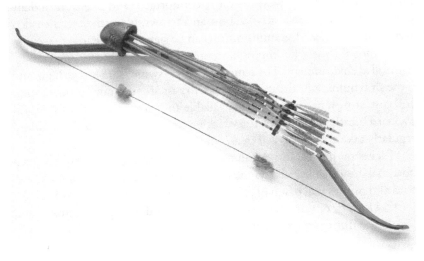

Regardless of style, the bow must have an ergonomic handle with a comfortable grip that allows you to shoot accurately.

A bow with a draw weight between 45–50 lb. (at your actual draw length) is recommended. Fifty pounds of draw weight is the minimum required to hunt moose, elk, and grizzly bear in many places, and 45 lb. of draw weight is enough for animals like deer and black bears as long as you have an appropriate broadhead point. Choose the minimum draw weight needed because your strength can deteriorate and make it difficult for you to shoot a heavier bow.

I highly recommend having the following accessories: string silencer (e.g., Beaver Balls), Bear Hair arrow rest, nocking points, two or three bowstrings, brush buttons, string wax, and arm guard. Brush buttons prevent your bow from getting tangled when bushwhacking in thick brush.

Bowstring wax helps keep the string in good shape. Strings break, so have two or three extras (a Flemish twist string is a bit more resilient than an endless loop). Keep your bow hung off the floor to deter mice from chewing your bowstring or silencers.

A modern recurve bow can be left strung for months without damage to the bow—avoid stringing one without a stringer. If you must string a recurve bow without aids, learn the proper technique (not the step-through method).

A bow-mounted quiver is a crucial accessory. The bow-mounted style is preferred for survival because it keeps both bow and arrows as a single unit. When you are hunting opportunistically while doing other activities, a bow-mounted quiver allows you to be ready to shoot at all times.

Arrows can be transported in a cheap telescopic drafting tube (cut two pieces of thick cardboard the same diameter as the tube and then punch holes for each arrow). A tube fits about 16 arrows, which is adequate. But don't trust the flimsy lid or the external strap.

Carbon fiber hunting arrows are the best option for use with a survival bow because they are strong and light. Ensure the arrows have an appropriate spine for their length and the bow's draw weight. And choose arrows with an appropriate mass for hunting large animals. The *total* weight of the arrow, including the point, should be 9–10 grains per lb. of your draw weight for best penetration and performance.

Use a carbon collar behind the point's insert to improve durability and minimize breakage at this juncture. For safety, regularly check carbon fiber arrows by flexing them to see if there are any cracks, as the arrow could splinter during a shot and impale your hand.

Choose brightly colored, contrasting feathers, and paint the arrow shafts to avoid losing your arrows. If you expect to hunt birds such as grouse, have a couple of flu-flu arrows (or glue extra feathers to your standard arrows). The flu-flu feathers will slow down the arrow so that it won't fly as far when aiming for animals in trees, and they make the arrow more visible.

Use "traditional vanes" instead of fletching in areas with lots of rain or for water shots. Traditional vanes can be shot off-the-shelf like fletching, but they resist water much better.

If you're shooting feathered arrows, learn to replace the feathers, as they will take a beating in the long run.

Choose heavier arrow points (150–200 gr.) if you plan on hunting large animals because they tend to have more kinetic "punch." Use a fixed broadhead that is easy to sharpen in the field. I like 2-blade broadheads with a single bevel like those made by Grizzly. Keeping your broadheads razor-sharp is paramount. Coat them with beeswax to avoid rust.

Use a small-game hunting blunt such as The Hammer for small animals. Keep in mind that some animals, like grouse, are sometimes hard to hunt with blunts because their wings may deflect the arrow; depending on the context, it might be best to use broadheads.

Keep it simple. There are many points with different features, but most features are just gimmicks in practice. All your points, regardless of style, should have the same consistent weight.

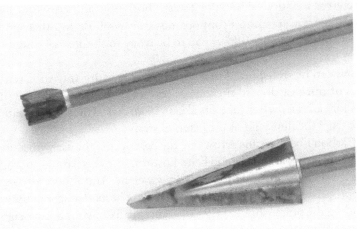

Survival bows generally don't have sights. Shooting is done with either unconscious (intuitive) or deliberate aiming. Intuitive aiming is best when shooting in less-than-ideal situations, such as when the animal is moving, is high up in a tree, or if it is hard to estimate the distance because of the terrain. Whatever style you choose, repeatability and consistency are key.

Practice shooting bare-handed (at least some of the time) because if you are hunting opportunistically in a survival context, there will be times when you'll be forced to shoot with bare hands.

It can be hard to maintain accuracy in the wild without target practice. You can shoot rotten tree stumps, but this can be hard on the arrows if the stumps are not punky enough. Other ways to improvise targets include using a pile of dirt, tightly tying a bunch of reeds together, or stacking layers of cut sod or floating mats.

There are various models of bows suitable for survival, like the Samick Sage, Samick Discovery ILF, Fleetwood Timber Ridge, and the Galaxy Sear ILF.

Ultimately, bows are not as practical as rifles for survival. Firearms give you a technological edge worth having when your life is on the line. The issue of limited ammunition is worth considering, but with careful rationing, it is not a concern unless you are in the wilderness for several years. Bows have the advantage of stealth, but that is unnecessary. The only strong case for bows over firearms is where regulations prohibit the use of firearms.

RAWHIDE AND TANNING

RAWHIDE

Rawhide is an animal skin that has had its flesh and fat scraped off, and often its hair as well. Rawhide works great for lashings, cases, snowshoe webbing, sled bindings, and moccasin soles.

When rawhide is wet, it is elastic, and as it dries, it shrinks and hardens. This process can also happen in reverse: rawhide will soften and stretch if it gets wet.

The basic process for making rawhide is to scrape off all the fat and flesh from a green (fresh) or soaked animal hide. Then, it is soaked in water to loosen up and remove the hair. The loosened hair is scraped on a log following the same direction of the hair. Finally, the hide is stretched tight on a frame or staked off the ground and left to dry *slowly* in the *shade*. When fully dry, rawhide will store almost indefinitely, but it may still be attacked by insects and mice.

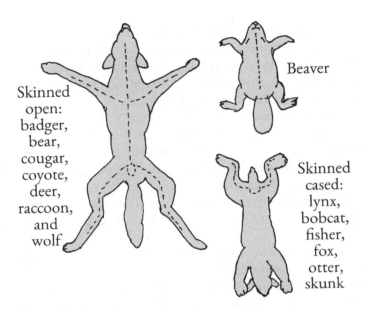

Skinned open: badger, bear, cougar, coyote, deer, raccoon, and wolf

Beaver

Skinned cased: lynx, bobcat, fisher, fox, otter, skunk

To make strong lashings, cut a thin, straight lace of rawhide. Soaking the rawhide makes it easier to cut.

Another method that creates a weaker lace—due to having one side slightly longer than the other—is to cut a circle from the rawhide in a continuous spiral. One effective way of cutting is to spike a razor-sharp knife into a stump and pull the rawhide into the blade.

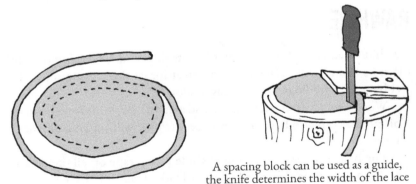

A spacing block can be used as a guide, the knife determines the width of the lace

To use rawhide, soak the lace until it is elastic, tie your lashings, and let them dry. Keep in mind the lace will stretch when wet. To reduce the loosening effect of moisture, stretch the *wet* lace tight between two trees, and let it dry.

BRAINTANNING

Braintanning is a time- and energy-intensive process that is unnecessary in most survival contexts. Ideally, you should be fully prepared with enough clothing and sleeping gear. Just staying fed is strenuous enough, and adding an unnecessary workload is not smart. Nevertheless, I've included this section for reference. This section was done with lots of help from Woniya Thibeault; I also referenced her unpublished book about buckskin sewing, *Buckskin Revolution*.

The aim of braintanning is to preserve the hide in a stable and supple state that won't rot or stiffen up. The three main processes needed for this are dressing (brain solution), softening (stretching and pulling), and smoking.

Do your best to start with a hide without slash marks (knife marks), for those will likely become holes during tanning. When skinning an animal, limit the use of a knife as much as possible and use a combination of pulling and pushing by hand instead.

FLESHING

Fleshing is the removal of the muscle and fat (as well as some membrane and veins) from the hide. This process of scraping is usually done over a round, peeled log, and with a broad scraper, such as a bone with a section removed, or a squared or beveled dull metal scraper, such as a drawknife. Large hides can be laced onto a frame and fleshed with a toothed bone flesher.

Fleshing can be done on a hide staked on the ground, but the two most common ways of fleshing and scraping are with an upright beam and a waist beam:

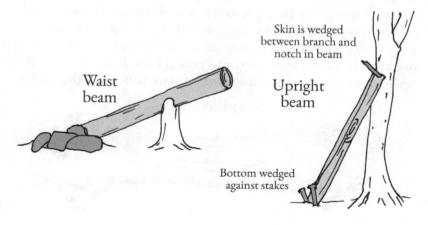

Waist beam

Upright beam

Skin is wedged between branch and notch in beam

Bottom wedged against stakes

Upright beam: lean the log against a tree at a steep angle. Place the skin flesh-side up on the log, and position it so that the hide's top is pinched between the log and tree. Use the scraper as a plow to remove all the fat and flesh.

Waist beam: angle the log high enough so it is at a comfortable height to work on. The hide is pinched between the log and the person's belly.

At this point, the fleshed hides may be stored frozen or dried, but drying will make the grain harder to scrape. In addition, a dried hide will need to be soaked for a longer time for wet-scraping.

SCRAPING

To make buckskin, the hide must be scraped to remove the layers above and below the dermis (mid-dermal layer). For clarity, the removal of the epidermis and grain (hair side) is referred to as *graining* and the removal of the membrane (flesh side) is referred to as *membraning*. Graining is done before membraning to facilitate the scraping of the membrane.

SCRAPING TOOLS

Scraping tools can be made from metal or stone. Chert or flint is used for stone scrapers. Bone and hardwood can also be used for wet-scraping. A rib, ulna, radius, or long leg bone (with a section removed) is often used for bone scrapers. Wooden scrapers must be made out of solid hardwood.

A broad scraper should have a square or beveled edge for use in conjunction with a log base. A beveled edge works better with soft materials, such as bone, while a square edge works better with metal scrapers. To make a bone scraper, remove most of one side of the bone, and sharpen one edge. To cut the bone, score two parallel lines. Then strike it with a stone or tool to break and remove a section of the bone. Smooth the edges.

Broad scraper

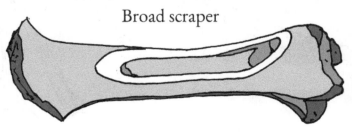

DRY-SCRAPING VERSUS WET-SCRAPING

Two general methods are used to scrape the hide: dry-scraping (often using a rack) and wet-scraping (often using a log).

Dry-scraping is generally used for larger and tougher hides, and should be done in dry weather. In dry-scraping, the hide is laced tightly to a rack while wet, so it dries flat and stiff. A sharp scraper is used to remove the hair and grain. In a dry state, there is no obvious distinction between the grain and dermis, so some of the dermis is scraped along with the grain, which weakens the hide. Dry-scraping is easier to perform with stone tools than wet-scraping.

In wet-scraping, the hair, epidermis, and grain are removed while the hide is wet and pliable. The epidermis and hair come off easily. In contrast, the grain (upper dermis) is thicker and requires vigorous efforts to remove.

WET-SCRAPING

The aim of wet-scraping is to leave the dermis intact and remove the other layers. The hide should be soaked in water to let the bacteria loosen the bonds between the dermis and grain.

Soaking can be done in a bucket, a stream, or a lake. The hide should be soaked long enough for the bacteria to weaken the bonds, but not long enough for them to weaken the dermis. It should be carefully monitored and pulled out once the hair "slips" (pulls out easily by hand). It could take between three days to a week, depending on the air temperature. The hide is being actively broken down by bacteria so it must be carefully monitored or it could rot.

Graining Once soaked, the hide is scraped over a beam, hair-side up, with a dull tool (but sharp enough to scrape the grain). Working the neck first—the hardest section—makes all the following steps easier, but some people recommend beginning with other areas first.

Start in a small patch, and work as hard as possible. Be aggressive. A common mistake is to remove some superficial hide gunk but leave the grain. The top layer of skin is easily scraped off, but the thick grain layer below is harder to remove. Matt Richards (*Deerskins to Buckskins*) writes that if the tool is not sharp, you can't scrape too deep. Once the grain is removed, an evidently different surface will show at a closer look: grain looks smooth and shiny while dermis looks more textured and matte.

Scrape in the general direction of the hair. Try to remove as much tissue as possible with each stroke; every stroke must overlap the last.

After a small patch is done, keep working from there. Always work from a scraped section into bordering sections, like a plow. Overlap each stroke. Focusing intensely on a tiny area will show you if you need to be more aggressive. Pay close attention to the finished areas, and expand slowly from there, removing the grain fully. If you jump around without fully removing the grain, you'll have difficulty later distinguishing the well-scraped areas. Hair can be a good indicator of where you've worked. Rewetting the skin will make the grain appear raised and shiny when looked at closely.

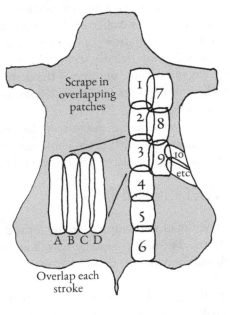

Scrape in overlapping patches

Overlap each stroke

Work carefully near holes and cuts. Only scrape toward the hole; don't pass over it. Scrape only up to the edge, or you will likely tear the skin. Don't scrape over folds.

If the skin is drying too fast, moisten it with water. Plan on spending a couple hours graining it.

MEMBRANING

Work carefully over the flesh side once you've done the grain side. Membraning is easier and less critical. Use the same techniques as before, but this time do longer, broader strokes and be less methodical. Scraping and removing the membrane allows the brain solution to penetrate deeper. But if there is a tiny bit of membrane left, don't worry. The hide must be wet and pliable during this process; if it dries out, you must resoak it. Be careful not to scrape over folds and cut the hide. The flesh side is easier to cut by accident.

After graining and membraning, there is an opportunity to dry and store the hide. Storing the hide also helps remove the mucous fluid (ground substance) that coats the hide. Stretch the hide on a rack or stake it on the ground. Hides in this stage are susceptible to damage from insects and critters.

BRAIN SOLUTION

It's said that an animal has enough brain mass to tan its hide, but that mass may not be sufficient. You might need additional additives, such as liver and spinal column contents in conjunction with the brain. Other possible additives are light oils, fats, and bone marrow. But it's the natural emulsifiers contained in the brain that allow the fats to penetrate the fibers and mix with the watery coating of the hide. This solution acts like a sort of lubricant that allows the fibers to dry—while being constantly stretched and pulled—without sticking to each other.

The brain can be removed by inserting a stick into the opening at the base of the skull. If there is a relevant possibility that the animal carried rabies or prions (e.g., chronic wasting disease), avoid touching the brain and spinal fluids.

Another option instead of using a stick is to open the skull with an axe: start at the nose and split it down the center until the two halves can be pried apart. Once the brain is out of the skull, it should be used or preserved. If the brain will be used within two to three days, leaving it in the head intact is practical.

The brain can be frozen or dried for preservation. To dry it in the field, mix the brain thoroughly with absorbent moss, dry grass, or lichen. Form the mix into cakes and dry them under the sun or next to a fire. To use the cakes, dissolve them in hot water and remove the plant material.

WRINGING

To encourage the absorption of the brain solution, the hide should be slightly damp but not moist. Wringing helps get rid of excess moisture and also encourages the soaking of the fibers. To wring out the hide, place it neck-down over a solid, smooth horizontal pole as shown. Overlap a few inches of the hide to form a roll or a sleeve.

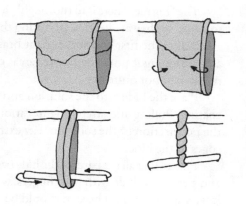

Then roll up the ends of the sleeve towards the center until you form a loop with the hide. Insert a robust and smooth stick into the loop and press against the bottom of the sleeve. Rotate the stick. Twist medium and thick hides as hard as you can, but don't twist thin hides too hard. Wait for the skin to finish dripping and twist the other way.

Grab the top of the sleeve and rotate it downwards to wring it again in a slightly different position. Wring it out eight times in four different positions as described above.

Unfold the hide to check if it was wrung out thoroughly. Its color should be translucent white with only a few gray, soggy spots. If there are numerous bluish, moist spots, another wringing is needed.

Stretch the hide using either your knee, fleshing log, stake, or wringing branch. The hide should look more leather-like and lose its transparency as it stretches.

Soggy spots must be squeegeed out. You can also stretch the hide and use a cloth to absorb the moisture. Wringing thoroughly directly impacts how soft your buckskin will be.

Don't let the hide dry at this point; ensure you're ready to soak it in the brain solution or place it in a plastic bag for braining later.

BRAINING

Using a container is more practical for braining, but it is not necessary. Instead, the brains can be mashed and smeared onto the skin with a bit of water. Try to conserve the tanning solution as much as possible. To ensure you leave enough for more than one treatment, rub the brains in a thin layer, and save the liquids for reuse. The animal's stomach may also be used as a container for braining.

The "big idea" here is to thoroughly impregnate the fibers with the brain solution so they are lubricated during the softening and stretching stage.

Before the first and subsequent brainings, stretch and work the skin as if softening it until the thicker areas turn whitish. The hide should be nearly, but not quite dry.

Place the hide into the solution and make sure everything gets a good coating. Pulling and stretching in various directions will greatly improve the penetration of the solution. Pay extra attention around holes and the edges of the hide.

Ensure that all the parts of the hide become thoroughly saturated. Knead and stretch the hide with your fingers, working over the whole skin. Don't leave any stiff areas. The skin should be as flexible as when it was fresh.

Immerse the skin fully for 20 minutes and up to a few hours, or overnight. The hide will begin to deteriorate if left too long. You can add water to cover the skin entirely. Working the hide while in the solution will help a lot more than simply soaking it for longer.

Wring out the skin between immersions, and work the difficult-to-penetrate areas. Do two to four cycles of braining, wringing, and working, depending on the skin's thickness. After the final wringing, be sure to examine the skin and wring out any remaining soggy spots.

If there are holes in the hide, this is a good time for sewing them; otherwise, the softening process can make them bigger.

SOFTENING AND STRETCHING

Softening is best done on a warm, sunny day but out of direct sunlight if it's too hot. It is the most labor-intensive step. Generally, it is wise to follow through on the softening phase once you start it. From this stage on, the skin must be stretched and pulled the entire time it is drying. Any areas that go from wet to dry without being worked during the entire process will remain stiff. The "big idea" here is to constantly work the fibers to impede them from getting "glued" together as they dry.

There are two common ways to soften hides: on a rack where they are worked with a stick (see the "Pelt tanning" section), or with the hands where they are pulled and stretched (often with aids, such as a stake).

I'll describe the process of using a stake to stretch the hide. Adapt these suggestions if you are using another method, such as a rack.

The stake is made by cutting a three-inch-wide sapling that is 3 ft. (1 m) above the ground. The sapling should have a wedge-shaped top with a slightly rounded edge. The hide is pulled, pushed, and stretched aggressively over the stake.

A strong, smooth overhanging branch can also be used for stretching. Drape the hide over the branch, and grab each edge. Slide it back and forth, pulling hard, as if you were using a wire saw. Another option is to frame the hide and use a dull tool (e.g., axe handle or paddle) to stretch it.

Work every part of the hide. Focus particularly on the fast-drying areas (i.e., the edges, the belly, and the legs). Work the edges frequently until they are dry and soft. Stretch the hide aggressively; it won't tear, but be careful around holes.

As the hide dries, glazed spots may develop on both sides. Stiff spots on the outside may need to be rubbed with something rough, like sandstone or pumice stone. Problem areas and stiffness on the inside can be softened with aggressive stretching on the stake or branch. Stretch the skin in every possible direction. To learn to read the hide, look at it carefully as a whole and then in small sections.

If clean, the fully dried skin should be soft, stretchy, and white. Do not let the hide get wet or you'll be back to square one.

SMOKING

Smoking is the critical final stage that prevents water from undoing all the hard work done throughout the tanning process. Typically, two hides and a cotton skirt are sewn together into a bag and placed over a smoky fire.

But in a pinch, a framework of green willow sticks over a pit works. Arrange the hide close to the ground to slow down the escaping smoke and quicken the process.

Use dry, rotten wood to smoke the skins. Avoid resinous punkwood from conifers. Don't let the smoky mass flare up. The fire should fluctuate between smoldering and smoking only. You'll need to attend to the hide the entire time. Watch and listen to the fire closely, as it can flare up quickly. If the smoking does flare up, remove the skin at once. And if it starts to get a hot spot, cover it with more punkwood.

Smoke the grain side first until a golden color bleeds through to the flesh side. Shift the skin regularly to smoke the spots in contact with the frame. Smoking the flesh side is optional. The hide is fully smoked once it is permeated by a rich golden color.

If the skin gets wet, treat it like a wool sweater and lay it flat to dry. You may hang it once it's almost dry.

STORING GREEN HIDES

The simplest way of storing a fresh hide for tanning later is to roll it in a tight bundle, put it in a sealed bag, and freeze it (the bag prevents the skin from freeze-drying). Fleshing is optional but encouraged.

The other simple method is to dry it. Unfortunately, dried skins are more challenging to soak, requiring much stretching and pulling in water to get them saturated. Typically, if the hides are stored dry for a long time, the scraping process will be harder while the softening process will be easier.

To dry a skin, first flesh it thoroughly. Remove all the fat to avoid grease-burning it; rubbing sawdust or dry sand onto the skin helps remove the fat. Then stake the hide several inches above the ground to allow air to circulate. Hides dried this way can be rolled and stored.

PELT TANNING

Tanning with the hair intact is a bit similar to the process for tanning skins, but it can be more work, depending on how soft you want the pelt to be. In addition, the tools and techniques are slightly different. The membrane, flesh, and fat must be removed entirely. Not removing them completely is a common mistake.

When tanning pelts, the objective is to soften and preserve the hide while keeping the hair intact. Therefore, skip the steps that encourage the hair to loosen up: don't wring the pelt by twisting, and don't immerse the skin in the brain solution. When the hide is dried quickly, the hair sets in very well, but the hair will fall out if the skin is left wet or green for a long time.

Commonly, pelts are softened on a rack or by hand (see "Braintanning" section).

The skin may be tied to a rack or staked while fresh off the animal. Then it should be fleshed and dried rapidly or tanned right away. Hides that have been fleshed and dried must be soaked thoroughly, but quickly, before being racked.

The rack is a large wooden

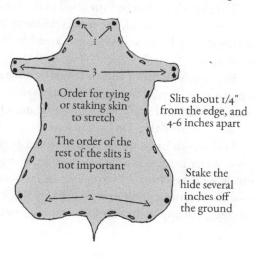

Order for tying or staking skin to stretch

The order of the rest of the slits is not important

Slits about 1/4" from the edge, and 4-6 inches apart

Stake the hide several inches off the ground

frame. The skin is laced into the frame. It's best to make the frame 5"–6" larger than the skin.

Cut slits 0.5" long, parallel to the edge—about 0.25"–0.5" away from it and 3"–4" apart. An efficient method of racking a hide is to lace the top of the rack first and then lace the bottom with another cord. The skin is stretched this way, and then the sides are laced, adjusting as you go to remove the wrinkles. Avoid over-tightening the hide.

Lean the rack against a tree and use a toothed scraper to flesh and membrane the skin. The toothed scraper is much more effective than a toothless tool. This bone scraper is simpler to make, but it requires frequent sharpening and re-cutting of its teeth. To make one, score a deep diagonal line around the end of a straight leg bone, such as the tibia. Use a rock to break the bone along the scored line and shape it into a chisel. Scoring bone is difficult, but the deeper you score, the more chances of success. The edge is serrated with a saw or file. When the bone is fresh, it can be shaped with a hatchet and file.

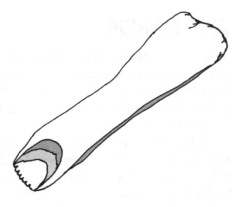

Braining and pre-softening are all performed in repeated cycles.

The skin shouldn't be immersed in the brain solution, or it can result in hair slippage. Instead, the flesh side must be thoroughly rubbed and saturated with brain solution, but avoid wetting the hair side with the solution.

Braining is more difficult and must be done almost twice as many times. You can't over-brain. When the solution dries into a coating, you'll have to scrape it off and apply the solution again. On the final braining, apply the solution until the skin is saturated.

Hides with hair cannot be wrung out as with buckskin. Instead, the excess water is squeezed by hand, and the skin is racked. Work the skin multiple times with a dull squeegee-like tool to remove as much water as possible. A canoe paddle may be used for this step. The squeegee is used as a scraper, starting at the top and scraping towards the bottom.

A long stick of wood sharpened to a flat, double-beveled edge is used to stretch the racked hide. The skin is poked, scraped, and rubbed on the flesh side with the stick as it dries.

To soften the hide, thoroughly break or work it as it dries. The stretching process is harder than with a hairless hide. Depending on the final use for the pelt, it may not need to be softened as much.

The final step is to smoke it. Smoking is crucial and also helps protect the pelt from bugs. Only the flesh side needs to be smoked.

BUSHCRAFT

WOOD CARVING

Wood carving is easier with softwoods, but sometimes you'll have to work with hardwoods. Use a mallet, hatchet, or saw to speed up the process.

JOGGED AND WEDGED SPLICE

This splice is used to join two logs or sticks together end to end. Two wedges are inserted to secure the splice.

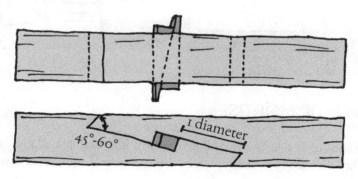

DOVETAIL NOTCH

The dovetail notch is a handy way to make items such as a mallet or a table. Start dovetail notches at about halfway through the diameter of the piece of wood. It's best to carve the notch first and then adapt the stick to the notch, and not the other way around.

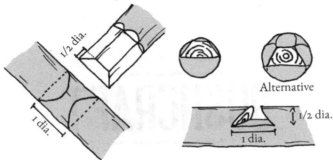

Alternative

SPEAR NOTCH

The spear notch is used for fitting arrowheads and for other projects. A stick with a straight grain is best for this purpose. The V notches *A* and *B* shouldn't be deeper than one-third of the diameter, or the stick will break. Notches *X* and *Y* should be made one-quarter deep at a narrow angle. Once the notches are cut, the stick is laid on a flat surface with the surface's edge below the *X* and *Y* notches. The stick is then hit with increasingly harder blows until a snap is heard. Turn the stick and repeat the process to split the other side. Then move the stick back and forth until the notch breaks away.

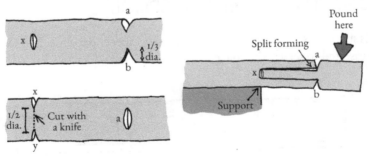

KNIFE TIP MORTISE

The stick must first be carved down to cut a hole with just a knife. Then the knife is used to cut a square hole through both sides. Making a round hole is messier. These holes are helpful for making some primitive snares, such as the Anishinaabe bird snare.

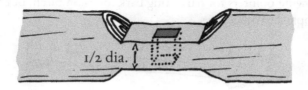

BURN AND SCRAPE

Burn and scrape is a handy primitive technique for making holes and cuts and hollowing out wood. Softwoods are easier to burn with a coal.

Make a fire with hardwoods to make a few good coals. Then use green sticks as chopsticks to grab the coals. Make a small hole or depression in the wood with your knife to place the coals in. Blow onto the coals to burn out the wood. A blowtube will speed up the process. You may use moist mud to cover areas you don't want to burn. Every once in a while, remove the coals and scrape the charred material.

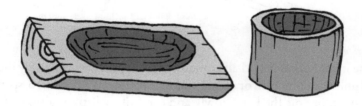

STEAM BENDING

Steam and boiling water can be used to bend and shape wood. When moist heat is applied, the wood fibers get loose. Then they realign into the new shape as they cool down, but they need to be held in place during this cooling down period. This technique is useful for straightening wooden arrows and making sleds.

Thin green sticks may be heated directly over coals and bent into shape, but using steam and boiling water works best. In addition to placing wood directly in boiling water, you can wrap some cloth around the wood and pour boiling water over it.

HARVESTING BARK

The following pointers for harvesting bark focus on birch, but they can also be applied to other trees.

Bark is generally harvested in the spring or early summer when the sap flows and the bark peels off the tree easily. Bark that is harvested during a winter thaw or in early spring is a bit more solid than bark gathered later in the year. Summer bark separates into layers more easily.

Choose a tree devoid of branches and with a smooth trunk. Place some skids for the trunk to fall on (as shown) or fell the tree from one side only. Then, cut two circles around the tree and join them in a straight line.

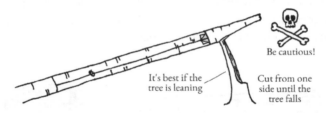

Be cautious!

It's best if the tree is leaning

Cut from one side until the tree falls

If the inner bark is peeled all around the trunk, the tree will likely die, so peel only the outer bark or use the tree for firewood. With a sharp, spatula-like stick, pry off the bark slowly and carefully, a little at a time. Then continue peeling with your hands.

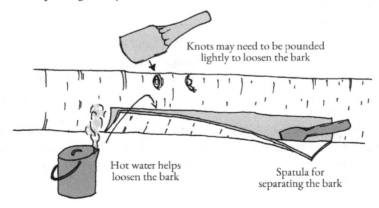

Knots may need to be pounded lightly to loosen the bark

Hot water helps loosen the bark

Spatula for separating the bark

Large pieces may be stripped from the trunk using wooden wedges. Hot water can facilitate the separation, and problematic areas may be gently pounded to loosen the bark.

It's best to use bark while it is fresh. Keep it cool and in the shade, and don't let it dry out. Keeping bark damp or submerged keeps it fresh and flexible, but it may mildew if left for too long.

PINE PITCH

Pine pitch can be used as an improvised glue or sealant. To make pine pitch, collect pine resin from tree wounds. Avoid old sap, as it's more brittle. Use gummy resin instead. Pure resin works better, so you might have to heat it into a liquid and filter out any debris.

Heat the resin, and as soon as it turns liquid, maintain or reduce the heat. Do not overheat it or it will turn brittle. Then, add a little bit of temper material to strengthen the pitch, but not too much, or it will turn brittle. Ground charcoal is often used as temper, but rabbit droppings, hardwood ash, and sawdust work.

You can dip a stick into the pitch and let the pitch harden around the stick for later use and storage. Proper pine pitch should retain some flexibility once it cools down.

METAL TOOLS

MULTI-TOOLS

Multi-tools have many uses in the wilderness. Their pliers are handy for removing fishhooks (from fish and humans alike), making repairs, and working with wire and metal. I recommend the models made by Leatherman, such as the Surge or the G10 Charge+. In addition to pliers, multi-tools often have small saws, files, and other implements that can be very useful in a remote environment.

I recommend two multi-tool modifications: swapping the serrated knife for a regular blade and sharpening the screwdriver into a chisel.

For cold regions, I recommend the G10 Charge+ because the composite scales are more ergonomic and reduce contact with cold metal. I attach a short piece of paracord to my multi-tool to make it more visible if dropped in deep snow.

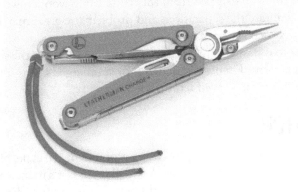

AUGERS

Augers are pretty useful for making camp furniture and building structures. A 1″ auger is the most versatile and can be used for making chairs, tables, tools, and other general projects. **BlackRaven.com** sells scotch eye augers that are portable and allow you to use a stick as an improvised handle.

Some ways of keeping wooden pins in place are to make the pegs square, nick them, or peg them with a small wedge.

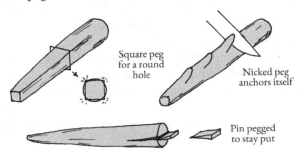

Square peg for a round hole

Nicked peg anchors itself

Pin pegged to stay put

SHOVELS

A compact shovel or entrenching tool (e-tool) can be a great addition to your kit. In many places of the boreal forest, the ground is not very deep—due to the Canadian Shield rock—and there is deep snow in winter, so a snow shovel makes more sense than an e-tool.

In lower latitudes, portable shovels can be quite valuable. I recommend the Cold Steel shovel or the Russian-made titanium shovel. The titanium shovel weighs about 40% less than the Cold Steel shovel, but it can't be sharpened for cutting—which is not a deal-breaker. Both shovels feature zero moving parts, and their handles can be easily replaced. These shovels are ideal for long-term situations, as you can just pack the blade and screws and carve out a much longer and more practical handle in the field.

IMPROVISED TOOLS

BUCKSAWS

It's always best to have the right tool for the job, but you may be constrained by its weight or bulk. Saw blades are very cheap and lightweight, so they can be a last-resort alternative for a ready-made saw.

The improvised bucksaw shown on the next page is the H bucksaw variation created by Kelly Harlton. Shave the bark off all the parts of the bucksaw to speed up the drying process and thus reduce the saw's weight. Spruce or pine works reasonably well for this type of field saw.

This bucksaw takes more time to make but provides great saw-blade tension, making the saw cut more efficiently.

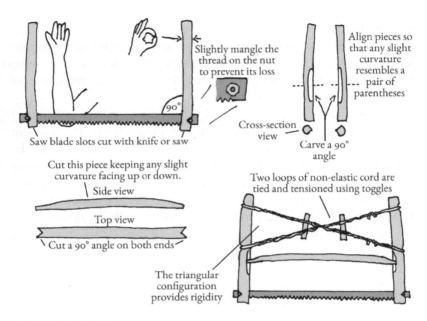

Slightly mangle the thread on the nut to prevent its loss

Align pieces so that any slight curvature resembles a pair of parentheses

Saw blade slots cut with knife or saw

Cross-section view

Carve a 90° angle

Cut this piece keeping any slight curvature facing up or down.

Side view

Top view

Cut a 90° angle on both ends

Two loops of non-elastic cord are tied and tensioned using toggles

The triangular configuration provides rigidity

BOW SAWS

The fastest way to improvise a saw is to curve a green sapling and make a bow saw. The saw blade can be retained with bolts, nails, hardwood pegs, split rings, wire, or lashings.

Trim off the branches from a straight, green sapling of birch, spruce, or pine. Curve the sapling and tie it into shape. Then, cut to length, make slots for the saw blade, and carve notches to keep the bolts in place. Fit the blade and untie the sapling.

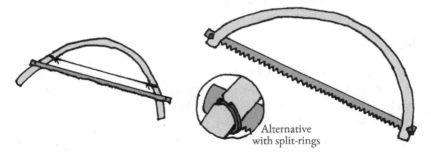

Alternative with split-rings

MALLET

If you are relying on a metal stove, you'll need to split wood, and this is where the mallet shines. In a long-term situation, you might be exhausted and have less-than-ideal tools to work with, which can be a dangerous combination. With a mallet, you can use a hatchet to split wood and make kindling more safely and in the comfort of your shelter. The mallet also comes in handy for numerous bushcraft projects.

There are various ways of making a mallet, but I prefer to start with a solid, heavy log and carve out a slim handle from the same piece using a saw and an axe.

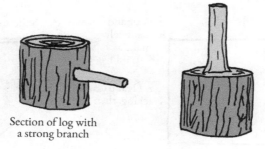

Section of log with
a strong branch

DIGGING STICK

Digging sticks can be quickly improvised from green hardwoods, and they are useful for digging up roots and tubers. Often the end of the stick is fire-hardened, but this is not necessary. The designs below allow you to use your foot to dig, like with a shovel.

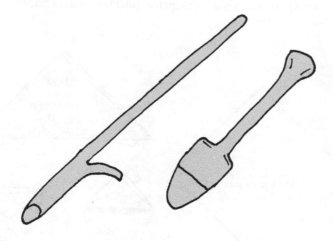

BIRCH BARK CONTAINERS

To make the bark more flexible, soak it briefly in hot water. Soaking too long may cause it to curl up. Shape the container while it's warm. Once cooled, the bark will hold the shape it had while warm.

The simplest bark container to make is a seamless—thus waterproof—pan. The folded corners can be quickly fastened with a few stitches of cord or spruce roots, or with a willow pin.

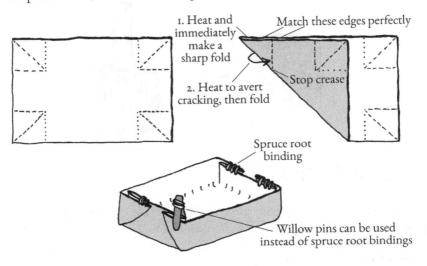

1. Heat and immediately make a sharp fold

Match these edges perfectly

Stop crease

2. Heat to avert cracking, then fold

Spruce root binding

Willow pins can be used instead of spruce root bindings

Below is a well-known origami design for quickly making a folded cup with birchbark.

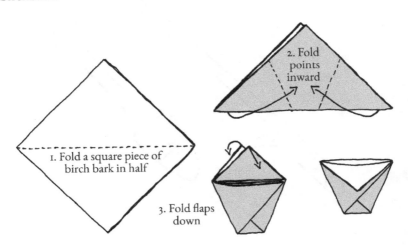

1. Fold a square piece of birch bark in half

2. Fold points inward

3. Fold flaps down

Making a pail or deep container is more complicated and requires more care. In traditional designs, the bottom is rectangular, the top has a circular rim, and the rim is often reinforced. Small containers are made from layers of split bark, and larger containers are made from thick bark. The pattern should be large enough to allow the seams to overlap. If the container must be waterproof, use pine pitch to seal the seams and stitches.

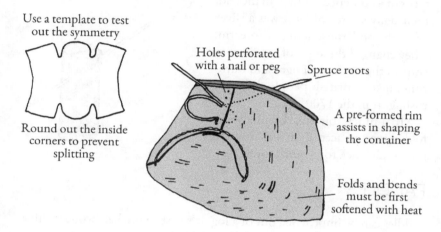

Use a template to test out the symmetry

Round out the inside corners to prevent splitting

Holes perforated with a nail or peg

Spruce roots

A pre-formed rim assists in shaping the container

Folds and bends must be first softened with heat

CUTTING BOARD

Cutting boards can be improvised by sawing a log at an acute angle.

30°

BUSH CANDLE

The challenge of having a sustainable source of light in the wild has long intrigued me. There are plenty of ways for making oil lamps, pine pitch "candles," and torches. The problem with oil lamps is that fat is generally too valuable to be used for purposes other than nutrition. The problem with pitch and torches is that they are too smoky and burn quickly.

After reading *Lost in the Taiga*, I finally learned of a viable option for a truly practical long-term light source. The Lykov family spent 40 years in isolation, and they tried many types of improvised candles. In the end, their daily source of light was a sliver of birchwood, the length of a forearm. They changed the angle of the sliver to control the amount of light and burn-time, just as British people did with rushlights in the 1700s.

In a pinch, birchbark can also be folded into an accordion and inserted into a split stick for a quick torch.

PADDLES

Paddles can be improvised out of a log. It's best to use hardwoods with a straight grain and without knots. Split the log in two, and thin down one split. Check for rot or irregularities. Then, roughly sketch the shape of the paddle on the split. If you have a saw, you can make a series of cuts perpendicular to the paddle to facilitate cutting it into shape. Once the paddle is roughly carved with the axe, use a knife to carefully finish the rest of the work. Hang the paddle as it dries to limit any warpage.

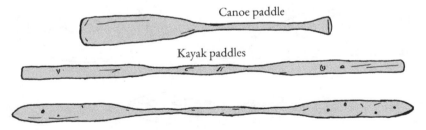

Canoe paddle

Kayak paddles

SNOW GOGGLES

Snow goggles can be quickly cut out of birch bark, and more elaborate goggles can be carved from wood.

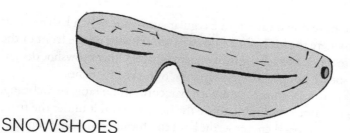

SNOWSHOES

There are many styles of improvised snowshoes. The snow depth, terrain, and available materials will encourage a particular design over another.

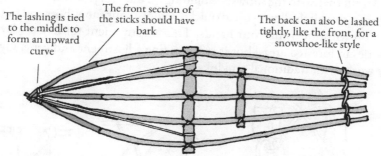

The lashing is tied to the middle to form an upward curve

The front section of the sticks should have bark

The back can also be lashed tightly, like the front, for a snowshoe-like style

This basic design can be adjusted to be longer and function as a ski-shoe

The Roycraft ski-shoe is made from 4–5 ft. (1.2–1.5 m) long poles and cross-sticks 0.75″ (2 cm) thick and 10″ (25 cm) long. In total, 10 poles and four cross-sticks are needed.

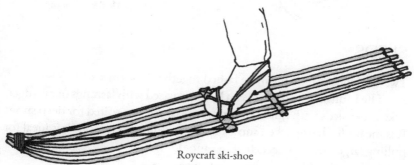

Roycraft ski-shoe

Lay down five poles parallel to each other on the ground and tie them loosely at the tip. Stripping the bark off helps the bindings stay tight, but leave a section of bark at the front of the snowshoe. Lift the poles horizontally to find their balance points and mark them. The tail is lashed crosswise with paracord. And the front cross-stick is bound just forward of the midpoint, where the toes of the boot step on. Leave some allowance for the tip of

Improvised tools | 341

the toes to move downward as in a regular snowshoe. Then lash another cross-stick where the heel of the boot will rest. Finally, tie the front of the snowshoe to the cross-stick to give it a curved shape. Other snowshoe designs use dense spruce boughs, flexible saplings, or forked branches.

Bindings can be improvised with paracord, mule tape, or webbing. Start with the rope's midpoint above the heel, and run it under the front cross-piece. Then pass them across the boot toe, forming an *X*, and continue as shown below. When walking, the bindings should allow your toes to move down while your heel rises, and the front of the snowshoe should rise above the snow.

An alternative to the snowshoe binding on the left is the Indian hitch. In theory, this hitch allows you to quickly remove your snowshoes and put them on without using your hands. This is convenient for day-to-day activities in forested areas, but it requires fine adjustment and generally only works with traditional mukluks.

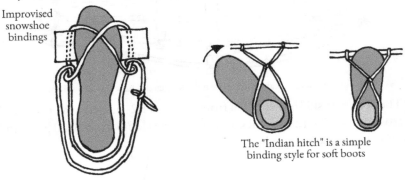

Improvised snowshoe bindings

The "Indian hitch" is a simple binding style for soft boots

SLEDS

Two Roycraft ski shoes can be lashed together to form a sled.

The Inuit sled (*qamutik*) can be improvised with lashings or an auger. Like other sleds with minimal surface areas, it is not suited for deep snow. It is meant for hardpacked snow or slushy snow over ice, but it is ideal for pulling large, heavy objects (e.g., a canoe).

The sled design below, built with an auger and steam-bent runners, is similar to the sled Dick Proenneke crafted and used in Alaska.

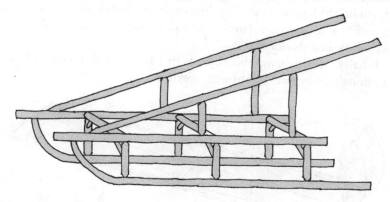

Toboggans are narrow and better suited for deep snow. They are made from two or three thin boards of green birch (preferred) or dry tamarack, each about 6–10 ft. (2–3 m) long, 3"–7" (8–18 cm) wide, and 1/4"–3/8" (7–10 mm) thick.

The board's end from the lowest part of the trunk is more flexible, so it is positioned toward the front of the sled. Keep in mind that the wood closest to the bark bends better. A birch log about 12" (30 cm) in diameter can yield two boards about 7" (18 cm) wide each.

Cut two grooves 1.5" (4 cm) deep on the top and bottom. Use an axe and wedges to split the log. The inner sides of the splits are hewed down to obtain 8" (20 cm) wide boards; the dried and finished boards will end up about 7" wide. Aim to hew the boards to a thickness of 3/8", which will result in a dried and finished board 1/4" thick.

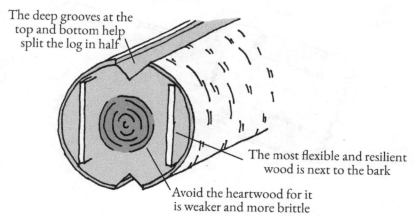

The deep grooves at the top and bottom help split the log in half

The most flexible and resilient wood is next to the bark

Avoid the heartwood for it is weaker and more brittle

The reference lines for hewing the boards can be made by rubbing charcoal onto a cord, stringing it in a straight line, and then pulling it and snapping it down on the log. Score the log close to the desired depth with a saw or axe, and hew it using the scores as an aid. Expect to spend a full day of work on the boards alone.

Finally, steam-bend the boards and fasten a few cross-pieces. Traditionally, they were lashed with rawhide.

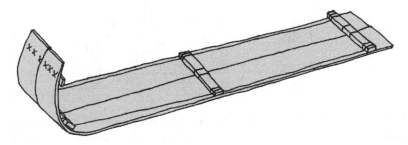

SNOW SHOVELS

A snow shovel can be improvised following an Inuit design by using two or three wooden boards and a wooden handle, and joining everything with rawhide stitches. Finally, a hand strap is attached to the middle of the shovel. Traditionally, the shovels had a piece of bone at the blade's tip to protect the boards.

Another way to improvise a snow shovel is to make a wooden paddle with a concave blade.

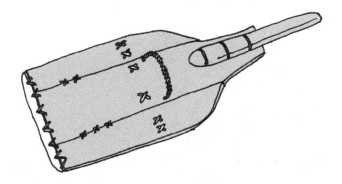

CAMP FURNITURE

BED

A bed frame can be improvised with sticks and poles. Some people make a bush mattress straight on the ground or over a pile of compacted snow between two wide logs, but I prefer a bed about the height of a chair. In an insulated shelter, the higher the bed, the warmer it is. In addition, high beds can be built on uneven ground, and they provide dry storage underneath.

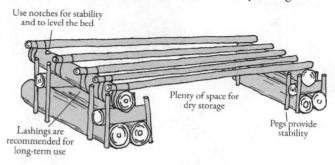

Use notches for stability and to level the bed

Plenty of space for dry storage

Lashings are recommended for long-term use

Pegs provide stability

These frames don't move as much as you might think; nevertheless, you can minimize any movement by using stakes, lashings, or rough notches.

Balsam fir boughs are an excellent material for the top of a bush mattress. Save the softest and best boughs for last and concentrate them around the part where your trunk and head will rest. The problem with balsam fir is that the needles flatten and drop more quickly than spruce. It's best to have spruce as the bulk of the cushioning and add a top layer of balsam fir for softness, but the spruce layer is what gives the bed its springiness. Boughs can be laid one by one for multiple layers or in a single layer of small handfuls, if time is of the essence.

Pay attention to the boughs' curves and lay them with an upright arch. Depending on how much comfort and insulation you need, you'll need a compressed thickness of at least four fingers to one handspan. Remember that your weight will compress the mattress overnight to about one-third of the starting thickness, so you'll have to add a fresh layer of boughs after a couple of days.

Where pine boughs are unavailable, you can use multiple layers of thin sticks, brush, reeds, grass, and leaves; these beds can be just as comfortable as spruce bough beds as long as you use progressively finer materials and make the top layers quite thick.

CHAIR

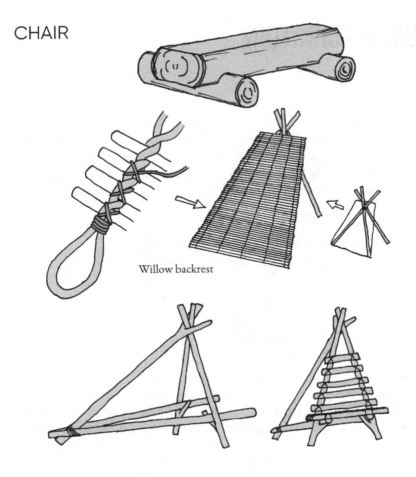

Willow backrest

AUGER-MADE FURNITURE

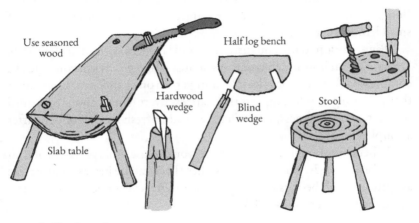

Use seasoned wood

Slab table

Hardwood wedge

Half log bench

Blind wedge

Stool

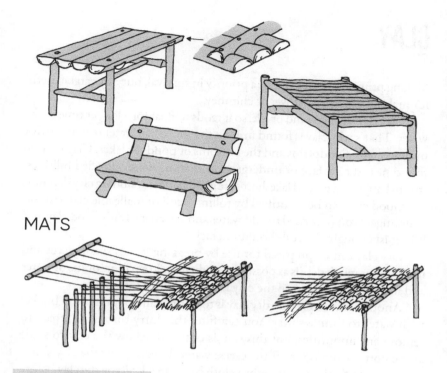

MATS

BASKETRY

Making rudimentary baskets is quite simple once you learn the fundamentals. Start with two sets of flexible, green sticks (warps), lay them in a cross, and add an odd stick so that the weave alternates over and under in the following rows. Weave a few rows to hold the sticks in place, spread them apart, and weave over and under each stick. I recommend using willow splints for the warps and spruce roots for the wefts. Curve the warps and weave tightly to give the basket its curvature.

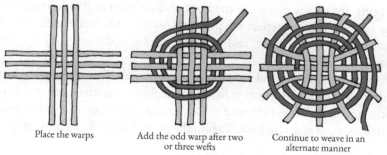

Place the warps   Add the odd warp after two   Continue to weave in an
                                or three wefts   alternate manner

CLAY

Making primitive pottery is not a priority in survival, but clay can be useful for making a fireplace, stove, or chimney.

Clay is finer than sand or silt, so it tends to float for a longer time in the water. That's why clay is found in areas that once had water over them; for instance, river floodplains and the bottoms of ponds or lakes. Clay is often found near the surface or underground at some depth. Eroded hillsides, stream banks, and eroded lakeshores are good places for finding clay deposits.

Good clay can be identified by rolling a coil of malleable clay around your finger (you may need to add water and knead it). If it's good clay and it's moist enough, the coil shouldn't crack.

Dry clay can be prepared for use by breaking it into small pieces and removing as much debris as possible. Gradually add small amounts of water and mix it in. Repeat until the clay is easily molded into shape.

Another way to prepare dry clay is to crush it and pour it into a bucket with water to form a slurry. You can filter the slurry through a screen to remove any impurities, but this step is optional. Allow the clay to settle at the bottom and pour off the excess water. Finally, pour the clay slurry over a tarp to dry it, or place it in a cloth bag instead. Shape the clay before it dries completely.

If you find clay that is already naturally moist, just remove as much foreign matter as possible to use it.

Even if you don't have an obvious source of clay, you can use two buckets to extract clay from soil with a high clay content. This is also an effective way of separating debris. Fill a bucket half-full with soil and fill the rest with water. Stir the soil and water until it is evenly mixed. Then, just let it settle until the water clears up. The clay will settle at the top layer. Carefully pour out the water without mixing up the layers of clay and soil. Then slowly pour the clay layer into another bucket, trying not to bring any of the dirt from the bottom layer with it. To clean out the clay further, you can repeat the previous process: add water, mix it, let it settle, pour out the water, and separate the clay at the top. Dry the clay slurry as described earlier.

Before shaping the clay, it must be tempered. Temper helps reduce shrinking and cracking during firing and makes the pottery better able to withstand heat shock. Fine sand makes a good temper, as do some organic materials, such as cattail fuzz. To find the proper ratio of clay and temper, mix some samples—with different ratios—into pencil-sized pieces, and let them dry. The ones that do not crack are likely good ratios.

Form clay into a thick pancake and cut a 1/4 piece off

Form a dam with the removed piece

Fill the void with temper

Usually, a temper of 20% works well. To get that ratio, make a pancake with clay, remove a quarter of it, and fill that part with a temper, as shown above.

If your pottery keeps cracking after trying different approaches, break up and grind down the cracked pottery and use the powder as a temper.

Parts sand	Parts clay	Temper
1	9	10%
1	6	14%
1	4	20%
1	3	25%
1	2	33%

PRIMITIVE POTTERY

Making primitive pottery that can be used for holding water and cooking is more complex than making a clay fireplace. For making vessels, the steps for drying and firing need to be done much more gradually and carefully.

The next step after tempering is to dry the pottery. To prevent cracks, it should be dried as slowly as possible, so place it in the shade and out of the wind.

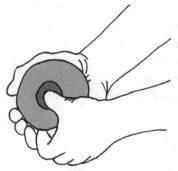
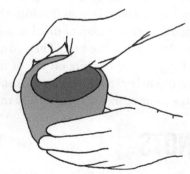

Roll the clay into a ball and push your thumb into the center

Gradually pinch the sides to make them thinner

Roll out a coil

To enlarge a pinch pot,
add a coil to the top while
the clay is still moist

Smooth the coil
into the pot

Once the pottery is dry, place it in the sunlight or near a fire to remove any residual moisture before firing it. But don't heat it too quickly or it may crack. If it develops a crack, it's best to crush the pottery and start over.

Roll the clay into a pancake
on a piece of cloth

Work the clay into a bowl,
which will serve as a mold

When firing, the aim is to heat the pottery slowly and evenly from all sides, eventually building up to a very high temperature. One simple way to do this is to place the pots over a pile of small, thumb-sized sticks and place some medium-sized logs at the sides of the fire. Cover the pots with organic material, such as pieces of dried manure, punkwood, or wood chips; this layer slows down the heat. Then cover the pile with sticks and logs. The final step is to start a fire on top of the woodpile. That way, the fire will burn top to bottom in a slower manner. After the fire dies down, you can scrape some coals away, but ensure the pottery cools down slowly.

KNOTS

This section will reference many useful knots, hitches, and lashings, but you can make do with only a handful of them. The most important knot for survival is the bowline. You can accomplish 80% of the tasks for survival with a bowline and its variants. The other 20% can be done with the figure-eight bend, trucker's hitch, friction hitch, girth hitch, clove hitch, Klemheist knot, Prusik knot, jam knot, and a tripod lashing, among other types.

I emphasize practical and versatile knots that can be untied even if tightly pulled under heavy loads. That is very important in a survival context where synthetic cordage is limited and cutting cordage is almost taboo.

CORDAGE

Have three or four cords of different diameters. Avoid earth-toned cords because they are easy to lose. Modern cordage is extremely valuable in the wild, so you'll have to be very strategic when rationing it. Try not to use cordage that is stronger than what is needed. Don't count on using paracord inner strands or cannibalizing other cords; that is a last resort, not a plan.

Paracord should be the largest diameter cord. Anything stronger is overkill and adds unnecessary weight and bulk for most circumstances.

Genuine MIL-SPEC 550 parachute cord is a static cord with seven inner strands and a minimum strength of 550 lb. (250 kg). Authentic MIL-SPEC paracord is best because its inner strands have three strands each instead of only two. The three-ply strands work much better for various applications, while the inner strands of commercial paracord unravel easily.

Paracord can be used for bear hangs, tripod lashings, or shelter lashings. Pack about 150 ft. (45 m) of paracord.

As a precaution, consider the *safe* working load of paracord to be half of its rated strength. Paracord should never be used for climbing because it is not a dynamic cord, and the force exerted in a fall (mass times acceleration) easily exceeds its strength.

Bank line is an excellent option for anything water-related, such as trotlines and setting nets. Pack about 150 ft. of tarred braided nylon line of 200 lb. test (Catahoula #30).

Furthermore, pack 300 ft. (100 m) of cheap, lightweight 1.8–2 mm diameter cord for multiple uses. This guyline-type cord is likely what you'll use the most.

Finally, if you want a thinner cord, pack 150 ft. (45 m) of braided fishing line, 0.4 mm in diameter (50–65 lb. test). Keep in mind that braided line is often waxed, so knots may slip.

BOWLINE

The bowline is a very secure and easy-to-tie knot. An essential feature of this knot is that it will loosen up even if pulled extremely tight.

A useful variant of the bowline is the running bowline. This knot allows you to quickly tie and untie things without undoing the bowline.

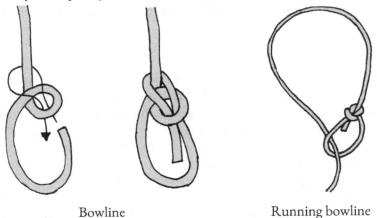

Bowline   Running bowline

BOWLINE ON A BIGHT

The bowline on a bight is useful for creating a loop in the middle of a cord, and if the bowline gets tight, it is easier to untie than a regular overhand knot.

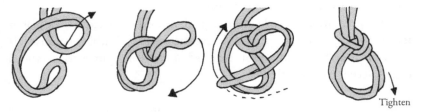

Tighten

FIGURE-EIGHT BEND

For joining two cords, use the reverse traced figure-eight bend (Flemish bend) instead of the double fisherman's knot. The figure-eight bend may take a bit longer to tie, but the advantage of this knot over an overhand knot or a double fisherman's knot is that, if the cord is pulled under very heavy tension, it can be untied much more easily than the other knots. A regular overhand knot will generally do if the two cords are tied permanently.

FRICTION HITCH

The friction hitch can be very strong, but its reliability depends on multiple factors: each knot is unique. To be clear, don't use it for situations that could put someone in danger.

I like the friction hitch because it is extremely simple and unties without difficulty, no matter how tightly it was pulled. It can be adjusted relatively easily (like the taut-line hitch) and tied and untied with mitts. To tie the hitch, just roll a long cord around a solid tree or branch a couple of times. That's it.

Due to the texture and surface area of a tree or branch, the rope won't come loose no matter how hard you pull. If the cord only allows you a couple of turns, it's best to tie the loose end; otherwise, you can finish it however you want. You can pass it underneath the rope to hold it or let it hang. The main drawback of the friction hitch is that you need a long cord.

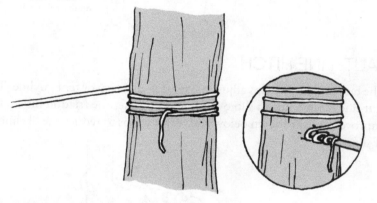

DOUBLE HALF-HITCH

The double half-hitch is handy when working with a short rope end and when finishing lashings and other knots, but it's not very secure if used by itself. Add extra half-hitches for more security. This knot is not easy to untie when tied as the primary knot. That's why I usually use it for the excess tail of a different knot.

TRUCKER'S HITCH

The trucker's hitch allows you to pull a rope really tight by using a knot in the rope as a sort of pulley to leverage your pull's force. It is useful when using rope for a shelter's ridgeline or whenever you need the rope to be very tight.

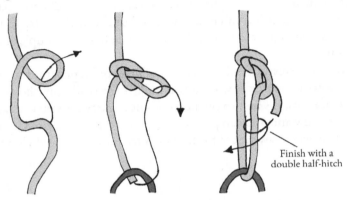

Finish with a
double half-hitch

TAUT-LINE HITCH

The taut-line hitch helps adjust the tension of a tarp or tent guyline. The taut-line hitch tends to slip over time, so I prefer the friction hitch. The improved variant shown below adds extra wraps to reduce the likelihood of slippage.

EVENKI QUICK-RELEASE HITCH

The Evenki hitch (Siberian hitch) is a quick-release knot that is quick and easy to tie and release even with mitts on. It is only moderately secure, so don't use it in critical contexts. The traditional way of tying this knot is best learned by watching a video (**bit.ly/e-hitch**). It takes a bit of practice at first, but it's worth remembering because it's quick and simple to tie. When tied, it looks like a "slipped" figure eight.

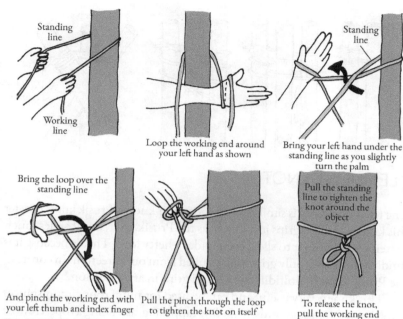

Standing line

Working line

Loop the working end around your left hand as shown

Standing line

Bring your left hand under the standing line as you slightly turn the palm

Bring the loop over the standing line

And pinch the working end with your left thumb and index finger

Pull the pinch through the loop to tighten the knot on itself

Pull the standing line to tighten the knot around the object

To release the knot, pull the working end

CLOVE HITCH

The clove hitch is a simple and essential hitch that works well with natural cordage. It is advantageous when the length of the running ends may need to be adjusted. The clove hitch gets tighter as you pull, but it comes apart easily when the pressure is released.

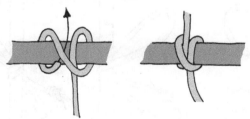

TRIPOD LASHING

The figure-eight lashing is one way to tie a sturdy tripod. Start with a clove hitch or constrictor knot and follow the steps below. Tripods are one of the simplest but most robust structures. It is important to cross the poles as shown for structural strength.

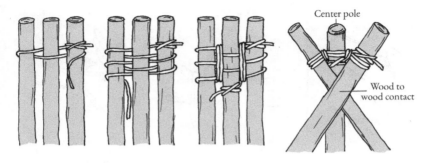

Center pole

Wood to
wood contact

KLEMHEIST KNOT

The Klemheist knot is similar to the more well-known Prusik knot. I prefer this knot because it grips just as well as the Prusik knot, but it slides much better when I need it to slide, even under a hefty load. That is because it is unidirectional and only grips when pulled from one direction. In contrast, the Prusik knot is multidirectional and grips in any direction.

This knot is very useful and can be used for numerous circumstances involving webbing and cords, including rappelling, ascending a rope, crevasse rescue, unpinning a whitewater canoe, setting up a bear hang, and so on. Add or decrease the wraps to adjust the gripping power. To slide the knot, release the tension and grab the wraps.

Unfortunately, the Klemheist knot requires a cord with a smaller diameter than the main cord: use a cord that is no wider than half the diameter of the main cord.

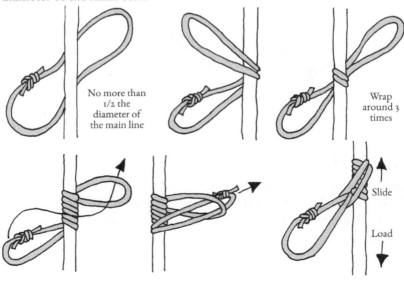

No more than
1/2 the
diameter of
the main line

Wrap
around 3
times

Slide

Load

PRUSIK KNOT

The Prusik knot has similar uses to the Klemheist knot. One of its advantages is that it can be used on a main cord of the same diameter, although this is not recommended.

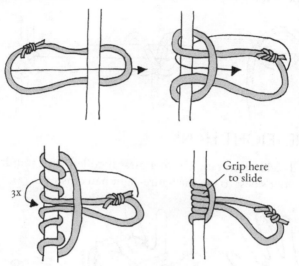

3x

Grip here to slide

JAM KNOT

The jam knot (Arbor knot) is excellent for tying a tight knot with a minimal amount of cord. It is useful for *permanent* lashings with modern cordage such as paracord (due to its slight elasticity). The downside is that you end up cutting the cord, and it is very hard to reuse it. Mors Kochanski regarded this knot as the most important knot for wilderness survival.

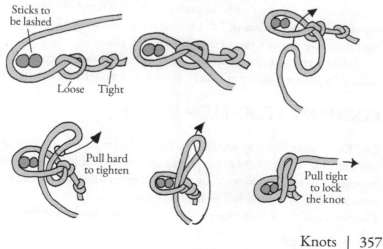

Sticks to be lashed

Loose   Tight

Pull hard to tighten

Pull tight to lock the knot

CONSTRICTOR KNOT

The constrictor knot can be used as an alternative to the jam knot when a low-profile knot is needed; for instance, when tying a splintered paddle. This knot can be tied slightly tighter than the jam knot, but it uses more cord.

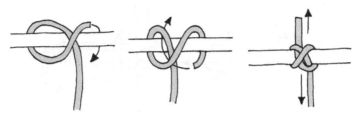

FIGURE-EIGHT HANK

Thin cords will often tangle into a mess if coiled with standard coiling methods, so it's best to use the figure-eight hank instead.

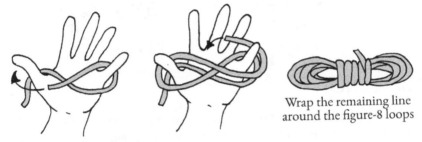

Wrap the remaining line around the figure-8 loops

Another quick method that works with short cords is to grab both ends of the line with one hand and the midpoint with the other. Then, join the midpoint with the ends and hold them in your left hand. Bring the end that is hanging together with the ends on your left hand. Repeat the same steps until the "coil" is about 1 ft. (30 cm) long. Finally, tie a loose overhand knot using the entire wrap to keep the cord in place.

I still haven't found a good way of coiling excessively long cords of a thin diameter without tangling as I undo the coil, so I wrap them around a stick.

KOCHANSKI FLIP-FLOP WINCH

The Kochanski flip-flop winch can be used to rescue a stuck canoe or snowmobile when there is no pulley system available. It is extremely important to use a rope without elasticity; otherwise, the kinetic energy stored by winding the windlass may be lethal.

The power of this winch tends to break any knot attached to the anchor, so use a friction hitch first, then tie the end with a secure knot. Another safety precaution is to place a heavy blanket over the rope to direct a possible rupture downward.

As you wind up the winch, always keep the rope neatly arranged (not going over itself) or it could break from the pressure.

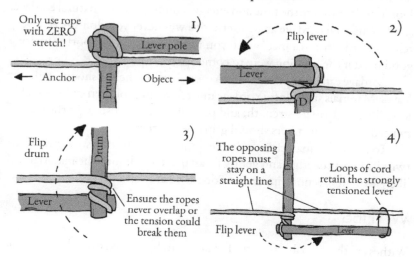

After step 4, flip the drum pole and continue again from step 2.

WHIPPING

Nowadays, there isn't much need for whipping cords because burning the ends is faster. But whipping is helpful for things like adding a handle to an improvised knife, having cordage handy, or repairing a fishing rod with cord and epoxy.

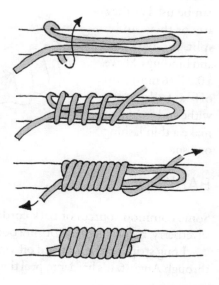

IMPROVISED CORDAGE

It's best not to plan on using much natural cordage. The reality is that natural cordage is far less strong, durable, and versatile than modern cordage. Don't underestimate the time and energy required to make natural cordage.

Use natural cordage as an alternative whenever you don't need a very reliable cord—for instance, when you wouldn't miss an opportunity for a good meal if the binding were to come apart.

Cordage can be improvised from roots, bark, branches, shoots, stems, or leaves. Materials suitable for cordage must have three properties: reasonably long fibers, adequate strength, and pliability when twisted. In the case of twisted cordage, its fibers should grip one another.

To assess if a material is suitable, pull on it to test its strength. Then twist its fibers together and gently tie an overhand knot. The material will likely work if it is not slippery and doesn't cut itself open.

WITHES

Withes are thin, flexible shoots of willow, birch, ash, red osier dogwood, or hazelnut. Choose the longest shoot or branch you can find for your task, and trim its branches. Twist the shoot until the fibers pop. Twist back and forth to slightly separate the fibers and increase their flexibility until the entire length has been twisted. Then, cut the shoot from the tree or ground. Withes can be used as they are, or they can be split for basketry and bindings. Shave a 0.25″ (6 mm) strip off a full-length withe and twist it to make a thin lashing or a snare.

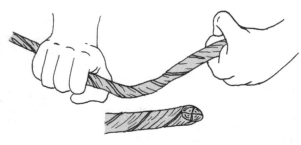

BARK

Some common sources of bark cordage are willow, basswood, juniper, silverberry, maple, poplar, cottonwood, and elm.

Long strips can be stripped off when the sap flows, usually from May through August. It's harder to peel the bark out of season, but it can still be loosened by pounding the tree limbs with a smooth mallet. Use a smooth branch to support the limb while pounding.

Another method to use when the bark is hard to peel is to split a stick into halves or quarters and heat the bark side over the campfire. Toast the whole bark surface over the fire until it is crusty, but don't burn it. While still hot, bend the stick, so only the wood snaps and the bark peels away.

Bark strips are much stiffer than cordage. Nevertheless, they make relatively strong bindings due to their rough texture and flat shape.

The best bark strips come from small limbs, as their bark is thinner. An effective way for peeling the bark in even sizes is to cut down a living shoot or branch between 1.5"–4" (4–10 cm) thick. Make a cut along the length of the stick, and peel the bark off into one or two strips. If a tree has been recently felled, the trunk's bark can also be peeled for cordage.

You may need to use a wooden chisel to peel the bark off. Those strips can be split again if needed.

The outer layer of bark is not useful for cordage, so it must be separated. Make a very shallow score perpendicular to the bark strips and then fold the bark at that point to separate the inner layers from the outer layers.

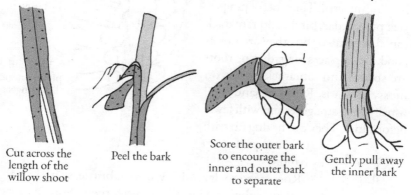

Cut across the length of the willow shoot

Peel the bark

Score the outer bark to encourage the inner and outer bark to separate

Gently pull away the inner bark

Submerge the bark for a few weeks to loosen up the inner bark layers. Or, if you need the cordage straight away, boil the bark in a mix of ash and water. The longer it's boiled, the softer and weaker the fibers will become.

The strips can be dried for later use then resoaked for a while before twisting them into cordage. This drying and soaking makes cordage less prone to shrinking and loosening.

Cedar bark also makes good cordage. Cut and peel the bark and use the whitish inner layer. Cedar bark can be soaked for a few days to loosen the outer and inner bark layers, but it's not required. Use the bark fibers as they are, or twist them into cordage.

SINEW

Sinew can be obtained from the leg tendons and from the silverskin from the backstraps of deer and other ungulates.

Sinew is very strong and can be used like rawhide. When it's wet, it is very malleable and may come loose. It shrinks as it dries.

Pitch can be applied as a waterproof coating to sinew bindings.

Unlike leg tendons, the silverskin on the backstrap must be separated from the meat by scraping it off with a dull edge.

The sinew fibers are dried flat and straight. Then, they are either shredded or pounded with a smooth, round stone, or both. These dried fibers will keep indefinitely if kept dry. The sinew fibers can then be twisted into very strong cordage.

Leg and backstrap sinew have the same uses, but backstrap is ideal because its fibers are longer and relatively easier to process.

ROOTS

Spruce roots are often used as a binding material. The roots of juniper, jack pine, cedar, birch, and tamarack can also be used, but they are not as good. Good places for gathering roots are spruce and tamarack stands on mossy grounds. Roots in sandy soil usually grow straighter and with fewer deformities. They can be dug up with a stick and pulled up by hand.

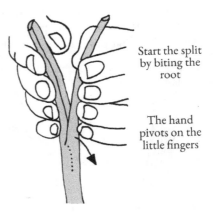

Start the split by biting the root

The hand pivots on the little fingers

Root stripper

Roots tend to dry quickly and get brittle, so it's best to keep them submerged until you need them. Spruce roots can also be boiled to increase their flexibility and make them less prone to turning brittle when dried. The outer bark of the roots is generally removed by rubbing it off, using a root stripper, or passing the root between two tightly held sticks. Debarking roots is usually easier immediately after harvesting them. Roots can be split many times to reduce their thickness. Take only a few roots from each tree to avoid killing it.

NETTLE AND THISTLE

Plants such as nettle, dogbane, thistle, and fireweed have fibers in their stems useful for cordage.

Nettle makes particularly strong cordage. Old, tall nettles provide the best fibers. Although the fibers can be extracted from green plants, it's best to gather them after the plants have turned brown and the leaves have fallen off.

Wear gloves when handling the fresh plant. To strip the remaining leaves from the nettle, grasp the base of the stem and pull your clenched fist up.

Crush the stem between your fingers or by pounding lightly with a stick. Then, split and flatten the stem and separate the bark layer.

The fibers can be torn into strips of two to four strands. Let them dry out and become thinner. Finally, soak the fibers for a while, then twist them into cordage.

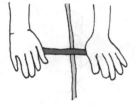  

| Roll a round stick back and forth on the stalk, pressing down hard to crush it | Bend the stalk in the middle to break away and separate the inner pith from the outer fibers | Carefully peel the fibers found just under the outer skin |

Most thistles contain fibers that are strong enough for snares. To extract the fibers, cut the plant near the ground and strip the fibers from the bottom to the top.

TWISTING CORDAGE

Two-ply cordage is made by reverse-wrapping fibers in the opposite direction of the main twist in the cord. This type of cordage is very strong, durable, and can be made with many materials.

Start by twisting the fibers until they form a loop. Always leave one side longer than the other so that the splices don't line up in the same area. Twist tightly and evenly with your hands, as shown below, until you form a short piece. To provide tension as you continue the reverse wrap, pass a thin stick through the end loop and grasp the stick with your toes.

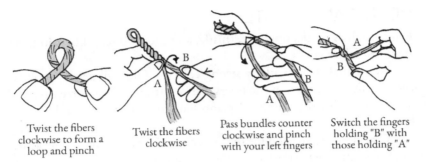

Twist the fibers clockwise to form a loop and pinch

Twist the fibers clockwise

Pass bundles counter clockwise and pinch with your left fingers

Switch the fingers holding "B" with those holding "A"

Once one end of the strands starts to get thinner or is close to ending, grab another fiber of similar thickness and pinch it on top, and continue twisting as before. To produce very strong cordage, the free end of newly added fibers should be folded onto the opposite fiber bundle to "lock" them in. Try to maintain an even thickness.

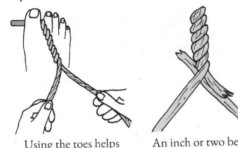

Using the toes helps speed up the process

An inch or two before a strand ends, add a new strand behind

Twist the new and short strands together as one to continue

Thigh rolling is a quicker method useful for making thinner cordage. Pinch the fibers at the starting loop and, while keeping the two strands separated in your other hand, roll them with the entire length of your hand over your bare thigh. Hold the fibers between your hand and thigh after each stroke and release the cord with the other hand. The strands should twist a bit. You can also encourage this twisting with your free hand. Repeat the cycle.

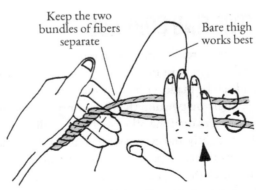

Keep the two bundles of fibers separate

Bare thigh works best

After a few twists, hold bundles with the right hand and release the left hand so that the cord winds itself

THREE-PLY CORDAGE

A three-ply cord can be made by making a two-ply cord first and then adding a third single strand using a reverse wrap; this almost doubles the strength and durability of the cordage.

Turn clockwise

The same thickness and amount of twist as each of the other strands

Wrap around the two-ply cord in a counterclockwise manner

BRAIDING

Fibers, withes, and roots can be braided instead of reverse-wrapped, but this is more time-consuming. Inner paracord strands can be braided to obtain very strong cordage.

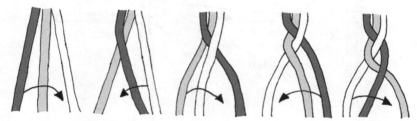

ROPE SPINNER

A rope spinner is a simple tool consisting of a rotating stick and a handle. The rope spinner is useful for making two-ply cords or conventional rope out of twine, improvised cord, or paracord inner strands. It is also useful for twisting a long strand, such as when making a rabbit-skin blanket.

The most practical technique to use with a rope spinner is to simply twist a cord in the same direction as it is twisted already until the cord is very tight and starts to kink if you give the cord some slack. The tightly twisted cord is held at its midpoint and suspended high from the ground. Then, its ends are released so that they twist naturally into a two-strand rope. This method yields half the length of the original strands and is useful for making quick cordage out of inner paracord strands, dental floss, and other thin cords.

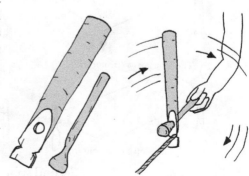

The other method has more steps and creates a very strong and durable cord. Unfortunately, this method yields only about one-tenth of the original length of the strands.

First, find an anchor stick that allows you to slip the loops of the cord on and off easily. Tie the cord to the rope twister. Then, pass it around the anchor stick and the rope twister, and then loop the end over the anchor stick as shown. For really long strands, a rope twister can be used at each end.

Stretch the cord a bit to ensure the three strands are under even tension. Then, use the rope twister to twist the cord in the same direction as the original twist in its strands. Once you feel moderate tension from twisting, the first spin is done.

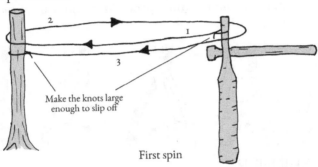

Make the knots large enough to slip off

First spin

For the second spin, you must loop the cord around the anchor stick and the rope twister, as shown, while maintaining tension in the cord to avoid kinks. Stretch the strands evenly and twist them in the opposite direction of the first spin. Overtighten the twist, and pull the cord tightly to set it. Then, release the cord to let it settle. Finally, whip or melt the ends.

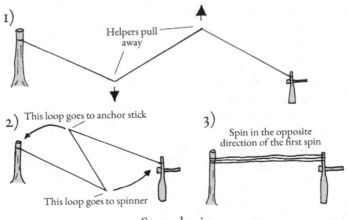

1)

Helpers pull away

2) This loop goes to anchor stick

This loop goes to spinner

3)

Spin in the opposite direction of the first spin

Second spin

KNOTS FOR NATURAL BINDINGS

Natural cordage is not often as strong or as flexible as regular cordage. The knots shown below work better with rough, natural bindings, such as grass, withes, or roots.

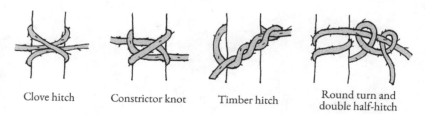

Clove hitch   Constrictor knot   Timber hitch   Round turn and double half-hitch

PLASTIC CORDAGE

To make plastic cordage out of a plastic bottle, cut the first bit of cordage manually. Then rig up a knife and stump as shown below, and feed the bit of cord between the blade and stump. Then, pull the cordage through to cut more of it.

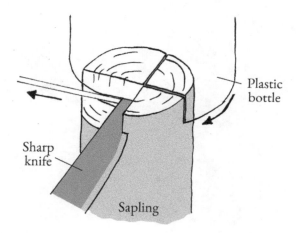

Plastic bottle

Sharp knife

Sapling

WINTER

LONG-TERM WINTER TIPS

Mind map dealing with cold

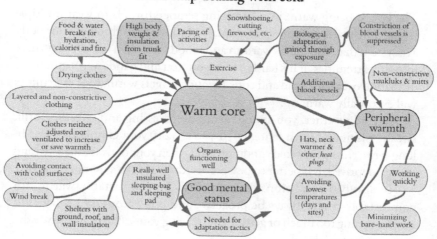

Modified from *Boreal forest adaptations*.

FALLING THROUGH ICE

In the "Travel" chapter, you'll find the procedure for getting out of a hole in the ice; here, you'll find what to do afterward in subfreezing conditions.

After your boots or clothes get soaked, some people recommend rolling in the snow so that the snow absorbs some of the moisture. In practice, rolling won't make much of a difference if you are entirely soaked. You're better off just focusing on creating a long-lasting fire and finding a place where you can spend a few hours drying your clothes. Or, if you have a dry set of clothes, change into them and get inside a sleeping bag; otherwise, follow the steps below.

If you can manage to walk with boots full of water, don't bother taking them off. At this stage, removing and wringing your clothes and boots is unnecessary. Even if you do, everything will still stay wet, and water from your upper clothing will move downward and soak your footwear again.

Stay active and make a fire. Then sit by the fire, wring your clothes, and dry them at a safe distance. You might have to do this one piece of clothing at a time, starting at the top.

If making a fire is not possible, wring your clothes as best as possible, get inside your shelter, and crawl into a *synthetic* sleeping bag. Eating will help you warm up.

LAYERING

The key to being warm in subfreezing temperatures is to wear multiple layers of insulating clothing. It's equally important to think of your body as a system that distributes warmth and blood flow from its central furnace into the extremities. If it's hard to keep your feet and hands warm, put more insulation over your head and core. If your core gets warm, your extremities will eventually warm up.

In cold weather, you should avoid overdressing and sweating. Still, sweating is not a "death sentence" if you can dry your clothes by a fire. In long-term, chronically cold conditions and when your body is exhausted and energy-deprived, it is better to be a bit overdressed than a bit underdressed.

In survival conditions, the aim is to be comfortably warm, not comfortably cool. Always be proactive and put on or take off layers to avoid sweating too much or getting cold. Pacing yourself to prevent excessive sweating is crucial.

Slightly overdressing and rarely adjusting clothing can be a deliberate tactic to increase the core temperature as a buffer against the cold, particularly in preparation for periods of inactivity. The techniques mentioned above are essential when the temperatures are freezing, and your body finds it hard to warm up due to food deprivation, fatigue, and chronic cold.

MITTEN HARNESS

Mittens can be crossed and thrown toward the back when fine dexterity is needed.

SOCKS

It isn't easy to keep winter socks in optimal condition when they are constantly being used. Have at least two pairs of winter socks per month of use.

Socks must be turned out often and fluffed up to prevent their fibers from matting and staying compressed. Insoles can be switched from foot to foot to avoid constantly compressing the same spots.

PRE-WARMING CLOTHES

It is helpful to warm up clothes before putting them on in the extreme cold. Try to pre-warm everything! Place any clothes you'll wear (e.g., hats, gloves, socks, boot liners) inside your sleeping bag overnight so that they are warm in the morning. Dressing inside a sleeping bag is also an excellent way to warm up. Keep metal contact gloves in a warm pocket as close to your body as possible, ready for use.

If you are forced to put on cold footwear, an effective Northerner trick is to place your bare feet in the snow until there's a lot of blood circulating. Then, wipe your feet dry and put on your socks and boots. The enhanced blood flow should quickly warm up the insulation in your boots.

REWARMING HANDS AND FEET

Arm windmills force warm blood down into the tiny capillaries of the fingers for temporary warmth.

Shoulder shrugs with hands at a 90-degree angle pump a surprising amount of blood and warmth into the hands.

While not as effective as arm windmills, a similar technique can force warm blood down into the feet.

It's best to increase your heart rate and warm up your core with jumping jacks, deep squats, and constant movement.

Ice fishermen sometimes submerge their hands in water to warm them up in extremely cold conditions; although the water is cold, it is warmer than the freezing air.

IMPROVISED BOOT INSULATION

With a slower metabolism and chronic cold, you might need to insulate your boots a bit more. Traditionally, Indigenous peoples in the North would add grass or moss to insulate their mukluks. Remember, it's important not to constrict any blood flowing toward your toes.

Another option is the Hudson Bay duffle. It is a triangular piece of wool duffle used to improvise a foot covering. The Hudson Bay duffle can be improvised with two to four layers of 30″ (76 cm) cloth squares. Fold the squares to form a triangle, and fold the sides over your foot like below.

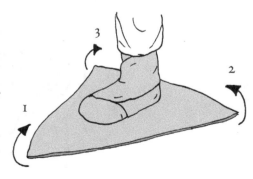

FIREARMS

In cold weather, store firearms in a sheltered, cold spot. Avoid moving them from the cold outdoors to a warm shelter because the condensation will rust the firearm.

Remove grease and oil from the firearm and replace them with graphite powder or nonfreezing oil. You can use the firearm without lubrication, or you can rub the moving parts with a pencil if you don't have the suggested replacements.

Cover the contact points of the firearm with tape to protect your hands from cold contact.

POOPING IN THE FREEZING COLD

During bad winter storms, or if you are tired of roughing it, poop inside your warm shelter or by a fire. Lay some bark down in a crisscross fashion and poop over it. Birchbark is excellent for this. Then, cover the excrement with bark, moss, snow, and whatever else you used to wipe yourself with, and toss everything in an appropriate spot.

If you have a pee bottle handy, my advice is to collect your urine and use it while it's warm to wipe yourself after pooping. Then use snow to finish wiping. In severe cold, using urine makes the whole process much more comfortable.

PEE BOTTLE

Anyone that has ever done some serious winter trips will tell you that having a pee bottle is quite nice. During winter, you should stay well hydrated. Still, some people stay a little dehydrated to avoid getting up to pee during the night. But dehydration will wear you out in the long run. The problem with getting out of your sleeping bag in extreme cold is that it's harder to warm up your bag again after going outside, especially when your metabolism is at its lowest point. So it's best to use a bottle to pee while staying in your sleeping bag.

If you will experience temperatures under -5°F (-20°C) often, I recommend a metal pee bottle so that, if it freezes, you can easily melt the pee. If you rarely experience those temperatures, your pee is not likely to freeze, especially if you store your bottle in an insulated spot.

Another freeze-resistant bottle alternative is the Wide Mouth UVPE bottle from Nalgene. A one-liter bottle should hold enough pee if you don't overdrink.

HOT WATER BOTTLE

For extreme cold conditions, I strongly recommend having a hot water bottle.

The hot water bottle is useful for when you are forced to expose your bare or thinly gloved hands to extreme cold. These conditions are challenging because they take away your dexterity in minutes. With a hot water bottle, you can quickly rewarm your hands after they start to lose dexterity so that you can continue working.

Another benefit of hot water bottles is that they can give you an extra boost when it is freezing and you are not generating much body heat. You can place the bottle over top your inner layers and be warm even when motionless.

Bottles that seal tight and secure like Nalgene and hot water bottles work well. Place some socks or a cozy over the bottle to protect your skin and extend the heat-release time. Place the bottle in areas of high heat transfer, like the stomach and groin, for maximum warmth. Single-layer metal bottles work, but they must be covered with thick fabric, or they will burn your skin or cause chilblains.

There is a risk when using hot water bottles. During my 100-day winter trip, I developed chilblains on the soles of my feet. I believe it was because I used a hot water bottle (with boiling water!) inside my sleeping bag without enough insulation between the bottle and my skin. The bottle warmed my feet up too quickly. It felt nice at the time, but after a few days, I noticed that the skin on my soles was no longer able to regulate blood flow properly. The blood vessels had become damaged due to the very rapid temperature changes. That reduced my ability to feel how warm or cold my feet were—something quite important—and caused me chronic pain for the rest of the trip.

If you don't have an appropriate bottle, you can substitute the hot water with a sock and a warm—but not too hot—rock.

STORING WATER OVERNIGHT

Snow is an excellent insulator: even if the temperature dips to -40°F (-40°C), water in a bottle will remain largely unfrozen if placed under a foot of snow. Make sure you store the bottle upside down. If some water does freeze, it will freeze at the bottom of the bottle and not where the lid is. If you have a stove or fireplace, just leave the water in a pot in a warm place (with thermal mass); it shouldn't freeze completely.

WINTER GEAR

ICE CHISEL

An ice chisel is a vital tool for long-term survival in places where bodies of water freeze. An axe can substitute for the ice chisel in areas where the ice is very thin. But in the North, where the ice is regularly more than 2 ft. (60 cm) deep, you need an ice chisel. The ice chisel lets you fish, set fishing nets under the ice, and get water quickly during winter. You can find them at commercial fishing stores in northern regions.

The most efficient way of cutting a hole in the ice is to make a square hole; this makes digging out the ice chips easier and faster. It's good practice to secure the chisel to your wrist with a lanyard so that you don't lose it if your grip is not firm and you punch through the ice.

Ice chisels can be improvised by sharpening the portion of the antler that attaches to the skull; this is the strongest part of an antler. Do not use bone as it is too brittle.

The chisel-axe hybrid (see the "Fire" chapter) is capable of chiseling through thick ice, so it covers the need for an ice chisel if you are gear-constrained.

SHOVELS

Snow shovels are essential if you are digging holes in the ice and there is a lot of snow around. After high winds, snow from the surrounding area will collect in any place that has been previously dug out, so you will need to clear it out again. Takedown aluminum shovels work great, and if you want to reduce their weight, you could even pack just the shovel's blade.

SLUSH SCOOP

The slush scoop is handy if you are digging holes in the ice every day. You can improvise a scoop from natural materials, but having a plastic or metal one is well worth it. The scoop is used to remove ice chips while cutting a hole with the chisel, and to clean the hole once it's open.

GOGGLES

Goggles are an optional winter item. Having snow goggles is a good idea if you expect to be outside during bad weather for prolonged periods. If you'll be able to hunker down during high winds and snowstorms, then you can probably make do with only a good pair of sunglasses. Another option if you are worried about snow blindness is to get glacier or alpine sunglasses.

HEALTH

Influence of wilderness environments on performance

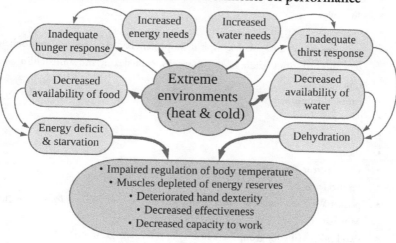

Modified from *Wilderness Medicine*.

FIRST AID KIT

I highly recommend taking a 40- or 80-hour wilderness first aid course (WAFA or WFR, respectively) to learn how to manage emergencies and use a first aid kit in remote areas.

To build a first aid kit, start with a good quality prebuilt kit, such as the ones sold by Adventure Medical Kits (like the Mountain Explorer and Mountain Guide kits) and add items specific to your circumstances.

Some recommendations for additional items are:

- hypothermia thermometer
- dishwashing soap
- single-use superglue or medical glue (for superficial wound closure)
- SAM Splint
- duct tape
- ziplock bags
- gloves
- antiseptic towelettes
- first aid tape
- waterproof notepad and pencils for SAMPLE/SOAP notes
- suture kit (for particular circumstances, and only under full knowledge of the risks)
- extra gauze and bandages
- clove oil
- emergency dental kit
- over-the-counter meds, such as aspirin, ibuprofen, Benadryl, and acetaminophen
- general antibiotics, such as ciprofloxacin, cephalexin, and amoxicillin (see appendix)
- antibiotic ointment
- lighter
- knife
- shears
- signal mirror
- Fresnel lens
- pocket WFA manual (*The Field Guide of Wilderness & Rescue Medicine* by Jim Morrissey)
- two EpiPens (if your group has a history of severe allergic reactions)
- compression bandages
- combat application tourniquet (CAT)
- triangular bandages

Always keep the first aid kit inside a waterproof dry bag, as many of its contents must always stay dry. The appendix goes more in depth into WFA kits and special considerations for long-term contexts.

MONITORING YOUR HEALTH

In remote and challenging environments, it's wise to be proactive and monitor your overall health. Don't wait until you have an issue to start monitoring. There are various signs and symptoms that are relatively easy to notice.

HYDRATION

Good hydration is extremely important because dehydration severely decreases your mental and physical performances. For that reason, dehydration can quickly lead—directly or indirectly—to an emergency.

Staying well hydrated in survival contexts can be particularly challenging depending on the availability of water, the energy and time needed for water treatment, the climate, and your level of exertion.

The color of your urine is one of the best ways of monitoring your hydration. Darker, yellow-colored urine indicates a water deficiency, and paler, lemonade-colored urine suggests adequate hydration.

SIGNS

Your resting heart rate is an easy sign to monitor if you have a watch, but be consistent with taking the measurements at the same time and in the same context each day. It's best to check your resting heart rate right after waking up. If your heart rate tends to be significantly higher or lower than your usual heart rate, that's a warning sign.

Blood pressure can't be accurately measured without instruments, but you can be aware of it indirectly. During a long-term survival situation, it's likely that your blood pressure will drop, and you'll often suffer a head rush whenever you stand up quickly.

Your stool can be a good way of checking how your digestive system is doing. Pay attention to your stool's consistency and adjust your diet if possible.

If you feel pain, monitor it over time by keeping a journal based on the OPQRST mnemonic: onset, provokes, quality, radiates, severity, and time.

ENERGY

Keep a rough log of how much food you are eating. Also, observe and note how much fat you have throughout your body and how the distribution of fat changes as you lose weight.

Keep track of how many hours you are sleeping. If you look up at the sky and it appears to be receding, you're probably exhausted.

In a survival context, sexual drive can help signal overall energy levels and physical condition.

MIND

Some symptoms that you should note are forgetfulness, distraction, and irritability.

STARVATION

Starvation is quite the slippery slope; you must avoid getting onto the steep part. For someone who has never gone truly hungry—over a few days or even several weeks—the experience can hit them like a truck. The lack of energy can quickly become a vicious cycle because you need energy to forage. That is why having a significant reserve of fat and pacing yourself is crucial for delaying the effects of starvation.

Adults can survive for weeks or months without food, depending on the amount of fat in their bodies, among other factors. A well-nourished adult has sufficient fat stores to live without food for 40 to 60 days. Fat stores vary, but they are typically between 22–33 lb. (10–15 kg) or about 27% of an adult's bodyweight. Each pound of body fat holds approximately 3,500 kcal of energy (1 kg of body fat = 7,700 kcal). Protein is another emergency source of energy. An average male weighing 154 lb. (70 kg) may have about 13 lb. (6 kg) of muscle or protein, roughly 20,000 kcal. A healthy, nonobese adult may die practically any time after 50% of their starting weight has diminished.

People who have undertaken prolonged starvation may suffer from low sodium (hyponatremia), low calcium, low serum magnesium, severe anemia, and impaired membrane and cardiovascular functions. Taking a multivitamin and half salt (salt and potassium chloride blend) might help counteract some of those effects.

Starving people do not adapt well to temperature extremes; the cold is particularly difficult to deal with because shivering uses lots of energy. One of the first things the body does when it's starving is to reduce its energy use. It lowers its metabolism and reduces its readily available energy. That is an effective life-prolonging strategy, but unfortunately, it makes the body susceptible to the cold.

I was cold during the last stage of my 180 days in the wild even though I didn't experience severely cold weather. I experienced living in a constant state of "hitting the wall" in terms of lacking energy and feeling cold. I learned a good lesson: have lots of warm clothes and a very warm sleeping bag (or two).

Mors Kochanski advocated fasting for *short-term* survival. He argued that it was preferable not to eat at all than to eat less than the minimum number of calories needed by the body (basal metabolic rate or BMR). For fasting, he recommended drinking far more water than usual, and boiling it and drinking it as hot as possible.

If gathering your daily energy needs in a long-term context is next to impossible, it is easier to manage your energy budget by fasting rather than attempting to forage enough food. You must ensure that you spend less energy gathering, processing, and digesting food than what you gain from that food. That is incredibly hard to manage in an unsuitable or restrictive environment. Moreover, fasting causes physiological changes that save energy and help the body prolong its life in a context of severe food deprivation.

Another advantage of fasting is that it reduces the discomfort from hunger pangs. In addition, fasting leaves more time for resting and other activities.

Obviously, fasting is not sustainable in the long term, but it may be forced on you by extreme environments and conditions. If possible, leave that area.

I suspect the most effective way to combine the physiological advantages of fasting with those of eating in a survival context is by doing interval fasting. If you fast for a few days, preserve food for later, and then eat for a few days—meeting the BMR energy needs of your body—you should get some of the benefits of fasting (energy preservation) as well as some much-needed nourishment. On the other hand, you may also find that eating a little everyday instead of interval fasting is better for your body.

If you are refeeding after a long period without food, start with 400 kcals and gradually go from there as needed. Some of the variables used when calculating the amount of calories for refeeding are bodyweight, length of fast, recent food intake, and various medical risk factors. Avoid carbs, salty foods, and sugars, and focus on probiotics, fats, and proteins.

The problem with increasing food intake too quickly is that you could develop refeeding syndrome. This metabolic disturbance can lead to death if severe enough. Increase your food intake slowly and gradually until your body rebalances its electrolytes. Watch out for signs of fluid and electrolyte imbalances, such as swollen ankles (early warning) or erratic vital signs during the first days of refeeding.

PROTEIN POISONING

It's widely known that you can't survive by just eating rabbits, and that is because rabbits have very lean meat. If you eat lots of lean meat for several days, you'll get what is known as rabbit starvation or protein poisoning. When more than 45% of your energy intake comes from protein, your kidneys cannot get rid of the byproducts of breaking down the protein quickly enough.

Symptoms can develop within a week. They include nausea, vomiting, diarrhea, headaches, feeling chronically hungry (despite eating lots of meat), and a lack of energy.

But the 45% figure doesn't show a clear picture. For survival, a more appropriate way to think about protein intake is as the maximum amount of protein that the body can handle per day. In theory, a 175 lb. (80 kg) adult can process 10–13 oz. (285–365 g) of protein per day—or about 2.2 lb. (1 kg) of lean meat.

It's best to prevent protein poisoning by eating as much fat and carbs as possible and reducing your consumption of lean meat. Eat the bone marrow and the fat around the organs (e.g., intestines) and brain. Focus on eating fattier animals, such as beaver, moose, and fish. In this context, having rations of fats and carbs to complement lean meat is a huge advantage.

Symptoms in mild cases may quickly recede if you increase your fat consumption to more than 55% of your energy intake.

GENERAL ISSUES

DEHYDRATION

After oxygen, water is the most important substance for maintaining bodily functions. Water is an essential ingredient for most chemical reactions and processes happening inside our bodies. If we lack water, these vital reactions can't occur.

Dehydration is a slippery slope that can lead to hallucinations and death, sometimes within hours or days. Do not rely on feeling thirsty as a way to signal that you are dehydrated; often, there is a significant lag in this trigger.

Even mild dehydration will begin to impair your mental status, making it easy to make dumb mistakes that can lead to worse mistakes, and so on. The best defense against this slippery slope is to always be adequately hydrated and to recognize the early warning signs of dehydration.

First signs and symptoms of dehydration:
- thirst
- headache
- decreased urination
- dark, strong-smelling urine
- light-headedness, dizziness, or fainting when standing up

Checking the color of your urine is an excellent way to assess your hydration levels.

In the winter, you may get complacent because you don't have other environmental triggers, like the hot sun and heat, to remind you to drink water. But water is as essential in the winter as in the summer. In addition, the body can handle the cold much better when it is adequately hydrated.

Generally, drinking about 17–25 fl. oz. (500 – 750 mL) of water per hour should be more than enough when dehydration may be an issue. Nevertheless, there are many variables, so it's best to be mindful of your body and watch for any warning signs.

HYPONATREMIA

Hyponatremia is the lack of sodium. Not eating enough food and sweating a lot can result in losing too much sodium, leading to dizziness, fainting, and even collapsing. That can be prevented by consuming one teaspoon (5 g) of table salt per day. If salt is not available, then avoid sweating excessively.

Another way of getting a deficit of sodium is through dilutional hyponatremia. It is the same mechanism as in the previous paragraph, but with the added factor of drinking too much water. And it can happen in both hot and cold environments.

Dilutional hyponatremia is extremely rare when regular meals are taken, but in a food deprivation context, it is something to watch out for—and for those reasons, packing rations makes sense.

LEG CRAMPS

Leg cramps can become a painful issue when you do not have adequate nutrition. They will usually happen at night as you stretch or point your toes down. These cramps may be caused by a deficiency of potassium, calcium, or magnesium.

Doing calf-stretching exercises before sleeping may reduce the chances of leg cramps. But by far, the most effective way to manage them is to go easy on your legs; doing less physical activity should eliminate the cramps. Leg cramps are one way your body tells you to slow down.

LOW BLOOD PRESSURE

One of the most common issues you may encounter in a long-term survival situation is low blood pressure. It is often due to malnutrition, a ketogenic diet, or dehydration.

If you have low blood pressure, you may black out, faint, or feel light-headed after standing up.

The symptoms can feel quite similar to dehydration, which could be confusing. If you notice that you are drinking lots of water but the symptoms are persisting, it might be low blood pressure instead.

There are some ways to manage low blood pressure. One is to be mindful of your condition and always stand up slowly. Another is to perform the Anti-G Straining Maneuver whenever you feel a head rush starting.

The Anti-G Straining Maneuver (AGSM) was developed during WWII and is widely used by pilots today to counteract g-forces, but it also works great as a way to avoid fainting when you have low blood pressure.

The purpose of the AGSM is to retain as much blood and oxygen in the brain as possible to avoid fainting. That is achieved through two simultaneous techniques. The first technique is to exhale quickly (less than one second) while making a "hick" sound to close the respiratory tract. Then, after two or three seconds, inhale quickly and repeat the cycle from the start, as needed. The second technique is to contract the muscles in your abdomen, chest, and legs.

Another strategy for counteracting low blood pressure is ensuring you are as fully hydrated as possible. That helps slightly, but it's not a solution.

FOOT CARE

Foot care is critical in the wilderness. One of the best ways to take care of your feet is to dry them regularly. During the day, find the time to take your socks and shoes off and dry your feet (and also dry your socks and shoes).

Dry your insoles, shoes, boot liners, and socks every night. Some nights, take your socks off while sleeping so that your feet can dry.

BLISTERS

An effective way of preventing blisters on your feet is to remove your shoes every few hours and dry your feet and socks.

Most blisters are harmless, but some can be so big or painful that they become a handicap. If a blister is problematic and hindering your ability to function, drain it with a sterilized needle and thread. Unfortunately, this increases your risk of infection, so it's a matter of risk versus reward. A drained blister won't be as painful, and most problematic blisters eventually break anyway. Being proactive ensures you have tiny holes rather than a big tear.

Clean your hands and the outside of the blister. Then heat a sewing needle with a lighter for a few seconds until it becomes red-hot. Let the needle cool down, then thread it. Then run the needle and thread through the blister. Depending on how thick the blister is, you may need to pass the needle and thread through a few times. Detach the needle and let the thread hang out of the holes. The thread ensures the holes don't close and allows the liquid to escape, which helps the blister dry out and heal. Cover the blister with a pad if necessary.

DRY SKIN

An improvised remedy for dry skin and deep cracks is to make a paste from crushed, oily nuts and use it as an oil balm. Animal fat also works.

SUNBURN

The best way to prevent sunburn is to wear good hats and long-sleeve shirts. If you need some extra protection, the white powder on trembling aspens can be used as an improvised sunblock.

URINARY TRACT INFECTION

Urinary tract infections (UTIs) are common in the wilderness. Women are more likely to get them because of the close distance between the involved body parts. The most common cause of UTIs is *E. coli*. One of the more common symptoms is a burning sensation while urinating. Another symptom may be more frequent or intensely sudden urges to urinate—the body is trying to flush out the infection.

The best way to prevent UTIs is to maintain as good hygiene as possible. UTIs can be a real PITA in the wilderness, particularly in winter, so wash your clothes and body often.

If you get a UTI, drink more water than usual; urinating more helps the body expel the infection. A natural remedy is kinnikinnick (*Arctostaphylos uva-ursi*) leaf tea. The grand majority of UTIs resolve themselves. But if you want to be more aggressive, you could run a course of oral antibiotics: ciprofloxacin 250–500 mg PO q12h × 3 days, or cephalexin 250–500 mg PO q6h × 3 days.

CONJUNCTIVITIS

Conjunctivitis is an infection or inflammation of the eye, and it's pretty common in the wild. Irritants and pathogens can cause it. Some of the symptoms are redness, itchiness, and discharge or crustiness in the eyes in the mornings.

It is tough to determine the source of the irritation in the field because there are many irritants, like smoke, dirt, and bacteria. Often smoke is a major factor. The best approach to prevent and manage conjunctivitis is to minimize smoke exposure, wash your face with clean water, and avoid touching your eyes. If the conjunctivitis is mild, it should resolve itself naturally.

Antibiotic eye drops are a good treatment if you suspect the conjunctivitis is caused by an infection (if there is a yellowish discharge). If the infection is prolonged, you can try antibiotic eye drops or an oral antibiotic like doxycycline (100 mg q12h × 7–14 days).

SMOKE INHALATION

Smoke inhalation can happen in just a few hours if you're next to a very smoky fire. If you are breathing in a lot of smoke, do something about it! Keep your fire well-tended, with an adequate balance of heat, oxygen, and fuel. Or put it out.

One of the symptoms of mild smoke inhalation is difficulty breathing. Smoke irritates your respiratory system, and it feels as if your respiratory tract is constricted and not letting enough oxygen pass through. You may also be disorientated and have headaches and nausea. The best thing to do—other than preventing it—is to get fresh air.

TOOTHACHE

You only need to watch *Cast Away* once to understand why it's crucial to have a dental checkup before a long expedition.

If you have many dental fillings, carry temporary fillings like Dentemp or Cavit. Adventure Medical Kits sells a simple dental kit that includes a tube of temporary cavity filling, a wax stick for filling cavities or stabilizing loose teeth, and an anesthetic gel for pain.

You can also improvise: cotton can be used to cover a cavity, and candle wax can be used to improvise a temporary filling. The wax must be melted and left to cool until soft and malleable. Then it can be placed over the tooth and shaped with a finger. Biting down helps hold it in place. Aspirin powder or toothpaste may be used to temporarily fill a thoroughly cleaned cavity.

If you have a broken tooth, you may find some relief in covering the tooth's nerve with a paste of finely crushed, fresh plantain (*Plantago major*) leaves. Chewing yarrow roots (*Achilea millefolium*) may help numb your gum or tooth.

Consider taking oral antibiotics if you suspect an infection is causing the toothache (preferred: amoxicillin-clavulanic acid 875 mg/125 mg PO q12h × 7–10 days, or less-than-ideal: cephalexin 500 mg PO q6h × 7 – 10 days).

REMOVING A TOOTH

This section describes a last-resort procedure to be taken at your own risk, and only if all other options are unavailable. Use common sense!

A general rule of thumb is that 90% of dental emergencies can be treated by extracting the tooth. But an extraction could go wrong (like a broken root) and worsen an issue, so extreme care is necessary.

Teeth with one root can be loosened by twisting, and teeth with two or three roots must be loosened by moving back and forth. Unlike baby teeth, a permanent tooth isn't likely to come out by wiggling it with your hand or tying it to a door and slamming it. The danger when removing a tooth is breaking it and leaving the root inside, so be extremely careful. The tooth should be loosened up as much as possible before extraction. Separate the gum from the tooth by carefully inserting something in-between. The main thing is to grab the tooth as close as possible to its root. Sometimes the root can be loosened by alternating 30 seconds of steady pressure toward the cheek with 30 seconds of steady force in the opposite direction.

After extraction, check that the root was fully extracted (it could have broken), and cover the gum with cotton gauze. The gauze should be held firmly in place for 30 minutes, and it should hold the gums close to the bone to encourage healing. Don't rinse for 12 hours to protect the clot.

Take ibuprofen 600 mg PO q6h, or hydrocodone-acetaminophen 5 mg/500 mg (Vicodin) PO q4–6h for pain. Only use an antibiotic (such as those mentioned in the "Toothache" section) if there are complications.

From what I've gathered from someone who has pulled his tooth in isolated conditions, taking the time to loosen the troublesome tooth over a couple of days may be best. Some alternatives to slamming a door are: tie the tooth to a rock and let it drop (this won't work with bottom teeth) or tie the tooth to a solid object and use your neck muscles to pull while you loosen the tooth with your fingers.

FISHHOOK REMOVAL

The first step for removing a fishhook is to clean the area thoroughly with antiseptic solution or soap. The barb is what makes the removal process challenging. The easiest way to remove a fishhook that made two punctures is to cut off the barbed end with pliers. If the hook is too strong to cut, remove or flatten the barb, and remove the hook the way it entered.

Recommended way: For fishhooks that made just one puncture, you can push the hook in a way that disengages the barb and use a loop to pull out the fishhook (see below). Rewash the area and cover it with a bandage.

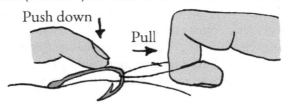

Push down

Pull

Bad barb: If it seems like the barb will do a lot of damage, you can advance the fishhook until the barbed end comes out. That way, you can cut off that end and remove the fishhook. Rewash the area and cover it with a bandage.

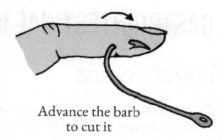

Advance the barb
to cut it

ANIMAL BITES

Animal bites—particularly from animals that eat meat—should be treated as if they are contaminated with pathogens. First, wash the wound thoroughly with soap and boiled water or a 1% povidone-iodine solution. Then rinse the wound a couple of times with plenty of boiled water. If you don't have an irrigation syringe, you can improvise one using a clean plastic bag with a small hole.

If the animal is suspected to be rabid, aggressive washing is the most effective first aid treatment. Use 2% benzalkonium chloride for washing the wound if available. If you were bitten by a raccoon, wolf, skunk, opossum, fox, or coyote, get a rabies shot (see "Rabies" section).

A high-risk animal bite is considered a dirty wound, so it should not be taped, sutured, or stapled right away. Clean the wound frequently and apply antiseptic ointment (Polysporin or bacitracin). Do not plug deep wounds with ointment; let them drain. Watch the wound for signs of infection: redness, swelling, or oozing. If needed, low-risk animal bites may be closed with tape. Cover the wound with a sterile dressing.

For high-risk animal bites, consider preventive antibiotics, such as amoxicillin-clavulanate or ciprofloxacin and start treatment immediately for improved effectiveness (amoxicillin–clavulanic acid 875/125 mg PO q12h × 3–5 days, or ciprofloxacin 500 mg PO q12h × 3–5 days). Five days of preventive antibiotics should be more than sufficient for uninfected bites; otherwise, do an entire course. Having a tetanus shot is wise for those who haven't been vaccinated in the last five years.

GASTROINTESTINAL ISSUES

HUNGER PANGS

Drinking lots of water or tea helps reduce hunger pangs considerably. They dial down after a few days or weeks of food deprivation, and fasting is another way to minimize them.

CONSTIPATION

There are two general definitions for constipation: infrequent bowel movements and consistently difficult bowel movements.

Not having bowel movements for several weeks should be expected in a state of food deprivation. I've experienced this in survival contexts without complications. If you haven't had a bowel movement in several days in a food-deprived context, do not panic or force your body at all costs. Take a moderate path, listen, and trust your body.

If you don't have laxatives, you can try the following remedies. Drink a bit of soap solution or fat to stimulate a bowel movement. Another method is to drink half a liter of cold water, followed by a mug of hot tea.

It helps to massage your abdomen: start at the bottom right and move clockwise, making circles and using gentle pressure.

Not drinking enough water or not consuming enough fiber can make passing stools more difficult. The more time feces sits in the lower intestine, the drier and harder it becomes. This kind of constipation could lead to fecal impaction (dry, hard stool) if not addressed. Fecal impaction is a dangerous type of constipation. If this occurs, you might have to insert a lubricated, gloved finger in the anus to break up the impaction and pull it out.

To increase your dietary fiber, eat birch leaves, chopped pine needles, and other edible leaves. Chewing the bones of animals, birds, and fish may help or worsen the issue depending on the quantities you consume. Make sure to stay well hydrated.

If you are constipated in a survival context, you might find blood in your stool. If there is only a trace of blood, you probably don't need to worry too much. Solve the constipation, and the wound should heal.

FOOD POISONING

Food poisoning is caused by eating food contaminated with bacterial toxins. Abdominal cramps, diarrhea, nausea, and vomiting are common symptoms that can appear one to 12 hours after ingestion. The problem usually resolves itself. Stay well hydrated, replace electrolytes, and monitor for new signs.

DIARRHEA

With diarrhea, the main issue is to stay well hydrated and with an adequate level of electrolytes. Drink water, tea, and broth, and eat fruits. Improvise a rehydration solution by adding one teaspoon of salt and eight teaspoons of sugar to a liter of water. Drink 300 mL of the solution every hour, along with plenty of plain water, until your urine looks clear. Take one tablet of Imodium after each explosion.

INTESTINAL PARASITES

Intestinal parasites can be a problem in the wilderness due to inadequate hygiene and contact with soil, water, and raw meat. Parasites won't necessarily cause strong symptoms, and you may be okay with them. But if the symptoms become more serious, try a broad-spectrum antiparasitic drug, like albendazole (Albenza) or mebendazole (Vermox). The World Health Organization (WHO) recommends a single dose of either albendazole (400 mg) or mebendazole (500 mg) for mass deworming campaigns. Both medications work against hookworm, whipworm, roundworm, pinworm, and the intestinal form of trichinosis. But they shouldn't be used by pregnant women or by children less than two years of age.

If you don't have antiparasitic drugs, you may resort to one of the following last-resort remedies. But don't make the cure worse than the disease!

- Mix four tablespoons of salt in one liter of warm water and drink (do not repeat).
- Eat one or one and a half cigarettes (repeat in 48 hours if necessary).

CRYPTOSPORIDIUM

Cryptosporidium is a protozoan parasite. Often, it results in diarrhea that resolves itself. The incubation period is usually seven to 10 days. People can experience no symptoms or have mild symptoms for five or six days.

Common symptoms include watery diarrhea (without blood or pus), abdominal cramps, nausea, flatulence, and sometimes vomiting and mild fever.

Most people recover without treatment within one to two weeks. In order to facilitate a full recovery, try to minimize vomiting and dehydration.

GIARDIASIS

Giardiasis (beaver fever) is an illness caused by protozoan parasites. Giardia is primarily transmitted through drinking water, and has an incubation period of one to two weeks. Around half of people with giardiasis have no symptoms.

The symptoms can be quite variable. Sometimes there is a sudden onset of explosive diarrhea, abdominal cramps, flatulence, fever, and vomiting. Usually, this stage lasts three to four days. Then, the symptoms decrease in intensity and come and go. The stools can be soft and foul-smelling, but there is no blood or pus.

Metronidazole can be used to treat giardiasis (250 mg q6h × 5–7 days), but it can cause nausea and discomfort.

E. COLI

E. coli bacteria is the most common cause of traveler's diarrhea. Some of *E. coli*'s strains can cause severe food poisoning. The main symptoms are persistent diarrhea (sometimes bloody), stomach cramps, nausea, and vomiting. Traveler's diarrhea usually resolves itself, so focus on proper hydration.

COLD WEATHER ISSUES

HYPOTHERMIA

Hypothermia is the drop in temperature of the body's core. The following conditions make the perfect recipe for hypothermia: cold, wet, and windy conditions; inadequate clothing; insufficient water and food intake; and fatigue.

It's important to recognize and deal with mild hypothermia early on when the body can quickly be warmed back up. But if moderate or severe hypothermia develops, it will turn into a full-scale emergency.

If you can't rely on others to notice a sudden lack of coordination or mental deficit in you, then you must be very conscious and notice even the slightest signs of hypothermia. If you miss those early signs while you can still recover, the hypothermia will worsen and eventually, you are done. Once your ability to function and think properly is gone, it will be practically impossible to rescue yourself.

Some first clues to watch for are feeling very cold and shivering. Although these clues don't necessarily mean your core temperature is low, they should trigger you to correct your situation.

MILD HYPOTHERMIA

With mild hypothermia—a core temperature of 95°–90°F (35°C–32°C)—the temperature regulation mechanisms in your body still work normally. One of these mechanisms is shivering, which is mainly how the body warms itself unless it has no energy left or you consumed drugs. Exercise and prolonged starvation may also inhibit shivering, making it difficult for you to notice the onset of hypothermia.

Uncontrollable shivering occurs when the core temperature falls to about 93°F (34°C). The inability to touch your thumb to the little finger of the same hand or shivering aggressively is the final warning for you to warm up. These circumstances signal the last chance for self-help.

Fine motor skills are impaired first, followed by gross motor skills. Mental impairment follows once the core temperature approaches 90°F (32°C).

The mildly hypothermic individual "umbles":
- Fumbles (fine motor)
- Stumbles (gross motor)
- Tumbles (gross motor)
- Mumbles (mental)
- Grumbles (mental)

MODERATE AND SEVERE HYPOTHERMIA

The core temperature of someone experiencing moderate hypothermia ranges from 90°F–82°F (32°C–28°C). In this stage, the body's warming responses die down or stop. Although people respond differently, consciousness is usually lost at 86°F (30°C).

Severe hypothermia is defined as a core temperature below 82°F (28°C); at this stage, death is imminent.

Moderate to severe hypothermia signs and symptoms:
- slow pulse and breathing
- uncoordinated walking
- altered mental status (slurred speech or lack of response to verbal or pain stimulation)
- no shivering (this may also be caused by exhaustion or starvation)

Hypo-thermia	Core temperature	Person's ability to rewarm without external heat	Signs	
Mild	95°F –90°F (35°C –32°C)	Good	Physical impairment "Umbles"	Mental impairment complex and simple
Moderate	90°F –82°F (32°C –28°C)	Limited	Below 90°F (32°C), shivering stops. Below 86°F (30°C), consciousness is lost.	
Severe	Below 82°F (28°C)	Unable	Rigidity, vital signs reduced or absent, severe risk of arrhythmia caused by rough handling	
	Below 77°F (25°C)	Unable	Spontaneous arrhythmia, cardiac arrest	

Modified from *Hypothermia, Frostbite and Other Cold Injuries*

TREATING MILD HYPOTHERMIA

Cold individuals who are not yet hypothermic—shivering lightly but behaving normally—can be warmed by exercise, such as walking or setting up camp. But if they are hypothermic, suffering from the "umbles," shivering vigorously, or showing signs of more severe hypothermia, they should be treated in a warm place.

If a medical facility is more than 30 to 60 minutes away, the hypothermic person should be rewarmed. If the person can be insulated, shivering vigorously inside a hypothermia wrap will be effective. The person should also consume energy-rich drinks and foods. Hot water bottles (wrapped in clothing) may be placed under the arms, in the groin, on the chest, or around the neck. Be careful of burning the person. If it's not practical to regularly change the hot water bottles, remove them because they can otherwise be counterproductive. Skin-to-skin contact with a warm person helps with rewarming.

The hypothermia wrap uses sleeping pads, sleeping bags, clothes, and tarps to form an insulated "burrito" and keeps the hypothermic person insulated from the ground and the environment (see below).

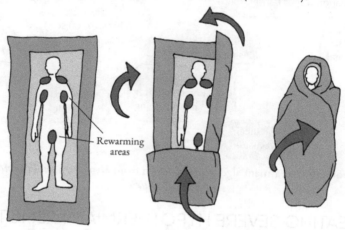

Rewarming areas

TREATING MODERATE TO SEVERE HYPOTHERMIA WITH SIGNS OF LIFE

Medical evacuation (medevac) is the primary way to treat someone with moderate to severe hypothermia, but it must be done gently to avoid precipitating cardiac arrest. Package the person horizontally in a well-insulated hypothermia wrap.

If the person is breathing or has a pulse, they should be rewarmed gradually, as outlined before, with the following exceptions: they must not sit or stand until rewarmed, they should not be given fluids or food, and they should not attempt to exercise or walk. Watch out for an afterdrop in core temperature.

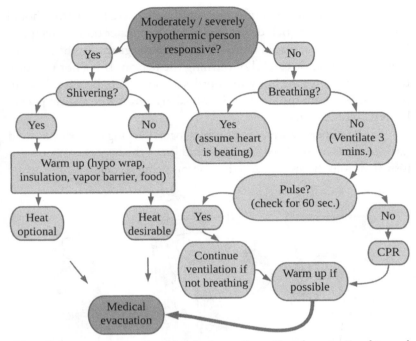

Hypothermia treatment algorithm (redrawn from *Hypothermia, Frostbite and Other Cold Injuries*).

TREATING SEVERE HYPOTHERMIA IN REMOTE AREAS

If medevac is delayed or not viable, the severely hypothermic person should be warmed up. Rewarming in the field may take up to 24 hours or more, and rescuers must have the equipment (tents, sleeping bags, and clothing) and the supplies (fuel, food, and water) to perform it.

The hypothermic person should be fully insulated and moved into a warm shelter. If there is no shelter, a fire should be built. The fire doesn't effectively warm an insulated hypothermic person, but it keeps them dry and reduces heat loss. It also provides warmth to the rescuers, allows clothing to dry, and may be used for hot water bottles. Perform the rewarming methods described earlier. Remember: "No one is dead until they are warm and dead."

COLD WATER IMMERSION

Contrary to popular belief, people that fall into cold water generally don't perish from hypothermia. It takes more than 30 minutes for someone submerged in ice water (wearing winter clothing) to become hypothermic, but most deaths happen within 20 minutes (from drowning or cardiac arrest).

THE STAGES OF COLD WATER IMMERSION

Cold shock is the initial reaction. It can kill within two minutes by leading to drowning or cardiac arrest.

Focus on surviving the first minute: suppress the urge to panic, and get your breath under control. Once you are in control of your breath, look around and take action.

Cold incapacitation occurs within 30 minutes of immersion. It impairs the ability to help yourself and swim, leading to drowning. Remember these tips:

- *Escape:* pull yourself out of the water.
- *Minimize exposure:* if escaping is not possible, get as much of your body out of the water as you can.
- *Secure solid flotation*: put on a flotation device, attach yourself to an object, or freeze your sleeves to the ice so that you won't drown if you fall unconscious.
- *Signal for help:* blow a whistle, wave your hands, and activate a personal locator beacon.

Hypothermia develops after 30 minutes or more of immersion and progresses until shivering stops and the person becomes unconscious. Once unconscious, the person may drown unless the head is supported above water, in which case the core will cool down until it leads to a cardiac standstill.

Focus on minimizing heat loss: use a posture that maximizes body heat retention.

Circum-rescue collapse can occur just before, during, or several hours after rescue. The effects range from fainting to a cardiac standstill. It occurs due to blood pressure loss, metabolic problems, or afterdrop cooling down of the heart.

The sudden relaxation of the person's stress response may cause a drop in their blood pressure, leading to fainting or drowning. The cold, stressed heart is quite vulnerable, so the person should be rescued as gently as possible, in a horizontal position.

1:10:1 RULE FOR COLD WATER IMMERSION

After falling into freezing water, you have:
- **1 minute** to get your breath under control (avoid panicking)
- **10 minutes** of useful movement (get out of the water or secure solid flotation)
- **1 hour** before becoming unconscious due to hypothermia (avoid unnecessary movement to extend the window of time for rescue).
- A person wearing a PFD may have an extra hour.

CHILBLAINS

Chilblains (pernio) are skin injuries caused by chronic exposure to cold and wet environments. This condition happens when the tiny blood vessels in the skin become impaired: there is persistent dilation of the smaller, superficial vessels while the larger vessels remain persistently constricted.

In a long-term situation, it's important to prevent chilblains because if you get it, it probably won't resolve itself until you are in a warm and dry environment. Chilblains may become a gateway for severe damage because it's harder to guard against trench foot or frostbite if your sense of feeling is impaired.

Chilblains may result from rapid temperature changes, such as putting cold feet close to a fire or onto a very hot water bottle.

Common signs of chilblains are tenderness, itching, numbness, burning or tingling, swelling, increased temperature in the area, and reddish or purplish lesions. Sometimes blisters develop, and it is common to be sensitive to the pressure caused by footwear. Chilblains may occur on the hands, ears, lower legs, and feet. Flaking and scaling may occur, but deep tissue damage won't happen. The damage should resolve itself over one to three weeks once you're in a warm and dry environment.

Chilblains may be prevented with these guidelines:
- Wear proper, warm clothing and stay inside a warm shelter.
- Keep feet dry. Maintain dry socks and footwear.
- Do not sleep with moist socks. Sleep with dry, warm socks.

- Practice good foot hygiene. Wash and dry your feet.
- Avoid tight-fitting socks and footwear.
- Avoid layering socks (unless you have large boots that do not constrict your feet).
- Rewarm gently and slowly with warm water bottles or soak in warm water. Do not use strong heat.
- Do not rub the skin. Use passive skin contact.

TRENCH FOOT

Trench foot (or immersion foot) is a severe, nonfreezing cold injury that happens when the skin of the feet is exposed to moisture and the cold for prolonged periods.

The most common cause of trench foot is wearing wet socks and footwear for a long time. In that context, the blood circulation in the feet is reduced. The body's core—which is trying to stay warm—restricts circulation to the feet, and tight footwear makes matters worse. This lack of oxygen and circulation—usually for periods of 12 hours or more—eventually leads to tissue death.

People who are not in combat should very rarely have their feet wet and cold for days at a time. Even in extreme circumstances, make a serious effort to warm up and dry your feet at night.

If you are at risk of trench foot, loosen up or remove constricting socks and footwear, and keep your feet dry and warm. Follow the measures for preventing and treating chilblains. Always have a spare pair of dry socks. Dry and change your socks on an ongoing basis, and remove your boots and dry your feet once or twice a day.

Signs of trench foot include numbness, prickling or tingling sensations (like electric shocks), itching, pain or sensitivity, swelling, burning, blue or spotted skin, blisters, and skin fissures or maceration. The pain often makes sleep difficult, and bearing weight on the feet in the mornings can become almost intolerable.

There is not much that can be done to treat trench foot in the wild; the treatment protocol is a medevac.

If the damage is not severe, little treatment is required. Keep feet clean, warm, and dry, and elevate them above the heart. Take anti-inflammatory drugs, and don't walk on injured feet (except for a medevac). It may take 12 to 48 hours for the severity of the damage to become fully apparent.

Almost no one recovers fully from trench foot: most are left with a permanently reduced tolerance to cold. If the injuries are severe, gangrene may occur, and amputation may be necessary.

FROSTNIP

Frostnip is the freezing of the skin's surface (first-degree frostbite). It usually occurs on noses, cheeks, earlobes, and fingertips. The skin may have a white frost spot and feel waxy, numb, and cold, but it will still be relatively soft. Frostnip may look like a superficial burn (first-degree burn). Wind chill is the usual cause for frostnip on the face, and contact with cold metal is the typical cause for frostnip on fingertips.

Frostnip is relatively common and not serious. To treat frostnip, thaw the spot with a warm hand or warm water until the skin returns to normal. It should take a few seconds. Never rub the area. The outer layer of skin may turn reddish and later peel, like a sunburn. If frostnip is not dealt with in time, it can progress to partial-thickness frostbite (second-degree frostbite).

FROSTBITE

Be aware of the threat of frostbite, recognize it, and treat it early. Early symptoms of frostbite begin with pain, then progress to numbness. As the freezing deepens, all sensation, including pain, disappears. However, people can experience different symptoms.

Partial-thickness frostbite (second-degree frostbite) is a more severe skin freezing injury. The skin may initially resemble frostnip: white, waxy, numb, and cold. However, it will feel harder and will dent if pressed. Often, it is impossible to assess the depth of damage before rewarming. When second-degree frostbite is thawed, a blister will form within minutes, or even hours later. Protect the blister with dressings, and avoid bursting or freezing it.

Full-thickness frostbite (third-degree frostbite) means the skin appears pale white and is frozen solid, and the person will have no sensation in the area. Again, the total damage can only be assessed after rewarming. The tissue damaged by third-degree frostbite dies, but part of the extremity could be saved. Once thawed, third-degree frostbitten extremities can't be used due to the excruciating pain.

The treatment for second- and third-degree frostbite is rapid rewarming and minimizing the post-warming circulatory impairment. Rapid rewarming reduces the severity of the damage, but it shouldn't be performed if the area may freeze again or if the person needs to walk on third-degree frostbitten feet for a medevac. If there is a risk of accidentally refreezing the tissue, it's best not to thaw it, for the cycle of thawing and refreezing inflicts far more damage.

To thaw the injury, submerge the affected part in a warm water bath at a temperature of 99° F–102°F (37°C–39°C). Heating the water to above the recommended temperature is more painful for the injury, doesn't improve the situation, and may cause burns. Do not use dry heat (campfires) to thaw the tissue! And don't rub! Too much time in warm water (overthawing) is better than not enough time (underthawing). Monitor the temperature to keep it at an appropriate warmth; add warm water often. If you don't have a thermometer, dip your bare elbow in the water. It should feel comfortably warm but not hot.

Once the area is fully thawed, air-dry the skin then cover it in antibiotic ointment and dressings and keep it elevated. Protect the injury from trauma and irritation. One or two aspirin tablets should be taken while the tissues are still frozen and every six hours afterward to improve blood circulation in the area. Strong painkillers are recommended.

SNOW BLINDNESS

Snow blindness can be crippling and quite painful, but it's easy to prevent by wearing dark sunglasses. Clear glasses can be smoked or taped, and snow goggles may be improvised with tape or birchbark.

If you expose your eyes to excessive amounts of sunlight, you risk severe pain in your eyes a few hours later. A cold, water-soaked cloth might offer relief. Keep your eyes covered, and remain in a dark place. If the exposure was not severe, you might feel better the following day. Otherwise, snow blindness may last up to three days. Fortunately, it usually heals by itself.

OTHER INFECTIONS AND DISEASES

The following diseases are relatively rare, but anyone handling wild meats has a higher risk of contracting them. Use gloves whenever you handle uncooked meat, wash your hands afterward, and cook meat thoroughly.

TRICHINOSIS

Trichinosis is an infection caused by microscopic roundworms. It is contracted by eating undercooked meat and fat containing trichinella cysts.

The adult worms reproduce in the intestines, and the young worms travel throughout the body to form cysts in different places. Trichinosis is generally carried by omnivores and carnivores like bears, hogs, bobcats, wolves, coyotes, foxes, raccoons, and skunks.

To prevent trichinosis, cook food to an internal temperature of 170°F (75°C). Boiling is an easy way to tell you've reached a high enough temperature. Otherwise, roast the meat until it is thoroughly heated. Then, slice through the thickest part and check for signs of steaming, or insert your finger: if you can't touch the meat for more than a second, you have probably reached the proper temperature. Keep the meat in the heat for a few minutes, just to be sure. Freezing or drying the meat is not effective against trichinosis.

The first symptoms of trichinosis include abdominal discomfort, diarrhea, nausea, fatigue, and fever. They are usually followed by muscle pain, fever with chills, aching joints, swelling around the eyes, and bleeding around the fingernails and in the whites of the eyes. Symptoms may appear after a few hours to five days after ingestion, and they may persist for up to six weeks before the infection clears. A severe case could lead to death.

No safe, effective drug is available for combating the larvae. Mebendazole (400 mg q8h × 13 days) or albendazole (400 mg q12h × 8–14 days) works against adult worms in the intestine, but these drugs won't work for worms outside it. Supplement them with prednisone (30–60 mg/day PO × 10–30 days) to relieve severe swelling.

TULAREMIA

Tularemia (rabbit fever) is a bacterial infection commonly associated with rabbits, but it is also carried by rodents, hares, moles, hogs, beavers, muskrats, squirrels, rats, mice, grouse, and ticks. It is transmitted by handling dead animals, eating undercooked meat, drinking contaminated water, as well as from tick and fly bites. Animals usually get it from water contaminated with carcasses, and carriers typically have small white spots on their livers, spleens, lungs, or kidneys.

The symptoms begin with an abrupt fever, cough, vomiting, and headache. The symptoms may relapse several days after a period of abatement and can affect many parts of the body. The lymph nodes may swell, and a small boil-like eruption or an ulcer may appear at the site of the infection. Symptoms usually appear in two to four days, and the disease lasts about two weeks.

Early diagnosis may be difficult, but tularemia is easily treated with antibiotics. Streptomycin (administered intramuscularly) is the preferred drug for treatment. Alternative antibiotics include oral tetracycline or chloramphenicol (both 50–60 mg/kg/day distributed q6h × 14 days) or ciprofloxacin if no other antibiotic is available. Relapse may occur with oral antibiotics.

HANTAVIRUS

Hantavirus pulmonary syndrome is a severe but rare viral illness carried primarily by wild mice—it's found in their saliva, feces, and urine. Hantavirus does not harm mice, but it's dangerous to humans (around 30%–35% of hospitalized cases are lethal). Humans usually contract it by inhaling the dust of deer mice nests. There have been hantavirus cases all along the range of deer mice, which spans most of North America. There is no effective treatment other than support, such as mechanical ventilation.

Symptoms include chills, fever, headache, nausea, vomiting, and cough, and progress rapidly to acute respiratory distress caused by fluid in the lungs.

Prevention includes:

- avoiding mice feces and nests
- wetting down mice nests before clearing them
- wearing gloves
- thoroughly cooking rodents
- using N95 filter masks (or N100)

The risk of exposure is greater in closed spaces such as inside a cabin. Hantavirus is an example in which the risk might not be worth the reward. Some survival experts recommend not eating mice for this reason.

BOTULISM

Botulism is a paralytic disease caused by the toxins of the *Clostridium botulinum* bacteria. The botulinum toxin is produced when the bacteria are exposed to low oxygen levels and specific temperatures. It may occur in improperly canned, dried, or fermented foods. And it is the most poisonous substance known to humankind. Assume that any found animal carcass has it.

Where it may get confusing is that to destroy the spores—which, given time and the right conditions, will eventually develop and produce the toxin—you need to heat the food to be preserved to a temperature of

250°F (120°C) for five minutes (some foods require more time). That is impractical in the outdoors and not needed if you are properly drying or dehydrating meat. But it is a must for canning food.

If you suspect that your food contains botulinum toxins, you will want to neutralize them. In that case, it is as simple as cooking the thinly sliced food to a rolling boil (five minutes if you are at a high elevation) or for five minutes at 185°F (85°C) to neutralize the toxins. But the spores won't be destroyed. The food must be eaten immediately because the spores can germinate, grow, and produce the toxin in two hours above 70°F (21°C), 11 hours at 50°F–70°F (10°C–21°C), and in seven days at 38°F–41°F (3.3°C–5°C).

The first symptoms appear 12 to 36 hours after ingestion, and include nausea, vomiting, abdominal pain, and diarrhea. They are followed by dry mouth; difficulty breathing, swallowing, and speaking; blurred or double vision; drooping eyelids; and facial paralysis, eventually causing respiratory failure. Treatment consists of giving botulinum antitoxin and using a mechanical ventilator. If left untreated, botulism has a mortality rate of 40%–50%.

RABIES

Rabies is quite rare, but it cannot be cured! This lethal virus attacks the nerves and brain, and it is primarily transmitted through bites (saliva) and excretions (bats). Its leading carriers are raccoons, wolves, skunks, opossums, foxes, coyotes, and bats.

The incubation period is about two weeks to three months (but can be anywhere from nine days to a year). Once you have the symptoms—severe pain, muscle spasms, paralysis, seizures, difficulty swallowing, and excessive salivation—there is no cure, and practically no one survives.

There are preventive vaccines that will boost the effectiveness of the postexposure vaccines. Postexposure vaccines only work if they are given before the symptoms start.

The best prevention is to avoid getting bit. If you get bit by an aggressive animal or one that acts out of character, assume it has rabies. Evacuate and get vaccinated.

HYGIENE

ORAL HYGIENE

Pack toothpaste and a toothbrush because they don't add much bulk or weight. Dental floss also helps and should be part of a repair kit anyway. Toothpaste is not required but helps morale.

Although not as effective, an improvised toothbrush can be made from a soft, green twig. Chew its end until it frays, and use it as a brush. Mountain ash, dogwood, and alder are said to work well. Or wrap a stick or your finger with a clean cloth and use it as a brush.

Toothpaste may be improvised with a paste made of water and charcoal (or even ash, as alder ash is said to work well).

You may improvise a mouthwash with clean salt water in coastal areas. Willow bark tea as well as juniper berry tea is also recommended. Usnea (see "Medicinal plants" section) or juniper berries can also be used as an antibacterial or an anticavity mouthwash.

SOAP

Soap makes a big difference when bathing and washing clothes, and it's also important for first aid.

Improvised soap won't be half as good as proper soap, but there are a few natural sources that may work.

- Birch leaves: select young leaves and place them in a container with boiling water. Mix until the saponin in the leaves dissolves into a natural soap.
- Wood ash: mix hardwood ash with boiling water and let stand for a few hours. This creates a really weak lye solution. Strain it. Don't use it too often because it dries out your skin.
- Soapberry (buffalo berry): *Shepherdia canadensis* is found in the US and Canada. Crush the berries and soak them in water.
- Soapberry tree: *Sapindus* is found in the Southern US. Dry the fruits thoroughly, grind them to dust, and then use them as powdered soap. Or soak the fruits for a couple of days and squeeze them.
- Soaproot: *Chlorogalum* is found in California. Peel the outer layers of its bulb and mix a few inner layers with water.
- Yucca: found in the Southwestern US. Separate the leaf fibers into very thin strands and mix with water.

BATHING

Wash your body with soap regularly to avoid having a thick layer of grime. Sunbathing and smoke bathing are two alternatives to water and soap. The sun's UV rays kill bacteria and provide vitamin D.

Smoke bathing helps mask odors and has limited antimicrobial effects, although juniper smoke has some antibacterial properties. The smoke from willow and birch smells good.

POOPING IN THE WILD

It is not necessary to build a camp latrine unless you are a group of more than two people and you stay in the same spot for several months. It's enough to delineate an area, bury the poop properly, and mark each location.

When pooping, I like to find a big fallen log or big rock to use as hand support and partially squat, or sometimes I grab a solid tree and squat.

In truly remote areas where humans rarely roam, you can just cover the poop with some leaves, moss, rocks, or sticks and mark the spot with a vertical stick or tripod so that your group won't step in it.

In high-use areas, you must dig about 6″ (15 cm) deep and cover and mark the spot. Marking is more effective than burying at preventing someone from stepping in the poop.

Shown below is another way to make a simple latrine, but you may have to dig through tree roots with this approach.

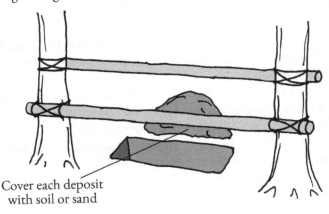

Cover each deposit
with soil or sand

TOILET PAPER

Toilet paper is impractical to carry on long-term trips without resupplies, but it can be improvised with the following materials:

- Rocks: round textured rocks are good if they are not too cold or hot.
- Grass: a bundle works great folded onto itself.
- Moss: it's excellent.
- Leaves: make sure they are not an irritant. Use multiple overlapping leaves or your fingers might pop through!
- Sticks and pieces of bark: not ideal, and be mindful of sharp ends.
- Snow: it wipes and cleans very effectively. But this invigorating experience gets old soon. For long-term trips, I use other materials first and then finish with snow to minimize any discomfort.
- Urine: is particularly useful in the cold.

Often the best approach is to use a combination of materials—e.g., start with moss and finish with snow.

WINTER HYGIENE

In winter, staying clean is a bit harder. Try to wash your face and hands daily. Even if you can't wash your whole body, wash your feet, crotch, and armpits weekly (a moist snowball works), and change your socks often. You can also warm up a cup of water and pour it on a washcloth to wash your body. Lastly, mustaches can be kept short to avoid ice buildup.

CUTTING YOUR HAIR

Keeping your hair short in the wild is a bit difficult without scissors. If your hair is long, a knife will do the job, but if your hair is short, the knife will have to be razor-sharp.

An alternative is to burn your hair off with a lighter. Work on a small patch and extinguish it with your palm once the heat is intolerable. Then start again. Don't do this inside a shelter, or it will stink. I have resorted to burning my hair off, and it works well, but your hair will stink for a few days.

FEMALE-SPECIFIC HYGIENE

Menstrual cups (e.g., DivaCup) and reusable cloth pads (e.g., Tree Hugger Cloth Pads) are great, long-term ways of managing menstruation. A menstrual cup could be enough, but some women may need both the menstrual cup and the cloth pad if they have a heavy flow.

BUGS

MOSQUITOES AND FLIES

In some areas, mosquitoes and flies can be a significant problem. If this sounds like your area, you must have an effective strategy to deal with them.

My preferred strategy for long-term contexts is to wear a loose-fitting, long-sleeved shirt, loose pants, and midheight shoes (to cover my ankles). That is adequate most of the time. Wear a hat and a mosquito net to protect your face during particularly bad periods.

Full bug jackets are way too hot, so I don't recommend them, and bug pants and socks are trash.

An integral part of the strategy above is to avoid areas with too many mosquitoes. Set up your camp in a dry and windy area during peak bug season. Stay inside a mosquito-proof shelter before sunrise and after sunset to avoid peak mosquito hours.

The U.S. armed forces' way to deal with areas heavy with mosquitoes is to use permethrin-treated clothes (**bit.ly/perm-c**) and DEET. In addition to covering your clothes and skin with potentially harmful chemicals, both permethrin and DEET wear off in the long term.

Factory-treated permethrin clothes last much longer than the ones you treat yourself (manufacturers claim over 25 machine washings).

DEET is highly effective, but it smells terrible. If you are going to pack DEET, take the 98% solution, for it is more compact. Ration it wisely, or dilute it. DEET is not needed, and it can be replaced with a head net and loose clothing.

If the options above are not available to you, you can resort to the following less effective techniques. A smoldering fire is one of the only natural, moderately effective defenses against mosquitoes. Make a smoldering fire in a can with dried animal dung, punkwood, moss, or leaves. A more desperate alternative is to use mud to cover your skin. Finally, the best approach is to stay in a spot without mosquitoes, such as a small rocky island in the middle of a lake or a very windy site.

TICKS

Ticks are not challenging to deal with. These simple strategies work well:

- Wear light-colored clothes (to spot ticks easily).
- Wear long sleeves.
- Tuck your pants into your boots.
- Perform daily tick checks during the tick seasons.

The most important thing is to perform daily tick checks of your entire body, including your hairline, backs of knees, waistline, crotch, armpits, and all nooks and crannies. That will ensure that even if a Lyme-disease carrying tick were to bite you, you won't allow it to stay attached for the 36 hours required to transmit the disease.

Not all ticks carry Lyme disease. Only a few species can spread it, and only a fraction of those tick populations actually have it (the percentage varies widely from place to place). Nevertheless, it's important to be careful because many tick species transmit various pathogens.

The most common ticks are the dog tick (*Dermacentor variabilis*) and the wood tick (*Dermacentor andersoni*); fortunately, neither carries Lyme disease.

Adult dog tick (*Dermacentor variabilis*, female)

On the other hand, the black-legged tick—aka deer tick (*Ixodes scapularis*)—and the western black-legged tick (*Ixodes pacificus*) can carry Lyme disease. These ticks are smaller, and they are pretty distinct from wood ticks.

Adult deer tick (*Ixodes scapularis*, female)

REMOVING A TICK

Regardless of species, all ticks should be removed as soon as they are discovered. Use tweezers to grasp the tick as close to the skin as possible and remove it straight up in a steady motion. That will give you the best chance of pulling it out intact. Don't twist, turn, or jerk. If removed at an angle, the mouthparts sometimes remain in the skin and can cause slight irritation.

Don't burn or squeeze ticks because they may vomit into the bite and introduce pathogens. If you don't have tweezers, use a toothpick-sized stick to gently dislodge the tick.

LYME DISEASE

Lyme disease is usually transmitted by the black-legged tick *Ixodes scapularis* (aka deer tick) and the western black-legged tick *Ixodes pacificus*. Typically, the ticks must be attached for more than 36 hours to transmit the disease.

The symptoms usually begin seven to 10 days after the bite and include fever, chills, headache, fatigue, and muscle and joint aches. Usually, a distinctive rash develops at the bite site: it starts as a red circle, and as it expands, it may resemble a bull's-eye target. The symptoms later include severe headaches, neck stiffness, facial palsy, pain along the body, irregular heartbeat, and arthritis.

When the disease is diagnosed early in a medical facility, these oral antibiotics are given: amoxicillin (500 mg q8h ×14 days) or doxycycline (100 mg q12h ×14 days).

In the wild, you could try a single dose of doxycycline (200 mg for adults) as a preventive measure if *all* the following criteria are met:

1. the attached tick is an adult or nymphal black-legged tick;
2. the tick was attached for over 36 hours (engorgement or time estimate);
3. the antibiotics will be given within 72 hours of the tick's removal; and
4. the person is not under eight years of age, pregnant, or lactating (doxycycline is contraindicated in those cases).

LEECHES

Leeches shouldn't be pulled off like ticks because they have serrated teeth. If you find a leech early enough before it bites, you may pull it off, as long as you make sure it's hanging from its big end (its bottom) and not its small end (its mouth).

If the leech is already attached, place your fingernail next to its mouth and gently push the mouth sideways. Or try poking its mouth gently with a toothpick-sized stick. Try a sprinkle of salt or ash on its body if it doesn't release, or touch it with a lit stick. Try the gentle ways first to minimize the risk of the leech vomiting into the bite.

POISONOUS PLANTS

POISON IVY

Typically, poison ivy (*Toxicodendron radicans* and *T. rydbergii*) grows east of the Rocky Mountains, and poison oak grows west of the Rocky Mountains.

Posion ivy has three separate leaflets each 1.2″–4.7″ (3–12 cm) long. It is a climbing shrub often found in wooded areas growing up the trunks of trees. The stems holding the leaves alternate on each side, rather than branching off directly opposite from each other. The middle stem holding the largest leaflet is always longer.

Toxicodendron radicans

Poison oak is found in wooded areas on the west coast of North America. It is a shrub with multiple stems that form three leaflets shaped like oak leaves.

Toxicodendron diversilobum

POISON IVY REMEDIES

The leaves of these plants are coated with urushiol, and their sap also contains this irritant. Urushiol is a substance that causes a skin reaction in 50%–70% of people. After being in contact with urushiol, you have five minutes to one hour to wash it off, depending on your sensitivity.

Wash the area with strong soap, and use *cold* water—hot water often worsens the reaction. Then, wash your clothes and hands with soap.

Usually, the reaction starts after two to six hours after contact, and sometimes it takes days. The irritation resolves itself naturally in around seven days, but it may last two or three weeks.

Soaking in very hot water can provide hours of relief. The sap released from crushed common plantain is said to help with the itch.

Depending on the severity and the size of the area affected, you can try the following medications: oral antihistamine (diphenhydramine/Benadryl 25–50 mg q4–6h), calamine lotion (drying agent), hydrocortisone cream (1/2%–1%) before any blisters develop, and oral steroids if the reaction is severe (prednisone 60 mg/day × 5 days, then 30 mg × 5 days, then 15 mg × 5 days).

ERGOT

Ergot (*Claviceps* spp.) is a toxic fungus that infects the grains of grass plants. It may cause painful seizures and spasms, burning feelings in the limbs,

hallucinations, paralysis, psychosis, and gangrene. This parasitic fungus takes the place of grain kernels and looks dark purple, white-purple, or black. Usually, ergot kernels are slightly larger than typical grains, and they look quite distinct.

If you are harvesting a grass like wild rice, you should be on the lookout for this fungus. You'll likely harvest multiple ergot kernels among your wild rice. Pick the ergot kernels by hand or try submerging the grains in salty or plain water to remove them. Most of them should float. Look for any remaining ergot kernels among the grains.

It is not the end of the world if you eat a few kernels by accident. Poisoning happens when moderate or high doses are eaten in a short time.

MEDICINAL PLANTS

USNEA

Usnea spp. (old man's beard) is a lichen found year-round hanging from trees. It is usually gray to pale green and contains usnic acid. This acid has antibiotic, anti-inflammatory, and pain-relieving properties. It has been used throughout the world to treat various ailments.

To distinguish *Usnea* from similar species, break it to confirm that it contains a slightly elastic white inner core.

Usnea makes excellent bandages for wounds, superficial infections, and skin rashes from allergies. Soft and wispy *Usnea* can be applied directly to the problem areas. Another option is to grind the lichen into a powder and sprinkle it directly on wounds.

To ingest it, make a strong tea and let it sit for a long time. *Usnea* is not safe to drink in high concentrations because it is known to cause liver failure.

PLANTAIN

The common broadleaf plantain (*Plantago major*) and narrow-leaved plantain (*Plantago lanceolata*) are medicinal plants that have been used traditionally for stings, bites, and irritations. Folk medicine suggests that crushed plantain leaves reduce the itch caused by poison ivy and may help relieve a toothache.

A paste of finely crushed plantain leaves helps treat superficial wounds, as well as stings or bites from mildly venomous insects. The crushed leaves have anti-allergic, antimicrobial, and anesthetic properties.

Robert Flogaus-Faust/CC-BY-4.0

YARROW

Yarrow (*Achillea millefolium*) is one of the most widely used medicinal plants. It has sedative, clotting, antimicrobial, and anti-inflammatory properties. It is excellent for digestive issues. Its leaves can be used in poultices and applied to wounds. But the leaves help stop bleeds more effectively when dried, powdered, and sprinkled onto wounds.

STINGING NETTLE

Stinging nettle (*Urtica dioica*) is a highly nutritious plant: it is particularly rich in iron, magnesium, and calcium. Boil and eat its young shoots and leaves. Avoid old plants, for they don't taste as good and are more fibrous. Leaves and shoots can also be eaten raw if rubbed between two cloth towels to remove the stinging hairs.

Wear long sleeves and gloves when collecting stinging nettles. The acid from stinging nettles can cause itching and burning for a few minutes and up to a couple of days. Nettles can also be cut down and left to decay for a few hours to weaken the stinging hairs in their leaves, but the stem hairs will take longer to wither. The stinging compounds are destroyed by cooking or drying.

Stinging nettle leaf tea is rich in minerals and iron. Let it steep for a few hours to get the most out of it. The leaves are best gathered in May for medicinal use before the plant flowers.

ELECTRONICS

SOLAR PANELS

Solar chargers with integrated battery packs are problematic because lithium-ion batteries won't charge when they are too hot or too cold. Integrated batteries introduce numerous points of failure and reduce the versatility of the chargers.

The most resilient chargers are just simple solar panels that can directly charge electronics without an intermediate battery. These solar panels must feature a restart function that kicks in after a cloud passes by, for most devices will stop charging after the current decreases, and they won't resume charging even if the current goes back up again.

The solar panel should have an output of at least 5–7 W if it's a high-quality panel, but I would recommend at least 10 W and 1.7 A. Keep in mind that advertised wattage tends to be higher than the actual output. The panel should also feature a regular female USB port. The surface area of the solar cells is crucial: small panels don't work well.

To get the advantages of a solar charger with an integrated battery but without the drawbacks, have multiple battery packs. That way, you can charge the battery packs during the day and then charge the devices at night.

Check the operating temperature of your solar panel if you will experience extreme cold.

A challenge when using solar panels is repositioning the panel throughout the day to face the sun. Rain, snow, and clouds are also an issue.

You can place the solar panel and battery pack inside a waterproof map case when water protection is crucial, such as when canoeing.

Despite all their drawbacks, solar panels are still the best recharging option because they work reasonably well without taking up much time from your day.

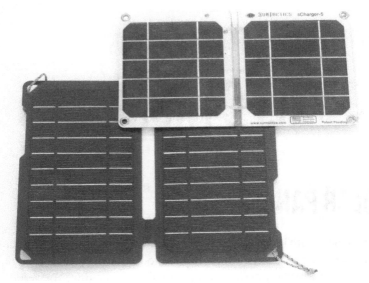

I recommend the Renogy E-Flex 10W (bottom left) and the Suntactics S5 (top right) solar panels. Both panels are light, simple, water-resistant, and reliable.

BATTERY PACKS

Battery packs are the other component needed for solar charging. You can get by without them by charging your devices directly from the solar panels, but it is inconvenient, and solar panels can't store energy for overcast days.

Battery packs should be waterproof, shockproof, and have a capacity of at least 6000–10,000 mAh to make full use of an entire day of charging.

Lithium-ion batteries won't charge in subfreezing temperatures, so the battery pack must be kept warm and insulated. You can wrap a hot water bottle and battery pack together inside a bundle of insulated clothes and connect the battery pack to the solar panel to charge. You can also substitute the hot water bottle for a rock that has been heated near a fire—make sure it's not too hot, or it could melt the battery pack or clothes.

BATTERIES

For headlamps and other electronics, the best option is to use rechargeable NiMH AA batteries and have extras for clouded periods as well.

Neither NiMH nor lithium-ion batteries charge at freezing temperatures; they must be warm to charge.

Cables are a point of failure, so have spares and avoid twisting them. Have long cables so you can charge your battery packs and devices from inside your shelter. Short cables are quite durable because they don't twist much.

For charging AA batteries, I recommend the Olight Universal Charger because it's compact and simple, but it only charges one battery at a time.

HEADLAMPS

There is no doubt that headlamps are more versatile and practical than flashlights. Having a reliable headlamp with a long battery life is crucial, especially throughout the winter in northern latitudes when the darkness dominates.

Headlamps with different brightness levels allow you to increase their run time if needed. In an emergency, conserving your battery could be a big deal.

Nothing ruins your night vision faster than a bright light. Contrary to popular belief, the color of the light is not as important for preserving your night vision as is the ability to dim the light really low. Use the dimmest setting. When you use your night vision, you retain your peripheral vision and awareness and the ability to see outside the range of the light.

A survival headlamp must be fully waterproof: certified to IPX7 or IPX8 standards, meaning the device can stay submerged for at least 30 minutes under 1 m of water.

It should also work with a single AA rechargeable battery. The reason why the AA battery is the way to go is because a device that takes AA batteries can also work with a AAA battery with the help of some aluminum foil. In contrast, a headlamp that takes AAA batteries can't use a AA battery. Although both batteries contain about the same energy per weight, it's best to have AA batteries because they pack more charge.

Some headlamps use lithium-ion batteries, but it's cheaper and more practical to stick with high-quality NiMH rechargeable batteries.

I've used NiMH batteries at -22°F (-30°C), and although their charge doesn't last as long, they still work.

Headlamps that use two or three batteries sometimes won't drain the batteries evenly. Headlamps that only use a single battery eliminate this problem and makes it easier to swap out batteries in the dark.

In cold temperatures, being able to use a headlamp without taking your gloves off is essential, so the power button should stand out.

On the other hand, headlamps often turn on by accident, and their batteries run out. One way to avoid this is by unscrewing the battery cap slightly.

Some ideal headlamps for survival are the Fenix HM23 and those made by ZebraLight. A neat feature of ZebraLight headlamps is that they tell you the energy level left in the battery.

WATCH

The only extra features that are advantageous in watches are tide tables and barometers. I recommend having a watch with a barometer for weather observation, and if you are by the coast, a watch with a tide function is quite helpful. Watches with digital compasses are convenient, but they require constant recalibrating and verifying with a proper compass.

GPS watches might be handy when used with a good map, but an actual GPS device or smartphone with an offline GPS app is more useful.

THERMOMETERS

Watch thermometers are not very useful because you must take off the watch and wait 15 to 20 minutes for an accurate temperature reading. In addition, most watch thermometers won't take readings if it is colder than 14°F (-10°C), which is precisely when knowing the temperature is important. For these reasons, I highly recommend having a field thermometer.

Most keychain thermometers are highly inaccurate, so the only ones I recommend are the Digital Zipogage by Sun Company, or a liquid-in-glass field thermometer (with an integrated metal case and window).

SMARTPHONES AND TABLETS

At first glance, smartphones and tablets don't seem like they belong in the wilderness, but smartphones and tablets can be a considerable aid for long-term survival. There are clear benefits of having them: satellite imagery, topographic maps, offline GPS, and a medical library.

You can store thousands of books on a smartphone. Some books that are particularly useful are field guides on wild edibles and medical books for researching specific health issues. Check the references at the end of this book for some suggestions.

I recommend having a few e-books on the topics of wilderness, remote, and expedition medicine and a few in-depth medical books, such as medical guides for ships and a recent copy of the Physicians' Desk Reference.

Install a few apps to read e-books and PDFs, such as Librera Reader and Moon+ Reader for Android or iBooks for iOS. Another considerable help—particularly if you have a vast library—is an app for searching text inside multiple e-books or PDFs at once. I recommend DocSearch+ for Android or QuickSearch PDF Reader for iOS.

In addition to books on survival, I suggest you store copies of the operating manuals of all the relevant electronic devices and other references.

Furthermore, download the Kiwix.org app on your device and store a ZIM file of the entire Wikipedia (40–90 GB) or just its medical section (800 MB–1.8 GB) in a microSD card for offline use.

Videos are another good reference to have. Download a good video player app like VLC Media Player and store videos of wilderness skills—for instance, net-making or moose calling.

If you use satellite communications, check if there are companion apps available. For example, when using a Garmin inReach device, it's convenient to pair it with a smartphone and send texts messages from the Garmin Earthmate app.

Use your mobile device to record voice notes, and view and take written notes (Google Docs).

Smartphones are also great for entertainment. I recommend storing books, particularly true survival stories, audiobooks, music, and podcasts.

In terms of navigation, have a GPS app that can store topographic maps for offline use, like Topo Maps for iOS. If you want custom map sources and satellite imagery for offline use, download the BackCountry Navigator PRO app for Android and Guru Maps Pro for iOS.

To download large offline maps for mobile devices from a desktop computer, I recommend the Mobile Atlas Creator (MOBAC). The previous two apps mentioned can read MOBAC map files.

It is unlikely, but a mobile device could get corrupted and might need to be factory reset in the field. If this happens, you will lose anything saved on your device except for what is stored on an SD card; that's why I recommend Android phones with SD card slots. Store everything critical on the SD card, and keep a copy of all your essential apps there so that you can reinstall them after a factory reset. Use the *APK Extractor* app by Natthapon Pinyo (privacy-friendly and free) to extract the app files of your important apps and copy them to the SD card.

If you have extra SD cards (e.g., for satellite imagery or Wikipedia), I recommend having an OTG microSD reader. It allows you to reference various microSD cards quickly.

WHICH READING DEVICE IS BEST?

There are three main options: an e-reader, a smartphone, and a tablet. Because e-readers are less versatile, I don't recommend them. Smartphones work reasonably well as a GPS and allow you to read books, but they are not very comfortable for reading. Tablets typically lack a GPS chip, but they make good e-readers. If you don't need a GPS, then pack a tablet, and if you want a GPS, then pack a smartphone.

A smartphone needs to have some essential characteristics for outdoor use. Ideally, it should be waterproof (IPX7 or IPX8). Another option is to buy a waterproof case: the LifeProof FRĒ cases work well as long as they are not too worn out. It's best to have a big screen (at least 5"). You will need a lot of storage for e-books and maps, so it should have an SD card slot. For redundancy and reliability, a phone with a removable battery is best (pack an extra battery as a backup).

Tablets are not likely to be waterproof or have waterproof cases, but because they will probably be used only at camp, they are easy to keep protected. For reading books, a tablet makes much more sense than a smartphone.

Although packing a smartphone or tablet adds weight and complexity, you could have a vast resource of information and maps in the palm of your hand. For example, a survival book weighs about 20 oz. and a smartphone with a case and solar charger weighs about 14 oz.

I recommend the Samsung Galaxy XCover 5 because it is waterproof and has an SD card slot and a removable battery; most smartphones lack one of those features.

SATELLITE COMMUNICATION

There are satellite phones and text-based satellite communicators, but text devices are more affordable and reliable. The best devices for satellite text messaging are made by Garmin inReach.

The main advantage of having two-way communication is that you can provide important information to your emergency contacts or search and rescue personnel during a rescue. Satellite comms also help you cope with isolation.

The main disadvantages are their high cost and subscription fees. They also give you a false sense of security, which can lead you to take on more risks.

The inReach is a great tool that allows you to send your location, texts, and emails, as well as receive weather forecasts, communicate with other inReach devices, and send an SOS. A great feature is that when the inReach sends a message, the device lets you know if the satellite network received it.

I recommend having a list of important contacts saved on the device. Have a proper protocol in place so that your contacts don't trigger an unnecessary rescue if the weather—or some unforeseen circumstance—prevents you from sending a check-in. Also, keep in mind that the device might get lost or malfunction, so your protocol should include those situations. I also recommend having instructions on performing a soft reset if the device "freezes."

PERSONAL LOCATOR BEACONS

Personal locator beacons (PLB) are the most resilient and reliable way of sending an SOS. They require no service fees, but they're used only for emergencies when life or limb is in danger. PLBs are pretty simple to use, and because they are not meant to be used casually, their battery can be depended upon for several years. Most PLBs transmit at 5 W of power while the inReach transmits at around 1.5 W and SPOTs around 0.1–0.2 W.

There is an optional paid service with PLBs that allows you to send a limited amount of check-ins to your contacts through 406link.com. But the service is not reliable because there is no way for you to know if a satellite received a check-in (i.e., your contacts may not receive them).

PLBs are the best SOS signaling devices because they are very reliable and straightforward and don't need a subscription. I recommend the compact Ocean Signal rescueME PLB1 (bit.ly/resc-M).

TWO-WAY RADIOS

Two-way radios are nice for coordinating people in different locations and for emergencies. Based on frequencies and wattage restrictions, the best hand-held radios for outdoor use in the wilderness, roughly ordered from best to worst, are Ham, VHF, MURS, GMRS, and FRS. Regulations depend on your local government and may change every few years, so do your research.

A rule of thumb is that a taller antenna has better range than a shorter antenna, and having more transmission power is better for range.

Ham radios are the most versatile option because they can operate in multiple bands and at higher power, but they require a license. VHF radios are another high-power, hand-held option for paddlers (it requires a certification in Canada). The next options are MURS radios (US only) and GMRS/FRS radios.

I would recommend a 5 W dual-band Ham radio like the inexpensive Baofeng radios, but you must be a Ham operator to use them. If used appropriately—at the power allowed for unlicensed use in your country on MURS/GMRS/FRS radios—it is very unlikely that anyone will notice or fine you, but this practice is technically illegal.

Most consumer radios don't use the total output permitted by regulations, and the very few that do are not waterproof. Before buying a radio, search online for its FCC ID to see their actual power output at fccid.io.

Many two-way radios can also receive weather radio broadcasts, but coverage may not be available in remote spots. Check these maps for approximate coverage: US (bit.ly/US-Wx) and Canada (bit.ly/Can-Wx).

FRS/GMRS Frequencies

Channel	Frequency (MHz)	Power	Power US (GMRS with a license)
1	462.5625	2 W	5 W
2	462.5875	2 W	5 W
3	462.6125	2 W	5 W
4	462.6375	2 W	5 W
5	462.6625	2 W	5 W
6	462.6875	2 W	5 W
7	462.7125	2 W	5 W
8	467.5625	0.5 W	0.5 W
9	467.5875	0.5 W	0.5 W
10	467.6125	0.5 W	0.5 W
11	467.6375	0.5 W	0.5 W
12	467.6625	0.5 W	0.5 W
13	467.6875	0.5 W	0.5 W
14	467.7125	0.5 W	0.5 W
15	462.55	2 W	50 W
16	462.575	2 W	50 W
17	462.6	2 W	50 W
18	462.625	2 W	50 W
19	462.65	2 W	50 W
20	462.675	2 W	50 W
21	462.7	2 W	50 W
22	462.725	2 W	50 W

MURS

Channel	Frequency (MHz)	US only
1	151.82	2 W
2	151.88	2 W
3	151.94	2 W
4	154.57	2 W
5	154.6	2 W

Weather radio

Channel	Frequency (MHz)
WX1	162.55
WX2	162.4
WX3	162.475
WX4	162.425
WX5	162.45
WX6	162.5
WX7	162.525

RADIO RECEIVERS

A pocket AM/FM or shortwave radio is a good tool for entertainment, boosting your morale, listening to weather forecasts, and keeping loneliness at bay. Many pocket radios can also receive weather radio channels.

The radio should have an external antenna or a headphone jack antenna so that you are able to wrap wire around it to extend it and get better reception.

NATURAL HAZARDS

LIGHTNING

There is no place in the wild that is safe from lightning, except for substantial buildings—with wiring and plumbing—and metal-topped vehicles. There are two general approaches to lightning in the wilderness: avoid the risk and stay indoors or accept that there is a lightning risk. Sitting on a pad, positioning your body a certain way, and staying inside a tent won't lower the risk. Depending on their size and height, small shelters may actually increase the risk because sideflashes can hit the occupants.

When a storm is approaching, avoid exposed areas, such as ridges, open water, isolated tall objects, or the bases of trees. Lightning may travel as far as 10 mi. (16 km) or more from a thunderstorm, and it can strike before, during, and after the storm.

The 30/30 rule—seek shelter when the time between the flash and crash is less than 30 seconds and remain there 30 minutes after the last flash or crash—is meant for civilization and is often impractical to follow in the wilderness. But keep it in mind.

If you're caught in the forest, seek shelter in a low area, under a thick growth of saplings or small trees. If you're in a group, spread out at least 20–50 ft. (6–15 m), but keep visual contact. Get low and insulate yourself from the ground as much as possible (e.g., using sleeping pads, ropes, or PFDs); this may help if the strike hits nearby.

LIGHTNING POSITION

The lightning position may help slightly reduce the chance of a direct strike and some effects of lightning, but it is no substitute for getting to a safer place. There is controversy around how much difference the lightning position makes, but there is at least comfort in action.

The lightning position consists of putting your feet together to significantly reduce the effects of ground current and squatting or crouching and balling up to slightly mitigate the impact of sideflashes. In addition, wrapping your arms around your legs, closing your eyes, and covering your ears helps reduce the effects of the current and blast.

The lightning position is challenging to hold for a long time, so it is more practical to sit down on your bum with your legs crossed or stretched out in front of you, and your arms around your legs. Keep your feet together, and place an insulating object underneath you if you can.

Ears covered

Eyes closed

On an insulating object

Feet together and minimizing contact with the ground

WILDFIRES

Evacuation is the ideal way of dealing with wildfires. If you are in an area near large bodies of water, those could provide a safer area to retreat to instead of doing a full evacuation. But smoke inhalation and radiant heat could still be significant issues.

If all protection and prevention measures have been exhausted, and you're down to desperate choices, this is what you can do:

LAST-RESORT WILDFIRE SURVIVAL TECHNIQUES

RETREAT INTO A SAFE ZONE

1. Go to an area that won't burn; the bigger, the better. Or choose an area with the least combustible material.
2. Use every means possible to protect yourself from the heat and hot air currents.

3. Protect your airway from the heat at all costs, and minimize smoke inhalation.
4. Remain as calm as possible.

Unless there is an apparent escape, do not run. Move downhill. Conserve your strength. If you become exhausted, you will be more prone to heatstroke, and you might miss an opportunity to take refuge.

BURN OUT A SAFETY AREA

If you are in dry grass or low shrubs and the flames are too high to run through, burn out an area as large as you can between you and the fire front. It takes time for the vegetation to burn down, so this may not be effective as a last-ditch attempt, nor does this work well in an intense fire. Go into the burned-out area, and hunker down, covering as much of your skin as possible.

HUNKER DOWN IN PLACE

Protect yourself from the heat at all costs. Many people die way before the flames reach them. The heat from a fire can quickly cause heatstroke, so find cover from it in an area that won't burn, such as a hole, large rock, stream, pond, or lake. Cover your head and skin with clothing or dirt to protect yourself from the heat.

Slow down your breathing. Avoid inhaling smoke: keep your face close to the ground, where there is less smoke. Hold a damp cloth over your nose, and try to breathe in the least amount of smoke. If breathing excessively hot air is a possibility, place a dry—not moist—cloth over your mouth. The lungs can withstand dry heat better than moist heat.

Lie facedown in an area that won't burn. If the fire overtakes you, you have a better chance of survival in this position than standing upright or kneeling.

RUN THROUGH THE FIRE
INTO A BURNED-OUT AREA

Running through the flames into a burned area can be a viable last resort in dry grass or low shrubs. Enter the burned area whenever and wherever possible. Move quickly, parallel to the fire front. Choose a place where the flames are less than 3 ft. (1 m) deep, where you can see through them clearly, and where the vegetation behind the fire has been largely consumed. Cover your skin and take several breaths. Follow the relevant recommendations in the previous paragraph. Then, move through the flames as fast as possible. If necessary, get low to breathe fresh air and see better.

WILDLIFE ENCOUNTERS

Typically, you only need to prepare for encounters with bears. Wolf attacks are practically unheard of, and cougar and coyote attacks are rare—and they are generally directed toward unattended children. Nevertheless, almost any animal could be dangerous if you trigger its fight-or-flight response or if it is in a perturbed state.

BEARS

Like most wild animals, bears don't like to waste energy or get injured. Severe injuries in the wild are often a death sentence, so bears are generally not looking for a fight. Nevertheless, bears can get scared and attack in reflex, and they can feel threatened and defend their cubs. In addition, a small minority of bears prey on humans. The main ways to manage bear encounters are to minimize the chance of an encounter, avoid provoking attacks, minimize injuries, and prevent predatory behavior.

AVOID SURPRISING A BEAR

- Make noise to alert bears of your presence. A casual conversation works, but you may need to be louder near streams or if it's windy. Bear bells are not loud enough.
- Be on the lookout for bears. Rain, fog, wind, and noise can prevent a bear from noticing that you are nearby.

AVOID PROVOKING AN ATTACK

- Let the bear know you are a human. Allow the bear to see you fully. Don't hide or act like prey. Talk in a calm and firm voice.
- Don't make sudden movements or scream, particularly with a grizzly bear. The bear may view this behavior as aggressive and respond in kind.

- Do not stare directly at the bear. Look to the side or stand sideways, but stand your ground. Let the bear know you are willing to defend yourself.
- Don't climb a tree or run. Doing that may prevent the bear from identifying you as a human. Besides, bears are great climbers and runners.

Be ready to use bear spray if you have it. If you are charged, stand quietly in a nonaggressive manner. Usually, the bear will stop the charge without making contact or causing an injury. Carefully retreat away from the bear. If it continues to charge, your response depends on the type of bear: if it's brown, lie down. If it's black, fight back.

GRIZZLY BEAR: MINIMIZE INJURIES

1. Don't fight, run, climb a tree, or scream. But if you have a high-caliber firearm, consider using it.
2. Drop facedown to the ground and protect your head by interlocking your hands behind your head (at ear level) and tilting your head forward. Use your elbows to protect your face if the bear turns you over.
3. Don't use your arms or hands to block an attack. And never look at the bear during an attack because it leaves your face exposed to injuries.
4. Stay down after an attack until you are sure the bear has left. Generally, those victims who got up before the bear had left got attacked again.
5. Only leave once you are sure the bear has left.

Generally, those who protect themselves immediately and do not try to run or fight receive minor injuries. In contrast, those who try to run, fight, or stand up before the grizzly bear leaves receive severe injuries.

BLACK BEAR: RESPOND ASSERTIVELY

Black bear aggression must be met with aggression. Scream, throw rocks, swing a stick, and use whatever is available. Never lie down in a submissive position because black bears are more likely to prey on humans during a physical attack.

PREVENT PREDATORY BEAR BEHAVIOR

Hungry bears and bears accustomed to humans sometimes lose their fear of humans and start to see them as a potential food source. The primary way to avoid predatory behavior is by not attracting a bear to your camp.

- Avoid camping where bears travel or feed.
- Use bear-resistant food storage containers or caches.
- Cook and eat away from your shelter to reduce odors.
- Do not leave garbage or food around the camp.

Bears rarely enter a campsite to prey on humans, but it has happened. So it's crucial to have a plan, just in case. Take notice of potential escape routes. If there are "problem" bears in the area, keeping your sleeping bag partially unzipped for a quick exit is a good idea. Have a headlamp ready inside your shelter and bear spray or a firearm. If a bear enters your tent, assume the bear is trying to prey on you; use all available defenses. During typical bear encounters, bears are driven by a fight-or-flight response, but a predatory bear is driven by hunger. This bear is not trying to pick a fight; it wants to drag someone to a nearby spot and eat them—often alive. Therefore, your group must respond in a swift, coordinated, and aggressive manner.

BEAR DETERRENTS

In grizzly bear territory, the best practice is to always carry bear spray on a holster. Bear spray is the deterrent of choice because it's simple, handy, and the most effective. To use:

1. Spray a charging bear once it is within 20 ft. (6 m) of you. Fire 1–2 sec. blasts, aiming at its head. If the bear is moving fast, start spraying from a longer distance away, as far as 30–60 ft. (10–20 m).
2. Don't stop spraying until it backs down.
3. Be very mindful of the wind direction when firing bear spray.

Keep your bear spray rapidly accessible. Practice deploying it unexpectedly: have a companion randomly say draw. It shouldn't take you more than two seconds to deploy.

Firearms are not recommended as the first line of defense because bear spray has been statistically more successful. Nevertheless, if you want to have the means to stop a bear lethally, consider carrying a firearm—in addition to bear spray.

Finally, bear deterrents are no substitute for general awareness and knowing how to respond appropriately to a bear encounter.

AFTERWORD

Surviving in the wilderness for an extended period is a widespread idea in the survival, bushcraft, and prepper communities.

The idea of bugging out to the woods in case of a widespread disaster or societal collapse is a bit misguided: you are wiser to shelter in place in a resilient community.

I wrote this book with a long-term perspective because it can be useful for those who live at the edge of civilization and those interested in long-term wilderness living and survival.

FUNDAMENTAL PRINCIPLES OF LONG-TERM SURVIVAL

- **Work with nature:** work smart by following the rhythms of nature instead of struggling against the infinite or imposing yourself on nature's rhythms.

- **Improvise, experiment, and adapt:** make do with what you have, be creative and think laterally, change your expectations and mindset, and adjust to the changing conditions.

- **Have an edge:** don't stay stuck in the past. Don't bring a knife to a gunfight. The context in which our hunter-gatherer ancestors lived was very different: they lived in tribes and in a world where wild foods were more abundant. Use any available advantage, but be respectful.

- **Err on the side of caution**: don't take unnecessary risks. Always keep in mind the risk versus reward of your actions.

- **Develop a resilient mindset:** exercise and practice a survivor attitude. Your mindset can either be your greatest asset or your greatest liability.

- **Experience trumps skills and knowledge:** you can be well-versed in the skills and know all the theory around survival, but dirt time really matters. With enough experience, you'll naturally learn the skills and knowledge. And you'll know which questions to ask!

- **Be efficient:** improve your energy return on investment by minimizing the energy and time you spend and maximizing the energy and time you gain.

- **Imitate the ultimate survivalists:** the local animals and plants use strategies that have been developed over millennia. Those strategies work.

- **Respect nature:** cultivate an attitude of gratitude and humility. Without respect and sustainability, the ability to survive long-term is unattainable.

- **There are no rules in survival:** there are only guidelines. Ultimately, you'll have to adapt those guidelines to each unique context.

APPENDIX

SHELTER

PATTERN FOR A TENT

Having spent an entire winter in the boreal forest in a homemade sil-nylon tent, I think a good size for a long-term tent for one or two people is 8 ft. × 10 ft. (2.4 ×3 m), a 3 ft. (90 cm) sidewall, and a 7.5–8 ft. (2.3–2.4 m) tall ridge. Shorter sidewalls significantly reduce the usable space, and taller sidewalls collect more snow. The ridge height leaves some room for hanging things and increases the usable space on the sides. The overall area allows enough space for a portable stove and two beds.

Unlike canvas tents, waterproof wall tents gather lots of condensation. That is not a complete deal-breaker, but it is something to consider. To reduce condensation problems in a DIY sil-nylon tent, keep the roof's angle shorter than 80 degrees so that condensation slides to the sidewalls instead of dripping over your sleeping bag.

I highly recommend adding windows of marine-grade, cold-resistant PVC or vinyl. That increases the illumination inside the tent and boosts morale a lot. But the windows should be attached to the tent with Velcro to make them easily removable. That allows you to set up the tent and warm up the rolled windows inside it. Once warmed, the PVC windows can be easily unrolled (they can't be folded and unfolded in freezing temperatures or they will crack). The windows must be rolled up before packing and storing;

otherwise, they may break at the folds if folded. Position the windows close to the stove to minimize condensation, frost, and ice blocking the view.

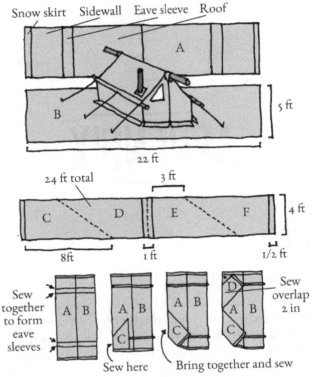

Suggested materials: Polyurethane coated 1.9 oz. (70D) ripstop nylon (tent); 1.1 oz. uncalendered ripstop nylon (optional liner); noseeum mesh (bug net); #8 zippers; MARA 70 thread; stove jack material; guyline cord; and 1″ nylon webbing.

FOOD AND FORAGING

EDIBLE WEIGHTS OF WILDLIFE

Note: the edible weights and calories are intentionally conservative. Unfortunately, studies on edible weights are scarce, so take these figures with a grain of salt.

Animal	Edible weight	Calories
Caribou	100 lb. (45 kg)	57,150
Woodland caribou	150 lb. (68 kg)	86,360
Moose	438 lb. (199 kg)	202,980
Mountain goat	80–150 lb. (36–68 kg)	39,240–74,120
Dall sheep	70–150 lb. (32–68 kg)	–
Deer	80 lb. (36 kg)	43,200
Mule deer	100 lb. (45 kg)	54,000
White-tailed deer	100 lb. (45 kg)	54,000
Elk	300 lb. (140 kg)	155,400
Snowshoe hare	2 lb. (0.9 kg)	1,026
Muskrat	1–1.4 lb. (0.45–0.64 kg)	–
Beaver	17–30 lb. (8–13 kg)	11,680–18,980
Porcupine	10.5 lb. (4.7 kg)	–
Squirrel	0.9 lb. (0.4 kg)	480
Otter	10.5 lb. (4.7 kg)	–
Lynx	8.5 lb. (4 kg)	–
Black bear	150–210 lb. (68–95 kg)	109,480–152,950
Grizzly bear	200 lb. (90 kg)	–
Waterfowl	1.4 lb. (0.67 kg)	–
Geese	3.5 lb. (1.6 kg)	2,128
Canada geese	4.7 lb. (2.1 kg)	2,793
Ducks	1.7–2.6 lb. (0.7–1.2 kg)	861–1,476
Mallard	1.9 lb. (0.85 kg)	–
Swan	10.4 lb. (4.75 kg)	–
Loon	2.5 lb. (1.1 kg)	–
Grouse	0.7–1 lb. (0.3–0.5 kg)	336–560
Sandhill crane	9 lb. (4.1 kg)	–

Trout, whitefish, grayling, pike, walleye	1.76 lb. (0.8 kg)	1,280
Whitefish	1.8–2.7 lb. (0.8–1.25 kg)	1,240–1,937
Lake trout	2.6 lb. (1.2 kg)	2,016
Northern pike	2.2–4.4 lb. (1–2 kg)	880–1,760
Walleye	1.1–1.6 lb. (0.5–0.73 kg)	465–678

Source: Edible Weights of Wildlife Species used for Country Food in the Northwest Territories and Nunavut, Bruce Ashley, 2002; and USDA FoodData Central.

NUTRITION IN WILD FOODS

Mammals

Raw portion 3.5 oz / 100g	Kcal	Protein %	Fat %	Raw portion 3.5 oz / 100g	Kcal	Protein %	Fat %
Antelope	114	22.3	2.03	Goat (roasted)	143	27.1	3
Beaver	146	24.05	4.8	Moose	102	22.4	0.74
Bear	161	20.1	8.3	Muskrat	162	20.76	8.1
Buffalo	99	20.39	1.37	Opossum (roasted)	221	30.2	10.2
Caribou	127	22.63	6.42	Rabbit	114	21.79	2.32
Deer	120	22.96	2.42	Squirrel	120	21.3	3.21
Elk	111	22.95	1.45	Wild boar	122	21.51	3.33

Birds

Raw portion 3.5 oz / 100g	Kcal	Protein %	Fat %
Goose, Canada (meat only)	133	24.3	4
Duck (meat only)	123	19.8	4.25
Grouse, ruffed	112	25.9	29.3

Raw portion 3.5 oz / 100g	Kcal	Protein %	Fat %
Pheasant	133	23.57	3.64
Wild turkey (meat only)	112	22.64	1.93

Fish

Raw portion 3.5 oz / 100g	Kcal	Protein %	Fat %
Bass (small and largemouth)	104	18.8	2.6
Bluefish	117	20.5	3.3
Buffalo fish	113	17.5	4.2
Bullhead	84	16.3	1.6
Burbot (lawyer)	82	17.4	0.9
Butterfish	169	18.1	10.2

Raw portion 3.5 oz / 100g	Kcal	Protein %	Fat %
Pompano	166	18.8	9.5
Porgy and scup	112	19	3.4
Red, gray snappers	93	19.8	0.9
Redhorse, silver	98	18	2.3
Rockfish	97	18.9	1.8
Roe (carp, cod, haddock, herring, pike and shad)	130	24.4	2.3

Carp	115	18	4.2
Catfish (freshwater)	103	17.6	3.1
Caviar (sturgeon)	262	15	26.9
Chiton, gumboot	83	17.1	1.6
Chub	145	15.3	8.8
Clam (meat only)	82	14	1.9
Cod	78	17.6	0.3
Crab (cooked, steamed)	93	17.3	1.9
Crappie	79	16.8	0.8
Crayfish (freshwater)	72	14.6	0.5
Croaker	96	17.8	2.2
Cusk	75	17.2	0.2
Dogfish, spiny (grayfish)	156	17.6	9
Drum, freshwater (sheeps head)	121	17.3	5.2
Eel, American	233	15.9	18.3
Roe (salmon, sturgeon and turbot)	207	25.2	10.4
Sablefish	190	13	14.9
Salmon, Atlantic	217	22.5	13.4
Salmon, chinook (king)	222	19.1	15.6
Salmon, chum	120	20.1	3.7
Salmon, coho (silver)	136	21.5	5.7
Salmon, pink	119	20	3.7
Salmon, sockeye (red)	143	20.3	6.9
sauger	84	17.9	0.8
Scallop (bay and sea)	81	15.3	0.2
Sea cucumber	56	13	0.4
Sea urchin	172	13.2	2.82
Seabass (white)	96	21.4	0.5
Shrimp	91	18.1	0.8
Skate	98	21.5	0.7

Flounder	79	16.7	0.8		Slipper shell	61	8.4	1.8
Grouper	87	19.3	0.5		Smelt (eulachon)	98	18.6	2.1
Haddock	79	18.3	0.1		Snail	90	16.1	1.4
Hake	74	16.5	0.4		Sole	79	16.7	0.8
Halibut	100	20.9	1.2		Spanish mackerel	177	19.5	10.4
Lake herring (cisco)	96	17.7	2.3		Squid	84	16.4	0.9
Lake trout	168	18.3	10		Sturgeon	94	18.1	1.9
Lake trout (siscoette, over 6.5 lb.)	524	7.9	54.4		Sucker	104	20.6	1.8
Lake trout (siscoette, under 6.5 lb.)	241	14.3	19.9		Swordfish	174	28	6
Lingcod	84	17.9	0.8		Tautog (blackfish)	89	18.6	1.1
Lobster (whole)	91	16.9	1.9		Tilapia	88	22	4.4
Mullet, striped	146	19.6	6.9		Tilefish	79	17.5	0.5
Muskellunge (musky)	109	20.2	2.5		Trout, brook	101	19.2	2.1
Mussels (meat only)	95	14.4	2.2		Trout, rainbow (steelhead)	195	21.5	11.4
Octopus	73	15.3	0.8		Tuna (raw)	145	25.2	4.1
Oyster (meat only)	66	8.4	1.8		Walleye	93	19.3	1.2
Perch, ocean (redfish)	88	18	1.2		Weakfish	121	16.5	5.6

Perch, yellow (lake perch)	91	19.5	0.9	Whitefish, lake (freshwater)	155	18.9	8.2
Pike, northern	88	18.3	1.1	Whiting	105	18.3	3
Pollack	95	20.4	0.9				

Amphibians

Raw portion 3.5 oz / 100g	Calories	Protein %	Fat %	Raw portion 3.5 oz / 100g	Calories	Protein %	Fat %
Frog (legs)	73	0.3	16.4	Green turtle	89	0.5	19.8

Insects

Dry portion 3.5 oz / 100g	Kcal	Protein %	Fat %	Dry portion 3.5 oz / 100g	Kcal	Protein %	Fat %
Crickets	120	9.6	5.6	Meal-worm	138	20	13
Grass-hopper	96	14.3	3.3	Red ants (cooked)	194	12.7	12.5
June beetle	78	14.3	3.3	Termites	124	12.4	1.3
Locust	179	18	21.5	Witchetty grub (dry)	325	16	29

Plants

Raw portion 3.5 oz / 100g	Kcal	Protein %	Fat %	Raw portion 3.5 oz / 100g	Kcal	Protein %	Fat %
Acorn (raw)	387	6.15	24	Perennial lily root	95.4	1.4	0.2
Arrowroot	65	4.24	0.2	Persimmon	127	0.8	0.4
Balsam poplar (bark)	230	1.9	-	Pigweed	56	6	0.9
Bitterroot (dry)	343	4	0.6	Plantain, greater (leaves)	61	2.5	0.3
Black cottonwood	31	0.2	0.5	Prickly pears	42	0.12	0.11
Black hawthorn	73	0.3	1.4	Purslane	20	2.3	0.36
Black walnuts	607	25.4	58.9	Red elderberry	110	2.9	4.8
Blackcap raspberry	87	1.2	1.4	Red huckleberry	56	0.8	0.5
Bog blueberry	51	0.7	0.6	Rice roots	102	2.9	0.3
Bunchberry	76	0.6	0.8	Rosehip	82	1.6	0.6
Burdock root	72	1.53	0.15	Salal berries	63	2.1	0.7
Butternut	629	23.7	61.2	Salmonberry	52	1.4	0.8
Cattail rhizome (dry)	-	7.7	4.9	Salmonberry shoots	31	0.5	0.6
Cattail shoots	25	1.18	0	Saskatoon berry	99	0.7	1.2
Chokecherry (pitted)	162	3.04	1.69	Seaweed, kelp	43	1.68	0.56
Cottonwood (inner bark)	27	0.2	0.5	Seaweed, laver	303	24.4	1.4

Cow parsnip stems	20	0.2	0.3	Sheep sorrel	48	1.1	0.6
Crowberry	45	0.2	0.7	Shepherd's purse	33	3	0.5
Curly dock	24	2.6	0.3	Silverweed roots (steamed)	136	3.1	0.6
Dandelion greens	45	2.7	0.7	Soapberry	80	1.8	0.7
Desert parsley roots	190	2.2	1	Sow thistle	20	1.9	0.3
Dulse (red algae) dry fronds	323	19.9	0.6	Spiny wood fern	128	2.5	1
Fireweed shoots	30	0.3	0.4	Springbank clover rhizomes	73	0.7	0.5
Goosefoot, lamb's quarters	43	4.2	0.8	Stinging nettle	44	1.8	0.6
Grey blueberry	54	1.1	0.5	Stink currant	70	0.8	1.2
Hazelnut, beaked	628	14.89	53	Sugar maple syrup	348	0.1	-
Hickory nuts (dried)	657	12.7	64	Swamp gooseberry	66	1.5	2.3
Highbush cranberry	42	0.1	0.4	Thimble-berry	110	1.7	1.2
Horsetails	20	2.1	-	Thimble-berry shoots	28	0.6	0.4
Jerusalem artichoke	77	2.6	0.5	Trembling aspen	-	1.3	-
Kelp, laminaria	43	1.7	0.6	Wapato (arrowhead)	99	5.3	0.29
Kinnikinnick berry	102	0.7	1.1	Watery blueberry	74	0.9	0.6

Licorice fern root	141	0.9	4.6
Lupine root	73	2	0.4
Mountain alder bark	270	4.3	-
Mountain bilberry	59	0.6	0.5
Mulberries	43	1.44	0.39
Ostrich fern (dried)	376	36	4
Pacific crabapple	79	1.2	1.6
Parsnip	75	1.2	0.3
Pawpaw	85	5.2	0.9

Western hemlock (cambium)	103	2.3	0.6
Wild black gooseberry	77	1.1	1.5
Wild blue currant	65	0.7	0.6
Wild leek, ramp	61	1.5	0.3
Wild onion	42.2	3.5	0.2
Wild raspberry	73	0.6	0.8
Wild rice	357	15	1.08
Wild strawberry	61	0.6	0.9
Wood sorrel	49	2.3	0.8

Mushrooms

Dry portion 3.5 oz / 100g	Calories	Protein %	Fat %
Black trumpets, *Craterellus cornucopioides*	378	69.4	4.8
Cauliflower mushroom, *Sparassis crispa*	283	32.6	5.2
Chanterel, *Cantharellus cibarius*	381	35.7	1.4
Chicken of the woods, *Laetiporus sulphureus*	341	10.6	2.9
Hedgehog mushroom, *Hydnum repandum*	434	34	6.3
Lion's mane or Bear's head, *Hericium*	190	22.3	3.5
Morel, *Morchella*	323	41.7	12
Oyster mushroom, *Pleurotus ostreatus*	193	23.8	2.1
Porcini mushroom, *Boletus edulis*	159	18	5.7

NUTRITIONAL PLANNING

Nutritional planning guide (Military Dietary Reference Intakes)

Nutrient	Unit	Men	Women
Energy; light activity	kcal/d	3,000	2,100
Energy; moderate activity	kcal/d	3,400	2,300
Energy; heavy activity	kcal/d	3,700	2,700
Protein	% kcal; g/d	10–35; 102 (68–136)	10–35; 83 (55–110)
Carbohydrate	% kcal; g/d	50–55; 510 (340–680)	50–55; 414 (276–552)
Fat	% kcal; g/d	25–30; <113 (100–157)	25–30; <113 (100–157)
Fiber	g/d	34	28
Linoleic acid	g/d	17	12
α-Linolenic acid	g/d	1.6	1.1
Vitamin A	μg RAE/d; IU/d	900; 3,000	700; 2,333
Vitamin D	IU/d	600	600
Vitamin E	mg/d	15	15
Vitamin K	μg/d	120	90
Vitamin C	mg/d	90	75
Thiamin (B1)	mg/d	1.2	1.1
Riboflavin (B2)	mg/d	1.3	1.1
Niacin	mg NE/d	16	14
Vitamin B6	mg/d	1.3	1.3
Vitamin B12	μg/d	2.4	2.4
Folate	μg DFE/d	400	400
Calcium	mg/d	1,000	1,000
Iron	mg/d	8	18

Magnesium	mg/d	420	320
Phosphorus	mg/d	700	700
Potassium	mg/d	4,700	4,700
Selenium	µg/d	55	55
Sodium	mg/d	<2,300	<2,300
Zinc	mg/d	11	8

Source: MDRI, Headquarters Departments of the Army, the Navy, and the Air Force, Washington, DC. Army Regulation 40–25, Nutrition and menu standards for human performance optimization. January 3, 2017.

The values for energy, protein, and other nutrients are expressed as average daily nutrient intakes based on moderate activity levels, and reference bodyweights of 187 lb. (85 kg) for military men and 152 lb. (69 kg) for military women.

BANNOCK RECIPE

1 cup flour
2 tsp baking powder
1/8 tsp salt
3/4 to 1½ cups of cold water

Mix the ingredients together to make a stiff dough for cooking on a stick or a runny dough for frying. Add oil to the pan before frying.

The white of wood ashes can be used as a crude baking soda or baking powder substitute. Hickory and dogwood produce the best ashes, but the ashes of balsam poplar, ash, and trembling aspen also work.

HUNTING

ANIMAL TRACKS

Moose 5-6"

Deer 2-3"

Elk 3.5-4.5"

Caribou 4-5"

Snowshoe hare 5-6"

Bobcat 2"

Lynx 3-4"

Cougar 3-4"

Red fox 2"

Coyote 2"

Skunk 2-3" 1-2"

Otter 2.5-3"

Squirrel 2.5"

Porcupine 2.5"

Opossum 2"

Raccoon 4" 2.5

Beaver 6" 3"

Black bear 6-9" 4-5"

Grizzly 10-12" 5-7"

Wolverine 3.5-4" 4-7.5"

Muskrat 2"

Crow 2-3"

Turkey 4-5"

Grouse 2-3"

ELECTRONICS

WEATHER FORECASTING

Expect:	Temperature	Winds	Air pressure	Clouds	Humidity
Weather to stay fair	Average for the season	West to northwest and gentle	Relatively steady	Climb and decrease in numbers	Stays low
Worse weather	Above or below average for the season	Shift between east and south	Falls steadily or rapidly	Get thicker, lower, and darker to the west	Goes up
Rain or snow	Rises	Increase in speed, usually from the east	Falls; the faster it falls, the sooner the precipitation arrives	Change from cirrus to lower types, or to rain or snow clouds	Goes up
Thunder storm	Cold front	Rapid increase in speed	Falls	Change from cumulus to cumulonimbus	—
Weather to clear	Rises after a warm front. Drops after a cold front.	Swing from east through south to west	Rises	Rise and break up	Goes down
Colder temperatures	Drops	From the north or northwest	Rises	—	—
Warmer temperatures	Rises	From the south	Falls	—	—

The barometer function in some watches is convenient for keeping an eye on sudden pressure changes, which signal changes in the weather. The table above is helpful for making rough predictions in North America.

Observe weather signals to determine if the weather conditions will remain stable or change. In addition to obvious clues like rain clouds, changes to air pressure and humidity can sometimes be felt or observed indirectly. It's a good idea to familiarize yourself with the prevailing winds and the typical weather patterns in your area. Observe from which direction certain weather comes from.

High humidity often causes sweat to accumulate, and sometimes rain can be smelled before it happens.

Generally, when smoke rises straight toward the sky, the air pressure is low, and when smoke stays low or travels horizontally, the air pressure is high.

Falling air pressure typically signals an approaching low-pressure system, bringing clouds and precipitation. On the other hand, rising air pressure typically signals an approaching high-pressure system bringing fine weather.

Baro* mb/hPa (in Hg)	Change	Wind direction	Weather
1016–1022 (30–30.20)	Steady	Westerly	Fair, slight temp. change for 1–2 days
1016–1022 (30–30.20)	Rising fast	Westerly	Fair, warm, and rain within 2 days
1016–1022 (30–30.20)	Falling fast	South to east	Warmer and rain within 12–24 h
≥ 1022 (30.20)	Falling fast	South to east	Warmer and rain within 36 h
≥ 1022 (30.20)	Falling fast	West to north	Cold and clear, followed by warmer rain
≥ 1022 (30.20)	Steady	Variable	No immediate changes
≤ 1016 (30.00)	Falling slowly	South to east	Rain within 18 h, continuing 1–2 days
≤ 1016 (30.00)	Falling fast	Southeast to northeast	Rain/wind, clearing and colder within 2 days
≤ 1016 (30.00)	Rising	South to west	Clearing and colder within 12 h
≤ 1009 (29.80)	Falling fast	South to east	Severe storm imminent, wind/rain/snow
≤ 1009 (29.80)	Rising fast	Shifting to west	Clearing, colder

Source: National Weather Service

*The barometer must be adjusted to show equivalent pressure at sea level for your current altitude. To correct your barometer for sea level, adjust it to match the readings reported by your local weather forecast.

COMMUNICATION CODES

Variations of the tap code and the International Morse Code may be used to communicate through simple messages by using light, whistles, or two-way radios (outside their range).

International Morse Code

1. The length of a dot is 1 unit.
2. The length of a dash is 3 units.
3. The space between parts of the same letter is one unit.
4. The space between letters is 3 units.
5. The space between words is 7 units.

A ● ▬
B ▬ ● ● ●
C ▬ ● ▬ ●
D ▬ ● ●
E ●
F ● ● ▬ ●
G ▬ ▬ ●
H ● ● ● ●
I ● ●
J ● ▬ ▬ ▬
K ▬ ● ▬
L ● ▬ ● ●
M ▬ ▬
N ▬ ●
O ▬ ▬ ▬
P ● ▬ ▬ ●
Q ▬ ▬ ● ▬
R ● ▬ ●
S ● ● ●
T ▬

U ● ● ▬
V ● ● ● ▬
W ● ▬ ▬
X ▬ ● ● ▬
Y ▬ ● ▬ ▬
Z ▬ ▬ ● ●

1 ● ▬ ▬ ▬ ▬
2 ● ● ▬ ▬ ▬
3 ● ● ● ▬ ▬
4 ● ● ● ● ▬
5 ● ● ● ● ●
6 ▬ ● ● ● ●
7 ▬ ▬ ● ● ●
8 ▬ ▬ ▬ ● ●
9 ▬ ▬ ▬ ▬ ●
0 ▬ ▬ ▬ ▬ ▬

TAP CODE

Each letter is transmitted by tapping two numbers: the first tap designates the row (down)—then pause—and the second tap specifies the column (across).

	1	2	3	4	5
1	A	B	C/K	D	E
2	F	G	H	I	J
3	L	M	N	O	P
4	Q	R	S	T	U
5	V	W	X	Y	Z

HEALTH

FIRST AID KIT EXTRAS

In addition to the first aid kit components mentioned in the "Health" chapter, add some of the following items depending on your specific needs for your wilderness first aid kit (WFAK).

Category	#	Item, type, and notes
Diagnostic tools	1	Digital hi/low thermometer w/ extra batteries (Adtemp 419 Digital Hypothermia Thermometer). For the evaluation of fever and hypothermia.
		Urine test strips (e.g., Clinitek). To evaluate abdominal pain, renal stones, and urinary symptoms.
Misc.	4	Examination gloves
	1	1″ × 10 yd. waterproof adhesive tape
	6	Cotton swabs (Q-tips)
		Duct tape
	4	Large safety pins
		Trauma shears and medical scissors
		Ziploc bags
		Headlamp and lighter
		Signal mirror/dental mirror
		Small, flat Fresnel-lens magnifier
		Permanent markers (Sharpie)
		Notepad
		SAMPLE/SOAP notes. To guide your first aid assessments (printables: bit.ly/SOAP-f, bit.ly/SOAP-b)
		WFA pocketbook: *The Field Guide of Wilderness & Rescue Medicine* by Jim Morrissey
Wound management	1	Dishwashing soap bottle or a small piece of solid soap
		Alcohol-based gel for hands
		Clean and sterile gloves
		Irrigation syringes (1 cc to 60 cc)
		Alcohol pads and gels
		Antiseptic towelettes

	5	Medium-sized suture strips
	3	#11 or #15 scalpel blades, sterile
	4	Absorbable suture kit
	1	Skin stapler (3M). Staples are easier to use than sutures, and it is a relatively low-risk procedure.
	4	Individual single-use cyanoacrylate skin glue (Dermabond, Krazy Glue singles)
	1	Combat Application Tourniquet (CAT). This tourniquet is easy to apply and can even be applied using one hand.
	1	3″ × 5 yd. (stretched) elastic bandage (ACE, Coban, Vet Wrap)
	1	3″ × 5 yd. (stretched) conforming roller gauze (Kling)
	8	Medium-sized (e.g., 3″ × 3″) gauze pads
	2	4″ × 4″ QuickClot Combat Gauze pads.
	2	OB-type compressed vaginal tampons
		Adhesive bandages (Band-Aid)
	1	SAM Splint (4.4″ × 36″; 15 × 110 cm)
	1	Triangular (cravat) bandage and safety pins
	1	Compression bandage (Israeli)
Dental		Cavit (7 g), IRM, Express Putty
		Paraffin (dental wax) stick
		Dental floss
		Dental mirror
		Cotton rolls and pellets

SAMPLE DRUGS FOR LONG-TERM WFAK

The list below is just an example. Your circumstances will dictate which items to keep in your kit and how many of them.

Category	#	Item and type	Dosage (adult)	Indications and notes
Pain meds	24	Naproxen 220 mg tabs (Aleve)	440 mg PO, then 220 mg q12h	Pain or cough. Ibuprofen alternative (more compact) can be combined with acetaminophen.
	48	Ibuprofen 200 mg (Advil, Motrin)	400–600 mg PO q4–6h; max 2400 mg/day	Pain reliever, anti-inflammatory, and fever reducer. Naproxen alternative can be combined with acetaminophen. Don't use if pregnant, dehydrated, or have GI bleeding.
	24	Acetaminophen 500 mg tabs (Tylenol, paracetamol)	500 mg PO q4–6h, max 4000 mg/day	Pain relief, fever reducer. May be combined with Ibuprofen/Naproxen.
	24	Acetaminophen-Codeine 300 mg/30 mg tabs (Tylenol #3, EMTEC)	300–600 mg/30–60 mg PO q4–6h	Mild-moderate pain relief.
	12	R Oxycodone 5 mg tabs (Percocet, OxyContin)	5–10 mg PO q4h PRN	Significant pain relief. Hydrocodone alternative.
	12	R Hydrocodone-Acetaminophen 5 mg/500 mg tabs (Vicodin, Lortab)	5 mg/500 mg q4–6h, max 8 tabs per day	Significant pain relief, cough suppressant; may cause severe constipation. Oxycodone alternative.
Allergy meds	2	R Injectable epinephrine (EpiPen)	IM injection in thigh, repeat after 5 min. if needed	Anaphylactic reaction, hypotension, cardiac arrest, severe asthma.
	12	Diphenhydramine 50 mg tabs (Benadryl)	25–50 mg PO q4–6h PRN	Allergies, itching, rashes, nasal congestion, sedation.
	4	R Prednisone 50 mg tabs (Deltasone, Pred-Pak)	50 mg PO QAM	Asthma, allergies; side effects include insomnia and nervousness.
GI Meds	8	Loperamide 2 mg tabs (Imodium)	4 mg PO, then 2 mg q4h, max 16 mg per day	Diarrhea; not recommended for patients with bloody diarrhea.

Cardiac meds	4	Aspirin 325 mg tabs (Bayer, ASA, Ecotrin)	325 mg PO daily	Chest pain.
Anti-biotics, etc.	1	3.5 g tube polymyxin/bacitracin (Polysporin) or bacitracin ophthalmic ointment	to skin BID	Antibiotic ointment for skin wounds. Ophthalmic ointment can be used for eyes and skin wounds.
	30	R Amoxicillin-clavulanic acid 875 mg/125 mg tabs (Augmentin)	875 mg/125 mg PO BID	Animal bites; oral, respiratory, and ear infections. Counterindicated in patients with penicillin allergy.
	30	R Ciprofloxacin 500-mg tabs (Cipro)	500 mg PO BID	GI infection (3–5 days), UTI (7–10 days), skin infection (5–20 days), pneumonia. To combat antibiotic resistance, continue for 10–14 days. For mild UTI 250 mg bid for 3 days.
	60	R Cephalexin 500 mg tabs (Keflex, Keftab)	500 mg PO q6h	Skin and wound infection, respiratory infection, UTI. Do not use if allergic to penicillin.
	30	R Doxycycline 100 mg tabs (Vibramycin)	100 mg PO daily or BID, 200 mg single dose for Lyme prevention	Malaria prophylaxis and treatment, fever of unknown origin.
Anti-septic	1	Povadone-iodine solution 10% bottle (Betadine)	10% for topical use; 1% for wound cleaning	—
Anti-fungal	6	R Fluconazole 150 mg tabs (Diflucan)	150 mg PO daily; BID-QID for skin/systemic	Yeast vaginitis, other fungal infections. Single dose treats vaginal candidiasis; higher, repeated doses treat systemic fungal infections.

Sources: Auerbach, Paul S. *Wilderness Medicine*; Morrissey, Jim. *The Field Guide of Wilderness & Rescue Medicine*; Conover, Keith. *Personal Wilderness Medical Kit.*

MEDICAL ABBREVIATIONS

Abbreviation	Definition	Abbreviation	Definition
PO	orally	q4h	every four hours
IM	intramuscularly	q6h	every six hours
BID	twice a day	PRN	as needed
QID	four times a day	QAM	Every morning

With some antibiotics, you may see improvements as early as three days or fewer. It's generally recommended to do an entire course to minimize antibiotic resistance. Still, emerging studies suggest this may not be the case. There is no evidence that longer courses discourage antibiotic resistance, and the opposite may be true. If you have limited supplies, it may be wise to continue antibiotic treatment only for two days after improvements.

PRESCRIPTION MEDICATIONS FOR A WFAK

One way to obtain controlled medications for your wilderness first aid kit is to request a prescription from your doctor. Another alternative can be to get meds for veterinarian use where they can be bought without a prescription. But it's crucial to ensure the medicinal ingredient is the sole ingredient because some veterinary drugs contain additives that could cause ill effects in humans. In addition, check the dosage in milligrams. Below is a sample of a few antibiotics and their veterinary equivalents.

Drug	Example veterinary drug	Dosage
Amoxicillin	Fish-Mox/Fish-Mox Forte	250mg/500mg
Cephalexin/Keflex	Fish-Flex/Fish-Flex Forte	250mg/500mg
Ciprofloxacin/Cipro	Fish-Flox/Fish-Flox Forte	250mg/500mg
Doxycycline	Fish-Doxy/Bird Biotic	100mg

When dealing with medications, always keep in mind the *five rights*: right person, right drug, right dose, right route, and right time.

When packing drugs in your kit, write down their common names, active ingredients, uses, doses in mg, and expiry dates, and store them in airtight or waterproof containers.

SHELF LIFE FOR DRUGS

In a survival context, expired drugs shouldn't be discarded immediately because their shelf life is generally intentionally conservative. Many expired drugs stored carefully in their original sealed containers can be used past expiration. Some factors reduce the shelf life of drugs (heat > moisture > oxygen > UV light); in addition, drugs in liquid and capsule forms degrade faster than tablets.

A study that used data from 122 different drugs from the Shelf Life Extension Program (for the U.S. Department of Defense) concluded the following: "Based on testing and stability assessment, 88% of the lots were extended at least one year beyond their original expiration date for an average extension of sixty-six months, but the additional stability period was highly variable." See the study (bit.ly/2drug9) and a related news article (archive.ph/tc2id) for more information.

PREPARATION

REPAIR KIT

A good repair kit should help you fix most of the issues you might encounter, such as problems with your canoe, sled, shoes, clothes, or snowshoes. You must be able to repair any critical gear.

Some of the contents I suggest for a field repair kit include a sewing kit with assorted needles (glovers, curved, sail), strong thread, unwaxed dental floss (heavy-duty thread), pieces of fabric, a thimble, and safety pins (assorted sizes); 20 gauge snare wire (steel and brass) and rebar tie wire; duct tape; hot glue sticks; shoe glue (rubber cement); epoxy (two-part resin or putty); zip ties (assorted); Kenyon K-Tape or ripstop nylon sail repair tape; sleeping pad patches; Aquaseal for waterproof repairs (in DIY single-use plastic straw containers); assorted nails and screws; heavy-duty aluminum foil; and assorted Ziploc bags.

LONG–TERM GEAR LIST SAMPLE

Category	Item	#	Sample model	Description and rationale
Bags	Rugged backpack	1	Karrimor Predator 80–130 PLCE	500 denier nylon, 80–130 L pack volume; durable, adjustable volume (large size for winter)
	Pack liner	1		Waterproof pack liner 90 L volume; protects gear against immersion, snow and rain
	Rugged sack	1	Ursack	Spectra-like, ultra tough sack; bear resistant, for hanging food and other uses
Navi-gation	Mirror or lensatic compass	1	Silva Ranger, Suunto, Cammenga	More rugged and accurate than baseplate compasses; land navigation
	Waterproof topo map			Waterproof 1:50,000 or 1:250,000 scale; land navigation
	Watch	1	Casio Pro Trek	Altimeter, barometer, temperature, compass, solar-powered, rugged woven wristband; time, navigation aid, and weather watching
	Smartphone	1	Samsung Galaxy S5 Neo or XCover 5	IPX7 Waterproof, removable battery, large screen; GPS, topo maps, e-books, satellite imagery, and lamp
	Waterproof smartphone case	1	LifeProof Case	IP67 Waterproof; shockproof and waterproof redundancy
	Extra smart-phone battery	1		Optional
Sleeping	3-Season Tent	1	Big Agnes Seedhouse SL2	Ultralight, green, 2-person (for 1-2 people); mosquito protection, and quick to set up on the move
	Synthetic winter sleeping bag	1		Mummy-style, synthetic insulation (moisture-resistant); used as an overbag with the down sleeping bag
	Down 3-season sleeping bag	1		Mummy-style, down insulation, Comfort rating of 22°F (-6°C); lighter than synthetic (inner-bag)
	Bivvy bag	1	Snugpak or USGI	Protects sleeping bag from rain and moisture; optional
	Compression sack	2		To store sleeping bags when traveling
	Sleeping pad	1	Therm-a-Rest Z Lite Sol	Closed-cell, full-length, virtually indestructible; an integral part of sleeping bag ratings

	Inflatable pad	1	Therm-a-Rest NeoAir XTherm	Inflatable, expedition quality pad with 5.7 R-value; optional
	Sil-nylon poncho tarp	1	Sea to Summit Poncho tarp	Ultralight sil-nylon; optional
	Sil-nylon guide tarp	1		Ultralight sil-nylon, high quality 10 × 13 ft. (4 × 3 m); large tarp for main shelter
Clothing	Backpacking boots		Salomon Quest 4D GTX Forces	Mid/high cut (to keep snow and rain out), GTX, for spring and fall; optional
	Hiking shoes		Salomon XA Forces Mid	Low/mid-cut, breathable (non-GTX) for 3-season use
	Rain jacket GTX			3-layered, GTX Pro jacket w/ zip vents large size; durable, rainproof jacket
	Rain pants GTX			3-layered, GTX Pro pants w/ thigh vents; durable, rainproof pants
	Fleece jacket	1	ECWCS Gen III or Patagonia R2/R3	Polartec fleece jacket; light, durable, warm when moist
	Extra fleece jacket	1	Mountain Hardwear or Melanzana	Polartec High Loft fleece jacket; optional
	Compressible jacket		Patagonia Nano/Micro Puff	Down or PrimaLoft ultra-portable jacket
	Base layers grid	1	ECWCS Level 2 or Polartec Power Grid	Top and bottom, grid wicking layer; must-have base layer for cold weather
	Base layers thin	1	Polartec Silkweight	Additional top and bottom, thin wicking layer; optional
	Underwear	1-2	ExOfficio	Synthetic
	Thin hiking socks	1-2	Darn Tough Micro Crew	Durable, merino wool; spring/summer socks
	Medium thickness socks	1-2	Darn Tough T4033	Durable, merino wool; fall/winter socks
	BUFF	2	BUFF bandanas	Polyester; multifunctional headwear
	Reinforced convertible pants	1	Prana + DIY reinforcements or RVRC	Convertible to shorts, rugged, cargo pants; durable, all seasons pants/shorts
	Long-sleeve shirt	1		Loose-fitting synthetic shirt for bug-resistance; bug protection, all seasons use

	Mosquito head net	1		
	Sun hat	1	Outdoor Research	Breathable or waterproof hat
	Light work gloves	1	Mechanix leather work gloves	Leather palm, not insulated; 3-season work gloves
	Filleting/ skinning gloves	1		Waterproof, cut resistant, nitrile coated; for hygiene and use in cold weather
	Waterproof gloves	1	SHOWA TEMRES 282-02	For filleting, working, fishing in cold weather; optional
	Belt	1		Adjusting for weight loss, holding tools
	Warm hat	1		Double-layered, fleece-lined beanie
	Gaiters	1		To keep snow out when not wearing winter boots; optional
	Fleece pants	1		For insulation in cold weather
Fire	Fresnel lens	2		Credit card size; backup firestarter
	Ferro rod	1		0.5″ thick ferrocerium rod; starts up to 2,500 fires, works if damp
	Lighter	3	BIC piezoelectric	Bright colors; starts up to 1,000 fires
Cooking	Pot 1L	1	MSR Alpine Stowaway Pot	Wide, 1 L stainless steel or titanium pot w/handle and lid; boiling, frying, baking, roasting, and food storage
	Spoon and fork	1		Titanium or stainless steel spoon and fork; won't melt or break like plastic utensils
Bow hunting	Bow	1		Lightweight, simple, rugged, 50 lb. draw weight; optional
	Bowstring	3		Strings have a limited life span; optional
	Bow wax	1		String maintenance; optional
	Arm guard	1		Minimalist arm guard; optional
	Finger glove	1		Leather finger glove; optional
	Arrows	12 – 18	Carbon-fiber hunting arrows	Durable, feathered for off-the-shelf shooting; optional
	Quiver	1	Selway	Bow-mounted, compact, quiet, hunting quiver; optional

	Arrow tube	1		For transporting up to 16 arrows; optional
	Broadheads	6		Fixed-blade broadheads for large animals; optional
	Blunt points	6		For target practice & hunting small animals; optional
Hunting	.22 Rifle	1	Ruger 10/22 or Henry AR-7	For hunting medium and small animals, w/ sling, scope & mags
	.22 ammo	1-3 p/ day	CCI high- or hyper-velocity	Hollow-points for heart, spine and lung shots, and solid points for headshots
	.308 Scout rifle	1		For hunting large animals, w/ sling; optional
	Rifle scope	1		With quick detach rings or mount for transport; optional
	.308 ammo	1-3 p/ wk		Optional
	Meat bags			
Trapping	Metal traps	2	220 or 280 Conibears	Body grip trap for medium-sized animals; optional
	Cable snares	12	1/16" cable snares	For small animals, w/ screws for attaching to a drag
	Snare wire		20 (stronger) or 22 ga. stainless steel wire	For rabbit and hare; also brass wire for crafts
Fishing	Fishing rod	1	Emmrod packer (6 coils) or telescopic	Light, durable w/ spinning reel; for active fishing and travel use
	Landing net	1	DIY	Just the net portion; a must-have for survival fishing
	Gill net	1-2	DIY	5" (12.5 cm) stretch mesh, 80 ft. long, mono line with floatline and lead-core lead line; a must-have for survival
	Braided fishing line	300 yd.		300 yd. of 10 lb. braided line; for fishing rod and trotlines
	Mono line			35 lb. mono line for handlining; optional
	Cuban yo-yo	1		For handlining and storing fishing line; optional

	Automatic fisherman	6 – 12		Optional
	Trotline kits		DIY	Hooks, leaders, sinkers, bobbers, anchor bags; for passive fishing
	Bankline	150 – 200 ft	Catahoula #30	Tarred braided nylon line of 200 lb. test
	Hooks	100		Assorted sizes stainless steel (circle hooks & trebles)
	Lures	20		High-quality lures and jigs; for fishing rod use
	Casting bobbers	12		Assorted bobbers; for fishing rod use in snaggy areas
Water	Metal water bottle	1	Stainless steel Nalgene	Wide-mouth; boiling water and melting snow
	Water filter	1	Sawyer Squeeze w/ cleaning coupling adapter	Simple and rugged, works with plastic bottles; optional
First aid	First aid kit	1	Adventure Medical Mountain Explorer	First aid kit + additional items
	Aluminum splint	1	SAM Splint	Much better than any improvised splint; for fractures
	Compression bandage	1	Israeli bandage	For bleeding wounds
Metal tools	Shovel		Cold Steel or titanium	Durable, simple, lightweight, multi-use; optional
	Knife	1	Mora Kansbol	Stainless steel, fixed blade, 3/4 tang; Carving, filleting, cooking, skinning
	Filleting knife	1		Much better for filleting than a regular knife; optional
	Axe	1	Schrade SCAXE2L or JP Paxe	Chopping axe w/ sheath, ~2 lb. (1 kg), 16″–24″ (40 – 60 cm); a full-length axe is not needed when paired with a saw
	Saw	1	Tuff Camp 30″ or Silky Big Boy	Needed for feeding a woodstove efficiently; cutting firewood efficiently
	Multi-tool	1	Leatherman G10 Charge+ or Surge	Heavy-duty multi-tool; very useful

	Sharpener	1	DMC Diafold	Fine and coarse pocket sharpener
	Axe sharpener	1	Lansky Puck	Dual-grit sharpener
	Auger		Black Raven	Scotch eye 1″ auger; optional
Electro-nics	Solar panel	1-2	Suntactics S5 or Renogy E.Flex 10 W	5–10 W, 5 V USB output, waterproof, folding, ultralight; for charging electronics and battery pack
	Battery pack	1-2		10,000 mAh battery, waterproof, lamp; to charge electronics
	USB cables	3		Long, high-quality cables
	Headlamp	1	TH20 or ZebraLight	Waterproof, adjustable intensity 1 × AA; low output for max battery life and night vision
	AA batteries	4	Eneloop	Rechargeable NiMH batteries for headlamp
	AAA batteries	3	Eneloop	Rechargeable NiMH batteries for radio; optional
	Battery charger	2	Olight UC Universal	Ultralight
	Radio receiver	1	Eaton Mini Radio	Shortwave, AM/FM radio for weather forecasts, news, loneliness; optional
	Field thermometer	1	Sun Company Digital Zipogage or liquid-in-glass	Accurate at low temperatures; optional
	Tablet	1	Android w/ microSD card port	Satellite imagery, maps, medical library, e-books; optional
	Satellite messenger	1	Garmin InReach	Two-way satellite messages; optional
	Personal locator beacon	1	Ocean Signal rescueME	5 W search and rescue beacon
	Two-way radio	1-2		5 W Ham, VHF, MURS, or GMRS w/ charger for group comms; optional
Miscella-neous	Paracord	150–200 ft.	550 type III paracord	45–60 m of MIL-SPEC paracord; bear hang and multipurpose
	2 mm nylon cord	300–600 ft.		100–200 m of 1.8–2 mm diameter guyline-type cord; multipurpose
	Braided line	150–300 ft.		45–100 m of braided fishing line, 0.4 mm diameter (50–65 lb. test)

	Repair kit		DIY	Rubber cement, wire, epoxy, superglue, sewing kit, fabric, dental floss, zip ties, glue sticks
	Duct tape	1		Multipurpose
	Notepad and pencils	1-2	Rite in the Rain or stone paper pad	Waterproof notepads and 4 pencils; journaling and notes
	Assorted Ziploc bags	12		Multipurpose
	Contractor bags	1-3		Multipurpose
	Cash			You never know
	Monocular			10 × 25 waterproof monocular; scouting
	Carabiner and pulley	1-2	Oval biner + Petzl Ultralegere pulley	Bear hang
	Ultralight biner	1-2	Camp Nano 22	Ultralight wiregate biner; optional
	Shemagh scarf			Multipurpose cotton scarf; optional
	Clear protective glasses			For bushwacking and cutting firewood; optional
	Earplugs			Very important for having a good sleep during storms
River specific	Canoe	1	Royalex or T-Formex	Whitewater 16–17 ft. expedition canoe; optional
	Paddle	1-2		Aluminum-plastic, T-grip for whitewater; optional
	Sandals	1	Keen Zerraport II	Protected toe sandals; optional
	Paddling accessories			Throw bag, painters, bailer, PFDs; optional
	Portage pack	1-2	SealLine Boundary	Waterproof 115 L pack; optional
Winter specific	Winter boots		Canadian Army Mukluks	Breathable, removable liners; cold weather boots
	Extra boot liners	1	Raber Duffle Sock	Double-layer wool liners

		Overshoes	1	Tingley rubber overshoe 10″	PVC overshoes as waterproof mukluks, fits boot liners; optional
		Winter socks	2 pairs / month	Canadian military-issue and Thermohair	Merino wool, thick winter socks
		Trapper hat			Fur hat; must-have for severe cold
		Neck warmer	1	DIY	Fleece neck gaiter with a sewn-in extra flap of fleece at the base; more versatile and practical than a balaclava
		Work mitts	1	DIY	Leather mitts w/ long cuffs and removable knitted wool mitt liners
		Waterproof mitts	1	JokaSafe	Removable liner, fully waterproof for winter fishing; optional
		Arctic mitts	1	Hy-Arctic Raber Mitts	Removable liner, cheek warmer, full sleeves; must-have for severe cold
		Liner gloves	1		Polyester-Lycra running/liner gloves
		Snowshoes	1	Military magnesium or MSR Evo/Revo	Flat and mountainous terrain snowshoes; for winter travel
		Ice chisel	1		Takedown, removable wood pole; for winter fishing
		Bibs	1-2	USGI Polartec Bib Overalls and Asbell Wool	Must-have for severe cold
		Vest	1		Down or synthetic vest; fits inside multiple layers without restricting movement
		Parka or jacket	1-2	ECWCS level 7 or Feathered Friends	Down or synthetic jacket
		Snow shovel	1		Aluminum collapsible snow shovel; winter fishing and shelter building
		Sled	1-2	Paris sled 60″ Expedition Pro	
		Sunglasses	1		To minimize snow blindness
		Titanium stove		Seek Outside XL	Large door, flat top for cooking and DIY mica glass window modification; must-have for severe cold
		Winter tent	1	DIY wall tent or Seek Outside 8 Person Tipi	Sil-nylon tent (or Snowtrekker tent if weight/bulk is no issue); must-have for severe cold

REFERENCES

Find below in bold letters some recommended reading. In addition, the letters in brackets indicate the chapters where the selected references were used: Preparation [PR], Mindset [MI], Clothing [CL], Travel [TV], Water [WA], Fire [FR], Shelter [SH], Food, Foraging, and Edible Plants [FF], Fishing [FS], Trapping [TP], Hunting [HU], Bushcraft [BU], Winter [WI], Health [HE], Electronics [EL], Natural Hazards [NH].

Agricultural Research Service (2019). *FoodData Central*. [online] FoodData Central. Available at: https://fdc.nal.usda.gov/ [Accessed 2021]. [FF]

Alford, M. (2013). *Winter Wise : Travel and Survival in Ice and Snow*. Heritage House Publishing. [TV, SH, BU, WI]

Alton, J. and Alton, A. (2013). *The Survival Medicine Handbook : a Guide for When Help Is Not on the Way*. Doom and Bloom. [HE]

Anon. (2005). *Survival and Austere Medicine : An introduction*. 2nd ed. The Remote, Austere, Wilderness and Third World Medicine Discussion Board Moderators. [HE]

Auerbach, P.S. (2007). **Wilderness Medicine**. 5th ed. Mosby Elsevier. [PR, CL, TV, WA, SH, FF, BU, HE, NH]

Auerbach, P.S., Constance, B.B. and Freer, L. (2013). **Field Guide to Wilderness Medicine**. 4th ed. Elsevier. [HE]

B. Allan Mackie (1972). *Building with Logs*. B. Allan Mackie. [FR, SH]

Baumeister, R.F., Tice, D.M. and Vohs, K.D. (2018). The Strength Model of Self-Regulation: Conclusions from the Second Decade of Willpower Research. *Perspectives on Psychological Science*, 13(2), pp.141–145. [MI]

Beard, D.C. (1916). **Shelters, Shacks and Shanties**. Charles Scribner's Sons. [SH]

Benson, R. (1980). *Survival Poaching*. Paladin Press. [FS, TP]

Benson, R. (1985). *Ragnar's Ten Best Traps : and a Few Others That Are Damn good, Too*. Paladin Press. [TP]

Biel, W. and Jaroszewska, A. (2017). The nutritional value of leaves of selected berry species. *Scientia Agricola*, 74(5), pp.405–410. [FF]

Bilsborough, S. and Mann, N. (2006). A Review of Issues of Dietary Protein Intake in Humans. *International Journal of Sport Nutrition and Exercise Metabolism*, 16(2), pp.129–152. [HE]

Blind Horse Knives and The Pathfinder School (2010). *Self Reliance Illustrated*, (1). [WA]

Blind Horse Knives and The Pathfinder School (2011). *Self Reliance Illustrated*, (5). [FR]

Bourne, W. (2011). *Basic Fishing : A Beginner's Guide*. Skyhorse Publishing. [FS]

Brandt, A. (1984). *Fish Catching Methods of the World*. Fishing News Books. [FS]

Brooks, R. (2009). *What's in the Water*. [online] NRS. Available at: nrs.com/learn/treating-backcountry-water. [WA]

Canadian Air Force (1982). **Never Say Die : The Canadian Air Force Survival Manual**. Paladin Press. [TV, FR, SH, FF]

Canterbury, D. (2014). *Bushcraft 101*. Adams Media. [TP]

Canterbury, D. (2015). *Advanced Bushcraft : an Expert Field Guide to the Art of Wilderness Survival*. Adams Media. [FR, FF, FS]

Centers for Disease Control and Prevention. (n.d.). *A Guide to Drinking Water Treatment and Sanitation for Backcountry and Travel Use*. [online] Available at: cdc.gov/healthywater/drinking/travel/backcountry_water_treatment.html [Accessed Apr. 2020]. [WA]

Chesbro, M. (2002). *Wilderness evasion : a guide to hiding out and eluding pursuit in remote areas*. Paladin Press. [PR, FS, TP, HU]

Cone, A.L. (1998). *Fishing Basics : a Prize Catch for Fresh and Salt Water Anglers*. Black Dog & Leventhal. [FS]

Conover, G. and Conover, A. (1995). **A Snow Walker's Companion : Winter Trail Skills from the Far North**. Ragged Mountain Press. [CL, TV, FR, SH, FS, BU, WI, HE]

Cooper, J.M. (1978). *Snares, Deadfalls, and other Traps of the Northern Algonquians and Northern Athapaskans*. AMS Press. [TP]

Dardick, G. (1986). *Home Butchering and Meat Preservation*. McGraw-Hill. [FF]

Davenport, G.J. (2001). *Wilderness Living*. Stackpole Books. [HE]

Davies, B. (2012). *SAS Mountain and Arctic Survival*. Skyhorse Publishing. [TV, FF, TP]

Deaton, J.E., Berg, S.W., Richlin, M. and Litrownik, A.J. (1977). *Coping Activities in Solitary Confinement of U.S. Navy POWs in Vietnam*. Journal of Applied Social Psychology, 7(3), pp.239–257. [MI]

Department Of Indian Affairs And Northern Development (1979). *Northern Survival*. Fitzhenry & Whiteside. [TV]

Department of the Army (2009). *The Ultimate Guide to U.S. Army Survival : Skills, Tactics, and Techniques*. Skyhorse Publishing. [HE]

Dickson, M., Bebermeyer, R., Hobdell, M. and Stevenson, G. (2010). *Where There Is No Dentist*. Hesperian Health Guides. [HE]

Divine, M. (2015). *Unbeatable Mind : Forging Mental Toughness*. CreateSpace. [MI]

Edholm, S. and Wilder, T. (2001). *Buckskin : The Ancient Art of Braintanning*. Paleotechnics. [HU]

Eisner, S. (1911). *Boy Scouts of America : Handbook For Boys*. Boy Scouts Of America. [BU]

Elbroch, M. and Pewtherer, M. (2006). *Wilderness Survival : Living off the Land with the Clothes on Your Back and the Knife on Your Belt*. McGraw-Hill. [FF, HE]

Elias, T.S. and Dykeman, P.A. (1990). *Edible Wild Plants : A North American Field Guide*. Sterling. [FF]

Etling, K. (2013). *Hunting Bears : the Ultimate Guide to Hunting Black, Brown, Grizzly, and Polar Bears*. Skyhorse Publishing. [HU]

Euell Gibbons (1987). *Stalking the Wild Asparagus*. A.C. Hood. [FF]

Evans, G.W., Stokols, D. and Carrere, S. (1988). *Human Adaptation to Isolated and Confined Environments Preliminary Findings of a Seven Month Antartic winter-over Human Factors study*. NASA Ames Research Center. [MI]

FalconGuides ed, (2014). *Basic Illustrated Freshwater Fishing*. Globe Pequot Press. [FS, BU]

Fitzwater, J.P.J., Arthur, C.A. and Hardy, L. (2018). The Tough Get Tougher: Mental Skills Training with Elite Military Recruits. *Sport, Exercise, and Performance Psychology*, 7(1), pp.93–107. [MI]

G., Y., Qiang, Y. and Che, T. (2011). Adaptation and Coping Strategies in Chinese Antarctic Expeditioners' Winter-over Life. *Advances in Polar Science*, 22(2), pp.111–117. [MI]

Gaaren, T. (2015). *Traditional Trout Fishing. Vol. 1 Fishing for Survival in the North*. CreateSpace. [FS, TP]

Gerke, R. (2010). *Outdoor Survival Guide*. Human Kinetics. [MI]

Gibby, E.H. (1994). *How to Make Primitive Pottery*. Eagles's View Publishing. [BU]

Gibson, W.H. (1901). *Camp Life in the Woods and the Tricks of Trapping and Trap Making*. Harper & Brothers. [TP]

Giesbrecht, G.G. and Wilkerson, J.A. (2006). *Hypothermia, Frostbite and Other Cold Injuries : Prevention, Survival, Rescue, and Treatment*. Mountaineers Books. [HE]

Gill, A.A. (1916). *Practical Basketry*. David McKay Pub. [BU]

Goggins, D. (2018). *Can't Hurt Me : Master Your Mind and Defy the Odds*. Lioncrest Publishing. [MI]

Gonzales, L. (2004). **Deep Survival : Who Lives, Who Dies, and Why**. W.W. Norton & Co. [MI]

Goodchild, P. (1999). *Survival Skills of the North American Indians*. Chicago Review Press. [FS, TP, HU]

Gorman, S. (1991). *AMC Guide to Winter Camping : Wilderness Travel and Adventure in the Cold-weather Months*. Appalachian Mountain Club. [TV, WI, HE]

Graves, R. (2013). **Bushcraft : The Ultimate Guide to Survival in the Wilderness**. Skyhorse Publishing. [FR, SH, FF, FS, TP, BU]

Greitens, E. (2015). *Resilience : Hard-won Wisdom for Living a Better Life*. Houghton Mifflin Harcourt. [MI]

Gruenwald, T. (1999). *Modern Methods of Ice Fishing*. Creative Publishing. [FS]

Hackenberg, R. (1988). *Becoming a Great Moose Hunter*. F. Amato Publications. [HU]

Hall, D. and Ulrich, J. (2015). *Winter in the Wilderness : a Field Guide to Primitive Survival Skills*. Cornell University Press. [HU]

Hanson, R. and Hanson, F. (2018). **Resilient : How to Grow an Unshakable Core of Calm, Strength, and Happiness**. Penguin Random House. [MI]

Harding, A.R. (1907). *Deadfalls and Snares: A Book of Instruction for Trappers About These and Other Home-Made Traps*. A. R. Harding. [TP]

Hart, C. and Hart, D. (1976). *Natural Basketry*. Watson-Guptill Publications. [BU]

Haslett, J. and Smith, C.M. (2009). *Wilderness Survival for Dummies*. Wiley Publishing. [FF]

Hawke, M. (2009). **Hawke's Green Beret Survival Manual**. Running Press. [PR, FF, FS, HE]

Hemming, B. (2009). *The New Buckshot's Complete Survival Trapping Guide*. Bruce Hemming. [TP, HU]

Hof, W. and Rosales, J. (2012). *Becoming the Iceman : Pushing Past Perceived Limits*. Mill City Press. [MI]

Jaeger, E. (1992). **Wildwood Wisdom**. Shelter Publications. [TV, FR, SH, FF, TP, HU, BU, HE]

Katz, H.N. (1917). *Kinks; a Book of 250 Helpful Hints for Hunters, Anglers and Outers*. The Outer's Book Co. [FS]

Kephart, H. (1957). *Camping and Woodcraft : a Handbook for Vacation Campers and for Travelers in the Wilderness*. The Macmillan Company. [FR]

Kidder, N. (1999). The Ties That Bind and The Bindings That Tie. *The Bulletin of Primitive Technology #17*. [BU]

Knapp, K. (2019). *Understanding Sleeping Bag Temperature Ratings*. [online] REI. Available at: rei.com/blog/camp/understanding-sleeping-bag-temperature-ratings. [SH]

Kochanski, M. (1988). **Northern Bushcraft**. Lone Pine. [FR, SH, FF, TP, HU, BU, HE]

Kochanski, M. (1999). *Top Seven Bush Knots and the use of the Windlass*. Karamat Wilderness Ways. [BU]

Kochanski, M. (2013). *Basic Safe Travel and Boreal Survival Handbook*. Karamat Wilderness Ways. [FR, SH, HE]

Kugach, G. (1993). **Fishing Basics : the Complete Illustrated Guide**. Stackpole Books. [FS]

Kuhnlein, H.V. and Turner, N.J. (1991). **Traditional Plant Foods of Canadian Indigenous Peoples : Nutrition, Botany and Use**. Gordon and Breach Publishers. [FF]

Kull, R. (2008). *Solitude : Seeking Wisdom in Extremes : a Year Alone in the Patagonia Wilderness.* New World Library. [MI, FF, HE]

Leach, J. (1994). *Survival Psychology.* Macmillan. [MI]

Lewis, G. (2008). *The Complete Guide to Hunting : Basic Techniques for Gun & Bow Hunters.* Creative Pub. International. [HU]

Lichter, J. and Forry, S. (2017). *Ultralight Winter Travel : the Ultimate Guide to Lightweight Winter camping, hiking, and Backpacking.* Falcon. [CL, TV, SH, WI]

Lips, J.E. (1936). *Traps Systems Among the Montagnais-Naskapi Indians of Labrador Peninsula.* Tryckeri Aktiebolaget Thule. [TP]

Lundin, C. (2003). **98.6 Degrees : The Art Of Keeping Your Ass Alive.** Gibbs Smith. [PR, MI, FR]

Lundin, C. (2007). *When All Hell Breaks Loose : Stuff You Need to Survive When Disaster Strikes.* Gibbs Smith. [PR, MI, HE]

MacKinnon, A., Kershaw, L., Arnason, J., Owen, P., Karst, A. and Chambers, F.H. (2014). **Edible & Medicinal Plants of Canada.** Lone Pine. [FF, HE]

MacWelch, T. and The Editors at OutdoorLife (2014). *Hunting & Gathering Survival Manual.* WeldonOwen. [TP]

Mann, D. and Pezzullo, R. (2012). *The U.S. Navy SEAL Survival Handbook : Learn the Survival Techniques and Strategies of America's Elite Warriors.* Skyhorse Publishing. [MI, FF, HE]

Marles, R.J., Clavelle, C., Monteleone, L., Tays, N. and Burns, D. (2000). *Aboriginal Plant Use in Canada's Northwest Boreal Forest.* UBC Press. [FF]

Martinez, N. (2012). **Subsistence : a Guide for the Modern Hunter Gatherer : Hunting, Trapping, Fishing & Foraging for a Living in Central Texas.** CreateSpace. [FF, FS, TP, HU, HE]

Martinez, N. (2017). *Trotlines : Artisanal Longlining for Food and Profit.* CreateSpace. [FS]

Mason, B.S. (2001). *Boy's Book of Camping and Wood Crafts.* Derrydale Press. [SH]

McDougall, L. (1992). *Practical Outdoor Survival : a Modern Approach to Staying Alive in the Wilderness.* Lyons & Burford. [HU]

McPherson, J. and McPherson, G. (2008). **Ultimate Guide to Wilderness Living : Surviving with Nothing but Your Bare Hands and What You Find in the Woods.** Ulysses Press. [TP, HU]

Mears, R. (1994). *Survival Handbook : A Practical Guide to Woodcraft and Woodlore.* Oxford Illustrated Press. [PR]

Mears, R. (2003). **Essential Bushcraft : a Handbook of Survival Skills from Around the World.** Hodder & Stoughton. [FR, FS, BU]

Mears, R. and Fält, L. (2016). **Out on the Land.** Bloomsbury Publishing. [BU]

Miles, C. (1963). *Indian and Eskimo Artifacts of North America.* Crown Publishers. [FS]

Minnesota Department of Health. (n.d.). *Causes and Symptoms of Waterborne Illness.* [online] Available at: health.state.mn.us/diseases/waterborne/basics.html [Accessed Jun. 2020]. [WA]

Monteclaro, H., Anraku, K. and Ishikawa, S. (2017). *Field Guidebook on Phillipine Fishing Gears.* Research Institute for Humanity and Nature. [FS]

Montgomery, D.R. (2000). *Mountainman Crafts & Skills : a Fully Illustrated Guide to Wilderness Living and Survival.* Lyons Press. [SH, TP]

Morrissey, J. and Johnson, D. (2017). **The Field Guide of Wilderness & Rescue Medicine : for Outdoor Professionals and Rescue Specialists.** Wilderness Medical Associates. [WA, HE]

Mountain Warfare Training Center (2002). *Summer Survival Course Handbook.* United States Marine Corps. [MI, TP]

O'Leary, J. (2010). *The Wilderness Survival Guide : the Practical Skills You Need for the Great Outdoors.* Watkins Publishing. [BU]

Olsen, L.D. (1997). *Outdoor Survival Skills.* 6th ed. Chicago Review Press. [TP]

Olson, M. (2014). *The Compassionate Hunter's Guidebook : Hunting from the Heart.* New Society Publishers. [FF, HU]

Peskov, V. (1994). *Lost in the Taiga : One Russian Family's Fifty-year Struggle for Survival and Religious Freedom in the Siberian Wilderness.* Doubleday. [FF, BU]

Pewtherer, M. (2010). *Wilderness Survival Handbook : Primitive Skills for Short-Term Survival and Long-Term Comfort.* McGraw-Hill. [HU]

Piantadosi, C.A. (2003). *The Biology of Human Survival : Life and Death in Extreme Environments.* Oxford University Press. [HE]

Pigliucci, M. (2017). *How To Be a Stoic : Using Ancient Philosophy to Live a Modern Life.* Perseus Books. [MI]

Plant, J. (2019). *Primitive Technology : a Survivalist's Guide to Building : Tools, Shelters & More in the Wild.* Penguin Random House. [SH]

Potter, E.C.E. and Pawson, M.G. (1991). *Gill Netting.* Ministry of Agriculture, Fisheries and Food. [FS]

Reich, J.W., Zautra, A.J. and Hall, J.S. eds, (2010). *Handbook of Adult Resilience.* The Guilford Press. [MI]

Richards, F.R. (2014). *An Introduction to Ice Fishing.* CreateSpace. [FS]

Richards, M. (1997). *Deerskins into Buckskins : How to Tan with Natural Materials ; a field guide for hunters and gatherers.* Backcountry Publishing. [HU]

Ridgeon, J. (n.d.). *Willow Bark Cordage.* [online] Jon's Bushcraft. Available at: https://www.jonsbushcraft.com/willow-bark-cordage.htm [Accessed 12 Apr. 2020]. [BU]

Rinella, S. (2015a). *The Complete Guide to Hunting, Butchering, and Cooking Wild Game : Vol II Small Game and Fowl.* Spiegel & Grau. [HU]

Rinella, S. (2015b). **The Complete Guide to Hunting, Butchering, and Cooking Wild Game : Volume I Big Game.** Spiegel & Grau. [HU]

Rosman, I. (1980). *Fishing with Bottom Gill Nets.* Food and Agriculture Organization of the United Nations. [FS]

Rutstrum, C. (1968). *Paradise Below Zero : a Complete Handbook on How to Camp in the Winter.* Macmillan. [TV, SH]

Rutstrum, C. (1975). *The Wilderness Cabin : How to Build Your Own Log, Frame, or Adobe Cabin and Where to Build It.* Macmillan. [SH]

Saskatchewan Education Northern Division (1990). *Saskatchewan Trapper Training Manual.* Saskatchewan Education Northern Division. [TP, HE]

Schneider, R.C. (1972). *Crafts of the North American Indians : a Craftsman's Manual.* Litton Educational Publishing. [BU]

Shubert, A.B. (1917). *Art of Trapping.* A. B. Shubert Inc. [TP]

Sloane, E. (1964). *A Museum of Early American Tools.* Ballantine. [FR]

Sloane, E. (1974). *A Reverence for Wood.* Ballantine Books. [FR]

Society of Primitive Technology (1999). *Primitive Technology : a Book of Earth Skills.* Gibbs Smith Publisher. [HE]

Song, T. (2015). *Extreme Survival Meat : a Guide for Safe Scavenging, Pemmican Making, and Roadkill.* Snow Wolf Publishing. [FF, HE]

Stackpole Books (2007). **Survival Wisdom & Know-how : Everything You Need to Know to Subsist in the Wilderness.** Black Dog & Leventhal. [TV, SH, FS]

Steegmann, A.T. (1983). **Boreal Forest Adaptations : the Northern Algonkians.** Plenum Press. [PR, FF, FS, TP, HU, WI]

Stefansson, V. (1945). *Arctic Manual.* Macmillan. [CL, FF, WI, HE]

Stewart, H. (1977). **Indian Fishing : Early Methods on the Northwest Coast.** The University of Washington Press. [FS]

Stroud, L. and Vlessides, M. (2009). *Survive! : Essential Skills and Tactics to Get You out of Anywhere - Alive.* HarperCollins. [SH, HE]

Tappan, M. (1981). *Tappan on Survival.* Paladin Press. [HU]

Taylor, J.D., Yarrow, G.K. and Miller, J.E. (2017). *Beavers.* U.S. Department of Agriculture. [TP]

Thayer, S. (2006). **The Forager's Harvest.** Forager's Harvest. [FF]

The Air Ministry (1953). *Arctic Survival.* H.M.S.O. [WI]

Thibeault, W. (unpublished). **Buckskin Revolution.** Buckskin Revolution. [HU]

Tilton, B. (2010). *Wilderness First Responder : How to Recognize, Treat, and Prevent Emergencies In The Backcountry.* 3rd ed. Falcon Guides. [HE]

Towell, C. (2009). **The Survival Handbook : Essential Skills for Outdoor Adventure.** DK Publishing. [CL, TV, FR, WA, FF, BU, HE]

Towell, C. (2011). *Essential Survival Skills : Key Tips and Techniques for the Great Outdoors.* DK Publishing. [BU]

Townsend, C. (2005). **The Backpacker's Handbook.** 3rd ed. McGraw-Hill. [HE]

U. S. Department of the Army (1968). *Basic cold weather manual.* Headquarters, Dept. of the Army. [WI]

U.S. Army Aviation Center (1993a). *Aviation Survival Part I : Survival Elements, Psychological Aspects, and Survival Medicine.* U.S. Army Aviation Center. [FF]

U.S. Army Aviation Center (n.d.). *Aviation Survival Part II : Protection From the Environment.* 7th ed. U.S. Army Aviation Center. [SH, WI]

U.S. Army Aviation Center (1993b). *Aviation Survival Part III : Sustenance.* U.S. Army Aviation Center. [FF, FS]

U.S. Department of Health and Human Services (2021). APPENDIX 4: Bacterial Pathogen Growth and Inactivation. In: *Fish and Fishery Products Hazards and Controls.* U.S. Department of Health and Human Services. [FF]

U.S. Department of the Army (2001). *Rigging Techniques, Procedures, and Applications.* Headquarters, Dept. of the Army. [BU]

United States Department of Agriculture (n.d.). *USDA Plants Database.* [online] Plants Database. Available at: https://plants.usda.gov/ [Accessed 2021]. [FF]

Vick, N. (2000). *Fishing on Ice.* Human Kinetics. [FS]

Vonhof, J. (2016). *Fixing Your Feet : Injury Prevention and Treatments for Athletes.* 6th ed. Wilderness Press. [HE]

Werner, D., Thuman, C. and Maxwell, J. (2011). *Where There Is No Doctor : A Village Health Care Handbook.* Hesperian Health Guides. [HE]

Wheat, M.M. (1977). *Survival Arts of the Primitive Paiutes.* University Of Nevada Press. [TP]

Wigginton, E. ed, (1972). *The Foxfire Book.* Anchor Books. [TP]

Wilkinson, E. (1992). *Snow Caves for Fun & Survival.* Johnson Books. [SH]

Wiseman, J. (2009). **SAS Survival Handbook : for Any Climate in Any Situation.** HarperCollins. [TV, FR, SH, FF, FS, HE]

Yoder, D., Blood, J. and Mason, R. (2005). *How Warm Were They? Thermal Properties of Rabbit Skin Robes and Blankets.* Journal of California and Great Basin Anthropology, 25(1), pp.55–68. [TP]

INDEX

PLEASE RATE MY BOOK,

I'D LOVE TO HEAR YOUR HONEST OPINION

Thank you for buying and reading my book. I am extremely grateful and hope you found value in reading it. **Please consider rating it on Amazon.** It only takes a few seconds and you may also write a review if you wish.

If you'd like to leave an honest rating, please go to bit.ly/rate-thrive or scan the code below. I read each review. — JP

ABOUT THE AUTHOR

Juan Pablo Quiñonez is a survival expert and outdoor professional with over 10 years of experience in outdoor recreation and survival.

His outdoor and survival experiences include backpacking the entire Pacific Crest Trail (2,650 miles) in 99 days; paddling over 1,500 miles during numerous remote whitewater canoe trips; living for six months in the wild with his partner, foraging to complement their meager rations; spending 100 days foraging in solitude during the winter in the boreal forest (supported only by small rations); and being a participant in Season 9 of the hit survival series *Alone*. He holds a degree in Applied Ecotourism and Outdoor Leadership.

The author loves adventure, enjoys type 2 fun, and is passionate about living off the land. He believes it's important to practice and share the skills and wisdom of our hunter-gatherer ancestors. In his eyes, strengthening a genuine connection to the land is essential for resilience in this age of ecological disruption and the decline of global civilization. He lives in Canada at the edge of the boreal forest and can be contacted at jp@jpquinonez.com.

Check out **jpquinonez.com** to find his latest blog posts, gear recommendations, and survival courses.